FAMILY ADDICTION

REFERENCE BOOKS
ON FAMILY ISSUES
(VOL. 21)

GARLAND REFERENCE LIBRARY
OF SOCIAL SCIENCE
(VOL. 732)

Reference Books On Family Issues

1. Resources for Early Childhood: *An Annotated Bibliography and Guide for Educators, Librarians, Health Care Professionals, and Parents*, Hannah Nuba Scheffler, General Editor
2. Problems of Early Childhood: *An Annotated Bibliography and Guide*, by Elisabeth S. Hirsch
3. Children and Divorce: *An Annotated Bibliography and Guide*, by Evelyn B. Hausslein
4. Stepfamilies: *A Guide to the Sources and Resources*, by Ellen J. Gruber
5. Experiencing Adolescents: *A Sourcebook for Parents, Teachers, and Teens*, by Richard M. Lerner and Nancy L. Galambos
6. Sex Guides: *Books and Films About Sexuality for Young Adults*, by Patty Campbell
7. Infancy: *A Guide to Research and Resources*, by Hannah Nuba-Scheffler, Deborah Lovitky Sheiman, and Kathleen Pullan Watkins
8. Postpartum Depression: *A Research Guide and International Bibliography*, by Laurence Kruckman and Chris Asmann-Finch
9. Childbirth: *An Annotated Bibliography and Guide*, by Rosemary Cline Diulio
10. Adoption: *An Annotated Bibliography and Guide*, by Lois Ruskai Melina
11. Parent-Child Attachment: *A Guide to Research*, by Kathleen Pullan Watkins
12. Resources for Middle Childhood: *A Source Book*, by Deborah Lovitky Sheiman and Maureen Slonim
13. Children and Adjustment to Divorce: *An Annotated Bibliography*, by Mary M. Nofsinger
14. One-Parent Children, The Growing Minority: *A Research Guide*, by Mary Noel Gouke and Arline McClarty Rollins
15. Child Abuse and Neglect: *An Information and Reference Guide*, by Timothy J. Iverson and Marilyn Segal
16. Adolescent Pregnancy and Parenthood: *An Annotated Guide*, by Ann Creighton-Zollar
17. Employed Mothers and Their Children, by Jacqueline V. Lerner and Nancy L. Galambos
18. Children, Culture, and Ethnicity: *Evaluating and Understanding the Impact*, by Maureen B. Slonim
19. Prosocial Development in Children: Caring, Helping, and Cooperating: *A Bibliographic Resource Guide*, by Alice Sterling Honig and Donna Sasse Wittmer
20. Hispanic Children and Youth in the United States: *A Resource Guide*, by Angela L. Carrasquillo
21. Family Addiction: *An Analytical Guide*, by Douglas H. Ruben

Jarrett Learning Center
East Texas Baptist University
Marshall, Texas 75670

FAMILY ADDICTION
An Analytical Guide

Douglas H. Ruben

GARLAND PUBLISHING, INC. • NEW YORK & LONDON
1993

Library of Congress Cataloging-in-Publication Data

Ruben, Douglas H.
Family addiction : an analytical guide / by Douglas H. Ruben.
p. cm. — (Reference books on family issues ; vol. 21) (Garland reference library of social science ; vol. 732)
Includes bibliographical references.
ISBN 0-8153-0031-X (alk. paper)
1. Narcotic addicts—Family relationships. 2. Narcotic addicts—Family relationships—Bibliography. 3. Alcoholics—Family relationships. 4. Alcoholics—Family relationships—Bibliography. 5. Family psychotherapy. 6. Family psychotherapy—Bibliography. I. Title. II. Series: Reference books on family issues ; v. 21. III. Series: Garland reference library of social science ; v. 732.
RC564.R8 1993
616.86—dc20 92-27787
CIP

Printed on acid-free, 250-year-life paper
Manufactured in the United States of America

Families live on through time,
thanks to generations of caring,
surviving parents and siblings,
who really believe in the
value of love.

With warmest devotion to my sisters

Ellyce and Nancy

and their Families

CONTENTS

FROM THE *AUTHOR*

Family relationships are remarkable phenomena. No matter how interpreted, family means being a part of something that is fully alive and evolves through time. How alive it is, and how much families develop depend on the sincerity, integrity, and ability of family members to overcome endless battles of survival. In clinical practice, I observe many family members losing these battles. Lost ambitions that tear the family fabric gradually spread like a cancer, affecting parents, brothers, sisters, and close relatives. Once nuclear familes lose their bond, reversing this damage becomes a lifelong commitment.

This is particularly so with families trapped in addiction. Families twisted by the complex world of alcohol and drug abusers wrestle with dilemmas of how to survive. Should we expose the abuser, or keep the abuse silent? Should we mobilize strength to restore dignity and cohesion in the family, or resist the barriers of conflict? Questions like these prompt undertakings like this book to assemble basic information about who the abusers are and what to do about it.

Inspiration for *Family Addiction* began in response to the compelling needs of clients for a compendia of guidelines toward self-understanding. A second inspiration was the dearth of academic handbooks available to students and faculty doing research in family addiction. A third inspiration is radical, perhaps, but reacts to the contemporary literature on family dysfunction that narrowly defines the phenomena in humanistic, unscientific ideas, focusing on anecdotes and inferences about personality. Lack of scientific principles and analysis deprives the topic of family addiction of an empirical sophistication it needs to advance its status equal to such natural sciences as biology, chemistry, and physics. Principles of family behavior deserve attention equal to that given to governing principles of individual behavior.

Toward this goal, I am grateful to many motivating individuals behind the scences of manuscript preparation. First I thank my wife, Marilyn, for her balance between work, family, and my writing schedule; a routine she masters with exceptional flexibility without inhibiting her own career growth. Her editorial insights also helped fine tune elements of theory and analysis in each chapter. To my parents Chuck and Belle I gratefully acknowledge their generous input on religious heritage and identity. Recognition is also extended to National Council on Alcoholism and Michigan Clearinghouse on Substance Abuse during research phases of the book.

D. H. R. 1992

INTRODUCTION & HOW TO USE THIS BOOK

Family Addiction presents a timely compendia of the effects of chemical dependency upon different family members. Chapters identify at-risk individuals directly abusing alcohol or drugs or afflicted by the systemic reactions addiction causes in psychological and social behavior. Research on dysfunctional effects is consolidated into sections on *etiology*, *effects upon the family*, and *priorities for intervention*. Unlike existing books on this topic that cover isolated issues (e.g., psychology, sociology, etc.), *Family Addiction* instead expands beyond by its interdisciplinary focus. Analysis covers origins and interventions from a systems approach, broadly explained for immediate practical application and research purposes. For the first time, as well, targeted family members are examined under the same cover, from adolescent addiction and children of alcoholics to elderly addicts. Chapters also supply readers with a resource bibliography listing key articles and books briefly annotated for reference.

Chapters follow an orderly fashion of first orienting the reader to the theoretical perspective regarding family structure. Chapter 1 details the conceptual schema of modern systems theory as derived from innovative works by J.R. Kantor, B.F. Skinner and current ecosystems investigators. A model of family addiction evolves into an ecobehavioral framework as new propositions about behavior replace the antiquated stimulus-response explanation. Principles of behavior governing the onset, continuity and cessation of addictive behavioral patterns are clarified for simpler clinical diagnosis of obvious family dynamics in one generation or across generations (intergenerationally). Finally, introduction of the ecobehavioral analysis justly revives hope for the dying breed of scientific psychologists displaced in recent years by cognitivism and the pressing revolt against learning theory.

Remaining chapters comprehensively explore the precarious role of an addicted family member within the family unit. Chapter 2 examines the addicted spouses and complications of marital and family treatment. Probing questions as to why spouses ignore, accept, deny or survive unbearable turmoil during addiction are answered in light of revealing types of dysfunctional marital patterns, perpetuated by fear of conflict, and many different varieties of avoidance and escape behaviors. The second part of the chapter asks whether solutions lie in family and marital treatment.

Chapter 3, on adolescent addiction, presents a critical comparative overview of research on how drug use and abuse start, and the peculiar patterns endemic to adolescence contributing to delinquency. Segments of the developmental continuum are isolated and closely inspected to unravel the warning signs that go unreported or are overlooked by unsuspecting parents. Issues regarding intervention strategies as well follow a different path. In addition to outpatient and inpatient options, the discussion also looks at problems of skill transfer from treatment to home, and alternative health care options for home, currently under research.

Chapter 4 surveys current undertakings to clarify the epidemic proportions of offspring from addicted families who now must face adult emotional dysfunctions. *Adult children of addiction* (ACOA) introduces, for the first time, empirically-based reasons for the evolving defective patterns in behavior, tracing them from punishment contingencies to formation of distorted rules (meta-rules) governing social behavior. Causal links also demonstrate that dysfunctional behavior is not exclusive to alcoholic parents but rather derives from *any* combination of addictions or abusive parents. Sections on treatment uncover explicit interventions typically overlooked in research on ACOA. Described are which behavior changes favor improvement over regression, expected limitations, and reactive problems among family members who inappropriately deal with these changes.

Chapter 5 covers an increasingly overlooked minority targeted as the number one victim of drug and alcohol problems in the decades ahead: The elderly. Growing old brings on many medical complications (polymorbidity), and numerous losses in physiological functions, socioeconomics, socialization, and emotional tolerance for change. Stressors imposed on the aged, from relocation to smaller quarters (apartment, nursing home, etc.) to self-medication of multiple drugs, force adjustment without the support of spouses (if deceased), children (if moved away), and friendships (if decentralized). Alienated from the social mainstream, elderly adults confront difficult obstacles for survival that easily interfere with their attention to healthy routines. Appetite decreases, bowels are irregular, insomnia increases, and mistakes occur in taking medicine. Medications are taken at wrong times, in the wrong order, and in wrong dosages. Mismedication not only is common, but poses severe diagnostic complications for physicians who cannot differentiate between normal physical problems of aging and mismedication symptoms. When mixed with alcoholism, degeneration of the person's physical and emotional condition is faster and again escapes diagnosis. This chapter draws needed attention to the types of hazards to be watchful for, and steps in prevention and intervention.

HOW TO USE THIS BOOK

Format for Item Entry

Entries for *articles and books* follow alphabetically by author and each entry contains sequentially the following information underneath the citation.

For research articles/books:

1. Language; 2. Focus; 3. Population; 4. Setting; 5. Target behavior; 6. Treatment/intervention; 7. Methods; 8. Measurements; 9. Results.

1. **Language:** Articles written in English or another language usually determine the accessibility and general orientation of the journal or book. While English is clearly dominant, articles in other languages will have abstracts in English.

2. **Focus:** This item identifies the generic focus of an article or book as either experimental or theoretical. Theoretical entries report analytical or summary of findings usually extracted, reviewed or rebutted from the experimental conclusions of another resource. Experimental entries, by contrast, report on manipulation of independent and dependent variables based on a null hypothesis. Types of experimental studies vary, from field applications in natural settings to pure laboratory research.

3. **Population:** Critical information relative to subjects in the study include (a) the number of subjects per sex (or age) and (b) a brief

description of their diagnostic category. If adolescents, for example, are they high school students? If adults, are they adult children of alcoholics (ACOA)?

4. **Setting:** Setting indicates the site of main activity in the study. An important rationale for this inclusion is that results may only apply to that setting despite impressive validity of findings. Nongeneralization to other settings occurs unless setting factors sufficiently resemble the conditions to which readers plan to apply similar procedures. Descriptors refer mostly to specific types of facilities or surroundings, such as a college campus, clinic, hospital, school, prison, and so forth.

5. **Target Behavior:** Disputes over what distinguishes dependent from independent variables in *true experiments* may change future definitions of this category. For now, target behaviors (dependent variable) are the behavior under question that is taught, measured or manipulated in an experiment. Target behaviors covered may include cognitive, emotional, attitudinal, biological, and social patterns.

6. **Treatment/Intervention:** Interventions are independent variables, or the procedures being implemented, measured, and used to manipulate target behaviors. Interventions are techniques, tasks, series of steps, testing, or exposure to several variables simultaneously.

7. **Methods:** Methods refer to the research design used within the study for data collection, and proof of validity and reliability. Methods vary widely depending on the number of subjects investigated, on the variables investigated, and on the theoretical orientation of researchers. Larger populations (*N's*), for example, usually warrant group comparison designs following a random sample of subjects into experimental and control groups. Smaller *N's* may go without a research design, use quasi-experimental designs, or rely on statistical correlational analyses. Fewer subjects also are appropriate for single case designs. These are powerful strategies calculated to demonstrate effects of variables manipulated in fewer days and on as few as one subject, by staggering interventions and comparing them to nonintervention periods. Single case, or *single-organism* designs include multiple baseline, reversal, and criterion designs.

8. **Measurements:** Measurements refer to assessment devices. Cited are all the psychometric devices or recording procedures employed in the study. Questionnaires, surveys, inventories, standard

diagnostic instruments such as the Minnesota Multiphasic Personality Inventory (MMPI), Sixteen Personality Factor Questionnaire (16PF), and a variety of intelligence and substance abuse scales all enter into this category.

9. **Results:** This section is a succinct statement regarding the conclusions drawn from experimental manipulations and implications of these findings for future study.

For theoretical/general articles/books:

1. Language; 2. Focus (theoretical); 3. Population; 4. Thesis (major argument/tenets briefly described); 5. Conclusions (suggestions for field).

1. **Language:** As with experimental studies, this category identifies the language in which the article or book is written.

2. **Focus:** Listed here is the resource that is "theoretical" and focuses on a certain area. Areas include clinical and review. Clinical issues examine treatment interventions, didactics or therapy dynamics based on qualitative or quantitative analyses. Reviews synthesize research findings on one or possibly two interventions, probing their underlying scientific constructs or operation, their benefits, limitations, and contraindications.

3. **Population:** As with "experimental" entries, population identifies the subjects discussed in the clinical or review article and book.

4. **Thesis:** Introduced in the article or book is an argument, position, hypothesis, or "thesis" under consideration. This thesis sets forth an assertion about variables or need for research modification. Evidence for this thesis may be entirely conceptual or a derivative of many empirical results.

5. **Conclusions:** Conclusions are the author's pragmatic statement on whether the hypothesis is valid, advances certain research goals, or can improve upon current technology in methods or clinical efficacy.

Family Addiction

Chapter 1

Family Structure

The family is the first and perhaps the most enduring context for growth. Adjustment within the family means identifying with models, accepting values, playing out family roles, developing affection, and eventually distinguishing one's own values and goals from those held by other family members. The term *family* refers to a variety of groupings including (a) a father, mother, and their children, (b) children of a father and mother, (c) a group of people living in the same house, (d) all of a person's relatives, (e) a group of related people, (f) a tribe, and (g) one's ancestors. Families essentially are adults and children living together for a long time.

Thinking about families is guided by these ideas:

1. The family is the main setting for the experiences of the child, particularly the young child.

2. The family is a dynamic set of relationships among all the people who live in the family.

3. Children's behavior, ideas, thoughts, and fantasies affect the lives of those with whom they live.

4. The behavior, ideas, thoughts, and fantasies of fathers and mothers affect the lives of their children.

5. This group has resources that are used to adjust to life.

Understanding what these five ideas mean requires a certain view about families. Families consist of structures, engineered together by continuous interactions. By "structure" is meant an order or system governing development of relationships, for example, between parent and child or between spouses. Families are architectural phenomena, constructed by social values and rules affecting all family members. Rules determining how relationships form and transactions occur within and outside of families can be very specific or very abstract depending on the theory or model proposed. This chapter introduces the many theoretical models advanced in contemporary family research but focuses more upon *systems* models. Addiction families are excellent subjects for analysis using systems models and particularly when the model has strong empirical foundation.

First we begin with *approaches to family structure,* and then examine more directly models having a systems orientation. The section on *system approaches* introduces tenets of systems theory followed by consideration of five empirically promising models of family change: *ecosystems, human ecology model, Kantor & Lehr's model, social exchange model* and *ecobehavioral model.*

APPROACHES TO FAMILY STRUCTURE

Tracing roots of family addiction through heritage must begin with a baseline analysis of how families evolve. In the last decade, renewal of family study sparked nearly revolutionary thinking in theory construction among sociologists and psychologists. Approaches to theory became less philosophical, less anchored in archaic concepts such as family *lifestyle,* or generic role differences between genders. Breakthroughs in theory tried desperately to increase explanation of phenomena as a science, compared to the physical sciences. From 1960 onward acceptance of more *empirical* models stimulated research investigation, collectively gaining valid measures of what *really* goes on during evolving stages of family growth. With research sophistication came a new belief that family theorizing only is possible if there are tenable assumptions, identifiable targets of application, and evidence that it was interdisciplinary (e.g., Nye, 1988; Sprey, 1988. Thomas & Wilcox, 1987).

Among the mainstream models circulated in the last decade, salient developments appear greatest for 16 of them. These include *institutional, symbolic-interactional, structure-functional, developmental, situational, role, demographic, small group, systems, exchange, conflict, structuralism, ecological, socio-historical, formal,* and *phenomenological*. Presented below is an overview of key assumptions, influences upon theory, and target focus for each of the models.

Institutional

Key Assumptions: Social units consist of distinct structural and cultural configurations. These units are interrelated at the societal level and change in response to historical and daily circumstances. Norms dictating social behavior largely impact upon conformity or nonconformity of institutional values (Buckley, 1967; Kantor, 1982).

Influences Upon Theory: Social philosophy, sociology.

Target Focus: Demography of population, larger societal structures.

Symbolic-Interactional

Key Assumptions: Social behavior is the exchange of meaningful symbols. Meaning is constructed during the process of social interaction (Parsons & Bales, 1955; Pratt, 1976).

Influences Upon Theory: Pragmatism, sociology.

Target Focus: Small groups, developmental stages, conflict models.

Structure-Functional

Key Assumptions: Social behavior is oriented toward some purpose and is governed by social constraints (Beutler, Burr, Bahr & Herrin, 1989; Nye & Berardo, 1973).

Influences Upon Theory: Sociology, anthropology.

Target Focus: Small groups, role development, family systems.

Developmental

Key Assumptions: The biography of a social unit follows an orderly sequence of change. Cycles of family development deal with changes in composition, tasks, role transitions and resource allocations (Baltes, 1978, 1987; Bronfenbrenner, 1986).

Influences Upon Theory: Symbolic-interactional, structure-functional, developmental psychology.

Target Focus: Individual family members.

Situational

Key Assumptions: Social behavior varies according to the situation in which it occurs. Definitions of the situation, role requirements, and the physical setting determine the situational context (Burr & Leigh, 1983).

Influences Upon Theory: Symbolic-interactional, ecological psychology.

Target Focus: Ecological analysis of behavior.

Role

Key Assumptions: Social behavior is a response to normative expectations about performance, rights, duties, and sanctions (Kantor & Lehr, 1975; Paolucci, Hall & Axinn, 1977).

Influences Upon Theory: Symbolic-interactional, structure-functional.

Target Focus: Human development, situational variables, small groups.

Demographic

Key Assumptions: Patterns of social behavior can be inferred from the spatial distributions and movements of the population (Kamerman & Kahn, 1981; Leibowitz, 1978).

Influences Upon Theory: Sociology, epidemiology, structure-functional.

Target Focus: Aggregate data such as rates of births, marriages, divorces and deaths.

Small Group

Key Assumptions: Social behavior occurs in groups and the structural and process aspects of groups constitute an appropriate unit of analysis Pilisuk & Parks, 1983; Reis, Barbera-Stein & Bennett, 1986).

Influences Upon Theory: Symbolic-interactional, structure-functional.

Target Focus: Dynamics of group process impact upon decision-making, cohesion, instrumental vs. expressive leadership, and communication channnels.

Systems

Key Assumptions: Social units are complex wholes with interrelated parts and linkages to external units. Units connect by feedback loops carrying family messages through input and output channels (Bennett, 1976; Odum, 1983).

Influences Upon Theory: Structure-functional, organization management, psychiatry.

Target Focus: Information processing, adaptation, transformation.

Exchange

Key Assumptions: Social actors attempt to maximize reward and minimize costs within the context of alternative courses of action and normative constraints (Burgess & Huston, 1979; Ekeh, 1974).

Influences Upon Theory: Symbolic-interactional, structure-functional.

Target Focus: Family reciprocity, marriages, reinforcement effects.

Conflict

Key Assumptions: Social conflict is an interaction process with multiple causes, strategies of management and outcomes. Two types of conflict recognized are interactional, and radical-critical. Interactional conflict arises out of individual autonomy against social expectations for conformity. Radical-critical conflict is the struggle over opposing interests (Hill, 1949; Klein, 1983; McCubbin & Patterson, 1983).

Influences Upon Theory: Social psychology, anthropology.

Target Focus: Analysis of cooperation vs. competition, trust, negotiation tactics, and constructive vs. destructive families.

Structuralism

Key Assumptions: Social behavior is structured or organized around implicit rules of conduct (Burr, 1973; Burrell & Morgan, 1979).

Influences Upon Theory: Anthropology, linguistics, developmental psychology, structural psychology.

Target Focus: Family thinking, cohesion, exchange dimensions.

Ecological

Key Assumptions: Social behavior occurs in a physical and social environment, is oriented toward the conditions in that environment, and includes transactions with that environment (Herrin & Wright, 1988; Wright & Herrin, 1988).

Influences Upon Theory: Systems psychology, cybernetics, behavioral psychology, home economics.

Target Focus: Family interaction, individual development, societal networks.

Socio-Historical

Key Assumptions: Social behavior in the present only can be understood in reference to social behavior in the past (Chafetz, 1978; Morton, 1957).

Influences Upon Theory: Historiography, epidemiology, psychology.

Target Focus: Role development, social groups.

Formal

Key Assumptions: Social theories are logically interrelated sets of propositions in causal or deductive form. The structure of theory is more important than its content (Giddens, 1974; Osmand, 1987).

Influences Upon Theory: Logical positivism.

Target Focus: Theory construction, conceptual schemes, logical calculus, empirical proofs.

Phenomenological

Key Assumptions: Social behavior is guided by the interpretations and understandings which social actors construct during the course of interaction (Mook, 1985; Rogers, 1983).

Influences Upon Theory: Symbolic-interactional, humanism.

Target Focus: Subject-object relations, introspection, and intrafamily dynamics.

The aforementioned models all share four common denominators besides dealing primarily with family issues. On conceptual grounds they are causally structured theories that propose relationships among variables without naming which cause is most important. Four properties of causality thus shared are (1) temporal precedence; (2) experimental manipulation; (3) intervening mechanisms; and (4) theoretical frameworks. Let us briefly review each property.

Temporal Precedence

Literature on family theory construction lacks consensus on whether causes must precede effects in time or whether causes and effects may be simultaneous or even whether effects may precede causes under special circumstances. The most generally held view is that causes precede events. However, causal models often do not permit such interpretations due to limitations of data collection (methodology) and also the common failure to specify the time lag between change in the cause and change in the effect.

Experimental Manipulation

Most sociological research lacks precise experimental manipulation of possible causes. Largely this failure is not an oversight but rather realistically accepting the fact that control over aggregate data is impossible, short of cluster data analysis. For theories to become testable they must undergo operational analysis, by re-defining family interactions as measurable behavioral units and clearly identifying independent and dependent variables.

Intervening Mechanisms

The effects which causes have are seldom directly or immediately felt. Causes and effects are suspicious because of some intervening mechanisms. In social theory, intervening mechanisms include institutional, cultural, political or even meteorological changes not controlled for in the analysis. For instance, two years ago applied research conducted in Charleston, South Carolina came to a shrieking halt when hurricanes hit the mainland. Loss of electrical power, manpower, and devastating destruction of environment contaminated the pristine research environment. Similar contamination appears in psychological theory. Motivation, perception and cognitive differences typically are unforeseen disturbances upon individual performance levels. Theories reviewed above do not explicitly incorporate precautions against intermediary or *confounding* variables and thereby lose precious validity on cause-effect relationships.

Theoretical Framework

Sometimes the assertion that a particular cause is operative rests on a general theoretical framework, a conceptual scheme that is logically derived from another conceptual scheme. Theories in social science commonly follow this principle of *shared foundation* rather than endeavor to verify these claims through original research.

SYSTEM APPROACHES

We now see that critical science begins with empirically relevant assumptions that are testable and have multicausal explanations. In a systems approach assumptions always derive from naturalistic or observable links among family members, and causality is never definitive. That advantage of systems analysis over dominantly theoretical analysis gives important status to system models for study of family addiction. This section first provides the rudiments of a systems model before launching into an examination of the current types of models relevant for clinical application.

General Systems Model

General systems theory (GST) aims to describe patterns and processes in a wide range of phenomena which are the same across disciplines and across levels of complexity and organization. It is mainly descriptive and qualitative, focusing on how a system evolved or prescribing what is necessary for that system to survive. Systems begin with an input that is processed by the system on its way to becoming an output. The process of transformation through the system is governed by rules of transformation, frequently called "feedback." Types of feedback regulate stability and allow the system to evolve through constant change. All objects in the system are reciprocally interdependent, causing changes in one person or object to have specific and broad consequences for other persons or objects interfaced in the system.

Theoretical Support

The basic assumption underlying GST is that time, energy, and space are properties of organization. Balance between these properties varies with different levels of *feedback* and *control*. Miller (1972), for example, proposed four particular levels affecting families. These included: (a) simple feedback, (b) cybernetic control, (c) morphogenesis, and (d) re-orientation or conversion.

(a) Simple feedback. This typically is a circular process in which inputs to a system convert into outputs producing a complete feedback loop, also called a positive feedback loop. Should the loop be delayed, disrupted or diverted, causing separation between inputs and outputs, then it is called "negative feedback loop." In addictive family relationships, "loops" translate into communicative messages exchanged between significant players such as between parents or parent and child. Lack of communication means any input from children or nonaddict parent is lost. The resulting negative loops distance family members and foster distrust.

(b) Cybernetic control. At this level the output of a system returns to a monitoring or inspection modality wherein adults judge it as correct or incorrect based on criteria or "meta-rules." Criteria

established and promulgated by the family may act as the standard for comparison. On a family level this means a child's grades "return" to stand trial against his parent's "meta-rules" of expectations. Failure to meet their criteria forces the child's grades (input) to be corrected before that child again can interact with external systems (the school). Before starting a new marking period, in other words, the child must suffer reprehensible consequences for poor grades. That way, cybernetically, his future grades (input) will reflect the family standards.

(c) Morphogenesis. This is an ideal situation. Here the monitoring system recognizes that its meta-rules are defective and must undergo change to prevent repetition of bad output. In theory this means families reflect upon their values, morals, and expectations toward a revision that best fits a child's realistic abilities in the world. Alcoholic families, however, would never partake in morphogenetic transition because it requires self-exploration, self-admission of mistakes, and self-correction. Disclosure of vulnerability threatens the insecurity of family members and they may bypass this level only to seek outside authority on how to change the system.

(d) Re-orientation or conversion. That's what this system is for. The main goal here is confrontation of the goals and principles governing a system. By dramatically altering a faulty system, input and output signals can resume a balanced flow with a positive loop. On a practical level, radical systemic changes rendered internally require members of that system to be objective to solve problems. Dysfunctional families simply cannot do this. This is why they seek the authority of therapists or experts upon whom they can lay the burden of changes. However, shirking responsibility backfires when the authority figure recommends systemic changes that are resisted by the family.

Ecosystems

Ecology is the science that studies interactions between living organisms and their environment. No living organism exists in isolation. The basic unit of organism-environment interaction resulting from the complex interplay of living and nonliving elements in a given area is called an *ecosystem* (Evans, 1956; Micklin, 1983). The ecosystem concept is central to "human ecology." This is the study of ecosystems as they affect or are affected by human beings. In its application to the family, emphasis is on families as systems interdependent with their natural physical-biological, human built, and social-cultural settings. This perspective emerged in the latter part of the 19th century, a period of social reform, urbanization, industrialization, and concern about health and welfare of families. It re-emerged in the 1960's with increased trends toward viewing psychological phenomena from a holistic and systems perspective.

Ecosystems can be used to study a wide range of problems related to families and their relationships with various environments and diverse levels and kinds of external systems (Andrew, Bubolz & Paolucci, 1980; Hook & Paolucci, 1970). It is appropriate for families of different structures, ethnic or racial backgrounds, or in different life stages and circumstances. Focus is upon individual family members as well as on the family as a whole, taking into account ways that families blend the many tasks and functions transacted in their daily lives.

Ecological framework offers an eclectic approach to examine interrelationships and interactions. Theories from psychoanalytic, behavioral, and developmental, among other systems, can be adapted to ecological concepts for inspection of system changes. Despite this flexibility, underlying assumptions of ecosystems all begin with the basic premise that the parts and wholes of families operate reciprocally with each other. Decisions, activities and essentially all psycho-social and physical-biological functions are interdependent and cannot be considered in isolation (cf. Herrin & Wright, 1988; Wright & Herrin, 1988). Ten other core assumptions regarding family ecosystems follow from this premise (cf. Bubolz & Sontag, in press):

1. In family ecology the properties of families and the environment, the structure of environmental settings, and the process taking place within and between them must be viewed as interdependent and analyzed as a system.

2. As human groups, families are part of the total life system, interdependent with other forms of life and the nonliving environment.

3. Families are semi-open, goal directed, dynamic adaptive systems. They can respond, change and develop, and can act on and modify their environment. Adaptation is a continuing process in family ecosystems.

4. All parts of the environment are interrelated and influence each other. The natural physical-biological environment provides the essential resource base for all of life; it is impacted upon by the socio-cultural and human built environment and also influences these environments.

5. Families require interactions with multiple environments.

6. Families are energy or transformation systems and need matter-energy for maintenance and survival, for interactions with other systems and for adaptive, creative functioning. Information organizes, activates, and transforms matter-energy in the family system.

7. Interactions between families and environments are guided by two sets of rules: immutable laws of nature which pivot around the capacity of the natural environment to supply energy and other essential resources and to process materials and waste; and human derived rules such as social norms and values, allocation of resources, role expectations, and distribution of power.

8. Environments do not determine human behavior but pose limitations and constraints as well as possibilities and opportunities for families.

9. Families have varying degrees of control and freedom with respect to environmental interactions.

10. Decision making is the central control process in families which directs actions for attaining individual and family goals. Collectively decisions and actions of families have an impact on society, culture, and natural environment.

Human Ecology Model

Human ecology model views family units as developmental and surrounded by a system of concentric circles of events, all equally causal. Pioneering research by Bronfenbrenner (1979, 1986) set the basic guidelines for analysis.

The model has four systems revolving around the child. These include microsystem, mesosystem, exosystem, and macrosystem. Microsystem is a pattern of activities, roles and interpersonal relations experienced by the developing child in a given setting. Mesosystem comprises the interrelations among two or more settings in which the developing child actively participates, such as school, church, and peers. Exosystem refers to one or more settings not involving the developing child as an active participant, but where the events occurring are affected by what happens in the setting containing the developing child. Finally, a macrosystem refers to consistencies at the level of subculture or the culture as a whole, along with belief systems or ideology underlying such consistencies.

Research support for Bronfenbrenner's model is optimistic. Dadds (1987) examined the relationship between family variables and child behavior, particularly that of oppositional disorders. Ecologically she showed that aggression is a function of three events: (1) it is determined by a network of subsystems that form the components of more complex systems, (2) at each level, components are interdependent in the way they function, and (3) each level is affected by the dynamics of levels above and below it.

This coalesces with Bronfenbrenner's (1979) micro-macrosystems model. Dadds also identified causes of the behavior problem as (a) trait-like behaviors, and (b) child's repertoire of deficits and excesses. Factors acting on the child included (a) interactions of child with primary caregivers, and (b) reaction to disruptive environment. Factors within the families acting upon parent and child included (a) maladjustment of family members as in case of stepparenting or having a second child, (b) mental illness in family, and (c) marital instability. Finally, community impacts described included (a) decline in extended family, (b) urbanicity versus rural isolationism, and (c) working parents.

In addictive families this ecomap reads like a blueprint. The *microsystem* consists of dysfunctional dynamics within the family household. Dynamics range from poor hygiene of children and disorganized, dirty living quarters, to parental mistreatment. The *mesosystems* are rare and inconsisent, regulated by the monopolizing parents who prevent outsiders from learning about problems at home. But there are many *exosystems* affected by addicted families. For example, friends of family and extended family alert to the child's adversities may be conspiring to confront the parents or rescue the children. School counselors, as one conspirator, frequently discover family abuse and take responsibility for informing protective services or other social welfare agencies that there is a need for intervention. The *macrosystem* supports moral beliefs about child rearing, about not drinking around kids, and about seeking advice from authority.

Kantor & Lehr's Model

Family types described in the conceptual model by Kantor & Lehr (1975) put the family into a different systems perspective. According to this model, process of interaction follows along three ecologic dimensions consisting *time, space,* and *energy.* How effectively integrative these dimensions are over time depends on the type of family system being either *closed, open,* or *random.* Further, determining the nature of open, closed, or random systems are casted roles that family members play for life adjustment. Let us consider each of these parameters separately before re-uniting them for an overall picture of how the model works.

Time, Space and Energy

Time refers to sequentially organizing the family so that players can assimilate rather than segregate their interactions. The more closely aligned or synchronized life schedules become over time, the better chance family cohesion remains stable. Likewise, loss of synchronicity threatens family unity as individuals diversify with uncontrollable and unpredictable movement that stifles communication and personal growth. Concepts that Kantor & Lehr use to describe time regulators are relatively common and include *orienting, clocking,* and *synchronizing.*

Orienting. This refers to family members' attitudes toward past, present and future temporal events affecting the total system. Alertness to progress or regression is relative to calendar dates.

Clocking. This regulates order of events by frequency, sequence, duration, pacing, and scheduling. Usually a family leader (parent, child, etc.) dictates whether events can be repeated, at what speed or rhythm and whether events deemed unsuitable and requiring change must be refereed by some or all family participants before its transformation.

Synchronizing. Setting the family pace is essentially to maximize productivity. Productive use of family time depends on one or many family members establishing guidelines on how to use and manage time, coordination of time schedules, and monitoring adherence to schedules once they are implemented.

Space describes physical boundaries deliberately or arbitrarily defined by the family or its designee around the family system. Its purpose is twofold. First is that boundaries keep out intruders and keep in members by surrounding the family with *impermeable* rules about outside communication. Censorship of or restricted communication narrowly defines the autonomy of family members to socialize in the world. Whereas, by contrast, *permeable* boundaries open channels of communication flow with the outside world. Three regulators imposed on family space include *bounding, linking,* and *centering.*

Bounding. This regulator establishes the firm perimeter of territory and how it will be defended if penetrated. Family roles serve to route traffic away from or patrol unopen boundaries, and to maintain perspective of the entire culture relative to family territory.

Linking. Distance is regulated between family and people outside the family. Members may bridge people in closer proximity, may buffer or move them farther away, or may under pressure *involuntarily* draw closer or deflect away people.

Centering. Spatial boundaries require evaluation on an ongoing basis. Parental leaders develop, maintain and extend evaluative responsibilities to other family members whose job it becomes to disseminate rules and norms about who the family enjoys contact with.

Energy is transformation of information. Where does it go, and how? Toward cohesion, family members agree upon ways of functionally using their actions and thoughts collectively rather than individualistically. Ideally this means dispersion of efforts are predetermined, predictable, and parallels the expectations, goals and values of parental authorities. However, less than ideal circumstances arise over time when, by sheer need to be creative, children deviate from pre-planned schedules of action and disrupt the equilibrium. Terms used to describe this energy process include *fueling, investing,* and *mobilizing*.

Fueling. Energy comes from somewhere. And fueling it is the acquisition step. Here family leaders or designees survey, tap, and requisition different sources of energy from which family cohesion can be expected.

Investing. Options for energy use force family decisions. Ways that energy can be expended or stored turn into an accounting and stock investment firm, where records are kept on ratios of gains and losses on margin investment. Following theories of market economy, reliable energy investments ultimately are ones that all family members or selected members earn dividends from. For example, efforts to build a friendship with neighbors must yield some foreseeable profit in terms of benefits of that friendship or what the friends will do for family members, or else the investment was poor.

Mobilizing. Guidelines to regulate flow of energy fall upon the shoulders of certain family members who take inventory of expenditures and recommend future directions for energy. This "budgeting" or management of energy alerts the family to when energy supply is high, low or balanced. Low energy supply demands compensatory efforts to restore balance. High energy supply forces emergency expenditures, even transducing energy from one medium or resource to another resource, as when doing homework assignments *replaces* watching television.

Closed, Open and Random Families

Differences between functional and dysfunctional families lie in the proper balance of time, space and energy dimensions. Evolving families regulate their patterns in one of three ways. The first is by rigidly limiting resources under fixed boundaries; this is the *closed* family. Families more loosely structured, in favor of autonomous individual growth, are *open* families. Extremes either way where diffusion of patterns is unpredictable, shifting like a pendulum between open and closed styles, represent the *random* family. Consider these distinctions as follows.

Closed family. Here parents or family designees tightly close boundaries making them impermeable and regulate all incoming and outgoing traffic. Activities follow highly synchronized time schedules, with steady energy and very little behavior deviation. Enforcement of rigorous standards usually requires punitive discipline for minor infractions, even for thoughts of infractions. For this reason, closed family systems manifest two diametrical reactions in affected children. First is that children rebel aggressively by defying guidelines and undermining parental authority to overthrow the oppression. Achievement of mutiny usually destroys what little family cohesion existed. A second reaction is passively surrendering to the oppression, hiding behind a mask of avoidance and escape behaviors.

Open family. One major difference from closed families is that opposition is open to discussion. Deviancy is regarded a reliable gauge of disequilibrium and of deterioration in relationships among family members. Energy is flexible, as members work together sustaining a strong unit while building ties with the outside world. Spatially, boundaries are permeable allowing for reciprocal traffic flow into and out of the family concourse. As time schedules vary, so it is that parents *trust* children to be curious, adventurous, and establish independence. Ironically, healthy open systems risk becoming too liberal if parents relinquish all regulating mechanisms and leave decisions entirely up to their children. When controls diminish, time, space, and energy suddenly lose continuity, as degrees of freedom distance family members and jeopardize what was once cohesive.

Random family. Chaotic families are ones whose routines are discordant and whose interests, goals and values are strikingly incompatible. The more twisted, illogical, unpredictable, and arbitrary patterns become, the more all three access dimensions (time, space, energy) completely vanish leaving not even a trace of family organization. Random families keep irregular or asynchronous time schedules, creating a fatalistic attitude among their members; that is, they never know what to expect and generally infer that home life is hostile, insecure, and inconsistent. Disengaged families have open and closed boundaries, vacillating without order or conviction. Energy is divergent, frequently antimobilized, as nobody is minding the shop. Under these conditions it is usual to find underdeveloped children with severe behavior deficits or excesses, in trouble at school or criminally, and prone to chronic psychiatric illness.

As in most dysfunctional families, character roles played out by different family members determine the strengths or weaknesses of a system. In Kantor & Lehr's analysis, player parts are either assigned or naturally evolve through survival of maladaptive conditions. Parts include *mover, follower, opposer,* and *bystander*. Movers take initiate directing the family toward some action and establish a context for either autocratic control or cooperation and negotiation. Opposers block the Mover's initiative, displeased with any and all suggestions for action or the context under which action might take place. Followers are bipartisan; they support either Movers' or Opposers' actions depending on who is strongest. Bystanders stay out of direct action by alienating themselves from decision making. They accomplish this distance either by (a) leaving the system field, (b) serving only as witness to the uproar, or (c) feigning support as means of neutrality.

Considering these principal players in view of access dimensions (time, space, energy) and family types (closed, open, random), it is no wonder that Kantor & Lehr speculated high risks of family stress in unstable homes. Families kept stable through tradition, by monitoring their interpersonal relationships and boundary transactions, are a rarity in American culture. Today families decentralize while children still are infants, as two working parents by necessity must trust external resources way beyond the home boundary. Daycare and aftercare programs force spatial disturbance but also force incredible synchronicity of time schedules and equally ambitious conservations of energy. Households on single or double incomes conserve money, effort, and skills as part of planning endeavors; planning to buy or build a house; planning to buy a car; planning to support a child through college. Endless lists of potential goals represent the family who may have loose boundaries but overcompensate for it by jointly sketching their future.

In addictive families the closed or random family buries hopes of cooperation and free choice. Movers and Opposers scramble for survival against adversarial parents or siblings whom they distrust and seek extensive distance from. Regulators decay, and Bystanders get lost in the shuffle, only later to resurface without any sense of family affiliation. Victims of destructive families, according to Kantor & Lehr, face inevitable recycling of their own fate once they begin a family and lose control over the boundaries. It starts all over again with the next generation. Sadly this decay never is spotted as history repeating itself, for introspection of that sort presumes the parent is aware of his mistakes.

Social Exchange Model

Social exchange proposes that social and interpersonal relationships operate according to economic principles of profit and loss (Burgess & Huston, 1979; Ekch, 1974; Heath, 1976; Simpson, 1972). Economy or "family economy" builds on the concept that resources are valuable commodities, transferable between family members or outside of families. Transfer of human resources determines the worth of that family relationship. Resources include not only such material forms as money, time, energy and productive skills, but also nonmaterial forms such as love, loyalty, pride, and status.

Several researchers have developed conceptual typologies for personal and interpersonal resources. Rettig (1985) focused on two typologies: economic exchange behavior, and social exchange behavior. Economic exchange behavior involves two-way or reciprocal transfer of objectively measured resources or services. Relationships between two parties depend on this equal or near-equal investment. Social exchange behavior involves subjectively measured resources or services transferred between two parties.

Foa and Foa (1974, 1980) linked these two typologies toward developing a more comprehensive resource exchange model. They proposed six essential resources within this model required to maintain familial equilibrium. Included are: (a) love, (2) status, (3) information exchange or "advice," (4) money as currency, (5) goods such as tangible products, and (6) services performed for one another. By way of category:

1. Love
2. Status
3. Information
4. Money
5. Goods (Products)

6. Services

All six resources address the underlying issue of whether individual life and family satisfaction fluctuate depending on dyadic gains and losses. Essentially, does one family member (giver) earn dividends on how he invests his own resources in another family member (receiver)? Does each family member reap equal shares of those dividends? To answer these questions, consider four assumptions about any exchange in a family:

1. That reciprocal needs develop chronologically through logical stages of personality or behavior changes along a continuum of time.

2. That all resources function as external or internal rewards or costs.

3. That reciprocal resources transfer via concrete-symbolic or particularistic-universal modalities.

4. That laws or principles of human behavior govern rules on reciprocity of rewards and losses, and the production of human happiness.

1. Reciprocal needs develop chronologically through logical stages of personality or behavior changes along a continuum of time.

This assumption basically proposes that needs evolve and differentiate in a hierarchy or sequential growth vis a vis the four-stage developmental schema by Foa & Foa (1980). Naturally different needs as a child or parent may also depend on such adaptive factors as success and failure of personal growth. How the environment receives or refuses the services and goods of family members may limit or even diversify Foa & Foa's stages. The order and formation of resource classes are not automatic.

2. That all resources function as external or internal rewards or costs.

Foa & Foa further argue that exchangeable resources function either to facilitate or hinder relationships. Services, status, goods, love, money--all possess properties internally or externally influential upon recipients or consumers and thereby must, like the environment, shape behavior of that recipient. Following this conditioning view, some resources seemingly encourage action without much personal experience, whereas other resources require direct experience by the recipient with that resource for action to occur. Love, for instance, supposedly is inherently reinforcing or unlearned, to which infants readily respond. Money and services--more universal and concrete--exert control over people by virtue of learning about their rewarding outcomes.

3. That reciprocal resources transfer via concrete-symbolic or particularistic-universal modalities.

Resources are plotted along two polar coordinates according to Foa & Foa's (1980) model. The concrete-symbolic continuum describes that certain resources are tangible, confrontable and overtly transmitted between people, such as goods and services. Status, love and paralingual behaviors transfer along less conspicuous routes, usually illustrated by words or remote outcomes. Feelings generated from receiving a job promotion or being in a position of authority are at times inarticulate but nonetheless strong. These are symbolic. When exchanges depend on "who" transfers resources, that is, when givers and takers affect quality of resources, that exchange is particularistic. Exchanges where the resource value is desirable or undesirable regardless of giver, for example, in the case of money, are universal.

4. That laws or principles of human behavior govern rules on reciprocity of rewards and losses, and the production of human happiness.

Of all the assumptions implied, none stir up positivistic overtones as great as claiming that exchange is orderly. Foa & Foa (1980) attempt levity by saying that "resource exchanges can be likened to a game in which participants give and take resources from one another" (p. 93). However, this is no game at all. Reference to "game" simply disguises the brute reality that social exchange theory follows basic principles of operant and respondent conditioning found at the core of behavioral psychology.

On a global level, exchange theory also directly provides rules or laws governing the orderliness of human behavior and social expectations. Foa & Foa (1980, pp. 93-94) summarize these governing laws in 13 rules they call "rules of the game." Rules describe transactions and their predictable outcomes based on gains and losses. These include:

1. The larger the amount of resource possessed by a person, the more likely it is to be given to others.

2. The smaller the amount of a resource possessed by a person, the more he is likely to take it away from others.

3. The nearer two resources are, the more likely they are to be exchanged with one another.

4. The nearer to love a resource is, the more likely it is to be exchanged with same resource. Love is exchanged for love, money is rarely exchanged with money.

5. The nearer to love a resource is, the narrower the range of resources with which it is likely to be exchanged.

6. For resources closer to money, the amount lost by the giver tends to approach the amount gained by the receiver (so that one's gain is the other's loss).

7. When a resource is not available for exchange, it is more likely to be submitted by a less particularistic than by a more particularistic person.

8. The simultaneous transmission of love and another resource increases the value of this other resource, or facilitates its transmission.

9. Taking away any resource (other than love) produces a loss of love.

10. The optimal range (neither too little or too much) of a resource is narrowest for love, and increases progressively for resources closer to money.

11. In the absence of an exchange, the amount of love possessed decreases, and the amount of love is greater for people closer to love.

12. Other conditions being equal, the probability of occurrence of a given exchange is contingent upon the institutional setting in which it may take place.

13. The probability of love exchange is higher in small groups. The opposite is true for money.

"Rules of the game" offer 13 trends observed in human resource exchanges. Underlying these propositions are basic economic propositions that shed light on why Foa & Foa's (1980) rules of the game seem plausible. That is, they answer the question, "Why do people engage in an exchange?"

1. There are multiple buyers and sellers.

2. There is a requirement for perfect information.

3. Margin utility is based on maximizing profit.

4. Conditions must be predictable.

5. Household production presupposes a connection between consumption and utility.

6. Household is a homogenous entity.

7. Economic activities require time for acquisition, consumption, utilization and expenditure (waste).

1. There are multiple buyers and sellers.

For any resource or number of resources, multiple family members may compete for sharing interest or investment in that resource.

2. There is a requirement for perfect information (consumers need accurate information to compare products, investments etc.).

Family members do not blindly request goods and services on transfer. They first inspect, assess, and weigh gains and losses among resources to determine degree of trust and safety before making a choice.

3. Margin utility is based on maximizing profit

Choice is calculated and depends on the least sacrifice of resources juxtaposed by the greatest gain potential. Parents may speculate "on margin" by restricting or delaying rewards to children who misbehave; premature investment (attention) may ruin the product (child may begin tantrum), whereas delayed investment (attention when child is quiet) may show a greater profit return (child's on-task behavior restored and increased).

4. Conditions must be predictable

Social exchange implies a "market economy. " As such, exchange theory anchored in uncertainty would misdirect participants. Family members must at least partially predict and control outcomes for their own purposes of planning, organizing, and selecting choices. Otherwise, exchange mechanisms deteriorate. Ambiguity of exchange distorts prediction, reduces probability of risk by family members, and leads to family decay.

5. Household production presupposes a connection between consumption and utility

Essentially this proposition claims a family resource must be "useful." Nonmaterial or material goods and services transferred all share properties of being needed by the family or part of regular routines or interactions such that its deprivation would disrupt the family cycle. Examples range from food (for mealtime) to love and affection.

6. Household is a homogeneous entity

Disparity of values and needs on a macroeconomic level yields diversity of products. The more selective a community, the greater the variety for accommodation. In a family, homogeneity assures more unanimity among resources; it assures that resources stand a better chance of equitable exchange among all family members, and thereby that family cohesion is stronger.

7. Economic activities require time for acquisition, consumption, utilization and expenditure (waste)

Human exchange, like human conditioning, is a temporal process. Slow or fast rates of exchange depend on whether the resource is already in a state for consumption and utilization. Love and affection, for example, require very little prerequisite ability for transfer, whereas permitting driving privileges to a child does require pre-existing or acquired skills in operating an automobile. In that case, resource transfers are contingent. Contingencies may also include how the child plans on utilizing the car and projected waste (of gas).

Ecobehavioral Model

Recent years have witnessed expansion of the unicausal behavioral model to a systems approach (Midgley & Morris, 1988; Wahler & Fox, 1981). Russo's (1990) Presidential address, for example, marks a crucial turning point in behavior therapy, arguing that multiple factors must be considered in both research and clinical endeavors. Enlarging the unit of analysis, from single to complex stimulus-response connections, echoes the sentiments of many behaviorists (Biglan, Glasgow & Singer, 1990; Morris, 1988) who support a "contextualist" approach. Such an approach promotes a "field-theory" concept following Aristotle's "interactionism" and Dewey-Bentley's (1949) "transactionalism." It replaces the artificial distinction between "behavior" and "stimulus." Principles of field theory describe human behavior "naturalistically" where stimulus and response constitute the overall transaction of events. Human behavior, in other words, is part of a process in a field of connected things and events, all reciprocally dependent.

Much of the history of field thinking can be traced to early writings of J.R. Kantor (1888-1984). Kantor essentially challenged the existing psychological constructs of mind and body and the formalization of intrapsychic dynamics (Kantor, 1959, 1970, 1976; Lichtenstein, 1984; Moore, 1984; Parrott, 1984; Smith, 1973, 1976, 1984). According to Kantor (1969), the psychological field is

> the entire system of things and conditions operating in any event taken in its available totality. It is only the entire system of factors which will provide proper descriptive and explanatory materials for the handling of events. It is not the reacting organism alone which makes up the event but also the stimulating things and conditions, as well as the setting factors. (p. 371).

Field thinking is unusual for a learning theory. It rejects heredity, environment, mind, cognition, stimuli, reinforcers, independent variables, and so on, as *exclusive* controlling forces in behavior. In fact, behavior itself must be totally redefined as an "event." Such events not only involve actions of an active organism, but also the stimulating objects, media of contact between organism and environment, functional stimulus and response attributes, and attending setting factors, all of which define the psychological field.

Antecedents and consequences are *one* among many interactive parts of the whole. Reinforcement, punishment, conditions of deprivation, pharmacologic interactions, and response properties more closely resemble kinetic energy in machinery. There are no singular units of action per se, but rather the synthesis of many larger aggregates of action (Thompson & Lubinski, 1986). For Kantor, as with avant garde field theorists, these fundamental units of a behavioral system act in constant motion along a time continuum.

Applications of the integrated-field models are evident in numerous clinical developments (Delprato, 1987; Ruben, 1984, 1986; Upson & Ray, 1984). Among these include theoretical and experimental research on aging (Herrick 1983a, 1983b; Ruben, 1990); anthropology and sociology (Herrick, 1974; MacRoberts & MacRoberts, 1983); child development (Bijou, 1976; Wahler, House & Stambaugh, 1976); substance abuse (Ruben, 1989, in press-a, in press-b) and methodological designs (Ray & Delprato, 1989). A systems alternative attests to the advancing potential of using a larger unit of applied behavior analysis as a conceptual scheme over traditional systems theory, human ecology, or traditional clinical models.

A case in point is the work by Wahler (Wahler, 1975; Wahler, Berland, Coe & Leske, 1977; Wahler & Hann, 1987). Wahler helped inspire a movement called "ecobehaviorism," essentially concerned with applying behavioral principles to marital and family problems within an integrated-field or ecological framework. Ecology, by definition, was different from a human ecology explanation. The term referred to a larger boundary or field of analysis wherein the same functions of responses and stimuli occurred, but the effects were spread over time and involved (a) multiple sequences of behavior, and (b) continuous, reciprocal exchanges of human-to-human contact. Delprato (1986; Delprato & McGlynn, 1986) later categorized these interdependent response patterns into two types: (a) concurrent response patterns; and (b) sequential response patterns. Briefly, the first type is when responses occur as, for example, when talking, walking and using gestures happen simultaneously. Sequential response patterns are responses in a chain link that depend on each for sources of reinforcement as well as from antecedents and consequences.

Ecobehaviorism Applied To Family Addiction

We now see that an ecobehavioral systems view of family addiction considers behaviors, setting events, and biological factors. But consider this clinical scenario for a moment. An addicted parent neglects or and mistreats his children and consequently destroys their adult lives.

Now, exactly where did the first "cause" start? Predicting the variables that cause this systemic family deterioration is not always so easy. Griffore & Phenice (1988) recently made this attempt. They traced ecological impacts upon human development in part following Bronfenbrenner's (1979) model and Aristotle's model of causality. Creatively they attributed disruptions in the flow of activity patterns and energy transfer in multilevel (ecobehavioral) systems to material, formal, efficient, and final causes. However, these four type of causes were too inexact for scientific predictions on how systems changed.

An alternative proposal is to advance the predictability of social exchange theory along with the principles of reinforcement and punishment. This poses interesting possibilities considering that Foa & Foa's (1980) model explicitly describes interactional outcomes of resources between a giver and receiver. Their rules of the game stipulate gains and losses, just as operant contingencies stipulate reinforces and punishers. In both cases the reciprocal exchange transacted determines whether those affected by the exchange will repeat their actions (i.e., increase probability of their behaviors) or inhibit their actions (i.e., decrease probability of their behaviors) in the future.

Combining both systems begins with a change in terminology. Let us substitute some words from Foa & Foa's list of rules with behavioral terms. Love, money, status, and other positive resources equal "rewards" (reward exchanges). Physical abuse, verbal abuse and hate will constitute negative resources, equal to "punishers" (punishing exchanges). The quality and quantity of resources can be described by measurable properties such as frequency, duration, magnitude, and intensity. The exchange itself is either "response-contingent" or "response-noncontingent." If it is response-contingent, resources may occur on a "schedule" or for something specific giver and receiver do. If it is response-noncontingent, no schedule or order of exchange exists (i.e., it is arbitrary, random), and it has nothing to do with what giver or receiver are doing.

With these changes in mind, consider the following revised "rules of the game" for a comprehensive ecobehavioral systems theory. Rules are divided into *reward exchanges, punishing exchanges,* and *simultaneous and delayed exchanges.*

Reward Exchanges

This is where the outcomes increase probability of either giver and receiver's actions:

1. The greater the amount (frequency and intensity) of rewards given by one person, the less the amount of rewards returned by another person.

2. The less the amount of rewards given by one person, the more the amount of punishers returned by another person.

3. The more the rewards are taken away after they are given, the higher the amount of punishers returned by another person.

4. When rewards are absent, it is more likely receivers demand substitutes or dispense punishers in return.

5. The more that rewards are given response-contingently, the faster rewards are returned by the receiver.

6. The more that rewards are given response-noncontingently, the slower rewards are returned by the receiver. But the higher the demand for rewards by receiver.

Punishing Exchanges

This is where the outcomes decrease probability of either giver and receiver's actions:

1. The greater the amount (frequency and intensity) of punishers given by one person, the less the amount of rewards returned by another person. And, there is a greater probability of punishers returned by receiver. Where there have been many punishing exchanges, the receiver may avoid the exchange entirely.

2. The less the amount of punishers given by one person, the more the amount of punishers given by another person.

3. The more that punishers are taken away after they are given, the higher the amount of rewards returned by another person. This is to avoid future recurrence of punishers.

4. When punishers are absent, there is a high amount of rewards given by receivers. This is to avoid future recurrence of punishers.

5. The more that punishers are given response-contingently, the more the amount of punishers returned by another person.

6. The more that punishers are given response-noncontingent, the less the punishers or rewards that are returned by the receiver. Where there have been many punishing exchanges, the receiver may avoid the exchange entirely.

Simultaneous and Delayed Exchanges (Transmissions) of Rewards and Punishers

This is where the outcomes increase or decrease probability of either giver and receiver's actions based on the timing of rewards and punishers.

1. When more rewards and less punishers are transmitted simultaneously, it is likely a receiver will react to the punisher and return with a punisher.

2. When less rewards and more punishers are transmitted simultaneously, it is likely a receiver will react to the punisher and return with a punisher.

3. When equal amount of rewards and punishers are transmitted simultaneously, it is likely a receiver will react to the punisher and return with a punisher.

4. When rewards are given, followed by punishers (within 30 min.), it is likely a receiver will react to the punisher and return with a punisher.

5. When punishers are given, followed by rewards (within 30 min.), it is likely a receiver will react with neither punisher nor reward.

Viewing ecobehaviorism as a leader among family system models recognizes the long struggle by sociologists and home economists for a basic science. Models reviewed in the first part of this chapter largely were theoretical, or derivations from existing models that were equally data impoverished. In the second half, on system approaches, applied models offered exemplary ways that phenomena so elusive as families could be harnessed in operational terms.

Ecosystems, human ecology, Kantor & Lehr's model, social exchange and ecobehaviorism all conform to the canons of valid research and represent new strides for future study of addiction families.

REFERENCES

Andrews, M.P., Bubolz, M.M. & Paolucci, B. (1980). An ecological approach to study of the family. *Marriage and Family Review, 3,* 29-49.

Baltes, P.B. (1987). Theoretical propositions of life-span developmental psychology on the dynamics between growth and decline. *Developmental Psychology,* 23, 611-626.

Bennett, J.W. (1976). *The ecological transition: Cultural anthropology and human adaptation.* NY: Pergamon Press.

Beutler, I.F., Burr, W.R., Bahr, K.S. & Herrin, D.A. (1979). The family realm: Theoretical contributions for understanding its uniqueness. *Journal of Marriage and The Family,* 51, 805-816.

Bijou, S. (1976). *Child development: The basic stage of early childhood.* Englewood Cliffs, NJ: Prentice-Hall.

Biglan, A., Glasgow, R.E. & Singer, G. (1990). The need for a science of larger social units: A contextual approach. *Behavior Therapy,* 21, 195-215.

Bronfenbrenner, U. (1977). Toward an experimental ecology of human development. *American Psychologist,* 52, 513-531.

Bronfenbrenner, U. (1979). *The ecology of human development.* Cambridge, MA: Harvard University Press.

Bronfenbrenner, U. (1986). Ecology of the family as a context for human development: Research perspectives. *Developmental Psychology,* 22, 723-742.

Bubolz, M.M. & Sontag, M.S. (in press). Human ecology theory. In P. Boss, W. Doherty, R. LaRossa, W. Schumm & S. Steinmetz (Eds.). *Sourcebook of family theories and methods: A contextual approach.* NY: Plenum.

Buckley, W. (1967). *Sociology and modern systems theory.* Englewood Cliffs, NJ: Prentice-Hall.

Burgess, R.G. & Huston, T.L. (1979). *Social exchange in developing relationships*. NY: Academic Press.

Burr, W.R. (1973). *Theory construction and the sociology of the family*. NY: John Wiley & Sons.

Burr, W.R. & Leigh, G.K. (1983). Famology: A new discipline. *Journal of Marriage and the Family*, 45, 467-480.

Burrell, G. & Morgan, G. (1979). *Sociological paradigms and organizational analysis*. London: Heinemann.

Chafetz, J.S. (1974). *A primer on the construction and testing of theories in sociology*. Itasca, IL: F.E. Peacock Publishers.

Dadds, M.R. (1987). Families and the origins of child behavior problems. *Family Relations*, 26, 341-357.

Delprato, D.J. (1986). Response patterns. In H. W. Reese & L.J. Parrott (Eds.). *Behavior science: Philosophical, methodological, and empirical advances*. Hillsdale, NJ: Lawrence Erlbaum Associates (pp. 61-113).

Delprato, D.J. (1987). Developmental interactionism: An integrative framework for behavior therapy. *Advances in Behaviour Research and Therapy*, 9, 173-205.

Delprato, D.J. & McGlynn, F.D. (1986). Innovations in behavioral medicine. In M. Hersen, R.M. Eisler & P.M. Miller (Eds.). *Progress in behavior modification*, vol. 20. Orlando, FL: Academic Press (pp. 67-122).

Dewey, J. & Bentley, A.F. (1949). *Knowing and the known*. Boston, MA: Beacon Press.

Ekeh, P.P. (1974). *Social exchange theory*. Cambridge, MA: Harvard University Press.

Evans, F. (1956). Ecosystem as the basic unit in ecology. *Science*, 123, 1127-1128.

Foa, E.G. & Foa, U.G. (1974). *Societal structures of the mind*. IL: Charles Thomas.

Foa, E.B. & Foa, U.G. (1980). Resource theory: Interpersonal behavior as exchange. In Gergen, S., Greenberg, T. & Willis, D. (Eds.). *Social exchange: Advances in theory and research.* NY: Plenum.

Foster, S.L. & Hoier, T.S. (1982). Behavioral and systems family therapies: A comparison of theoretical assumptions. *American Journal of Family Therapy,* 10, 13-23.

Gibbs, J.C. (1979). The meaning of ecologically oriented inquiry in contemporary psychology. *American Psychologist,* 34, 127-140.

Giddens, A. (1974). *Positivism and sociology.* London: Heinemann.

Griffore, R.J. & Phenice, L. (1988). Causality and the ecology of human development. *Psychological Record,* 38, 515-525.

Heath, A. (1976). *Rational choice and social exchange.* Cambridge, England: Cambridge University Press.

Herrick, J.W. (1974). Kantor's anticipations of current approaches to anthropology. *Psychological Record,* 24, 253-257.

Herrick, J.W. (1983a). Interbehavioral perspectives on aging. *International Journal of Aging and Human Development,* 16, 95-123.

Herrick, J.W. (1983b). The road to scientific ageism. In N.W. Smith, P.T. Mountjoy & D.H. Ruben (Eds.). *Reassessment in psychology: The interbehavioral alternative.* Washington, D.C.: University Press of America (pp. 269-275).

Herrin D.A. & Wright, S.C. (1988). Precursors to a family ecology: Interrelated threads of ecological thought. *Family Science Review,* 1, 163-184.

Hook, N. & Paolucci, B. (1970). The family as an ecosystem. *Journal of Home Economics,* 62, 315-318.

Kamerman, S.B. & Kahn, T. (1981). *Child care, family benefits, and working parents: A study in contemporary policy.* NY: Columbia University Press.

Kantor, D. & Lehr, W. (1975). *Inside the family: Toward a theory of family process.* NY: Harper.

Kantor, J.R. (1959). *Interbehavioral psychology.* Granville, OH: Principia Press.

Kantor, J.R. (1969). *The scientific evolution of psychology (vol. 2).* Chicago, IL: Principia.

Kantor, J.R. (1970). An analysis of the experimental analysis of behavior. *Journal of the Experimental Analysis of Behavior,* 13, 101-108.

Kantor, J.R. (1976). The origin and evolution of interbehavioral psychology. *Revista Mexicana de Analisis de la Conducta,* 2, 120-136.

Kantor, J.R. (1982). *Cultural psychology.* Chicago, IL: Principia Press.

Klein, D.M. (1983). Family problem solving and family stress. *Marriage and Family Process,* 6, 85-112.

Leibowitz, L. (1978). *Females, males, families: A biosocial approach.* North Scituate, MA: Duxbury.

Lichtenstein, P.E. (1984). Interbehaviorism in psychology and in the philosophy of science. *Psychological Record,* 34, 455-475.

McCubbin, H.I. & Patterson, J.M. (1983). The family stress process: The double ABCX model of adjustment and adaptation. *Marriage and Family Review,* 6, 7-37.

MacRoberts, M. H. & MacRoberts, B.R. (1983). An interbehavioral and historico-critical examination of anthropology, ethology and sociology. In N.W. Smith, P.T. Mountjoy & D.H. Ruben (Eds.). *Reassessment in psychology: The interbehavioral alternative.* Washington, D.C.: University Press of America (pp. 297-325).

Merton, R.K. (1957). *Social theory and social structure.* Glencoe, IL: Free Press.

Micklin, M. (1973). Introduction: A framework for the study of human ecology. In M. Micklin (Ed.). *Population, environment and social organization*. Hillsdale, IL: Dryden Press (pp. 2-19).

Midgely, B.D. & Morris, E.K. (1988). The integrated field: An alternative to the behavior-analytic conceptualization of behavioral units. *Psychological Record*, 38, 483-500.

Miller, J.G. (1972). *Living systems*. NY: John Wiley & Sons.

Mishler, E.G. (1979). Meaning in context: Is there any other kind? *Harvard Educational Review*, 49, 1-19.

Mook, B. (1985). Phenomenology, system theory and family therapy. *Journal of Phenomenological Psychology*, 16, 1-11.

Moore, J. (1984). Conceptual contributions of Kantor's interbehavioral psychology. *The Behavior Analyst*, 7, 188-196.

Morris, E.K. (1988). Contextualism: The world view of behavior analysis. *Journal of Experimental Child Psychology*, 46, 289-323.

Nye, F.I. (1988). Fifty years of family research, 1937-1987. *Journal of Marriage and the Family*, 50, 305-316.

Nye, F.I. & Berardo, F.M. (1973). *The family: Its structure and interaction*. NY: Macmillan.

Odum, H.S. (1983). *Systems ecology: An introduction*. NY: John Wiley & Sons.

Osmand, M. (1987). Radical-critical theories. In M. Sussman & S. Strinmetz (Eds.). *Handbook of marriage and the family*. NY: Plenum Press (pp. 102-124).

Pilisuk, M. & Parks, S.H. (1983). Social support and family stress. *Marriage and Family Review*, 6, 137-156.

Paolucci, B., Hall, O.A. & Axinn, N. (1977). *Family decision-making: An ecosystem approach*. NY: John Wiley & Sons.

Parrott, L.J. (1984). J.R. Kantor's contributions to psychology and philosophy: A guide to further study. *The Behavior Analyst, 7,* 169-181.

Parsons, T. & Bales, R. (1955). *Family, socialization and interaction process.* Glencoe, IL: Free Press.

Patterson, G.R. & Reid, J.B. (1984). Social interactional process in the family: the study of the moment by moment family transactions in which human social development is embedded. *Journal of Applied Developmental Psychology,* 5, 237-262.

Pratt, L. (1976). *Family structure and effective health behavior.* Boston, MA: Houghton-Mifflin.

Ray, R. & Delprato, D.J. (1989). Behavioral systems analysis: Methodological strategies and tactics. *Behavioral Science,* 34, 81-127.

Reese, H.W. & Parrott, L.J. (Eds.). (1986). *Behavior science: Philosophical, methodological, and empirical advances.* Hillsdale, NJ: Lawrence Erlbaum Associates.

Reis, J., Barbera-Stein, L. & Bennett, S. (1986). Ecological determinants of parenting. *Family Relations,* 35, 547-554.

Rettig, K. (1985). Conceptual issues for integrated economic and social exchange theories. *Journal of Consumer Studies and Home Economics,* 9, 43-62.

Rogers, M.F. (1983). *Sociology, ethnomethodology, and experiences: A phenomenological critique.* NY: Cambridge University Press.

Ruben, D.H. (1984). Major trends in interbehavioral psychology from articles published in "Psychological Record" (1937-1983). *Psychological Record,* 34, 589-617.

Ruben, D.H. (1986). The "interbehavioral" approach to treatment. *Journal of Contemporary Psychotherapy,* 16, 62-71.

Ruben, D.H. (1989). Behavioral predictors of alcoholics: A "systems" alternative. *Alcoholism Treatment Quarterly,* 5, 137-162.

Ruben, D.H. (1990). *The aging and drug effects: A planning manual for medication and alcohol abuse treatment of the elderly.* Jefferson, NC: McFarland & Company.

Ruben, D.H. (in press-a). Interbehavioral approach to treatment of substance abuse: A "new" systems model. *Alcoholism Treatment Quarterly.*

Ruben, D.H. (in press-b). *Avoidance syndrome* . St. Louis, MO: Warren Green.

Ruben, D.H. & Delprato, D.J. (Eds.). (1987). *New ideas in therapy: Introduction to an interdisciplinary approach.* Westport, CT: Greenwood Press.

Russo, D.C. (1990). A requiem for the passing of the three-term contingency. *Behavior Therapy,* 21, 153-165.

Simpson, R.L. (1972). *Theories of social exchange.* Morristown, NJ: General Learning Press.

Smith, N.W. (1973). Interbehavioral psychology: roots and branches. *Psychological Record,* 23, 153-167.

Smith, N.W. (1976). The works of J.R. Kantor: Pioneer in scientific psychology. *Revista Mexicana de Analisis de la Conducta,* 2, 137-148.

Smith, N.W. (1984). Fundamentals of interbehavioral psychology. *Psychological Record,* 34, 479-494.

Smith, N.W., Mountjoy, P.T. & Ruben, D.H. (Eds.). (1983). *Reassessment in psychology: The interbehavioral alternative.* Washington, D.C.: University Press of America.

Sprey, J. (1988). Current theorizing on the family: An appraisal. *Journal of Marriage and the Family,* 50, 875-890.

Thomas, D.L. & Wilcox, J.E. (1987). The rise of family theory: A historical and critical analysis. In M. Sussman & S. Steinmetz (Eds.). *Handbook of marriage and the family.* NY: Plenum (pp. 81-102).

Thompson, T. & Lubinski, D. (1986). Units of analysis and kinetic structure of behavioral repertoires. *Journal of the Experimental Analysis of Behavior,* 46, 219-242.

Upson, J.D. & Ray, R.D. (1984). An interbehavioral systems model for empirical investigation in psychology. *Psychological Record,* 34, 497-524.

Wahler, R.G. (1975). Some structural aspects of deviant child behavior. *Journal of Applied Behavior Analysis,* 8, 27-42.

Wahler, R.G., Berland, R.M., Coe., T.D. & Leske, G. (1977). Social systems analysis: implementing an alternative behavioral model. In A. Rogers-Warren & S. F. Warren (Eds.). *Ecological perspectives in behavior analysis.* MD: University Park Press.

Wahler, R.G. & Hann, D.M. (1987). An interbehavioral approach to clinical child psychology: Toward an understanding of troubled families. In D.H. Ruben & D.J. Delprato (Eds.) *New ideas in therapy: Introduction to an interdisciplinary approach.* Westport, CT: Greenwood Press (pp. 53-78).

Wahler, R.G., House, A.E. & Stambaugh, E.E. (1976). *Ecological assessment of child problem behavior.* NY: Pergamon Press.

Wahler, R.G. & Fox, J.J. (1981). Setting events in applied behavior analysis: Toward a conceptual and methodological expansion. *Journal of Applied Behavior Analysis,* 14, 327-338.

Wright, S.D. & Herrin, D.A. (1988). Ecology, human ecology, and the study of family: Part 2. *Family Science Review,* 1, 253-282.

SELECTED ANNOTATED RESOURCES

ANDREWS, M.P., BUBOLZ, M.M. & PAOLUCCI, B. (1980). An ecological approach to study of the family. *Marriage & Family Review*, 3, 29-49.

1. English; 2. Theoretical/review; 3. Family; 4. Presents interdependence of family members in a human ecosystems approach. Describes family as energy transformation in the production of human capital through building of individual competence. Competencies include the individual, family, community and societal; 5. Use of ecological tenets enhances understanding of relationship between behavior and environment and provides framework for clinical intervention programs.

BEUTLER, I.F., BURR, W.R., BAHR, K.S. & HERRIN, D.A. (1979). The family realm: Theoretical contributions for understanding its uniqueness. *Journal of Marriage and the Family*, 51, 805-816.

1. English; 2. Theoretical/review; 3. Family; 4. Describes "family realm" as unique phenomena characterized by seven factors that are evaluated according to four theories. Seven distinctive factors include (a) generational nature and permanence of family relationships, (b) concern with "total" persons, (c) the simultaneous process orientation that grows out of familial caregiving, (d) a unique and intense emotionality, (e) an emphasis on qualitative purposes and processes, (f) an altruistic orientation, and (g) a nurturing form of governance. Empirically derived theories forming what authors call "famological perspective" serve as catalyst in comparisons; 5. Value of characteristics illustrated best through theories of exchange, economy, and role theory.

BIJOU, SIDNEY, W. (1984). Cross-sectional and longitudinal analysis of development: The interbehavioral perspective. *Psychological Record*, 34, 525-535.

1. English; 2. Theoretical/review; 3. Children; 4. Reviews and extends J.R. Kantor's concept of life-span development divided into foundational, basic, and societal stages. A 6-stage cross-sectional analysis is proposed, instead, where the foundation stage remains the preverbal period, basic stage is subdivided into early and middle

childhood and adolescence, and societal stage is divided into maturity and old age; 5. This revision clarifies the orderly changes from origin to termination and transactions along dimensions of emotion, language, and cognitions.

BUBOLZ, M.M. & SONTAG, M.S. (in press). Human ecology theory. In P. Boss, W. Doherty, R. LaRossa, W. Schumm & S. Steinmetz (Eds.). *Sourcebook of family theories and methods: A contextual approach.* NY: Plenum.

1. English; 2. Theoretical/review; 3. Families; 4. Comprehensively examines the roots and currency of modern ecological thinking starting with leading theories and covering terms and concepts that define family ecology and human development; 5. Authors articulate their own theory called "human ecosystem" consisting of four components: (a) the family, (b) natural physical-biological environment, (c) human built environment, and (d) social-cultural environment.

BUBOLZ, M. M, EICHER, J.B. & SONTAG, M.S. (1979). The human ecosystem: A model. *Journal of Home Economics*, 71, 28-31.

1. English; 2. Theoretical; 3. Families and children; 4. Proposes conceptual scheme for human ecology that incorporates cultural values, human adjustment, and evolving physical or ecological changes. The model spotlights the human environment unit as centrally surrounded by (a) human behavioral environment, (b) human constructed environment, and (c) natural environment. Interaction among all three units is reciprocal and continuous; 5. Implications for rules governing and specifying interactions within human ecosystems are discussed.

CROSBIE-BURNETT, M. (1989). Application of family stress theory to remarriage: A model for assessing and helping stepfamilies. *Family Relations*, 38, 323-331.

1. English; 2. Clinical; 3. Family; 4. Application of ABCX model serves as basis for delineating hardships associated with remarriage and potential resources available to the stepfamily, meanings of remarriage, and communication breakdown. Case study illustrates how stressor event of remarriage interacts with family system causing family crisis; 5. Steps for assessment and clinical intervention can (a) improve family communication, (b) reconstitute meaning as family unit, and (c)

establish realistic goals in child raising, relieving fears of family detachment.

DUVALL, E.M. (1988). Family development's first forty years. *Family Relations*, 37, 127-134.

1. English; 2. Theoretical/review; 3. Family; 4. Reviews history of family development theories as well as universality of family cycle and assigned tasks among family members that functionally run the household. Transition of tasks considered during crises, family stress, generational support, and cultural and social class factors; 5. Its interdisciplinary origins and accretions unfortunately cause confusion and required are new hypotheses for validity testing.

EZELL, M.P., PAOLUCCI, B. & BUBOLZ, M.M. (1984). Developing family properties. *Home Economics Research Journal*, 12, 563-574.

1. English; 2. Experimental; 3. 107 randomly selected family constellations of husband, wife, and oldest child; 4. Rural community; 5. Perceptions of responsibility for household production and quality of life; 6. & 7. Self-report questionnaire adapted from work of Andrews & Withey (1976), scored along a seven point scale. Groups based on individuals taking the instrument (husband, wife, child); 8. Results computed using three models to measure family properties: (a) additive model (addition of family scores across items), (b) dispersive model (sum of discrepancy between family members' scores across items) and (c) discrete model (individual reports as discrete, independently valid family properties); 9. Triadic perceptions reveal congruency among family properties identified, but perceptions of quality of life as a whole were different. Implications for using family properties in operationally defined interactions are discussed.

GRIFFORE, R.J. & PHENICE, L.A. (1988). Causality and the ecology of human development. *Psychological Record*, 38, 515-525.

1. English; 2. Theoretical; 3. Adults; 4. Outlines multidimensional research approach using Aristotelian concepts of causality including material, formal, efficient, and final causes. Terms are redefined in Bronfenbrenner's ecological system showing organization of stage progression; 5. Direct implications of model are for evaluation of child maltreatment and related family dysfunction.

HERRICK, J.W. (1983). Interbehavioral perspectives on aging. *International Journal of Aging and Human Development*, 16, 95-123.

1. English; 2. Theoretical/review; 3. Elderly; 4. Questions assumptions that behavioral and mental incompetence accompanying aging is a natural process, or process accelerated by a cultural system closed to older people; 5. Proposed is alternative interbehavioral model eliminating erroneous, medieval concepts, negative stereotypes, replacing them with operational principles for further geropsychological research.

HERRIN, D.A. & WRIGHT, S.D. (1988). Precursors to a family ecology: Interrelated threads of ecological thought. *Family Science Review*, 1, 163-183.

1. English; 2. Theoretical; 3. Family; 4. Presents historical overview of relevant developments in ecology and human ecology spanning last 10 years, toward a unified approach to family study; 5. Growth of documented research points to common threads with bioecology and behavioral ecology over against sociology and traditional psychology.

KANTOR, J.R. (1982). Psychological retardation and interbehavioral maladjustments. *Psychological Record*, 32, 305-313.

1. English; 2. Clinical/review; 3. Adults, children; 4. Applauds the efforts of scientific psychologists on describing juvenile delinquency as abnormality along an event continuum, where psychological events interact continuously in tandem with biological development. Interbehaviorally, social pathology or retardation are products of simple maladjustments along different clinical types that are reviewed; 5. Concludes that extreme variations in psychological life must be considered in full context of field relationships.

KANTOR, J.R. (1980). Manifesto of interbehavioral psychology. *Revista Mexicana de Analisis de la Conducta*, 6, 117-128.

1. English; 2. Theoretical/review; 3. Adults; 4. Describes the genesis of interbehavioral psychology in reference to its postulation, data, operations, laws, and implications for contemporary science; 5. Premise states that practice of psychology requires a scientific foundation for thorough analysis of cultural and endemic human variables.

KIDD, R.V. & NATALICIO, L. (1981). Toward a radical interbehaviorism. *Revista Interamericana de Psicologia,* 15, 123-131.

1. Spanish; 2 . Theory/review; 3. Adults; 4. Interprets differences and similarities between systems of J.R. Kantor and B.F. Skinner regarding event field and tracing historical roots; 5. Authors argue that reconciliation between both positions depends upon forming new paradigm.

MCCUBBIN, H.I., & PATTERSON, J.M. (1983). The family stress process: The double ABCX model of adjustment and adaptation. *Marriage and Family Review,* 6, 7-37.

1. English; 2. Clinical/review; 3. Family; 4. Re-examines Hill's ABCX family crisis model and Burr's synthesis of family stress research, which states family outcomes are by-products of multiple factors in interaction with each other. That is, A (stressor event) --->interacting with B (the family's crisis—meeting resources)--->interacting with C (the definition the family makes of the event)--->produces X (the crisis). Additional components shaping family adjustment based on longitudinal observations of family under stress; 5. Improved version of the model expands research efforts to test the efficacy and limitations of the process.

MEDERER, H. & HILL, R. (1983). Critical transitions over the family life span: Theory and research. *Marriage and Family Review,* 6, 39-60.

1. English; 2. Theoretical/review; 3. Family; 4. Assesses circumstances that precipitate shifts in families from one stage of structural equilibrium to the next by reviewing work in family development and by drawing on the work on family stress and critical transition theories. Eight transitional phases explored include (1) establishment stage (newly married), (2) first parenthood (infant to 3 years of age), (3) family with preschool child (oldest 3-6 years), (4) family with school child (oldest 6-12 years), (5) family with adolescents (oldest 13-20 years), (6) family as launching center (leave taking of children), (7) family in middle years (empty nest), and (8) family in retirement (breadwinner 65 years and over); 5. Argues that developmental issues are interdisciplinary and require more elaborate methods to move beyond theories.

MIDGLEY, B.D. & MORRIS, E.K. (1988). The integrated field: An alternative to the behavior-analytic conceptualization of behavioral units. *Psychological Record*, 38, 483-500.

1. English; 2. Theoretical; 3. Family; 4. Proposes J.R. Kantor's behavioral field as an alternative behavioral unit to B.F. Skinner's operant. Historical background follows by analysis of three long-standing false dichotomies: organism vs. response as the subject matter, internal vs. external causation, and explanatory vs. descriptive analysis; 5. Field thinking emphasizes holistic orientation as opposed to reductionistic one and allows greater flexibility for methodological research and clinical applications.

MORRIS, E.K. (1984). Interbehavioral psychology and radical behaviorism: Some similarities and differences. *Behavior Analyst*, 7, 197-204.

1. English; 2. Theoretical/review; 3. Adult; 4. Explains that Kantor's psychology and Skinner's radical behaviorism, while sharing similar features, differ along many dimensions. Dimensions covered include the concept of field versus three-term contingency and evolving behavior patterns of adulthood; 5. Concludes that similarities largely are fundamental and that integration of both theories can facilitate development of science to greater plateau.

NYE, F. I. (1988). Fifty years of family research, 1937-1987. *Journal of Marriage and the Family*, 50, 305-316.

1. English; 2. Theoretical/review; 3. Family; 4. Assays the family research literature beginning in 1937 and evolving into a social science perspective by 1970's, with research methods surfacing by late 1980's. Major transitions brought about by the renewal of societal interest in home economics; 5. Competent family research invariably depends on reaffirmation of scientific values through more rigorous research applications.

PARROTT, LINDA J. (1984). J.R. Kantor's contributions to psychology and philosophy: A guide to further study. *Behavior Analyst*, 7, 169-181.

1. English; 2. Theoretical/review; 3. Adult; 4. Examines disregard for Kantor's interbehavioral systems theory within science proper, proposing that field thinking from 1917 to 1984 shaped modern

pragmatism into orderly concepts adopted later by Skinner's operant psychology; 5. Retrospective appreciation of Kantor's theories advances understanding of functionalism and organismic psychology.

PRONKO, N.H. (1982). From Dewey's reflex arc concept to transactionalism and beyond. *Behaviorism*, 10, 229-254.

1. English; 2. Theoretical/review; 3. Adult/children; 4. Traces the evolution of Dewey & Bentley's 1949 formation of transactional system from its antecedents to modern reformulations, prominently noting Kantor's philosophical and psychological field theory as sharing major premises and terminology; 5. Upon further evaluation author shows that Kantor's first presentations of systems theory go beyond Dewey and Bentley's unfractured observations.

RAY, M. (1988). An ecological model of the family. *Home Economics Forum*, 2, 9-15.

1. English; 2. Theoretical/review; 3. Family; 4. Argues that family theory must be problem-focused, value-laden, integrated, and multidisciplinary. Examines contributions by Bronfenbrenner, Kantor & Lehr, & Reiss; 5. Concludes based on multiple system levels that (1) American society does not value the welfare of families, (2) family welfare is essential to individual welfare, and (3) conceptualizations of family must focus simultaneously on individual and family welfare.

RIBES, E. (1984). The relation between interbehaviorism and the experimental analysis of behavior: The search for a paradigm. *Psychological Record*, 34, 567-573.

1. English; 2. Experimental/review; 3. Adult, children; 4. Outlines differences between Kantor's interbehavioral psychology and Skinner's analysis of causality and generality as interpreted through T.S. Kuhn's notions about rules of correspondence between language and nature and exemplary rules in scientific problem solving; 5. Concludes that interbehaviorism provides feasible meta-theory for study of anomalies and is more powerful than conditioning theory.

RUBEN, D. H. (1986). The "interbehavioral" approach to treatment. *Journal of Contemporary Psychotherapy*, 16, 62-71.

1. English; 2. Theoretical/clinical; 3. Adults; 4. Introduces and describes the "interbehavioral" approach to clinical intervention as an

interdisciplinary system where assessment and treatment encompass physical and psychological effects as continuous interactions. Tenets of theory based on J. R. Kantor's conceptualization, and interpreted for clinical training, application, and methods to overcome problems of skill generalization; 5. Advantages of integrated-field thinking over orthodox Skinnerian behaviorism range from development of a sophisticated clinical network to larger pool of variables considered in diagnosis and treatment phases.

RUBEN, D. H. (1984). Major trends in interbehavioral psychology from articles published in the "Psychological Record." *Psychological Record,* 34, 589-617.

1. English; 2. Theory, review; 3. Adults, children; 4. Major trends in interbehavioral psychology are examined retrospectively through articles published in the 33-volume history of the Psychological Record, given that this journal reflected evolution of the theory and practice. Articles assessed in terms of applied, experimental and interdisciplinary philosophical research, showing comparisons to noninterbehavioral research. Lists all interbehavioral terminology extracted from J.R. Kantor's introductory psychology textbook for systems approach, and provides annotations of articles; 5. Conclusions demonstrate re-emerging interest in field systems by behavioral and nonbehavioral researchers, with focus aimed at advancing it with a solid scientific foundation.

SMITH, N.W. (1984). Fundamentals of interbehavioral psychology. *Psychological Record,* 34, 479-494.

1. English; 2. Theoretical/review; 3. Adult, children; 4. Reviews the cognitive and behavioral models in contrast to interbehaviorism, confining itself to functional descriptions of terms and applications. Introduction offered on such terms as stimulus and response function, interactional history, setting, medium of contact, and field analysis of private events such as imaging, thinking, language, attending, perceiving, voluntary and involuntary conduct; 5. Directives for research and theory naturally follow from emphasis on applied problems.

SPREY, J. (1988). Current theorizing on the family: An appraisal. *Journal of Marriage and the Family,* 50, 875-890.

1. English; 2. Theoretical/review; 3. Family; 4. Central to discussion is re-evaluation of socio-cultural theories that dichotomize descriptive versus analytical approaches to family study. Problems of hermeneutics are shown to be too subjectively qualitative and negate progress toward natural sciences. Feminist theorizing blamed for being too epistemological and lacking methodological sophistication; 5. In light of speculative theories, goals of family study scholars must shift from realm of politics, philosophy and religion to that of family development, returning credibility to a defined discipline.

UPSON, J.D. & RAY, R.D. (1984). An interbehavioral systems model for empirical investigation in psychology. *Psychological Record*, 34, 497-524.

1. English; 2. Experimental/review; 3. Children/adults; 4. Discusses empirically based model for assessment of systems interactions among children and adults following J.R. Kantor's field initiatives. System encompasses macro events, mid-range micro events, and micro events existing at the level of nervous activity. Model stresses interdependent nature of these processes and need to evaluate them concurrently in, for example, sports, music, EEG, spectral analysis, hemispheric synchronization and information processing studies; 5. Authors imply that model assimilates bio-physical and psychological variables for a more comprehensive systems outlook.

WRIGHT, S.D. & HERRIN, D.A. (1988a). Family ecology: An approach to the interdisciplinary complexity of the study of family phenomena. *Family Science Review*, 1, 253-281.

1. English; 2. Theoretical/review; 3. Family; 4. Sequel to Herrin & Wright (1988) expanding the conceptual commonalties and differences between ecological and other behavioral science frameworks of family study. Shared perspectives include viewing (a) humans as ecological organisms, and (b) organismic and holistic orientations; 5. Implications of human ecology for family dynamics beyond developmental stages include new terminology, advanced models of reciprocal human conditioning, and assessments of good, healthy and normative family life.

WRIGHT, S.D. & HERRIN, D.A. (1988b). Toward a family ecology. *Home Economics Forum*, 2, 5-8.

1. English; 2. Theoretical; 3. Family; 4. Provides conceptual framework for understanding complexities of family dynamics derived from principles of ecology. Traces historical origins of theory and shows connections to research in family study along with advantages of this system over traditional models; 5. Summarizes its major purposes in four categories: (1) a philosophical approach that follows closely the orientations of an organismic and transactional worldview, (2) an integrated curriculum on family phenomena based on conceptual issues from complementary disciplines, (3) a methodological eclecticism for investigating family phenomena with both quantitative and qualitative methods, and (4) the promotion of policy and intervention programs for families.

Chapter 2

Spouse and Family Addiction

Family problems considered in the context of marriage raise many questions regarding spouse tolerance to the addicted partner. Questions like "why do clean spouses stay married to abusing spouses?" "How can family deterioration occur over years, possibly threatening effects upon children, without the clean spouse taking remedial action?" More times than not these paradoxical questions present case workers and clinicians with a serious problem. That of taking sides. Who is right? Who really is the addicted spouse? The one abusing the substance? Or, the supposed victim, who clearly enables the spouse's addiction and insulates the family from recognition of illness? Whose side deserves support? The answer in today's conception of spouse addiction is simple: neither receive support. The solution always is a team effort, where both parties own responsibility for the dysfunction.

This chapter carefully assails the factors contributing to and treating spouse and family addiction during early and aftercare stages of problems. More than discussing "marital problems," focus here is upon the assessed warning signs of marital degeneration, how it impacts the family, and why both spouses equally contribute to the addiction.

ETIOLOGY

Spouse Assessment

Tolstoy observed in *Anna Karenina,* "Happy families resemble one another: each unhappy family is unhappy in its own way." This theme recurs in all marital conflict, taking a variety of shapes and sizes but always dealing with similar issues. Issues include: Lack of communication; lack of caring and affection; lack of availability and accessibility to spouse; lack of responsibility; and lack of trust. Let's consider each issue relative to the complaining spouse.

Lack of Communication

Studies of husbands' and wives' emotional communication vary intensely by marital obstacles or anticipatory conflicts brought on by disclosure of problems. Guthrie and Synder (1988), for one, showed spouse's perceptions influenced by overall couple satisfaction or dissatisfaction. Obvious as this finding seems, conflict or dissatisfaction clearly interferes with honest revelations of spouse distress. The issue is not "that it happens," but rather "why this happens." Carefully examining spouse miscommunication shows explicit trends slowly evolving in the first 5 years of marriage. Trends go unspoken, unnoticed, and little if any risk at modification is attempted fearing exacerbation of conflict.

Consider, for preliminaries, a common series of questions asked of distressed couples in early intake sessions:

Can you:

1. Say sorry to your partner?
2. Ask your partner for comfort and concern?
3. Tell your partner what's nice about him?
4. Tell your partner what's making you mad?
5. Talk to your partner about how sad you feel?
6. Talk to your partner about a personal problem?
7. Admit to your partner you're nervous?
8. Laugh and have fun with your partner?
9. Tell your partner how good you feel?
10. Show your partner you're angry?
11. Behave sad and unhappy in front of your partner?

The repeated theme in each question is "how much can you tell your spouse?" Restriction of feelings, of openly sharing lifestyles and daily activities worsens because spouses experience severe fears that (a) they will produce conflict, (b) they will say things sounding stupid, (c) they will impose selfish needs upon their spouses, and (d) they will emotionally upset or hurt that spouse in turn causing them much guilt.

They will produce conflict. Anticipatory fears that bringing up a topic will anger the addicted spouse usually is sufficient reason not to pursue the topic. A spouse fears any process involving disagreements or problem solving or that may likely involve criticism against either spouse. Fears run deeply to avoid conflict and criticism because both spouses generally lack the assertiveness or prosocial interpersonal skills needed to overcome the emotional defeatism. Lacking, as well, are abilities to remain objectively focused and distant and to regard the spouse's comments in context rather than personalizing the cruel remarks as attacks against integrity. Failure to detach from hurt immediately seduces either spouse into self-doubt or into a torrent of defenses, mounted to attack the accuser, and ultimately to terminate the discussion.

Secondly, conflict never is resolved. It lingers obsessively in the household air, contaminating subsequent conversations or activities. Fear of resurrecting the conflict once it boils over prevents the couple from identifying underlying anger, dealing with it constructively, and cleaning the slate of interaction. Instead, interactions remain void of any conflict or confrontation in hopes that the marriage can operate more smoothly.

They will say things sounding stupid. Fear rises severely when a partner believes that anything spoken is perceived as invalid. High-risk (provoking conflict) or low-risk (ignored) statements deal on a number of personal issues and may even reflect the spouse's competency. Nonetheless, unless spouse feedback is positive, the other partner immediately questions whether his or her facts in the opinion are rational, relevant, and can be supported by facts should the listening spouse challenge him or her. Consequently the fearful partner carefully censors beforehand all statements to be said in the conversation. Rehearsed mentally is the dyadic where the spouse pictures saying the comments and either expects ridicule and feeling invalid, or prepares strategic answers deflecting that invalid feeling. One way or another, replaying the "private thinking tape" over and over puts the anxious spouse under enormous pressure to handle some aversive situation.

They will impose selfish needs upon their spouses. Equally anticipated is revealing information expected to burden the partner. That personal problems of one spouse, told to another spouse, is selfishly imposing needs upon that spouse's precious time and that some other route of ventilation should be pursued before opting for this one. When depressed spouses suppress their ideas they are assuming nobody really cares about them, and that hardships in life must be coped with entirely alone. Oddly, upsetting or personal issues told to them by their addicted spouse are embraced warmly. Willingness to discuss, even solve personal dilemmas of the addicted spouse is pursued vigorously, without expecting in return to have that spouse listen to them with their personal concerns. Feared spouses forfeit being helped so they will look caring, compassionate, and win approval despite marital problems.

They will emotionally upset or hurt that spouse in turn causing them much guilt. Initially high-risk and low-risk statements tried to penetrate the edifice of silence. The clean spouse crashed through with expressions of honest, personal feelings hoping that the addicted spouse might acknowledge these feelings, and establish a talking dialogue. Instead the wall crumbled on top of that caring spouse. Feeling statements upset the addicted spouse making the clean partner not resentful or annoyed, but deeply emotionally hurt. Words of pain inflicted on the abuser cause the clean spouse to re-think their intentions, their strategies, and own the shame and responsibility associated with imposing grief. Unable to depersonalize the situation, partners fully absorb shame for their actions and subsequently avoid confrontations threatening another assault upon the abuser. Each assault vicariously wounds the clean spouse and he or she blames themselves for the marital failure.

Lack of Caring and Affection

A second problem faced by spouses is feeling a lack of caring or affection by the abuser. Affection generally is not sexual, but involves casual and complimentary comments to the spouse or to another about that spouse, or physical gestures of compassion. Touching, holding, brief kisses, or even sitting together enter this category. Verbal affection, the more missed of the two, begins as compliments but consists of listening and understanding skills accompanied by being supportive.

Listening and understanding. Addicted spouses are too consumed by selfish urges to pay attention to needs expressed by their spouses or children. Listening and understanding are completely absent. Listening starts in prompting the spouse to discuss personally troubling problems affecting that person during the day or past few weeks. Passively listening just means collecting the data without offering input or advice. Actively listening means input is crucial to the momentum of discussion. Input also conveys genuine concern for the person's welfare, emotional frailty, and need for talking. Saving the person from vulnerability in either listening mode reassures the speaker the marriage is a sanctuary for hardships experienced in the outside world. However, denying that sanctuary deprives the spouse of a need for safe escape from the world and again repeats the dysfunctional message that "your personal problems are a burden."

Being supportive. Listening is a nice tool, but its deprivation stifles the clean spouse from actively pursuing marital communication. The same is true for being supportive. A supportive spouse compliments the partner, without prompting, on accomplishments or regarding physical attributes. Compliments extend to public places around eager listeners who are informed of the partner's contributions. Another form of support is defending the spouse under duress or simply augmenting the validity of the person's claims. Agreements, proofs of why these statements are valid, and taking the spouse's side in debates all represent support. By contrast, abandoning the spouse in debate strips that person of confidence, risk-taking efforts, and resonates the message loud and clear that marriage is a lonely occupation.

Lack of Availability and Accessibility to Spouse

Concerns also include the plain and simple absence of the spouse. Addicted spouses either are away from home and thus unavailable, or distracted from family needs while in the household. That limits contact and makes the person inaccessible. Unavailability occurs for several reasons. First, addicted spouses stay out late or do not return home due to drug or alcohol use, or activities thereof. Staying longer at local bars, at VFWs, or at friends' homes distracts from awareness of time and responsibilities. Second, addicted spouses may avoid home or the partner's repeated disappointments, anger, or confrontations likely to surface because of the addiction or marital problems. Avoidance delays returning to the aversive environment until the addicted individual is fully immune or prepared for the conflict. Immunity comes from intoxication, from getting high, or eliminating fear through whatever mind-altering means is possible for that person.

Inaccessibility is actually worse for the clean spouse who believes the drinking spouse is gone *deliberately*. But rarely is this true. Addicted spouses stay out of the mainstream of family activity, unaffected by soft requests or even harsh coercion from their spouses. Isolation is for several reasons. Among the most prominent include:

Lacks appropriate skills; afraid of criticism; dislikes spouse (and children); physically incapable of helping; and selfishly impulsive.

Lacks appropriate skills. Assumably, addicted spouses possess identical caretaking skills as their spouses and *should* share equal responsibilities in the marriage. Cooperative roles involve understanding the family system and having the capability to interact with discrete parts of that system. In parenting, the system entails acuity to stressful child problems or normal needs such as feeding, playing, sleeping, and physical affection. In marriage, the system entails communication, disclosure, affection, support, and co-participation. None of these factions may be detected, understood or properly processed in the overall scheme of daily interaction. Failure of alertness simply means the addicted spouse overlooks when and why events occur or that they hold any significance whatever.

Secondly, awareness may not be enough. Realizing child and spouse needs presupposes the next step; that the addicted spouse knows coping skills for them. Is the spouse equipped to handle a crying infant? A frustrating spouse? Can that spouse rescue aggravation from two siblings fighting? Assumed knowledge leads to assumed skills. The addicted parent and spouse may lack fundamental skills for dealing with life priorities and may avoid contact with them to hide this fact.

Afraid of criticism. Skills or no skills, avoidance is nearly always at the heart of inaccessibility. Addicted spouses may be terrified of spousal criticism marshalled for not performing exactly up to standards. That is, standards according to the complaining spouse. Failure to meet spouse expectations, for weak addicted spouses, plants seeds of self-doubt, fears of conflict, and leads to withdrawal from cooperative ventures. Rarely will withdrawn spouses express their resentment for being criticized or offer restitution for the family if anger or disapproval is given. Asserting this view could incite a riot and again provoke conflict. Instead, resistance from activities presumably signals this displaced resentment.

Dislikes spouse (and children). Quite frequently, addicted spouses hide from family because they literally dislike or have built up enormous hostility toward the spouse and children. Disclosure of feelings is out of the question given the anticipated horror of confrontation. The alternative is beating around the bush in avoidance and escape tactics that refuse active roles in any joint family ventures. When ventures are unavoidable or seemingly inescapable, such as holiday meals or family reunions, escape is found by drinking, by drug use, or by abusive behavior so repulsive to onlookers that it sabotages family unity and assures the addicted person's removal from the situation.

Physically incapable of helping. Extended drug use and abuse naturally has medical repercussions. Organ deterioration along with fatigue, poor concentration, and muscular atrophy, all plague repeated users and cause irreversible damage to other voluntary and involuntary nervous systems. These intrusions may realistically prohibit the intensity, frequency, or duration of addicted spouse's contribution to family and marital activities despite other reasons. No matter how lazy or insensitive the addict is, physical limitations such as pain or immobility impair performance. Affected are psychomotor and sensory capabilities that drastically reduce and even paralyze actions to the point where helping out would be pointless anyway.

Selfishly impulsive. These reasons considered, the narcissistic part of addiction still primarily accounts for being inaccessible. Addicts are selfishly impulsive by poorly controlling their physical and psychological urges for any particular wants, at any time during the day. Want of sleep, of food, of sex, of "peace and quiet," or of parts for some project, all spontaneously take mandatory priority regardless of ongoing activities, or needs of children and spouse. Persistence to satisfy impulsive needs destroys any organization of the family system. Times for play, for dinner, for work, or just routine schedules all are subject to unforeseen changes due to the unpredictable whims of addicted spouses. Reactions to this are twofold. Either clean spouses rebel against this impulsion, forcing the addict to act on his or her behalf without assistance from the family. Or, there is capitulation; surrender to the demands and pressure of impulsiveness to keep composure in the marriage and prevent onset of conflict.

Lack of Responsibility

Conflict nearly is certain when spouses are derelict of basic duties and obligations affecting the entire family. Neglecting financial and caretaking responsibilities carry the greatest weight. Financial delinquencies include unemployment or inconsistent earnings particularly when that spouse is the main source of income. Caretaking deficits range from inattention to spouse and children to not assisting with domestic errands such as grocery shopping, home repairs, major and minor purchases, and establishment of direction or goals in the family. Avoiding these commitments frees the addicted spouse of expectations and of diversions away from selfishly impulsive actions. The problem is that irresponsible behavior feeds on mistaken actions of the clean spouse. Two mistaken actions in particular are: Enabling, and rebellion.

Enabling. The literature is replete with case studies and biographies depicting the cyclical rise and fall of caring spouses who try pleasing the partner and family in spite of themselves, only to perpetuate the dysfunction. Classic enablers, in other words, might buy alcohol for their alcoholic spouses thinking it will please that person and keep the family together. Regretably, the plan backfires when the alcoholic's condition worsens, becomes totally dependent on that spouse's generosity, and this further increases the amount of spousal altruism. Rising to meet this need, enablers literally maintain irresponsible actions of the addicted spouse by preventing them from being independent or caring for family at the risk of things going wrong. Protection of the family from emotional injury, that is, from the addicted spouse spoiling the synchronicity and regularity of the household, keeps that spouse from ever learning what to do for other people.

Rebellion. Fear not only causes enabling, it also can manifest as fierce physical or verbal anger. Annoyed spouses, tired of unilaterally handling the family, may retaliate by aggression. Yelling, screaming, physically assaulting the addict, or even recurrent threats of separation or divorce might accompany tantrums. Eruptive outbursts deliver a strong message that this behavior is reprehensible and must change at any cost, although little follow-up on that threat takes place. Typically rage leads to a net reaction of deeply felt guilt and self-criticism for upsetting the family and particularly for assaulting the spouse. Apologies and rescindment of threats relieve the spouse of guilt and assumingly gives them a new lease on the relationship. Unfortunately other consequences double the trouble. Removal of threats also discredits the seriousness of change and permits the addict spouse continued escape from responsibility.

Lack of Trust

Marital duress is never over single instances. Cumulatively, frustrations and disappointments take their toll on tolerant spouses who turn the cheek or look for a light at the end of the tunnel. Ultimately this optimism fails because the addicted spouse cannot be trusted. Trust means the spouse (a) lacks consistency between words and actions, (b) lacks predictability by being so impulsive, and (c) engages in immoral, unethical behaviors or violations of the marriage contract.

Lacks consistency between words and actions. Discrepancy between words and actions is crucial to trust. Does the addicted person do as he or she says? Correspondence between promises and behavior usually indicate organization of lifestyle. Promises take two forms. First, promises are made for the spouse or family. Expectations set up for children (go roller skating on weekend), for spouse (go out to movies or dinner), or for other significants (parents, friends) persuade these people into believing the addict is responsible and even cooperative. Second, promises are for the addict himself or herself. Statements promise completion of certain chores, lists of extensive errands to be finished under unrealistic deadlines, and outright lies on self-action that may draw praise from the partner. Resolutions to stop drinking, for instance, might excite a troubled spouse and ease marital tensions. However, failure to fulfill expectations set for other people or the addict himself or herself terribly destroys the the partner's confidence and blind faith that future promises hold meaning.

Lacks predictability by being so impulsive. Destruction of trust also results from not being predictable. Selfishly impulsive actions described earlier normally interfere with organizing the family system. Constant disruptions force a change in plans, force flexibility in people who too frequently are flexible and causes massive disequilibrium. Left to adjust are bystanders such as partner and children who can no longer anticipate actions of the addict. Lack of prediction leads to not knowing how partner and children should respond to the simplest daily needs. Eating meals, for instance, is up for grabs. Either the addicted parent expects a hot meal or prepares a meal, or demands supper at a restaurant. Decisions are random and arbitrary. Control over this impulsive action is too difficult or frightening, and surrendering to its juvenile pattern also is frightening. The dilemma grows worse when frightened spouses and children begin to second-guess the outcome before it happens. Right or wrong, so much analyzing goes on ahead of time that family life loses its spontaneous, playful feelings. Stress is constant.

Engages in immoral, unethical behavior or violations of the marriage contract. Conventionally the explanation offered for distrust is that the addicted spouse violated the marriage vows. Infidelity and other shocks to the family system disrupt what little balance is left from coping with the addiction. Unethical or immoral undertakings display insensitivity to spouse and show that distancing has reached the outer boundary where the family is less important (not more important) than selfish ventures regardless of repercussions. Indulgence sadly detaches the addict from spousal influence, from loyalty to obligation, and from feeling guilty after committing such culpable actions.

Detachment sends a glaring message that trust neither exists nor does the individual possess the capacity to manage trust even if it did.

Therapist Assessment

Examination of dysfunctional marital variables partly relies on spousal self-reports during initial sessions as well as continuously throughout treatment. Subjective input identifies cognitive, emotional, behavioral and cultural aspects uniquely experienced by the clean and addicted spouse, their children, and effects upon the family unit. Information on these variables also is obtained from objective records. Data collection by the therapist is part of *assessment*. Asking questions naturally is one obvious way of achieving this end. Methods of assessment, however, vary greatly depending on the therapist's clinical orientation, time, energy and resources for data collection, and extent of patient trust. Higher trust in patients require less intensive surveillance of family data than lower or no trust in the patient.

Therapists presented with a substance abuse couple approach assessment by identifying, isolating, and analyzing the collected data that later determines the therapy goals. Jointly, the therapist must recruit the couple in the team effort of honestly observing and recording information for a short period of time (possibly one week after initial intake) constituting a *Baseline period*. During Baseline, problems in the natural environment remain unaltered as all observers gain a new perspective on the scope of interactions. Exactly what the team looks at, by what methods, and how it critically impacts the marital relationship may be divided into: (a) assessment options; (b) major parameters; and (c) types of dysfunctional control.

Assessment Options

Use of specific "instruments" in assessment poses several questions typically confronting the empirically-based clinician. "Should the data be exact?" "Should information reflect purely emotions, purely cognitions, or purely behaviors--maybe all of them together?" Traditionally, behavioral assessment was believed delinquent in gathering a gestalt of individual information by its strict prohibition against emotions, thoughts, and nonbehavioral indices. This "methodological behavioral" view clearly is obsolete among today's behavioral practitioners who adopt a healthier systematic attitude regarding the type of information collected. Essentially, it should be *concrete, observable, measurable, and confrontable* (Jacobson & Margolin, 1979; Ruben, 1986, 1988).

Concrete means the behavior is *topographically* and *functionally* specific and discrete enough for individual observation. Topography represents the shape, form or movement of behavior in space and time. An example is hitting behavior. Questions asked about topography include (a) how many times does he hit his wife?; Or, "how long does the abuse last?" Function of behavior refers to the immediate outcome of behavior upon people or things. Take physical abuse again. Questions asked about function include (a) who was hit?, (b) what did the person do?, and (c) what in turn did that consequence do to increase or decrease hitting by the abusive person? Isolating instances of behavior to discrete or concrete situations narrows the margin of ambiguity and makes the behavior recognizable among other actions.

Observable, measurable, and confrontable are additional criteria defining the detection and containment of behavior. Observability requires that any action the spouse does--behavior, thinking or feeling--be subject to public or private inspection using simple steps of awareness. Recording those observed actions by means of numbers gives them a status of quantity. Actions measured in terms of how much (frequency), how long (duration), how severe (intensity or magnitude), or in relation to other actions (latency) breaks out of inferences and assumptions and allows spouses a more solid basis for behavior change. That behavior is also confrontable, means it happens relative to interaction rather than when the spouse is sleeping or entirely sedentary. Confrontable action is action with events, people, objects or other stimuli forcing reactions of all sorts. Much spousal action is *public,* that is, appears visible between two parties during ongoing interaction, for example, provocations. Other actions like angry feelings or thoughts while being provoked, are *private.* Privacy protects the behavior from being observed by a second party, but it is just as confrontable as talking aloud.

Options that are available to access both public and private behaviors on the part of spouses are at the therapist's discretion. First to decide is the dimensions of assessment. There are five dimensions to consider (Jacobson & Margolin, 1979, p. 72): (a) observational targets; (b) observer sources; (c) observational methods; (d) timing; and (e) setting. Observational targets consist of types of behaviors observed such as relationship perceptions, interactions, and specific habits. Observer sources refer to the individuals under observation such as the spouses themselves or watching each other. Observational methods vary by technical sophistication but include interviews, questionnaires, behavioral rating forms, analogues, observational coding systems, and checklists. Timing defines the length of observation, either as continuous, daily, one-time measurement or another dimension.

Setting identifies the locus of observation ranging from home environment to the office, at other people's homes or in the community.

Five dimensions of assessment prepare the therapist with tools for early data collection. On drinking, for instance, one spouse might record the daily number of beers or mixed drinks consumed (frequency); or the length of time (duration) spent away from home following work hours per day or for the entire week. That same spouse, observing herself or himself, might keep track on paper or by another simple frequency device (e.g., grocery counter, switching paper clips between pockets, etc.) the number of enabling statements or actions made to the addicted spouse. Data also is possible on severity of arguments (intensity), how arguments impacted the family (magnitude), and length of time elapsed between drinking and arguments (latency). Spouses consenting to self-monitoring accept the risk that discovery of these behaviors can lead to higher awareness and more fruitful therapeutic outcomes. Nonconsenting spouses, such as the addict who refuses this "self-monitoring nonsense" may not sabotage the baseline process but avoid the risk of self-discovery.

Alternative measurements for the noncooperative spouse include checklists and analogues. While self-monitoring is best for the natural environment, checklists and analogues take place directly in the outpatient clinic. Checklists and marital surveys appropriate for this intervention are countless and essentially elicit inferences or opinions on retrospective actions of the past. Analogues, by contrast, are role-playing, enactments, and a variety of simulations (Ruben, 1983, 1989) can simulate the realistic dyadic between couples, closer to the natural phenomena seen at home. While both methods are inferior to direct naturalistic observation, analogues by far offer the best predictive validity for later diagnosis and formation of treatment plans.

Naturalistic or analogue assessments sometimes produce untoward effects that become clinically important after Baseline. Effects generally occur in two categories: (a) Hypersensitivity to self and spouse; and (b) intrusion of privacy.

Hypersensitivity to self and spouse. Self-monitoring during direct naturalistic observations clearly gains new information on behavior previously taken for granted or accepted as habitually part of the marriage. Under a microscope, that same information undergoes dissection. Details of the action, reaction or interaction scrupulously uncover response patterns, conspicuous connections to cues, urges, and thoughts. A sharper picture appears of why the spouse predictably behaves in certain ways, the triggers of that behavior, and outcomes usually expected given certain variables. Monitoring spouses who discover in themselves or their spouse insight that explains key dysfunctions can lose their detachment and objectivity they thought possible for data collection. Alertness becomes obsessive, as the spouse acutely spots every instance of dysfunctional behavior no matter who causes it, or reasons for the action. Sensitivity increases to events preceding, during or after the dysfunctional behavior, becoming completely preoccupied with analyzing it and waiting for its next occurrence.

Overenthusiastic monitoring not only produces hypersensitivity, but also transforms that monitoring from objective composure to inflamed anger. Suddenly spouses realize the breadth of abuse they suffered in the marriage and are deeply upset by their own inadequacies. Repeated offenses are perceived more clearly and promptly and reacted to with resentment. This animus continues until Baseline ends or the alert therapist pulls the plug on self-monitoring before it destroys the couple prior to starting the helping techniques.

Intrusion of privacy. Couples split on "this data collection idea" usually create an implicit battlefield right from the beginning. As one spouse monitors compliantly, tracking frequency and duration of behavior, the other spouse may resist this *intrusion of privacy* by escalating the problem that brought them to therapy. For addicted spouses, they might drink more or use drugs more frequently. Nonaddicted spouses may show resentment by aggression. Attempts to restore control mobilize the angry spouse to terrorize the compliant spouse until the monitoring ends. Intimidation by either spouse interferes with honest commitments to therapy, to behavior change, and to improving the marriage. It also plays into the irrational belief espoused by the victimized, compliant spouse that he or she "will retaliate against me for doing this—I know it!" Faced with this bootleg interference, therapists should disassemble the data collection process immediately and address, first, why the couple is resistant to observation. Second, shift direction to tools used within the clinic such as analogues or checklists.

Major Parameters

Exactly what information is clinically important? Roberts & Magrab (1991) recently proposed that practical assessment requires consideration of several basic family parameters. Combined with these are conditions described by Stuart (1980) for assessing quality of marriage.

Family strengths and needs. Identification of assets and liabilities of each spouse and the family system is essential. Gauged as assets are shared activities done frequently or at least enjoyed, or milestones reached by the couple together (childbirth, new home, new jobs, new cars, etc.). Materialistic or emotional strengths open the doors to new needs or provide closure to previously unmet needs.

Role of the family in the assessment process. Spouses, as a couple, represent only half of the systemic unit under assessment. The other half are children or significant others playing a direct role in the total picture or having daily contact with the couple. Observations of the children *in interaction with their parents* may be as productive as spouses monitoring one another. Interrelational family contact that adds to the dysfunction becomes a crucial part of the entire assessment and should be worked into the observational record.

Knowledge of specific disabling conditions. By habit many therapists conclude that chemical dependency of one sort or another underlies the need for marital and family therapy. That by identifying, containing, and eliminating substance abuse the collateral dysfunction stands an excellent chance of being eliminated. Correct one and it takes care of the other. However, extenuating limitations besides substance abuse may be present in the family or affect the addicted or clean spouse. Addicted spouses who are also legally blind or have multiple sclerosis, for instance, must cope with their disabilities in addition to goals of abstinence. Abusers of pain killers (Demorol, Percodan, etc.) who stop the drug abuse suddenly face the trauma of excruciating pain and the lack of any immediate relief matching the potency of the addicted drugs. Without finding relief, or alternatives to handle the pain, relapse to drug abuse is nearly certain. Disabilities, like other organic factors intrude upon assessment, even treatment goals, and must be realized as soon as possible.

Possible emotional sequelae of the condition. What is the emotional support system like? Does it exist? Families disturbed not only by addiction but by absence of spouse-to-spouse and parent-to-child support operate on a distance meter that keeps the family disintegrated. Cold, rigid, and controlling actions erase bonding or family rapport. Cohesion of family members suffers when a child is too afraid or naive to approach his parents, and both spouses are too selfish, afraid, or naive to break the cycle of alienation from their children. Deprived of comfort, children must survive on their own making arbitrary decisions and expecting nothing in return for gains of self-esteem. Dysfunction at this level undermines motivation for change and requires initial steps in rebuilding communication even before data collection has a fighting chance to succeed.

Cultural differences among spouses. Underrated in the last five years are racial, ethnic, religious, and socio-cultural differences among spouses improperly resolved during the marriage. Intermarriages automatically conflict with societal expectations and many values spouses have grown up with. Deviating from these values, from the promulgated norms, is only problematic if there remain certain spousal attributes that are polar opposites or that cause major adjustments. Interfaith marriages are a good example. Rising numbers of Jewish and Catholic marriages in the last five years reflects a serious defection from traditional roles. As couples, liturgy or the religious customs in their respective faiths may be irrelevant as both agree not to be practitioners--perhaps even to embrace atheism.

What contaminates this unanimous thinking are *values* or *habits* endemic to their the religious culturalization. Jewish spouses may have educational or occupational expectations diametrically opposed to those of their Catholic spouse. Postures on ambition, methods of child rearing, and familial activity may require compromises that neither spouse finds easy to make. However, spousal differences primarily are in interpersonal styles of interaction. Avoidance of conflict, mischanneled anger, and other obstructions to communication can dissolve family unity.

In other words, religiously the couple has little to worry about, unless they butt heads over how a child might be raised. More immediately they face disparities in handling conflict, in approaching life goals, and personally growing. Such differences rank very high on priority, nearly as important as the addiction.

Informal networks available. How much does the family exceed its tight boundary lines? A "regulated" or closed-boundary family (Kantor & Lehr, 1975) confines its dysfunctionality within the close quarters of living space and few if any outsiders are let in. Boundaries that are more open, or *permeable,* permit family members to trespass onto unfamiliar territory and risk interactions that later may upset the balance of control in the family. Interactions are informal or formal. Informal interactions are networks developed among friends, other families, or extended members of the same family living outside the nucleus. Contact is essential with outsiders for an outlet of personal problems and exposure to *normal* family civilization. Recognizing how life *should be,* family members return home in shame or in grief over their helpless situation.

Formal networks available. Formal networks refer to societal institutions with which the family must interact or chooses to interact for survival. These include school, place of employment, even state agencies such as departments of social services, vocational rehabilitation, and mental health. Contact is mandatory for functionally keeping the family in its habitual cycle of daily interaction. Contact also is maintained to protect the family image from looking dysfunctional. On the surface all the "right things" are happening and family members are abiding by normal civic or cultural rules that prevent conspicuous exposure of their flaws. However, just because formal networks are utilized by the family does not mean they will comfortably seek another service within that network on account of their problems. Parents already attending outpatient public health facilities for a routine physical examination may resist asking for a substance abuse counselor in an adjacent department. Insulation from revealing family problems remains quite thick.

Mate selection. Intermarriage prompts questions about mate selection. But there are other factors dictating mate selection that the couple may now find are irrelevant or seriously defective. Sexual compatibility, for example, may drive two maturing teenagers into lust that later evolves into early marriage. Now the carnal intensity is less meaningful or weak as the only adhesive holding the marriage together. Dominance is another common variable. Passive, dependent spouses who are attracted to domineering, impulsive spouses may gain security from feeling this stronger spouse fills a critical void in their weaker personality. Years into the marriage, however, responsibilities double and risk-taking increases thereby teaching the passive, dependent spouse more independence. Confidence rises in proportion to many ventures attempted alone and proven successful. The domineering, impulsive spouse resists this change in the mate's personality and it begins to crumble the marriage.

Age differences. The term *chronophobia* best describes this difference. Fear of age or of dating older/younger people typically plagues attracted couples undermined by value-conscious inhibitions regarding how old their mates must be. Age discrimination explicitly prevents new relationships from forming. At least that was the cultural climate a solid decade ago. The last ten years have witnessed amazing leaps and bounds beyond this ethic and into a genre where older women dating younger men and vice versa are now commonplace. Dating men five to ten years younger holds unparalleled excitement and frequently this couple marries. Age differences, as with religion in interfaith marriages, rarely manifest as problems for the couple. Problems do rise regarding values, and cultural indoctrination endemic to that spouse's rearing years. A 40-year-old experiencing young adulthood during the prime of the 1960s era of extreme rebellion and rugged individualism, greatly conflicts with the 25-year-old raised in the late 1970s and early 1980s. Peace, responsibility, and conservatism were dominant themes--much different from the 1960s. How does the couple handle their business or risk-taking affairs? Admittedly, with serious difficulty.

Marital and personal stages. Spousal reactions to the addicted spouse and the increasing marital and family dysfunction may be said to go through different stages of deterioration (cf. Nelson & Beach, 1990; Zweben, 1986). At first the spouse neglects admitting there is an addiction. Then meager attempts are made at controlling the addicted spouse, using the family as ammunition to threaten abandonment unless there is immediate cessation of the habit. The family begins to be socially isolated, partly as a protective strategy. Next phase is the clean spouse realizing the efforts are futile and that things are getting worse, not better. Feeling defeated, he or she surrenders to the helplessness of losing control. In short time, that spouse recuperates energy to "try again," pleading with the addicted spouse for treatment. If no improvement the marriage may break up or continue for years in a state called *circumvention*. The passive resignation to futility and adjustment around the addict's defective lifestyle (Edwards, 1982).

Changes in behavior observed during these phases (Edwards, 1982, p. 49) are continuous but have discrete observable characteristics about them. There is the *coping style,* where problems are avoided and confrontation abandoned. There is the *attack and manipulation style,* where the spouse zealously controls the addicted spouse, inducing shame, stress, humiliation and other deprivations hopefully to effect rapid changes. There is *spoiling;* here the enabler returns, nursing the addict through hangovers, or purposely inventing excuses to hide the foul addiction. *Constructive management* is where the clean spouse looks after the family making sure finances are in order and essentially remains active in spite of the addict's intrusion. Finally, *constructive help seeking* begins the first real admission of "it's out of my control" and involves going to see a family doctor or specialist, asking him to confront the addict.

Financial status. Managing the budget is a distraction away from managing an unmanageable drinker or drug user. However, finances get out of control more quickly under marital duress for several reasons. First, the controller of the finances may be the addicted spouse. Compulsive behaviors rapidly strip the family of critical savings or weekly allotments for bills. Under pressure to pay the mortgage or rent, and finding no way to juggle funds, addicts may borrow or steal money or seek impulsive solutions such as filing bankruptcy or taking out another (e.g., consolidated) loan. Second, controller of the finances may be the clean spouse. That person balances the budget and holds the fort together *until or unless* costs well exceed the income and funds simply do not exist for paying for the addict's impulse purchases. Even the clean spouse finds spending money an intoxicating escape. He or she may compulsively run up the credit cards or take lavish vacations expecting to magically pay for it later. When "later finally comes," funds are so short that even the clean spouse may resort to imprudent decisions just for stress relief.

Couples operating on smaller budgets hypothetically would seem to have less problems. Less money to spend might prevent them from overspending or becoming deeply in debt. But not true. Uncontrollable spenders usually are found in *any individuals, regardless of socioeconomic level or even socioeconomic upbringing,* providing they act on avoidance, on impulse, or derive feelings of self-esteem through materialistic gains.

Child-rearing problems. Marital dysfunction by and large contains major parenting problems (Azar & Barnes, 1986; Burgess & Conger, 1978; Peterson & Zill, 1986; Trickett & Kuczynski, 1986). Both clean and addicted spouse lack basic nurturing and disciplining skills and so resort to negatively correcting misbehavior. Tantrums, noncompliance, bedwetting, stealing, lying--all receive severe corporal punishment or verbal rebukes. Focus is entirely upon rapidly eliminating interruptions upon the adult parent's life, thinking the child will respect and honor their spoken instructions more obediently. Parents typically might yell, scream, spank, slap, pinch, pull, grab, and accidentally cause injury on repeated occasion. Parents also complain their children are (a) manipulative, (b) not minding, (c) defiant and disrespectful, (d) pushing their buttons, and (e) totally immature. In fact, these "bad" children are classic victims of naive parents who teach the children to be bad partially by how much negative attention they give to bad behavior, and partly by how little positive attention they give to constructive behaviors.

Type of Dysfunctional Control

Degeneration of trust can cause severe imbalance of control. *Control* in this context refers to decision-making power and assertively dominating the marriage and family life. Controlling spouses, whether addicted or clean, demand order in an otherwise random and arbitrary household, following rigidly a regimen of caretaking that offers little latitude for noncompliance. Strict enforcement of adherence by family members is part of the controlling style. Types of spousal control largely seen in addiction include: (a) Co-alcoholism; (b) co-dependency; and (c) refusal of assistance.

Co-alcoholism. Thus far in discussion the assumption is that one spouse is clean and another is addicted. However, marital decay accelerates when both couples are alcoholics. This is *co-alcoholism*. Drugs users, as well, follow the same pattern symptomatic of co-alcoholics. Patterns of behavior forcefully intensify right before and right after inebriation. Prior to, or during urges and minor withdrawal, frustrations elevate out of control and turn to aggression. Verbal and physical aggression conspire to intimidate the other spouse, who reciprocally is provoking and acting aggressive. Rising aggression leads to physical aggression or property destruction. Immediately after, escape behaviors occurs. That is, alert to the disaster of conflict, both spouses abort the argument by rushing off in opposite directions. Use of substances continues the avoidance and escape action. After intoxication, the couple at first is distant while suffering through their own hangovers or general physical discomfort. Once suffering subsides, at least one spouse, if not both weakens with a conviction not to be brutal in the future, followed by persistent pleas for affection or sexual intercourse. Intimacy reconciles the dispute and silences the resonating anger.

Co-alcoholics also have a constricted view of reality. Rarely can they think of the future and rarely does that future deal with being benevolent. They perceive their world through selfish eyes instead. Perceptions largely revolve around personal gratification, around things happening *now*, and around ways that other people can accommodate them. High-rolling and energetic addicts ingratiate themselves to caretaking types who subordinate to the impulsive demands without a struggle. If that caretaker also is an addict, that person may hide selfish needs from the spouse fearing his or her rejection. But selfish needs still pervade. In cases where wives disguise selfish needs, cruelty and aggression is frequently evident in response to her children. The children in effect get the brunt of impulsive demands from their mother, who is afraid to display these actions around her husband. Kept hidden is also the fear of looking stupid or vulnerable. Neither father (husband) nor mother (wife) can partially or completely admit mistakes without first blaming others or qualifying the mistake with rationalizations. As with selfish needs, blame is farmed out to the children who become prey to their parents' sadistic habits.

Co-dependency. Two addictive spouses pose a threat to a sane marriage. But so does a couple where one is addicted and the other *feels addicted*. Feeling addicted does not mean early stages of drug or alcoholic dependency. Dependency is of another sort, involving the desperate need to have a spouse at any price. Self-esteem is so low, self-identity is so absent, that the dependent spouse feels totally invisible and an imposter unless he or she can assume a *role or personality* by obsessively overachieving for the addicted spouse. This type of dependency is reciprocal. The addicted spouse *depends* on the security of marriage to continue substance abuse. Clean spouses *depend* on the security of marriage to functionally feel important. Several forms of co-dependency take place. The role of the enabler already has been discussed at great length. Other roles deal with *physical identity, social identity, and value identity.*

Physical identity is when the clean spouse feels self-importance by believing he or she is perceived by others as pretty, handsome, or greatly more attractive by association with the physically attractive spouse. They regard themselves as fortunate and enhanced with glamour so remarkably superior to their natural physical appearance, that the transformation depends on keeping the marriage alive. The more physically irresistible the addicted spouse is perceived, the higher the physical status of perfection felt by the other spouse.

Social identity. By analogy, social status rises through association with an affluent addicted spouse. The drinking aside, elitism or *perceived elitism* becomes an uncontrollable addiction for the clean spouse who must maintain the marriage for this privilege. It sounds manipulative, as if the clean spouse took calculated measures to lure and then marry this spouse only for social gains. Indeed, many marriages are set into motion for precisely this reason. But not marriages suffering from dysfunctional co-dependency. In co-dependency, pursuing the stakes of social status is not a premeditated, calculated process; the drive is conscious, but very consuming and extremely debilitating. The co-dependent person constantly fears that he or she is losing sanity, control, and will be left abandoned and alone. Fear of loneliness is so severe that every effort is made to be with the spouse and around his or her friends. Personal sacrifices are many if in return people approve of or gratefully value the clean spouse.

Value identity. Sense of esteem derived from physical and social status seems guaranteed as long as the dependent spouse stays married. Value identity requires the same commitment. It involves catering to an addicted person, which generates enormous pleasure. Caretaking is one variation of this. Another variation is by treating the marriage like a game of challenge. The objective is ultimately changing the partner without him or her knowing it and consequently the clean spouse proves to be worthwhile. Terms for a challenge seem peculiar but necessary. Addicted spouses must be aloof, insensitive, impulsive, and possibly abusive. Described, in effect, are attributes antithetical to the clean spouse who charges after these qualities with a vengeance.

This challenge excites energy and mobilizes the spouse into defeating the partner by working diligently on forcing that partner to be more and more like the clean spouse. However, there is never a victory. Success only backfires. When the addict reforms and behaves according to the clean spouse's profile, the challenge is over. It is no more. *That devastates the clean spouse who constantly requires a higher and higher dose of challenge to feel needed or dependent on the addicted spouse.*

Refusal of assistance. Impaired trust in marital relationships partly stems from chronic inconsistency and unpredictability of addictive spouses. Expectations disintegrate over time as promises never are fulfilled and lack any correspondence with subsequent behaviors. Consequently a clean spouse stops relying or selectively relies on the other spouse for personal needs. Damage to trust also occurs before the couple marry. Experiences may occur in childhood or early adulthood in which accelerated responsibilities were the consequence of irresponsible, uncaring parents. Children of alcoholics or of mentally ill or highly volatile parents lose valuable respect for their arbitrary, irrational, and distrusting parents. They are forced into miniature adult roles and made caretaker for parents and siblings. As surrogate parent, all household and scheduling cares fall upon the child's shoulders without assistance. Initially burdens are abundant, highly time-absorbing, and sporadically accomplished. In just months child homemakers gain amazing efficiency in home economics. Even at school, solitary activities are preferred over cooperation in groups. If group work is compulsory, the child homemaker takes control by leading the group. Depending on only themselves, frantic and meticulous effort goes into every chore. Higher and higher self-expectations of efficiency drive motivation not only well beyond their parents' capabilities, but into the traps of perfectionism.

Adult children of dysfunctional homes undergo adult development too rapidly and without the benefit of one childhood pleasure; that of being taken care of. Parental care, of which they were stripped, *provides the basic foundations for trust.* Because they never trusted their parents, they will distrust any other emotionally significant person for the rest of their lives. The spouse is only one person. Distrust permeates to all caring persons, especially authorities (bosses, relatives, etc.). Trust forced upon this adult is resisted at all costs. As it was in childhood, vulnerability is turned into taking control or leadership, instead of following other adults. But if control through leadership is not possible, fear sets in. He or she will scramble viciously for another shield against vulnerability; they will refuse to have others control their action. Yell, scream, threaten, even physically combat the unwelcome controller, as long as it restores personal control.

In marriage this means literally preventing the spouse, children, or any other person to help out in the household. All chores, planning, and budgets are consciously pursued without complaint. Family violators who try helping out receive criticism for acting out of line or not performing the task as efficiently. After a while, repeated criticism discourages voluntary efforts by family members and they naturally accept the passive role of being catered to. However, determination to control begins to weaken when responsibilities become excessive. Now the controlling parent blames the family and especially the spouse for inefficiency, laziness, and dereliction of duties. Accusations abound. The family remains apathetic, unmotivated by the many critical verbal assaults against them. Never does the controlling parent realize that years of refusing assistance conditioned the "ungrateful" family to be recipients instead of providers.

Specific Problems

Marital distress aggravated by dysfunction takes on unusual and highly immobilizing patterns that are different from the conventionally diagnosed marriage problems. Presenting complaints may sound the same, coupled by symptoms looking exactly like common symptoms, but there are key features that are important to keep an eye on. Let us examine these key features relative to (a) problems of health, (b) problems of disclosure, (c) problems of provokes, (d) problems of affection, and (e) problems of verbal and physical abuse.

Problems of Health

Health problems vary depending on the couple's education and sensitivity to fundamentals of nutrition, exercise, and stress control. Higher stressors, medically evinced by hypertension, irregularity of eating, irritable bowel disorder, or other gastrointestinal conditions, signal improper handling of tensions or tensions with substance abuse. Usually therapists suspecting medical complications arrange for a psychiatric or other physician consultation concurrent to regular therapy sessions. This way, examinations can reveal health hazards without interrupting the therapeutic process. Consultations are frequently routine and communication between referring therapist and examiner is no more than protocol requests. What gets lost in requesting consultations is *what exactly to look for and why there may be a problem.*

Physicians testing for medical abnormalities instead require more direction on exactly what could be wrong with the patient. A full medical exam may uncover organic pathology precipitating or produced by addictions. Spouses with high recidivism rates particularly are at risk of pathology, kept disguised by withdrawal symptoms and the rebound phenomenon (Light, 1985, 1986). Reviewed here are the type of problems detectable among addicted spouses and possibly not reported by the clean spouse:

Brain damage. The brain and spinal cord are particularly vulnerable to effects of drugs and alcohol. Heavy drinking may result in epileptic-like convulsions, coma or even death. Chronic, long-term drinkers sometimes go on to develop debilitating central nervous system syndromes.

Nerve damage. Chronic alcohol abusers also experience nerve damage to their peripheral nervous system. Damage shows up initially as slight loss of sensation in the hands or feet. In some cases, sufferers develop great difficulty in walking. In other cases, alcohol-induced nerve damage causes chronic impotence.

Delirium tremors (DTs). This syndrome occurs when chronic drinkers suddenly quit drinking and it often lasts for several days. Key symptoms seen include severe shaking, fever, sweating, hallucinations, and dehydration that is severe and occasionally life-threatening.

Liver damage. Because the liver contains enzymes necessary for metabolizing alcohol, it sustains more damage than most other organs in the body. Heavy drinkers risk developing alcohol hepatitis. This condition, characterized by jaundice and a buildup of toxins in the blood, is difficult to treat and potentially fatal. If drinking continues, the liver damage may progress to the point of cirrhosis. Cirrhosis occurs when the liver has become so scarred that blood flow through the organ is impaired. This impairment causes a dangerous back-pressure in the veins. To compensate, veins elsewhere in the body swell like aneurysms and sometimes rupture. Ruptured varicose veins can be deadly. Cirrhosis can also lead to ascites, an accumulation of fluid in the abdominal cavity. Eventually, cirrhosis leads to complete liver failure. This irreversible conditions leads inexorably to hepatic coma and death.

Pancreatitis. Chronic drinking causes this painful inflammation of the pancreas. Typically, pancreatitis hampers the body's ability to digest fats and certain other nutrients. If drinking continues, crucial insulin-producing islet cells in the pancreas sustain permanent damage. The result is developing diabetes.

Mouth and throat cancer. Chronic drinkers face a significantly increased risk of cancer of the mouth and throat, presumably because of the direct toxic effect of alcohol.

Low body weight. Chronic drinkers are more likely to be rail-thin than obese. They stop eating almost entirely and survive on alcohol's hollow calories. Rapid weight loss over weeks and months predictably reflects this physical dependency.

Vitamin deficiencies. Nutritional deficiencies that are almost unheard of in the general population such as scurvy, beriberi, etc., frequently show up in long-term drinkers because of poor nutrition.

Heart failure. Although some research suggests a drink a day benefits the heart, the risks of drinking far outweigh any possible benefits. Chronic drinking causes a pathological enlargement of the heart. This condition can progress to congestive heart failure, and from there, almost certain death.

Stomach pain. Alcohol irritates the delicate mucosal cells lining the esophagus and stomach. Although this irritation seldom leads to ulcers, it can cause a generalized stomach inflammation such as gastritis. Symptoms felt include pain in the gut, vomiting, and vomiting of blood.

Hormonal irregularities. Men who drink excessively over a period of time may lose body hair. Males also often experience a benign, but embarrassing enlargement of the breasts, known as gynecomastia. They also risk atrophy of the testes and consequently reduced fertility.

Reddening of the skin. Chronic drinking dilates small blood vessels just below the skin. This causes them to show through to the surface. Known as acne rosacea, this condition often results in reddish rash on the nose and cheeks.

Muscle damage. Chronic drinkers often develop pain and tenderness in the skeletal or voluntary muscles. This condition--skeletal myopathy--is generally not threatening in itself. However, breakdown of these muscles floods the bloodstream with proteins, severely damaging the kidneys.

Problems of Disclosure

Damage to marital and family stability usually reverberates in all areas of communication. Earlier, in spouse assessment, we reviewed deficits of communication causing severe anxiety for clean spouses and preventing confrontation with the substance abuse. One particular deficit inclined to deteriorate at a faster rate is self-disclosure. Self-disclosure is uninhibited release of protected, personal information, usually regarding flaws and mistakes, the exposure of which instantly invokes vulnerability. Causing that vulnerability is anticipatory fear that listeners will rebuke or punish for the expressed information, and that self-awareness of it might further jeopardize an already weak confidence.

Difficulties with self-disclosure happen for three reasons. First, the spouse is extremely self-critical and has censored any and all controversial admissions of fault risking condemnation from a listener. Virtually all acknowledgment of imperfection is repressed and deliberately avoided in private interpersonal discussions. Avoidance even includes not sharing personal details about themselves or their spouse to friends or family for fear that the conversation might uncover protected domains considered taboo. Anxious spouses become superb listeners, shifting the conversation away from themselves and onto another speaker, while they respond emphatically.

A second reason is literally never learning to articulate beliefs or faults about oneself around people. This develops from presuming nobody cares to know about it or that such topics are irrelevant to listeners. Spouses, as children, raised by passively quiet, unaffectionate parents learned the message that personal disclosure neither was encouraged nor discouraged--it just didn't happen. Nobody talked in the family and sharing seemed an unusual deviation of silence. As adults the same habit recurs of saying little about themselves thinking it's only their business and must be dealt with by themselves.

A third reason derives from fear and avoidance but unlike the first reason has no relationship to self-criticism. The spouse readily accepts faults, admits being fallible, but believes that sharing this information *imposes on people and causes other people grief. They wish solely to spare the spouse of being burdened by personal waste.* Hypersensitivity to the spouse's feelings and desire to minimize aggravation conspire to prevent self-disclosure. Apparently the pain vicariously observed in the spouse after telling him personal issues cuts deeply into the emotional fiber of the speaking spouse and automatically invokes fears of being a failure. A failure not because of imperfections, but because the speaker violated the belief that caretaking requires constant nurturing and providing an impeccable atmosphere of family happiness. The failure was making the spouse unhappy.

Types of self-disclosure fundamentally absent in family addiction fall into six categories, including: Neutral things, positive things, negative things, neutral things about self, positive things about self, and negative things about self.

Neutral things. This is disclosure of interactions with *other* people, objects or events not involving the person and that remain generically safe and distant. Discussing the Persian Gulf War after watching it on television is sharing neutral things.

Positive things. Disclosure of positive things again requires detachment and involves reporting events, objects, or interactions of a positive nature happening in the recent past. Sharing antics of a *M.A.S.H.* episode is sharing positive things.

Negative things. Expression of negative things is risky but ventures opinions about bad events, objects, or interactions happening to somebody else or somewhere else. Again, disclosure is an act of disembodiment. It deals not with the reporter himself or herself other than this or her opinions or feelings regarding the transaction.

Neutral things about self. At this stage self-disclosure implies trust. Even sharing neutral events experienced by the reporter assumes the listener will not abuse the information or show disinterest. Details shared are routine, normal habits, object or events occurring to that person in the recent past.

Positive things about self. Disclosure about positive things happening to the person is a higher risk and deeply confronts the internal fear of sounding pompous or conceited. Repression of self-affirmations, as mentioned earlier, prevents setting people's expectations too high and worrying about failing them.

Negative things about self. The ultimate test of fear is admission of bad, silly, humiliating, embarrassing, or outright stupid mistakes made by the person. Consider an innocent statement like, "Gee, honey, know what I did today? You won't believe it; I watered a fake plant." The humiliation felt by confessing this silly accident can unravel personal confidence and instantly force spouses into isolation if they are hypersensitive to another spouse's reactions, to their own self-criticism, or feel awful for grossly burdening the spouse with such a waste of time.

Problem of Provokes

Arguments are relatively commonplace for marital conflict. But why do they occur? Analyses take several different perspectives but nearly always deal with unresolved differences of opinion. In many instances, differences of opinion are healthy contributions to a conversation and add awareness of thoughts and feelings. Sharing of personal thoughts and feelings deteriorates the moment hostility escalates the exchange. Factors that directly cause this degeneration and upset the balance of control are called *provokes*. Provokes erupt from the following: (a) impure inferences; (b) persistence; and (c) repeating hostile or evocotive statements.

Pure and impure inferences. Ellis (1962; Ellis & Harper, 1975) correctly described irrational beliefs as subjective inferences strongly biasing opinions and destructively upsetting personal emotions. Beliefs regarding the way things or people *should be or ought to be* force hypothetical judgments upon expectations of other people including oneself. Variations of Ellis' original belief systems within cognitive-behavior therapy (Hayes, 1989; Hayes, Brownstein, Zettle, Rosenfarb & Korn, 1986; Ruben & Ruben, 1984, 1985; Zettle, 1990; Zettle & Hayes, 1982, 1986; Zettle & Young, 1987) further operationalize that fundamental assumptions start from having wrong rules about a situation or lack or information about the situation. Wrong rules, originally derived from *rule-governed behaviors* (Skinner, 1957, 1966, 1969), imply there are observed links between behavior and consequences that are incorrect or inconsistent with actual contingencies. Saying, for instance, that traffic jams occur at 8:00 am and again at 5:00 pm on the interstate in part depends on some facts. But empirically, traffic jams are not always that time-predictable and fluctuate depending on other variables. Likewise, assuming a spouse will be infuriated by telling him or her the credit card is overextended, draws from some but not all the historical contingencies observed in similar situations.

Predictions about behavior lose validity when assumptions interfere with the observation. That's what constitutes *pure and impure inferences.* A pure inference is guessing reasons for a person's behavior based on valid sources of data-words or actions of the person, history of reactions, and observations of unusual or collateral events affected by behavior (e.g., house doors left unlocked, more frequent long distance calls, etc.). Inferences, in other words, partly derive from facts or rules regarding *why the person has done this in the past relative to actions today.* Pure inferences lack total isomorphism with facts because inferred events remain unconfirmed, either by the observed person not admitting these reasons or lack of other forms of affirmation. *Impure inferences,* by contrast, stray even farther from realistic events by lacking both initial facts as well as lack empirical confirmation. Neither source of data establishes a foundation for the beliefs regarding another person's actions. Ellis' irrational beliefs fall into this category.

For example, stating that "my wife will return home from work today at 5:00 pm," indicates a pure inference. Cumulative historical data, or facts, reveal a behavioral pattern of this person's driving habits and hour of arrival after work, increasing the probability of this prediction. Lowering the probability is that the wife did not directly report that "she plans on being home at this hour" or express other confirmatory feedback. Were it to be an impure inference, the belief might go as follows: "She'll be late as usual." Here, little or no data is replaced by inflated beliefs regarding what the wife *always does, or typically does, or that she never is punctual.* Here the assumption contains an accusatory or stereotypical meaning, heavily biased by the observer's concept of what his wife should do or must do. *She should be home punctually, but typically is not. She must learn the importance of punctuality.* Rarely if ever are impure inferences dictated by accurate facts since they instead are cultivated from immediate preconceptions of *why* people behave and how this behavior violates a belief system of *proper behavior.*

Persistence. A second cause of provokes is persistence. Impure inferences initially equip a spouse with distorted, false beliefs regarding an incident that are presented once and repeated over and over until the listening spouse acknowledges them. Failure by the listening spouse to agree to the impure inferences results in two natural reactions. First is instant conflict wherein the observer defends the impure inference by presenting further generalizations, exaggerations of facts, and "false exhibits" as evidence. False exhibits are confabulated events based very loosely on actual interactions and twisted to confirm the impure inference at all costs. Citing the spouse's tardy return home yesterday as an exhibit deliberately overlooks definite facts that, for example, driving was hazardous and slow due to a two foot snowfall. Failure to consider these obvious facts refuting the impure inference adds intensity to the conflict. A second possible reaction is that the listening spouse passively withdrawls, surrenders to defeat and accepts the impure inference as judgment of behavior.

Repeating hostile or evocative statements. Where conflict is the primary reaction, exchanges typically escalate to hostile levels involving insistence by both parties that their convictions are correct. Arguments intensify when there is no recognition, clarification or defusal of the impure inference, and when defending inferences cause retaliatory challenges to the inference, usually by creating more impure inferences about the same situation (e.g., being tardy) or another situation (e.g., "and you also can't cook good"), or regarding events totally irrelevant to the impure inference and intended only to weaken the opposition (e.g., "and you don't love me anymore"). Ultimately altercations may degenerate to severe verbal and physical abuse or threats of divorce, property destruction or the disclosure of truthful or fabricated information targeted, again, to punish and weaken the opponent for "being stubborn."

Conflicts that frequently reach aggravative levels may simmer down in time. Reconciliation initiated by one or both spouses deflates the bitter feelings of antagonism and wrongful actions. However, no matter how long the reprieve exists, repeated conflicts have a peculiar conditioning effect upon most couples and especially addicted couples. Words and actions frequently visible during the arguments acquire "properties" to which the couple respond predictably. Raised voices, or use of profanity by one spouse might immediately evoke loud defensive remarks by the other spouse. Fists, a red face, or other body tension might be a "cue" triggering physical attack by the other spouse. "Cues" or discriminative stimuli, serve as a signals of impending behaviors and the consequences of those behaviors. Take, for instance, use of profanity. The very moment one spouse swears, especially if swearing rarely is heard unless in conflict, that action might signal to the other spouse that (a) conflict just began, (b) swearing may lead to yelling, to verbal or physical abuse, (c) frustration rises in the observer, and (c) neighbors might hear the altercation and call the police.

The listening spouse develops this discriminative reaction to any word or action associated with arguments. Like most discriminative learning, responses conditioned in the presence of some cues tend to recur in future situations involving those cues. One day later, for instance, one spouse brings up the same topic about the other being late. Any words, actions or interactions even slightly resembling the discriminative stimuli from that conflict *will predictably trigger the same agitative or aggressive behaviors seen in the original conflict.* This is essentially the basis of provokes. Repeating identical conflicts, or parts of the conflict, or behaviors used in that conflict, instantly *provoke* the reactor to respond in ways identical to previous conflict behaviors, regardless of how calm the person is at the moment of confrontation.

Problems of Affection

Assessment frequently unleashes complaints about affection. Disturbances of physical affection cover a wide variety of romantic overtures and sexual performance. Nonphysical affection in part covers listening and supportive behaviors discussed above, but also perceptions of the other person as an important or valuable contributor to the marriage. Let us carefully examine both components under the categories of (a) physical affection, and (b) perceptions of spouse.

Physical affection. Touching, for years, has symbolized intimate acceptance into a private, personal space and a development of trust. Affection also communicates a message of commitment, interest, and physical attractiveness, usually supported by sexuality. Howsoever construed, affection can deteriorate rapidly or be transformed into a controlling, abusive mechanism that exacerbates marital discordance. Types of deviations in physical affection most frequently diagnosed among addictive spouses include: (a) absence of any touching or intimacy; (b) touching or intimacy to prevent conflict; (c) unilateral touching or intimacy; (d) inhibition of touching around family or in public; and (e) abnormal touching or intimacy.

Absence of any touching or intimacy. Couples in distress complain that there is virtually no exchange of kisses, hugs, or intimacy either as the result of attrition over years or because it never or rarely occurred since the couple married. Prolonged absences deal, naturally, with harboring unresolved hostilities toward each other and the accumulation of marital problems. However, reasons may also include that (1) one or both spouses do not know how to be affectionate, (2) one or both spouses are afraid of intimacy stemming from the marriage or from childhood history, (3) one or both spouses find touching and intimacy usually the cause of conflicts or only used to resolve conflicts, and (4) one or both spouses experience physical discomfort or disturbance impeding touching and intimacy (premature ejaculation, frigidity, a physical disability, etc.)

Touching or intimacy to prevent conflict. Enablers who propagate the addictive cycle will frequently surrender to physical touching or intimacy if it allows for avoiding or escaping conflict. Either by prompting it themselves or passively accepting it if coerced, they elect for the humiliation of being a sexual object and consequently abhor all intimacy including their own needs for sexual gratification. Personal arousal is denied, blamed on being weak and vulnerable, and regarded as a waste of time. Aversion to sex or touching worsens once the addicted spouse comes to expect this reward for abusive behavior and demands it with threats to continue the conflict. Outwardly the enabling spouse may show enthusiasm, may participate in ritualistic games, wear enticing clothing, subordinate to the addicted spouse's peculiar positions or sexual preferences, and even fake sensuality and orgasms.

Unilateral touching or intimacy. Frequently the presenting problem is that only one spouse expresses physical affection. Absence of reciprocity intrudes on forming a trusting companionship. The "giving" spouse becomes suspicious, annoyed, and inductively assumes he or she is physically inadequate to satisfy personal needs of the spouse. Self-deprecation magnifies to greater fear that the uncaring, addicted spouse has high expectations for affection, toward which the caring spouse vigorously sets a course to fulfill. Or, fears concern the possibility that the uncaring spouse might abandon the family unless unilateral physical affection continues. Anticipation of this separation and loneliness has emotionally paralyzing effects that reverse the caring spouse's resistance, anger and opposition. Spouses simply accept the inequity as a condition of marital stability.

However, just as with absence of any touching or intimacy, unilateral affection typically is progressive over years of marriage and results from the uncaring spouse (1) lacking skills in touching and intimacy, (2) fearing rejection for the inadequate skills, (3) selfishly and impulsively depending on touching and intimacy like a child, (4) suffering physical impediments to touching and intimacy, and (5) feeling intimidated or unchallenged by excessive touching and intimacy.

This last one, feeling intimidated or unchallenged, raises a critical problem in dysfunctional relationships bound by control issues. Addicted spouses accustomed to being the controller and who receive excessive attention and affection lose motivation to be with the spouse. They no longer perceive the affectionate spouse as incompetent, needy, or deprived or requiring caretaking. Repairing that spouse at first was a definite challenge, excited by feeling personal value each time the spouse made improvements. Now that deficits are gone, so is the challenge. Emptiness in the relationship and loss of affectionate interest results from one spouse becoming healthy while the addicted, controlling spouse stays the same.

Inhibition of touching around family or in public. Mutual exchanges of affection may be very frequent and satisfying but only *in private.* Fears of exposing touching to significant family members or in public places traces to irrational beliefs (impure inferences) regarding body and sexual taboos. Adults raised by strict, inexpressive families prohibiting discussion about bodies, puberty and sexuality learned to be ashamed about physical contact and consequently are highly sensitive to exhibitions of this behavior. Instilled childhood fears resurface in thinking that other people (adults or children) who watch displays of affection will criticize them exactly as his or her parents did years ago. That criticism, assumed to occur, would cause emotional devastation and feelings of guilt. Childhood beliefs shift to adult impure inferences about *why it is simply bad to do these things.* Refusals to hold hands in the mall or kiss at an anniversary party feed on irrational beliefs as much as the strangeness or inexperience of touching in public.

Abnormal touching or intimacy. It is not unusual that spouse subordination reaches severely abusive stages where requirements for sexual satisfaction become abnormal. Diagnostically (e.g., DSM-IIIR) defined deviations such as fetishism and cross-dressing (transvestism), among others, are ritualistic steps a spouse believes are necessary to achieve presexual arousal sufficiently powerful enough to evolve into orgasm. Indulgence in costumes, games, or elaborate fantasies, even other partners during foreplay, all function as excitatory stimuli. Repeated rituals are usually unilateral, where the clean spouse unwillingly tolerates this subversion to avoid or escape conflict or assure marital stability. Increased ritualism, however, operates much like building up tolerance to alcohol or drugs. The more times it occurs, the more *of it* is needed to produce the *same effect* that initially required less amounts.

Perceptions of spouse. Regarding the spouse as "important" communicates in many ways. One obvious way, reported as delinquently missing or deficient, is through compliments. Intuitively, compliments pay attention to some physical or social feature or behavior of the spouse considered compatible or positive and thereby encourage more of that feature or behavior. Failure to provide this critical feedback on features or behavior conveys many messages that clean spouses may misinterpret or chronically personalize, and consequently decompensate in terms of self-importance. However, simply stating, "gee, you look nice or that was really great," is not always as easy as therapists think it is. Reasons exist for not complimenting the spouse that go beyond "not interested" and are endemic to addiction families. These consist of: (a) owing and obligation, (b) vulnerability, (c) absence of skills, (d) reserved compliments, and (d) aversion to compliments.

Owing and obligation. One difficulty with praising a spouse is feeling a necessary obligation to make the comment, or creating an obligation for the spouse after he or she receives the compliment. Owing is interpreted as a *must do,* and builds fearful expectations that compliments of any sort will fail, be viewed as stupid and incompetent, and draw negative criticism. Feeling compelled to make the compliment applies pressure to the person who historically may be afraid of pressure, or may avoid and escape it immediately. Secondary fears pertain to the complimented spouse who is believed to resent the obligation of now *owing a compliment back to his or her spouse for receiving one.* If anxiety over conflict is very high, if fear of rejection and criticism also is high, the spouse will be terribly apprehensive of drawing the other spouse into interactions that risk negative or unknown outcomes.

Vulnerability. A second emotional liability is feeling vulnerable. Complimenters are afraid that by singing the praises of the spouse they in turn look inferior. Competitively the spouse perceives self as the underdog, incapable of reaching the praiseworthy status or skill level of their mates. Self-criticism instantly reminds the spouse of their shortcomings, lack of lifelong accomplishments, and replays the horrible tune of *why I'm not a good person.* Excessive self-pity turns rapidly to resentment and anger directed to the spouse for excelling in areas, being confident or achieving goals.

Absence of skills. Overlooked frequently is the all too common problem that complimenting never was learned. It never occurs to the spouse to observe or comment on impressive traits of their mates because they never received compliments during childhood or early adulthood. Exactly what to say, how to say it, when to say it or outcomes expected to follow compliments are entirely unknown. Ignorance contributes to the alien or mechanical feelings when attempting to compliment the spouse; after one or two tries the spouse aborts the effort because the statements sound strange, peculiar, and unnatural.

Reserved compliments. Treatment of compliments during critical developmental periods creates another problem. Spouses recognize that praise is important but they reserve it for special occasions or exceptional behaviors beyond the call of duty. Extraordinary achievements deserve "honorable mention," whereas routine or ordinary tasks, even done efficiently, are expected and should be self-gratifying without the need for external approval. Prioritization of compliments traces to a rigid belief system that over-rewarded or -praised behavior spoils a person, gives them a swollen head, and leads to arrogance. Ironically, arrogance never develops; instead, spouses who refuse to give compliments, to themselves or others, until they perform some exceptional feat, generally become procrastinators, severely inefficient, and create unrealistically high expectations that typically exceed their abilities.

Aversion to compliments. Hatred for compliments increases sensitivity to receiving compliments as well as to giving compliments. A compliment represents a suspicious, distrusting statement believed to be made for some manipulative reason. The complimenter must be *up to something,* otherwise they never would pay attention in this way. Reared in a punitive environment, spouses cannot imagine they are worthy of praise or possess qualities exceptional to other people. Doubt destroys acceptance of any complimentary words received for any behavior, mediocre or extraordinary. Just as the spouse disqualifies compliments from others, so it is that giving compliments equally seems wrong. Immediately the spouse anticipates the partner dislikes compliments as much if not more than he or she does, and thereby spares the person of this aversion.

Problems of Verbal and Physical Abuse

Research is replete with studies showing domestic assault is on the rise and directly impacts groups of certain ethnic, racial, or economic denominators (Newberger & Bourne, 1985). The denominator of family addiction ranks high among leading predictors because there are response patterns in the marriage amenable to aggression. Reviewed here are eight ways verbal and physical aggression occur in troubled families. These include: (a) Biobehavioral, (b) emotional abuse, (c) isolation, (d) intimidation, (e) using male/female privilege, (f) threats, (g) using children, and (h) economic abuse.

Biobehavioral. Aggressive reactions by one or both spouses typically occur either before or during inebriation or drug usage. During these periods, uncontrolled urges produce two biobehavioral reactions in people. First, *pain* from the muscular or physical urges rising in anticipation of drug use increases frustration, anxiety, and compulsive reactions. Arousal of the autonomic nervous system (ANS) evokes speed of movement, irritability, distractibility, and acute sensitivity to the environment. Affected spouses are aware of everything around them, though feeling angry, suspicious, and prone to rage.

Second, during alcohol or drug use, and once urges get satisfied, there is a leveling off period lasting only as long as it takes for the body to absorb and react to the ingested substances. Substances that lower psychomotor activity and essentially slow the spouse's thinking (depressants) cause less threat of physical assaults than do stimulants. Cocaine, crack, and any amphetamine or bioequivalent agents raise autonomic functions at different rates and reach different peaks, the tip of which is disinhibition. That is, control over frustration or angry feelings is lifted and the spouse more freely risks confrontation.

Elevated levels of risk-taking at both predrug use and at actual drug use periods involve saying and doing things without the capacity for immediate self-awareness and self-censorship. Angry spouses usually lose touch with what words they say or the topic of argument and only focus upon the body's highly charged (stimulated) sensations. Self-monitoring of thoughts is nearly absent. All the spouse feels is the speed of pulsating sensations caused by frequent shifts between muscular constriction and muscular dilation. Tightening and loosening duplicates feelings of anger--of being upset; kinesthesia simulates effects produced by a gymnastic or athletic activity, but without the fatigue. Increases in adrenalin flow and in cardiovascularity induce a false physical state of aggression, so the person acts as if feeling aggressive, although precipitants to aggression are absent. Drug-induced aggression confuses observers, even the reactor, and behavior begins to subside once effects of the drug wear off.

Laboratory studies offer support for aggression under the influence of alcohol and drug use. Research has followed three basic forms of analysis: Direct cause, conditional, and situational. Direct cause studies have tried to posit a direct relationship between alcohol consumption and aggression. Studies on human subjects have been based on designs measuring aggression according to specified amounts of ethanol in the bloodstream, or on designs that studied the relationship between types of beverage (beer vs. distilled spirits) available to subjects on a free choice basis and perceived aggression (Boyatzis, 1974; Shuntich & Taylor, 1972). Boyatzis (1974), for example, found that persons who had a history of arguments and aggressive acts, and who scored low on measures of socialization, were more apt to display aggression after heavy drinking. However, Perskey, O'Brien, Fine, Howard, Khan & Beck (1977) in a controlled study failed to find a significant correlation between aggression and alcohol intoxication using a variety of measures.

Some laboratory studies have focused on limited conditional factors attempting to link the importance of intoxicated aggressive behavior to coping mechanisms employed by the individual. Jellinek & MacFarland (1940), for instance, tried to show that intoxicated coping devices were determined by the immediate situation. For others, the chain of events immediately leading up to the violent or aggressive act are the most relevant situational variables (Wilsnack, 1974; Mayfield, 1972).

Research designs that focus on the nature of conditioned variables also tend to see social settings and emotional states as relevant for examining alcohol use and aggression. Items such as male drinking company (Carpenter & Armenti, 1972), frustrating or stressful stimuli (Boyatzis, 1974, 1975), and cognitive structures have revealed the importance of testing for differences in social settings. However, the as yet undetermined link between emotional or stressful states and aggressive behavior has stymied systematic analyses between social settings, aggressive behavior, and alcohol use. Further, these studies generally have not taken into account the family as a particular social setting from which to study these links.

Observational and general population studies on alcohol and aggressive behaviors have tended to follow along the same lines of research employed in studies of alcohol's emotional effects. The two prime examples of observational approaches are tavern studies and anthropological studies of a variety of primitive cultures (MacAndrew & Edgerton, 1969; May, 1973). One focus of aggressive behavior examined through observational methods is the study of the escalatory process of behavior patterns resulting in violence (Aho, 1967; Mayfield, 1972; Washburne, 1961). All these studies explicitly imply linkage between alcohol and escalating violence, although no systematic attempts have been made to study domestic violence specifically.

Emotional abuse. Clear cases of emotional abuse involve directly insulting or making the clean spouse feel bad, calling them names, or making that spouse think he or she is literally crazy. To the degree blame shifts to the clean enabler, aggressive abusers feel they are exonerated. Upsetting the spouse becomes a daily obsession, with few recuperative plateaus. Acceptance of these assaults, or satisfying other needs in hopes of preventing subsequent criticisms, are useless and the enabler soon discovers expectations for pleasing the spouse are both unrealistic and constantly changing.

Isolation. Abuse takes the form of controlling what the clean spouse says and does even when absent from that spouse. Constant telephone calls checking up on the spouse or having "spies" keep surveillance, all undermine marital trust. Victimized spouses held hostage by ongoing monitoring such as reporting the car mileage, logging telephone calls, or asking permission before venturing outside the house, will rapidly develop a dependency on the feared spouse to prevent conflict. Fear-induced isolation causes a secondary complication in the clean spouse of anticipating intense anxiety in public, eventually evolving into agoraphobia.

Intimidation. Emotional immobility is further induced in clean spouses when the abuser physically displays property destruction or other aggressive actions suggesting the same violence against the clean spouse. Fear is brought on by actions, gestures, loud voices, smashing things, destroying special keepsakes or items having marital symbolism (wedding picture and frame). Excessive and repeated demonstrations exert control over the clean spouse's attempted disobedience.

Using male or female privilege. A common ploy is the abuser asserting his or her dominance simply by decree of gender. Male abusers insist they are the "boss," "master of the castle," and will make all family decisions. Female abusers declare they are "smarter," have "better intuition," and demand making all the family or child-related decisions. Gender privilege assumes a powerfully controlling role that restricts the other spouse from a cooperative role, largely out of avoidance of conflict and criticism. Beliefs regarding gender status unfortunately are impure inferences that never get clarified, or defused, and instead the inferences receive inadvertent support by both spouses simply accepting the situation as status quo.

Threats. Verbal insults also prescribe aggressive actions for the future. Threats are made to hurt the clean spouse, children, or other family members emotionally. Threats may pertain to others or the abuser himself or herself. Toward others, threats warn of physically hurting the spouse, having affairs, or exposure of sensitively confidential information entrusted between spouses. Removal of the children is another common manipulation. Abusers insist they will abscond with the children without a trace and force matters into a costly custody battle. Toward the abuser, threats are to commit suicide or liquidate all the family's assets. Warnings of self-infliction usually are grandiose, are stated impulsively immediately upon conflict, and even meager attempts to carry out plans nearly always bet on seeking sympathy from the frightened spouse.

Using children. Abusers lose parental respect for children when the children become diplomats of war. Attacks, physically or verbally, may be sent through the child like a messenger who reports "daddies' or mommies'" threats to the other spouse. Children also receive the brunt of blame for marital disputes. Abusers accuse the disobedient child of working in collusion with the clean spouse to sabotage power. Attacks worsen during marital separation or divorce. Visitation schedules act as bargaining chips when the abusive spouse refuses to pick up the children or arrives late, again blaming the clean spouse for insubordination and lack of love.

Economic abuse. Insulating the clean spouse from the outside world extends to all facets of social integration. Abusive spouses may refuse to let the clean spouse work a job, volunteer in community activities, or spend money. Economic sanctions do more than suppress employability. Threatened spouses lose a precious opportunity to expose their personal vulnerability at home and seek solutions from trusted members of the community. Refusals of money, for the clean spouse to buy clothes, supplies, or even to afford basic home improvements (e.g., repair of washing machine, dryer, dishwasher, etc.) minimize that spouse's re-entry into the public mainstream and force unwilling survival on a shortage of economic resources.

EFFECTS UPON FAMILY

Substantially more dysfunctional couples plagued by addiction in the last ten years have realized there is a gestalt or total family effect of the addiction. Concepts of "family disease" essentially describe the systemic or permeable reactions toward the addict and how lives of each family member deteriorate both during addiction phases as well as during addiction recovery. This is why assessment regarding effects upon family must consider how the spouse and each affected child fit into the total picture. In this section major problems arising in the family are reviewed.

Problems Facing Addiction and Recovery

In any social system, for every action there is a reaction; and the more intimate the social system, the more each participant expresses and influences the whole. This simple but critical concept is central to understanding predictable patterns brought on by an addicted spouse and perpetuated by enablers. Patterns that are silently or unobtrusively infecting lifestyles of each family member include the following: (a) distrust, (b) protectiveness, (c) unrealistic expectations, (d) newly surfaced resentment, and (e) recovery as threat to others in family.

Distrust

As discussed earlier, distrust guards against repeated emotional and even physical injury in an unpredictable family environment. Spouse or children uncertain when the next outburst or abuse might occur are walking on egg shells and hypersensitive to all precipitatory events. Doubt also arises during the addict's recovery in the fear of a relapse and being caught at the mercy of the abuser. It is virtually impossible for the family not to harbor distrust, even after months or years of abstinence, depending on the severity of previous abuse and whether the recovering spouse undergoes major behavior changes conducive to family interaction.

Protectiveness

Oddly, desertion from the addict can have reversal effects during recovery. While spouse and family members alienated themselves when abused, now that the addict accepts the chemical dependency, seeks treatment for it, and is legitimately making changes, family sympathy tends to increase. Strong interest in helping the addict reach recovery goals can become excessive. Anxious families often overprotect or overtreat the addict as too fragile to handle normal responsibilities, at least while in recuperation. Protection is believed to be a curative approach toward nonaddiction. However, it actually is leftover forms of enabling that resurface now that the addict needs their assistance and is grateful for their sacrifices.

Unrealistic Expectations

Damage from an addicted spouse already takes a heavy toll on family members. As they slowly recover from hurt, observing abstinence in the spouse or parent, beliefs quickly develop that the disaster is over and now the family can be happy. Expectations based on how *things should be or are with other families* encourage optimism and motivation to give the person a second chance. Expectations about treatment are that it brings a finite cure and now all past painful experiences can be ignored. Removal of past painful history is wishful thinking taken out of proportion and unrealistically applied to the family's ideas of normalcy. Pretending that all is fine, clean spouses and the children may overlook or ignore slips and episodic relapses and persist at blindly believing that mistakes are routine.

Newly Surfaced Resentment

Anger kept repressed during the addiction phases now has an option for release once the addictive spouse begins recovery. Family members manifest resentment for suffering emotional and physical abuse, for being neglected and abandoned, and for developing their own dysfunctions attributable to the recovering parent. Loyalty to the ex-addict also remains jeopardized. Restoring this loyalty means forgiving the parent for culpable actions and denying personal anguish undertaken to avoid and escape the horrors of conflict and havoc. Families that realize they have unrelenting anger typically must submit to major steps in reconstruction of the family unit including explicit steps on expressing opinions no matter the outcomes.

Recovery as Threat to Others in Family

Naturally the recuperation process involves ongoing adjustment. The personality of the ex-addict is unusual, perhaps diametrical to the past addictive behaviors, and behavior patterns expected under most circumstances no longer occur. Superficially the family applauds this reconstructive surgery of personality and internally believes the parent deserves a new lease on life. However, reacting to this personality change uncovers peculiar family patterns indicated as: (a) resistance to change, (b) overcompensating for change, and (c) distance from change.

Resistance to change. Observed changes in the addict's behavior signal a necessary family adjustment in ways that are foreign, uncomfortable, and thus avoided. Clean spouses are not accustomed to "communicating" with the ex-addict, just as children rarely expect hugs, kisses, money or gifts given unconditionally. Displays of affection and family interest frighten members away from the ex-addict, even causing them to aggressively resent this improvement. Resistance arises when the family must now engage in behaviors about which they are ignorant or have deficiencies, or forfeited long ago during addiction years.

Take affection, for instance. Being receptive to warm physical gestures, after uninterrupted years of physical or even sexual abuse (on parent, or incest with children), requires drastic revisions in *perceiving the person differently, allowing for physical touch, and possibly developing reciprocal feelings of caring.* Suppression of these actions and feelings made it possible to survive, and so trying to reverse the process bitterly conflicts with a history of punishment conditioning. Memories of punishment, along with literally not knowing how to do the behaviors, mitigate against cooperation, for even the best intentioned family.

Overcompensating for change. Families alert to this resistance and especially aware that they lack critical skills for change, may seek improvements too far in extreme. A wife realizing she is aorgasmic and wants normal sexual relations with her ex-addict husband may read literature on all the "right positions" or dress in seducing lingerie or possibly even attend self-help conferences on strengthening one's sensuality. Laborious effort goes into developing skills, into polishing those skills until they reach perfection, and finally putting those skills to the test in hopes of spousal approval. This overcompensation of skill-building in part is left over from approval-seeking and enabling behaviors of the addiction lifestyle. Again the spouse feels inadequate unless she receives positive feedback for her loyalty. Now that her ex-addict husband is sober, more affection, praise and approval seem available, in unlimited amounts, *if only she works hard enough to achieve it.*

Distance from change. Resistance to trying out new behaviors as part of adjustment has a familiar outcome. Affected spouses and children both during addiction phases and into recovery steps may alienate from the ex-addict at the expense of *keeping things the way they are.* Maintaining the status quo entirely predicates on avoidance of difficult or painfully contradictory thoughts, behaviors and emotions. For example, as alluded to earlier, pretending to love an incestuous parent now that the parent recants still feels hypocritical and repulsive. By leaving things as they are, family interactions slightly improve simply because there are no new surprises and psychological warfare has stopped. Intimacy never grows closer, and children essentially retain their biased, distrusting judgments toward the ex-addict without any opportunity to express these thoughts.

Coping with these Problems

In family reactions to spouse addiction, the one phenomenon clearly injurious to communication and trust is *family ambiguity.* Family ambiguity derives from concepts of role ambiguity (Ruben, 1986) and describes the continuous presentation of unavoidable and inescapable problems compounded upon spouse and children without relief. Unabated pressures force loss of autonomy, or independently responding to situations with the hope of producing positive outcomes. When actions and reactions only produce hazardous, punitive outcomes, responses undergo such shock that they initially paralyze the person, then responses slowly deteriorate, and ultimately actions and reactions fade entirely. A helpless state results. Gradual decay of behavior to the point where a person becomes immobile, apathetic, even depressed, is called *learned helplessness* (Garber & Seligman, 1980).

Extensive research on learned helplessness in animals and later reproduced in humans (Barbar & Winefield, 1986;Fincham & Cain, 1986; Nolen-Hoeksema, Girgus & Seligman, 1986), showed that repeated exposure to aversive situations is worse than response decrements or extinction. In other words, behavior just doesn't decrease until it disappears. Humans forced in hostile and especially painful environments replace *normal positive actions* with a series of predictable and sequential reactions as part of adaptation to the environment (cf., Seligman & Schulman, 1986). Clinical observations suggest that stages of the sequence include: (a) intensified anxiety; (b) intermittent productive behaviors, and (c) altruism and depression.

Intensified Anxiety

Under initial stress the person struggles aimlessly for escape hatches and tries vigorously to avoid future stressors. Struggles bring on acute anxiety, anticipatory doubts, and generalized fears that there is no prevention of problems or that escalated problems will only threaten a worse situation. At the heart of this anxiety are five unresolved forces: (1) roles are unclear; (2) lack of resources; (3) lack of skills; (4) lack of standards; and (5) lack of feedback or communication.

Roles are unclear. Confusion causes deadly consequences for the anxious spouse. That spouse may not know how he or she is to behave in the marriage; whether actions today are appropriate or will be criticized. Uncertainty inhibits handling normal decisions of childcare, house or office planning, and personal improvement.

Decisions of any sort risk rejection or attack for not complying with the addicted spouse's expectations. When expectations vary, and criticism is arbitrary and capricious, decisions simply are not made. However, refusal to make decisions also may draw criticism. Now the battered spouse receives punishment for making decisions, making wrong decisions, or not making decisions at all. Rebukes become totally unavoidable.

Lack of resources. Lack of resources means the clean spouse remains at the mercy of the addicted spouse for materials, money, transportation, food, or whatever is necessary to comply with the arbitrary and random expectations. Action taken alone is impossible because the addicted gatekeeper must be consulted before satisfying daily needs. Purchases all must pass the gatekeeper's inspection; likewise with destinations traveled by automobile. Without new resources, spouse and children live off of their reserves (old clothes, old appliances, etc.) or resort to undermining this moratorium by stealing resources from the gatekeeper or from places outside the family.

Lack of skills. Underlying ambiguity from all directions is absence of skills. Spouses and children are behaviorally illiterate in strategies or basic prosocial skills considered absolutely necessary to combat the addict or ex-addict's oppression. Skills in assertiveness, in conflict-resolution, in problem-solving and in relaxation that might allow risk-taking without anxiety and an anticipatory sense of doom are all weak. Deficits restrict mobility in the family to challenge the addict because the outcome of confrontation would leave such emotional scars and deepen the resentment, so that very little would be gained.

Lack of standards. A family tightly regulated by an addicted spouse has few approved opportunities to socialize in public. All information about the family dysfunction is kept hidden within the microcosm. The children rarely disclose their miseries in school, just as clean spouses keep a tight lid on matters when at work or among adult friends. However, silence cannot prevent vicarious observations of other family interactions, particularly positive ones, and envying the demonstrations of love, affection and communication. Created by these observations are standards--some accurate, some inflated--concerning how families *should behave toward one another*. Standards help the children identify what they are missing in their own families and set up contrasts with other observed families closer in profile to their own. Families they find that match their own family profile relieve a feeling of deviancy, of thinking of themselves as freaks. However, if observations prove otherwise, noticing more discrepancies than similarities in family profile, resentment toward those healthy, positive families is severe.

Lack of feedback or communication. Already discussed is the anxiety produced by negative feedback, either as criticism or rejection. Lack of feedback or communication induces a similar problem of family insecurity. Members constantly wonder if actions were appropriate, inappropriate, or met parental or spousal expectations. Limited comments generally create tension in three ways: (a) personalization of fault; (b) rebellious reaction; and (c) formation of irrational beliefs.

Personalization of fault. Silent households offer minimal feedback on routine behaviors or accomplishments of clean spouse and children. One normal reaction is assuming the behavior or accomplishment received no feedback because it was inadequate, delinquent. Imperfection instantly creates shame for *not knowing better or the having the ability to prevent the mistake.* This assumes that, had they known better or prevented the mistake, feedback would be available. Limited feedback, primarily as negative, further causes guilt. Family members surmise their actions not only are imperfect, but they themselves must be stupid, inane, or completely mindless for even trying those actions in the first place.

Rebellious reaction. Morsels of attention, particularly negativity, provoke an untoward reaction. Rather than regress, spouses and children may engage in outrageously rebellious behavior forcing the addict to react under situations where that person typically is silent. Impulsive screaming, hitting, threats, tantrums, and property destruction beg for attention. In reply the addict's hostile actions are sufficient to cause repetitions of the behavior on subsequent occasions.

Formation of irrational beliefs. Forming at this impressionable period of time for children is the belief that *this is the way families are.* Silence, reluctance to communicate, and expectations of negative or little positive feedback imprint rules regarding family dynamics that the children carry into adulthood. Later, when dating or in marriage, these adult children of dysfunctional families have virtually no concept of communication nor does it occur to them that there is a problem without it.

Intermittent Productive Behaviors

As struggles become futile, infliction of stress becomes both inescapable and unavoidable. Attempts at resisting it generate momentary relief, perhaps even artificially creating productive efforts, but the net result still is loss of control. These periods of strength are called *intermittent productive behaviors* because they are recuperative efforts that penetrate through the edifice of punishment. Family members show productive efforts in the following ways: (a) pleading, (b) negotiating, and (c) public disclosure.

Pleading. Desperate pleas beg the addict to seek help. During recovery, spouses and children beg for changes in behavior patterns besides the chemical dependency. Abstinence may be strong, but aggressive outbursts are still arbitrary and capricious. Repeated requests appeal to the addict's sentimentality and idealistic hopes for family cohesion. Failing at this, members temporarily resign to helplessness only to bounce back later with another appeasement.

Negotiating. Pleading only does so much. It presumes a subordinate role against the superiority of the addict with little or nothing to bargain with. Rising above this inferiority is the next step. Family members, particularly the clean spouse, try negotiating different deals conditionally tied to the addict seeking help. Refusal to seek help is regarded as disapproval of the spouse's terms for negotiation, not as resistance or denial or substance abuse problems. This mobilizes the spouse or children to renegotiate, offer more rewarding terms for acceptance, and even forfeit personal values, material goods, money or self-respect. Negotiating takes on a perpetual challenge to discover the addict's weakness, at whatever the cost to family members.

Public disclosure. Slowly there are leaks through the cement walls. Disclosure is the last ditch effort to escape from family ambiguity. The clean spouse may schedule only one appointment with a therapist. At the appointment there is catharsis on problems at home and desperation for intervention. Children may go a different route. Slow release of information usually is with peers, a trusted teacher, or possibly a parent of a friend. Once this privileged information is set free, it also redeems hope for family members, as they gain a momentary surge of courage. However, returning home to the restricted environment immediately bursts that courage if they re-experience fear and suddenly recede in shame over *what people will think of them for exposing this information.*

Altruism and Depression

The last step in learned helplessness is capitulation. Experimentally, tests of learned helplessness on dogs (Seligman, 1968; Seligman & Maier, 1967; Seligman, Maier & Geer, 1968) showed that repeated exposures to painful stimulation without chance of avoidance or escape produced a paralysis, or sudden cessation of responding. Years earlier, Ratner (1958; Ratner & Thompson, 1960) reported a similar phenomena called *tonic immobility* (see also Maser & Gallup, 1977). In both cases, response deceleration was gradual and reached a point where there were no further struggles. The human analogy is catatonia and states of depression. Humans exposed repeatedly to noise, or some aversive stimuli without avoidance or escape eventually lose response strength and, like the dogs, simply collapse in defeat.

Applied to addiction families, this last step of learned helplessness opens possibilities for another reaction consistent with withdrawal or depression. Family members stunted by punishment may simply do whatever the addict wants, not in hopes of preventing future pain, but because the delivery of pain is less intense, less frequent, and accompanied by minimal approval and caring. This is a type of altruism. In other words, two (tandem) schedules of contingencies operate simultaneously on the clean spouse or children. First is a punishment schedule that may be entirely or partially random and arbitrary. Second is a "reward" schedule that doesn't necessarily produce anything, like the punishment schedule does, but it delays and de-intensifies the punishment schedule. The sweeter, kinder, and more compliant family members are, the lighter the punishment; but it is still forthcoming. When punishment hits, the force is smaller, length of punishment is shorter, and possibly number of punishment attacks are fewer. Strangely, in between punishment are some gentle words of caring made by the addicted spouse. Altruism keeps this vicious cycle going with the two schedules in constant flux.

PRIORITIES FOR INTERVENTION

Correcting spouse and family addiction calls upon special expertise in two categories of interventions. First is the behavioral methodology largely based in scientific experimentation and heavily tested upon many distressed couples with varying problems. Strategies following this approach, called *behavioral marital therapy (BMT)* for couples and *behavioral family therapy (BFT)* for families, provides a platform for direct and structured re-training of dysfunctional patterns. Use of BMT or BFT alone is ineffective and can be best integrated within a systems model (e.g., Russell, Atilano, Anderson, Jurich & Bergen, 1984). However, many methods already exist for the *systems approach* that may have nothing to do with behavior therapy per se, and so this integration, for many, seems unwanted. That is why we start with a review of advantages and disadvantages of both approaches.

Behavioral and Systems Approaches To Family and Marital Therapy

Investigation of the dynamics leading to successful outcomes of marriage and family therapy is relatively new among research topics. Nearly two decades ago the clinical case study was sufficient documentation of treatment effects. Two factors, however, changed this reliance on case studies. One was a closer alliance between research and practitioner (Andreozzi, 1985; Barlow, Hayes & Nelson, 1984). A second factor was the increase in ethical and legal questions about the validity of therapy and training adequacy for prospective therapists (e.g., Hersen, 1979). Consequently research on interventions is more prolific and this trend especially is visible within family and marriage therapies.

A closer examination of differences between behavioral and systemic models can be made through: (a) efficacy of family and marital therapy, (b) methodological pitfalls, and (c) therapist factors .

Efficacy of Family and Marital Therapy

Approaches to family and marital therapy share a basic problem with approaches to individual therapy. The multiplicity and diversity of designs and theoretical orientations complicate attempts to uniformly measure treatment efficacy. Then, too, regardless of orientation, definitions of "efficacy" are elusive. For this discussion, two approaches to family and marital therapy (FMT) considered are the family systems approach and behavioral approach. An overview is provided of each approach, followed by components of purported effectiveness.

Family systems theory essentially addresses pathology as an integrated group, not as an individualistic problem, focusing on interdependent relationships among family members. Andrews, Bubolz & Paolucci (1980) redefined the central target of therapy as upon the energy transformation system. Earlier accounts (Bubolz, Eichner & Sontag, 1979; Ezell, Paolucci & Bubolz, 1964; Hook & Paolucci, 1970) clearly identified this system as consisting of time, space, boundary conflicts, and degree of coherency. Concepts borrowed from cybernetic and mathematical paradigms help describe families in terms of organizations, processes, and interactional sequences. Jackson (1965) further contended that sequences are ongoing, with no discernable beginning or end point. Cause and effect thereby are nonlinear, or mutually reciprocal such that individual behavior and surrounding physical environment are both equal parts of the macrosystem.

By contrast the orthodox behavioral models focus on organismic or individualistic problems. Therapies for individuals or groups (couples, families) derive in part from tested principles of operant and respondent conditioning. Pathology is considered conditioned, or learned, based on developmental and current consequences for one person. Whether or not the person behaves along a continuum of interpersonal interactions is secondary. Therapies for couples or families slightly differ in perspective. While models of conditioning prevail, focus is upon the "contingency" or function of behavior, consequence and setting as it affects family members. For example, contingencies of reinforcement, punishment and confusions thereof spark marital discord and imbalance among dysfunctional families (Epstein, Schlesinger & Dryden, 1989; Jacobson & Margolin, 1979; Stuart, 1980).

Both systems and behavioral approaches thus have important differences. Systems therapists might consider family alcoholism a holistic matter rooted in disturbances of asynchronicity, closed or random boundaries, and disequilibrium of energy (Constantine, 1989; Schwartzman, 1989). Viewing it behaviorally, identical symptoms may indicate maladaptivity, absence of feedback loops, dominance of punishment, and interpersonal dysfunctions. Foster & Hoier (1982) articulated these differences in four areas: (a) the locus of intervention (contingency sequences versus system structure), (b) explanations of interaction mechanisms and failure to change, (c) approaches to the maintenance of therapeutic gain, and (d) integration of assessment and treatment goals and methods. Their major similarity is focus upon parts or all of behavioral sequences rather than purely on the subjective or affective experiences of individual family members.

Based on their differences alone, it comes as no surprise that few definitive conclusions can be reached regarding the absolute effectiveness of either approach. Gurman (1973, 1978) reported data on outcome studies comparing psychoanalytic, behavioral and systems approaches. His findings, supported by Russell, Atilano, Anderson, Jurich & Bergen (1984), concluded that structured interventions, over nonstructured types, proved superior. Structured therapies directed toward the family unit especially were valid. Kniskern (1985) suggested this unit consist of the (a) identified patient, (b) the marriage, and (c) the total family system. A slight variation offered by Todd & Stanton (1983) was to assimilate behavioral technology and traditional systems such as Minuchin's family therapy model or Bowen's family systems theory.

Todd & Stanton (1983) acknowledged that the merits of behavioral combined with systems models must be evaluated empirically. Yet they were critical of behavioristic origins in therapy. The greatest deficiency cited was that "behaviorally oriented research has derived from what appears to us to be an overvaluing of the laboratory method" (p. 97). Of course, that "laboratory method" is precisely what enabled Jacobson (1978, 1979) to demonstrate repeatedly that behavioral marital and family therapies are significantly more effective than no treatment, minimal treatment, or purely systems treatment.

Interventions that are frequently shown as effective appear in multifaceted packages and include communication, problem-solving, behavior exchange, and contingency management. Jacobson (1977) demonstrated that solution generation did not occur unless the couple mutually agreed upon an exchange of rewards (contingency management). More recently he advanced his "exchange component" to include increasing demands of spouse changes proportional to more rewards earned (Jacobson & Follette, 1985). In the systems approach, techniques per se are less supported than are "therapies." Among therapies that have generated encouraging findings are (a) functional family therapy, (b) structural family therapy, and (c) Zuk's go-between therapy (e.g., Garrigan & Bambrick, 1979).

With few therapies identified, research in the systems approach appears headed in two directions. The first direction is generating data on individual problems in living consistent with the human ecosystems theory. Dysfunctional behavior, in other words, can be both intraorganismic as well as interorganismic. A second direction is specification of therapy methodology not only of benefit for replication, but also so that therapy can add etiological information to family problems.

Directions in behavior therapy, oddly enough, are moving toward systems (ecobehavioral) orientations. Recent interest appears to integrate field thinking, viewing family as a continuum, with stimulus-response methods. Secondly, like Jacobson, other researchers view the mutual spouse relationship as undervalued and requiring a more definitive technology for treatment.

Methodological Pitfalls

Conducting marital and family therapy research, as already mentioned, involves endless problems because of the divergent approaches (cf. Persons, 1991). But most methodological pitfalls pertain to the absence of control groups, the lack of adequate follow-up data, the use of questionable, poorly validated measures of treatment outcome, and treatment procedures that are so vague and poorly specified that they are unreplicable (Coleman, 1989; Jacobson & Bussod, 1983). Parloff (1980) concurred that frequently employed measures of marital satisfaction not only are unreliable and invalid, but also inconclusive. Outcome indicators usually overlook those influenced by familial improvements such as friends, therapists, and community members. He calls for expanding boundaries of data collection for a larger sample of treatment effects.

Toward one solution, Jacobson and his colleagues (Hahlweg & Jacobson, 1988; Jacobson & Gurman, 1988) outlined specific research design alternatives including use of single case methods. Single case or time-series strategies essentially measure independent and dependent variables in smaller groups (n=1) and replicate hypothesized effects rapidly and systematically without inferential statistics. The pragmatic benefits for supporting clinical behavior change are well documented in the literature (for a review, see Borkovec & Bauer, 1982; Kazdin, 1980). Methods such as reversal design, multiple-baseline design, multi-element design, and criterion design powerfully control for intrusions upon internal validity and can increase obtained scores of interobserver reliability far higher than obtained from traditional group design studies.

Despite these advantages, single case designs might be limited to outcome results. Process results are another story. Liberman, Wheller & Kuehnel (1983), for example, pinpoint failures in marital therapy due to factors undetected by single case as well as group designs. These include (a) noncompliance by one spouse with therapeutic assignments reinforced by the martyr role; (b) covert intention for separation that sabotages therapy; (c) marital therapy starting too late; (d) marital therapy starting too soon; (e) when only one partner will participate; (f) inability to move from the past; and (g) changes in one spouse that require painful adaptation in the other.

Identifying these deficiencies during or even after marital and family interventions thus requires an integrative model of research. Gurman & Kniskern (1971) postulated seven guidelines for assessing therapeutic change that in part derive from the operationalization of behavioral methods and also preserve a systemic perspective. Among the list includes measuring:

1. The identified patient
2. The marriage as a total system
3. The family as a total system
4. Same generation of identified patient (e.g., siblings)
5. Cross-generation of identified patient (e.g., parent, another child)

6. Same generation of a relationship to identified patient (e.g., friend)
7. Cross-generation of a relationship to identified patient (e.g., parents of nonfamily friends)

The criteria on outcome changes in effect becomes a measure of behaviors and perceptions of people directly and indirectly shaping the family subsystem.

Therapist Factors

A final pitfall impacting on therapeutic outcome is therapist training and competency of service delivery. Concerns for quality no doubt permeate across behavioral and nonbehavioral practice and are universally problematic within the clinical field. Let us consider how these pitfalls affect behavioral clinicians and the implications for marriage and family therapy in general.

Traditionally trained behavioral practitioners run into a common problem. They are so equipped in methodology that they may put behavior change goals ahead of client sensitivity (Herson, 1979). Consequently a torrent of studies emerged (e.g., Gardner, 1972; Wisocki & Sedney, 1978) aimed at preparing practitioners-to-be with more empathic, personal skills in dyadics. Isaacs, Embry & Baer (1982) for example, designed a training program to teach students family therapy skills. Among components taught were procedural descriptions for behavior methods *and* effectiveness skills to facilitate client rapport and maintenance of behavior changes. This was accomplished by having trainees become more alert to parents' verbal and nonverbal behaviors and to adjust accordingly the timing, tone, and content of their own comments.

Finely tuning "personal style" is a beginning but still verges on vague concepts such as therapist-client rapport, good interviewing skills and therapist likability. One alternative is to operationalize these concepts into specific measurable and learnable skills that are part of the clinical curricula (e.g., Fuqua & Miltenberger, 1985; Iwata, Wong, Riordon, Dorsey, & Lau, 1982). Out of this research appears categories for verbal and nonverbal presentation of therapist to client.

Family and marriage practitioners, as well, need two additional skills frequently omitted in research literature. First is flexibility. Second is adaptivity. Flexibility in this context refers to adjusting verbal and nonverbal responses higher or lower for adults and then for children. Choice of words, facial expressions, and explanatory emphasis must be consistent with the comprehension level of clients.

The second, adaptivity, refers to arranging and re-arranging sessions with different members of the family. At times scheduled sessions may be attended by selected parties--siblings only, parents only, or combinations of the two. However, with weekly family sessions, prior commitments or unexpected school and community activities disjoint session planning and this causes shifts in agenda or delays in goal attainment. Therapists sensitive to external intrusions can be prepared with alternative routes of intervention for whichever family members attend sessions.

Principles of Relationship Change

Thinking integratively, approaches to family and marital therapy operate on general principles of behavior change critically contributing to overall outcome success. Stuart (1980, pp. 370-371) proposed three categories of principles dealing with marital interaction that are adapted here for treatment of families as well. Categories include: (a) for understanding relationships; (b) for changing relationships; and (c) for understanding and changing communication.

For Understanding Relationships

A. *Open system principle:* All relationships change constantly as a result of reactions to external demands and shifting desires on the part of all people in the relationship. Therefore, change is the norm of all relationships.

B. *Best-bargain principle:* Behaviors that all parties in relationships display at any given moment represent the best means that each person believes he or she has available for obtaining desired satisfactions.

C. *The instability principle:* All relationships are intrinsically unstable in that any party may decide that the reward-cost balance of opting out of the relationship may be greater than the reward-cost balance of remaining within it.

For Changing Relationships

A. *The change-first principle:* For couples and families to overcome struggles, all parties must assume the responsibility of changing their own behaviors first in order to prompt behavior changes in others.

B. *The positive-change principle:* Relationships can be changed best through a search for positive behaviors that can take the place of negative exchanges.

C. *The small-steps principle:* Complex family and marital relationships can be changed only through small, planned sequential steps.

D. *The as-if principle:* To prompt the initiation of small, assertive, positive changes, it is important for each person to act as if the other has a definite interest in promoting relationship changes.

E. *The fear-of-change principle:* It is wise to expect that couples and families will be fearful of change even if by any objective standard that change is toward the relief of pain and the provision of pleasure. Therefore, some resistance to all change efforts is to be expected and cannot be taken as a negative sign.

F. *The testing principle:* All parties can be expected to test especially the most positive of changes in order to make certain that they can be trusted over time. Testing takes the form of time-limited return to earlier behaviors or audition of new behaviors, that can be overcome by reaffirmation of the desire for change.

G. *The predictability principle:* Relationships produce more comfort and more freedom for all principals when their norms are expressed as rules.

H. *The principle of irreversibility:* No act of any kind can ever be completely withdrawn, nor will it ever be completely forgotten. Therefore, tact and timing should be the benchmarks of all behavior.

I. *The all-win or no-win principle:* In every bargaining situation in families or marriages, no person can make more than a temporary gain unless all parties win.

J. *The principle of shared responsibility:* All parties to the relationship are jointly responsible for everything that happens— good or bad; and therefore, they must participate in any successful effort to promote relationship change.

K. *The principle of the urgent present:* It is necessary to concentrate attention on the present, forsaking the opportunities to exact penalties for the past in all efforts to promote and maintain relationship improvement.

For Understanding and Changing Communication

A. *The principle of constant communication:* One cannot *not* communicate, as every behavior, verbal or nonverbal, expresses both a specific content and a comment about the relationship between the parties.

B. *The principle of level consistency:* Because all communication has at least two levels, and because communicators often attend more closely to one level as opposed to the other(s), there are frequent inconsistencies between the varied levels of each communication.

C. *The principle of whispering words and shouting gestures.* When there are inconsistencies between spouses or among family members, the nonverbal message almost always has a greater impact than the spoken message. But the nonverbal message also destroys flow of communication more rapidly than the verbal message.

D. *The princess-and-the-pea principle:* Any negative dimension of any communication is likely to have a greater impact than the sum total of all of the positive dimensions of communication.

E. *The ownership principle:* It is important to take active ownership of every message sent whether in the form of a statement or in the form of a question, for that is the only way to enter into responsible communication.

F. *The principle of incomplete communication:* Because one can never be sure that the message sent is the message received, no communication cycle is complete until the message is sent and acknowledged.

In sum, the considerable body of research investigating family and marital therapy, systemic or behavioral, implicitly encourages a broader-based orientation when selecting specific interventions for relationship changes. Spouses seeking therapy alone or jointly represent a part of the microsystem, equally relevant as the role children play in the family unit. Omission of the children, leaving them for the "family therapist" to "pick up," seriously overlooks the interrelationships that contribute to martial discord, to permeable effects of the dysfunction, and whether other family members' behavior, if improved, might automatically ensure improvements in spouses' behavior. By carefully first assessing, and second, treating patterns of behavior, therapists stand a solid chance of narrowing the ambiguity of family issues in addiction.

REFERENCES

Aho, T. (1967). Alkoholi ja aggressiivinen K'yttatyminen. *Alkoholi-politikka,* 32, 179.

Andreozi, L.L. (1985). Why outcome research fails the family therapist. In L.L. Andreozi, (Ed.). *Integrating research and clinical practice.* NY: Aspens Systems.

Andrews, M.P., Bubolz, M.M. & Paolucci, B. (1980). An ecological approach to study of the family. *Marriage and Family Therapy,* 3, 29-49.

Azar, S.T. & Barnes, K.T. (1986). Developmental outcomes in physically abused children: Consequences of parental abuse or the effects of a more general breakdown in caregiving behaviors? *The Behavior Therapist,* 11, 27-32.

Barber, J. & Winefield, A.H. (1986). Learned helplessness as conditioned inattention to the target stimulus. *Journal of Experimental Psychology: General,* 115, 236-246.

Barlow, D.H., Hayes, S.C. & Nelson, R.O. (1984) *The scientist-practitioner: Research and accountability in clinical and educational settings.* NY: Pergamon.

Borkovec, T.D. & Bauer, R.M. (1982). Experimental design in group outcome research. In A.S. Bellack, M. Hersen & A.E. Kazdin (Eds.). *International handbook of behavior modification and therapy.* NY: Plenum.

Boyatzis, R.E. (1974). The effect of alcohol consumption on the aggressive behavior of men. *Quarterly Journal of Studies on Alcohol,* 35, 959-972.

Boyatzis, R.E. (1975). The predisposition toward alcohol-related interpersonal aggression in men. *Quarterly Journal of Studies on Alcohol,* 36, 1196-1207.

Bubolz, M.M., Eichner, J.B. & Sontag, M.S. (1979). The human ecosystem: A model. *Journal of Home Economics, 71*, 28-31.

Burgess, R.L. & Conger, R.D. (1978). Family interaction in abused, neglected and normal families. *Child Development, 49*, 1163-1173.

Coleman, S.B. (Ed.). (1989). *Failures in family therapy*. NY: Guilford.

Constantine, L.L. (1989). *Family paradigms: The practice of theory in family therapy*. NY: Guilford.

Edwards, G. (1982). *The treatment of drinking problems*. Boston, MA: Blackwell Scientific Publications.

Ellis, A. (1962). *Reason and emotion in psychotherapy*. Secaucus, NJ: Stuart.

Ellis, A. & Harper, R.A. (1975). *A new guide to rational living*. Englewood Cliffs, NJ: Prentice-Hall.

Epstein, N., Schlesinger, S.E. & Dryden, W. (1989) (Eds.). *Cognitive-behavioral therapy with families*. NY: Brunner/Mazel.

Ezell, M.P., Paolucci, B. & Bubolz, M.M. (1964). Developing family properties.*Home Economics Research Journal, 12*, 563-574.

Fincham, F.D. & Cain, K.M. (1986). Learned helplessness in humans: A developmental analysis. *Developmental Review, 6*, 301-333.

Foster, S. L. & Hoier, T.S. (1982). Behavioral and systems family therapies: A comparison of theoretical assumptions. *The American Journal of Family Therapy, 10*, 13-23.

Garber, J. & Seligman, M.E.P. (1980). *Human helplessness: Theory and applications*. NY: Academic Press.

Gardner, J.M. (1972). Training the trainers: A review of research on the teaching of behavior modification. In C.M. Franks & R. Rubin (Eds.). *Progress in behavior therapy*. NY: Academic Press.

Garrigan, J.J. & Bombrick, A.F. (1979). New findings in research on go-between process. *International Journal of Family Therapy*, 1, 76-85.

Gurman, A.S. (1973). Marital therapy: Emerging trends in research and practice. *Family Process*, 12, 45-54.

Gurman, A.S. (1978). Contemporary marital therapies: A critique and comparative analysis of psychoanalytic, behavioral and systems theory approaches. In T.J. Polino & B.S. McCrady (Eds.). *Marriage and marital therapy*. NY: Brunner/Mazel.

Gurman, A.S. & Kniskern, D.P. (1971). Research on marital and family therapy: Progress, perspective, and prospect. S.L. Garfield & A.E. Bergin (Eds.). *Handbook of psychotherapy and behavior change.* NY: John Wiley & Sons.

Guthrie, D.M. & Snyder, C.W. (1988). Spouses' self-evaluations for situations involving emotional communication. In Noller, P. & Fitzpatrick, M.A. (Eds.). *Perspectives on marital interaction.* Philadelphia, PA: Multilingual Matters Ltd. (pp. 123-152).

Hahlweg, K. & Jacobson, N. (Eds.). (1988). *Marital interaction.* NY: Guilford.

Hayes, S.C. (Ed.). (1989). *Rule governed behavior: cognition, contingencies and instructional control.* NY: Plenum.

Hayes, S.C., Brownstein, A.J., Zettle, R.D., Rosenfarb, I. & Korn, Z. (1986). Rule-governed behavior and sensitivity to changing consequences of responding. *Journal of the Experimental Analysis of Behavior*, 45, 237-256.

Hersen, M. (1979). Limitations and problems in the clinical application of behavioral techniques in psychiatric settings. *Behavior Therapy*, 10, 65-80.

Hook, N. & Paolucci, B. (1970). Family as ecosystem. *Journal of Home Economics*, 62, 315-318.

Isaacs, C.D., Embry, LH. & Baer, D.M. (1982). Training family therapists: An experimental analysis. *Journal of Applied Behavior Analysis*, 15, 505-520.

Iwata, B.A. Wong, S.E. Riordon, M.M., Dorsey, M.F. & Lau, M.M. (1982). Assessment and training of clinical interviewing skills: Analogue analysis and field replication. *Journal of Applied Behavior Analysis,* 15, 191-204.

Jackson, D.D. (1965). The study of the family. *Family Process,* 4, 1-20.

Jacobson, N.S. (1977). Problem solving and contingency contracting in the treatment of marital discord. *Journal of Consulting and Clinical Psychology,* 45, 92-100.

Jacobson, N.S. (1978) Specific and nonspecific factors in the effectiveness of a behavioral approach to the treatment of marital discord. *Journal of Consulting and Clinical Psychology,* 46, 442-452.

Jacobson, N.S. (1979). Behavioral treatments for marital discord: A critical appraisal. In M. Hersen, R.M. Eisler & P.M. Miller (Eds.). *Progress in behavior modification.* NY: Plenum.

Jacobson, N.S. (1985). Family therapy outcome research: Potential pitfalls and prospects. *Journal of Marital and Family Therapy,* 11, 149-158.

Jacobson, N.S. & Bussod, N. (1983). Marital and family therapy. In M. Hersen, A.E. Kazdin & A.S. Bellack (Eds.). *The clinical psychology handbook.* NY: Pergamon.

Jacobson, N.S. & Follette, W.C. (1985). Clinical significance of improvement resulting from two behavioral marital therapy components. *Behavior Therapy,* 16, 249-262.

Jacobson, N.S. & Gurman, A.S. (1988). *Clinical handbook of marital therapy.* NY: Guilford.

Jacobson, N.S. & Margolin, G. (1979). *Marital therapy: Strategies based on social learning and behavior exchange principles.* NY: Brunner/Mazel.

Jellinek, E.M. & MacFarland, R.A. (1940). Analysis of psychological experiments on the effects of alcohol. *Quarterly Journal of Studies on Alcohol,* 1, 272-273.

Kantor, D. & Lehr, W. (1975). *Inside the family: Toward a theory of family process*. NY: Harper Colophon.

Kazdin, A.E. (1980). *Research designs in clinical psychology*. NY: Harper & Row.

Kniskern, D.P. (1985). Climbing out of the pit: Further guidelines for family therapy research. *Journal of Marital and Family Therapy*, 11, 159-162.

Liberman, R.P., Wheller, E.G. & Kuehnel, J.M. (1983). Failures in behavioral marital therapy. In E.B. Foa & P.M.G. Emmelkamp (Eds.). *Failures in behavior therapy*. NY: John Wiley & Sons.

Light, William J. Haugen. (1985). *Alcoholism: Its natural history, chemistry and general metabolism*. Springfield, IL: Charles C. Thomas.

Light, William J. Haugen. (1986). *Neurobiology of alcohol abuse*. Springfield, IL: Charles C. Thomas.

MacAndrew, C. & Edgerton, R.B. (1969). *Drunken comportment*. Chicago, IL: Aldine.

Maser, J.D. & Gallup, G.G. (1977). Tonic immobility and related phenomena: A partially annotated, tricentennial bibliography, 1636-1976. *Psychological Record*, 1, 177-217.

May, J. (1973). *Drinking in a Rhodesian African township*. Occasional paper No. 8. Salisbury: Department of Sociology, University of Rhodesia.

Mayfield, D. (1972). *Alcoholism, alcohol intoxication and assaultitive behavior*. Paper presented at 30th International Congress on Alcoholism and Drug Dependence, Amsterdam.

Miltenberger, R.G. & Fuqua, R.W. (1985). Evaluation of a training manual for the acquisition of behavioral assessment interviewing skills. *Journal of Applied Behavior Analysis*, 18, 323-328.

Nelson, G.M. & Beach, S.R. (1990). Sequential interaction in depression: Effects of depressive behavior in spousal aggression. *Behavior Therapy*, 21, 167-182.

Newberger, E.H. & Bourne, R. (Eds.). (1985). *Unhappy families: Clinical and research perspectives on family violence.* Littleton, MA: PSG Publishing Company.

Nolen-Hoeksema, S., Girgus, J.S. & Seligman, M.E.P. (1986). Learned helplessness in children: A longitudinal study of depression, achievement and explanatory style. *Journal of Personality and Social Psychology*, 5, 435-442.

Noller, P. & Fitzpatrick, M.A. (Eds.). (1988). *Perspectives on marital interaction.* Philadelphia, PA: Multilingual Matters Ltd.

Orford, J. & Harwin, J. (Eds.). *Alcohol and the family*. London: Croom & Helm.

Olson, D.H., Sprenkle, D.H. & Russell, C.S. (1980). Marital and family therapy: A decade review. *Journal of Marriage and the Family*, 42, 973-994.

Parloff, M. (1980). *The efficacy and cost effectiveness of psychotherapy.* Washington, D.C.: Office of Technological Assessment.

Persky, H., O'Brien, C.P., Fine, E., Howard, W.J., Kahn, M.A. & Beck, R.W. (1977). The effect of alcohol and smoking on testosterone function and aggression in chronic alcoholics. *American Journal of Psychiatry*, 134, 621-625.

Persons, J.B. (1991). Psychotherapy outcome studies do not accurately represent current models of psychotherapy. *American Psychologist*, 46, 99-106.

Peterson, J.L. & Zill, N. (1986). Marital disruption, parent-child relations, and behavior problems in children. *Journal of Marriage and the Family*, 48, 295-307.

Ratner, S.C. (1958). Hypnotic reactions of rabbits. *Psychological Reports*, 4, 209-210.

Ratner, S.C. & Thompson, R.W. (1960). Immobility reactions (fear) of domestic fowl as a function of age and prior experience. *Animal Behaviour*, 8, 186-191.

Roberts, R.N. & Magrab, P.R. (1991). Psychologists' role in a family-centered approach to practice, training, and research with young children. *American Psychologist*, 46, 144-148.

Ruben, D.H. (1986). What is the "interbehavioral" approach to treatment? *Journal of Contemporary Psychotherapy*, 16, 62-71.

Ruben, D.H. (1988). *Behavioral handbook: Rapid solutions to difficult behavior*. Okemos, MI: Best Impressions International.

Ruben, D.H. (1989). Behavioral predictors of alcoholics: A "systems" alternative. *Alcoholism Treatment Quarterly*, 5, 137-162.

Ruben, D.H. (1983). Analogue assessments in the behavioral treatment of drug addictions. *The Catalyst*, 2, 69-77.

Ruben, D.H. & Ruben, M.J. (1984). Interviewing skills: implications for vocational counseling with alcoholic clients. *Alcoholism Treatment Quarterly*, 1, 133-140.

Ruben, D.H. & Ruben, M.J. (1985). Behavioral principles on the job: control or manipulation? *Personnel Magazine*, 62, 61-65.

Ruben, D.H. (1986). The management of role ambiguity in organizations. *Journal of Employment Counseling*, 23, 120-130.

Russell, C.S., Atilano, R.B., Anderson, S.A., Jurich, A.P. & Bergen, L.P. (1984). Intervention strategies: Predicting family therapy outcome. *Journal of Marital and Family Therapy*, 10, 241-251.

Schwartzman, J. (Ed.). (1989). *Families and other systems: The macrosystemic context of family therapy*. NY: Guilford.

Seligman, M.E & Schulman, P. (1986). Explanatory style as a predictor of productivity and quitting among life insurance sales agents. *Journal of Personality and Social Psychology*, 50, 832-838.

Shuntich, R.J. & Taylor, S. P. (1972). The effects of alcohol on human physical aggression. *Journal of Experimental Research on Personality*, 6, 34.

Skinner, B.F. (1957). *Verbal behavior*. NY: Appleton-Century Crofts.

Skinner, B.F. (1966). An operant analysis of problem solving. In B. Kleinmuntz (Ed.). *Problem-solving: Research, method, and theory*. NY: JohnWiley & Sons (pp. 225-257).

Skinner, B.F. (1969). *Contingencies of reinforcement: A theoretical analysis*. Englewood Cliffs, NJ: Prentice-Hall.

Stuart, R.B. (1980). *Helping couples change: A social learning approach to marital therapy*. NY: Guilford.

Todd, T.C. & Stanton, M.D. (1983). Research on marital family therapy: Answers, issues and recommendations. In B. Wolman & G. Striker (Eds.). *Handbook of family and marital therapy*. NY: Plenum.

Trickett, P.K. & Kuczynski, L. (1986). Children's misbehaviors and parental discipline strategies in abusive and nonabusive families. *Developmental Psychology*, 26, 115-123.

Vannicelli, M., Gingerich, S. & Ryback, R. (1983). Family problems related to the treatment and outcome of alcoholic patients. *British Journal of Addiction*, 18, 193-204.

Washburne, C. (1961). *Primitive drinking*. NY: College and University Press.

Wilsnack, S.C. (1974). The effects of social drinking on woman's fantasy. *Journal of Personality*, 42, 43.

Wisocki, P.A. & Sedney, M.A. (1979). Toward the development of behavioral clinicians. *Journal of Behaviour Therapy and Experimental Psychiatry*, 9, 141-147.

Zettle, R.D. (1990). Rule-governed behavior: A radical behavioral answer to the cognitive challenge. *Psychological Record*, 40, 41-49.

Zettle, R.D. & Hayes, S. C. (1982). Rule-governed behavior: A potential theoretical framework for cognitive-behavioral therapy. In P.C. Kendal (Ed.). *Advances in cognitive-behavioral research and therapy (Vol. 1).* NY: Academic Press (pp. 73-118).

Zettle, R.D. & Hayes, S.C. (1986). Dysfunctional control by client verbal behavior: The context of reason-giving. *The Analysis of Verbal Behavior,* 4, 30-38.

Zettle, R.D. & Young, M.J. (1987). Rule-following and human operant responding: Conceptual and methodological considerations. *The Analysis of Verbal Behavior,* 5, 33-39.

Zweben, A. (1986). Problem drinking and marital adjustment. *Journal of Studies on Alcohol,* 47, 167-172.

SELECTED ANNOTATED RESOURCES

Ackerman, R.J. (1987). Family response to alcoholism: Effects on children growing up in the shadow. *Focus on Family and Chemical Dependency*, 9, 25-27, 31, 39, 44.

1. English; 2. Clinical/review; 3. All family members; 4. Reactive phase of family response to parental alcoholism is examined regarding the emotional isolation and denial of healthy relationships; 5. Analysis shows that most significant impacts occur outside the dysfunctional family or for suffering children in their adulthood, considering that children of alcoholics disproportionately appear in juvenile courts, family courts, spouse and child abuse cases, and in divorce cases plagued with psychological or emotional problems.

Asher, R. & Brissett, D. (1988). Codependency: A view from women married to alcoholics. *International Journal of the Addictions*, 23, 331-350.

1. English; 2. Experimental; 3. Fifty-two wives of alcoholic men describing themselves as co-dependent; 4. Outpatient setting; 5. Degree of exploitation, abuse, or caretaking behavior patterns; 6., 7. & 8. Taped interviews identifying impact on self, longevity of problems, and distinctions made to alcohol-complicated marriages; 9. Self-labeling and self-debasement was reported with women's self-esteem compromised by their caretaking needs and false dedication. This perpetuates traditional view of women as more passive than active and that they have pathologies secondary to codependent behaviors.

Baughan, D.M. (1987). Crisis precipitation in alcoholism. *Connecticut Medicine*, 51, 18.

1. English; 2. Clinical/review; 3. Alcoholic family members; 4. Examines reasons for family barriers protecting the alcoholic member and dynamics of denial enabling exacerbation of the disturbance; 5. Recommends that many treatment programs adopt interventions that eliminate these barriers, confront the denial, and uncover emotional and behavioral inhibitions of family members.

Bennett, L.A., Wolin, S.J., Reiss, D. & Teitelbaum, M.A.(1987). Couples at risk for transmission of alcoholism: Protective influences. *Family Process,* 26, 111-129.

1. English; 2. Experimental; 3. Sixty-eight married children of alcoholic parents and their spouses; 4. Outpatient setting; 5. Intergenerational tendencies of alcoholism and drug dependencies; 6., 7. & 8. Group design, data recorded on dinner-time and holiday ritual practices in their families of origin, and heritage and ritual practices in the couples' current generation; 9. Predictor variables suggested high transmission of alcohol in alcoholic nuclear families, theorized by a general theme of "disengagement" and "re-engagement" for couples in families at risk.

Bilal, A.M., Kristof, J., Shaltout, A. & El-Islam, M.F. (1987). Treatment of alcoholism in Kuwait: A prospective follow-up study. *Drug and Alcohol Dependence,* 19, 131-144.

1. English; 2. Experimental; 3. One hundred alcohol-related patients; 4. Inpatient psychiatric hospital; 5. Adaptation in recovery versus relapse rates; 6., 7. & 8. Group design, assessments on nine post-treatment questions reflecting improvement or deterioration; 9. Longitudinal surveys showed that non-Kuwaitis do better than Kuwaitis in resuming employment and social reintegration. Patients of chronic benziodiazepine prescription were less prone to abstinence and had more readmissions. Analysis focused on cultural changes needed to alter the attitude toward alcoholism as a disease and causing family disintegration. Recommendations call for utilization of systems family approach involving the role of the Arab extended family in therapy.

Cloninger, C.R., Van Eerdewegh, P., Rice, J.P. & Mullaney, J. (1988). Secular trends in the familial transmission of alcoholism. *Alcoholism: Clinical and Experimental Research,* 12, 458-464.

1. English; 2. Experimental; 3. 831 first-degree relatives of alcoholics and 125 spouses; 4. Outpatient and hospital; 5. Identifying secularity and family intergenerational trends of alcoholism; 6. & 7. & 8. Multifactorial Model of Disease Transmission and "Tau Model of Familial Transmission" used; 9. Analyses confirmed that more recently born cohorts of individuals had increased expected lifetime prevalence of alcoholism and decreased ages of onset, when compared with older cohorts. Influence of parental transmissible factors was greater than that expected for polygenic transmission, strongly

suggesting the presence of intrafamilial nongenetic familial transmission between generations.

Connors, G.J., O'Farrell, T.J. & Pelcovits, M.A. (1988). Drinking outcome expectancies among male alcoholics during relapse situations. *British Journal of Addiction,* 83, 561-566.

1. English; 2. Experimental; 3. Twenty-two male alcoholic patients; 4. Outpatient treatment setting; 5. Relapse events; 6. Relapse prevention and restoration of control methods; 7. Group design; 8. Clinical interview; 9. Results showed that almost half of the expectancies reported dealt with drinking as an aid in coping with a social or marital situation. Data suggested importance of relapse expectations for couples and particularly for clean spouse who inflates the speed and success of recovery.

Davenport, Y.B. and Mathiasen, E.H. (1988). Couples psychotherapy group: Treatment of the married alcoholic. *Group,* 12, 67-75.

1. English; 2. Clinical; 3. Nine married couples (10 alcoholic members); 4. Outpatient setting; 5. Marital duress; 6. Open-ended marital and family therapy provided 1.5 hours once weekly; 7. Group design; 8. Case records; 9. Participation of both members counteracts the denial process and brings defenses into the open. Marital therapy including other family members offers significantly more cost-effective approach than individual therapy for married alcoholic.

DeFoe, J.R. & Breed, W. (1988). Response to the alcoholic by "the other" on prime time television. *Contemporary Drug Problems,* 15, 205-228.

1. English; 2. Review; 3. Television shows depicting "others" related to friends to alcoholics; 4. Data from eight seasons of television programming were examined showing the important of others promoting change by alcoholics; 5. Of 1,417 episodes recorded, 74 episodes included scenes where one character responded to an alcoholic, suggesting that sitcom and drama shows depicting alcoholism only are beginning to understand phenomena of codependency and relevance of alcoholic's environment upon bystanders.

Dolan, J.S.. (1987). Rediscovering the alcoholism field: New trends and needs. *Journal of Alcohol and Drug Education,* 32, 59-62.

1. English; 2. Clinical/review; 3. Alcoholics, children of alcoholics; 4. Summary presented of trends in college campus movements and prevention field regarding acceptance of alcoholism treatment in mainstream of American public health; 5. Trends toward outpatient and employee assistance programs are moving at accelerated rates establishing alcoholism as a legitimate illness and family disease, warranting a more systemic intervention.

Farrell, M.P. & David, A.S. (1988). Do psychiatric registrars take a proper drinking history? *British Medical Journal,* 296, 395-396.

1. English; 2. Experimental; 3. One hundred consecutive hospital admissions of alcohol treatment center; 4. Inpatient hospital; 5. Identified were diagnostic categories (e.g., affective psychoses, neurotic depression, schizophrenia, personality disorders, anorexia nervosa, etc.), and drinking and smoking disorders; 6., 7., & 8. Case review design; 9. Recorded profiles on admissions showed that primary diagnosis of alcoholism is missed due to apparent confusions on other psychiatric diagnoses and particularly for acute alcoholic cases.

French, S. (1987). Family approaches to alcoholism: Why the lack of interest among marriage and family professionals? *Journal of Drug Issues,* 17, 359-368.

1. English; 2. Clinical/review; 3. Alcoholic families and couples; 4. Reasons for lack of attention by marriage and family professionals to applications of family theories to treatment of alcohol problems are explored; 5. Review of literature suggests alcohol abuse falls outside of clinician's specialty, that cultural myths of alcoholism interfere with acceptance of client for treatment, and that greater emphasis is upon family structure over process, deflecting attention away from removal of alcoholic in families. Recommendations offered to redirect focus toward drug-dependency issues.

Gustafson, R. (1988). Relationship between alcohol intoxication and power in real-life non-alcoholic couples. *Drug and Alcohol Dependence,* 22, 55-62.

1. English; 2. Experimental; 3. Thirty couples of mixed and moderate drinking levels; 4. Outpatient setting; 5. Testing whether alcohol intoxication leads to shifts of power among couples; 6. Drinking and nondrinking groups under controlled conditions; 7. Group design (control, men-only drinking, women-only drinking); 8. Clinical

interview and observation methods; 9. Men were more powerful in terms of outcome both in control and women-drinking groups, but women became more powerful in men-only drinking group. Discussed was sex-role stereotyping and tendency for men to overestimate their influence of control.

Hamberger, L.K. & Hastings, J. (1988). Characteristics of male spouse abusers consistent with personality disorders. *Hospital and Community Psychiatry*, 39, 763-770.

1. English; 2. Clinical/review; 3. Male domestic assaulters and abusers, alcoholics; 4. Profiles analyzed of abuser's personality disorders according to DSM-IIIR and across characteristics of socioeconomic status, crime involvement, alcoholism, and violence; 5. Alcohol-abusing batterers present social challenges and likely to revert to violence during sobriety unless treatment directly targets abatement methods.

Hirschfeld, R.M.A., Kosier, T., Keller, M.B., Lavori, P.W. & Endicott, J. (1989). Influence of alcoholism on the course of depression. *Journal of Affective Disorders*, 16, 151-158.

1. English; 2. Experimental; 3. 268 inpatient and outpatient moderately depressed recovering alcoholics; 4.Tracking in patients' natural environment; 5. Recovery from depression, drinking relapse; 6. Repeated interviews over a 5-year period; 7. Group design (depressives with and those without alcoholism); 8. Clinical interview, case records; 9. Differences between both groups appeared in their psychosocial status. Alcoholic depressives reported lower levels of functioning through the 2-year follow-up, particularly in interpersonal relationships and marriages.

Jacob, T. & Leonard, K.E. (1988). Alcoholic-spouse interaction as a function of alcoholism subtype and alcoholism consumption. *Journal of Abnormal Psychology*, 97, 231-237.

1. English; 2. Experimental; 3. Forty-nine alcoholics and spouses; 4. Outpatient setting; 5. Links between drinking style and levels of marital satisfaction; 6. Systems family therapy; 7. Focus on problem solving tactics; 8. Clinical interviews; 9. Interactions displayed by episodic alcoholics and their spouses suggested a coercive control pattern. In contrast, steady alcoholics and spouses displayed patterns of high level problem solving. Additional research required to determine which

patterns are predictive of continued alcohol abuse or exacerbation of marital problems.

Jacob, T. & Krahn, G.L. (1988). Marital interactions of alcoholic couples: Comparison with depressed and nondistressed couples. *Journal of Consulting and Clinical Psychology,* 56, 73-79.

1. English; 2. Experimental; 3. Thirty-eight families with husbands alcoholic, 35 with husbands depressed, and 34 with husband a social drinker and no psychopathology; 4. Outpatient setting; 5. Observations of interpersonal and interactive style of couples during sessions after husbands consumed and did not consume alcohol; 6. Family systems approaches; 7. Group design; 8. Clinical interviews and observations; 9. Alcohol consumption lead to increased expression of affective behavior both positive and negative, critical and disagreeable, than depressed and nondepressed couples when husband's drank. Results suggest alcohol consumption disinhibits emotions but can interrupt problem solving process.

Jacob, T. (1987). *A family interaction perspective.* In P.C. Rivers (Ed.). Alcohol and addictive behavior. Lincoln, NE: University of Nebraska Press (159-206).

1. English; 2. Clinical/review; 3. Alcoholic families and adult children of alcoholics; 4. Literature on spouses of alcoholics and impact of drinking upon children reviewed; 5. Issues concerning codependency and dynamics of marital discordance analyzed in terms of the drinking husband and during recovery process.

Jacob, T., Seilhamer, R.A. & Rushe, R.H. (1989). Alcoholism and family interaction: An experimental paradigm. *American Journal of Drug and Alcohol Abuse,* 15, 73-91.

1. English; 2. Experimental; 3. Intact families with a member having psychiatric problem (depression, alcoholism, etc.); 4. Outpatient clinic, natural environment; 5. Observation of dinnertime interaction, of social dyadic, and problem solving; 6. Observational recording; 7. Group design (two control groups, plus two experimental groups); 8 & 9. Results revealed nondistressed couples displayed more positive behaviors than couples disturbed by alcoholism or depression. Data also showed episodic and steady drinkers react differently in the marriage, greatly diminishing such family dynamics as communication and intimacy skills.

Jacobson, N.S., Holtzworth-Munroe, A. & Schmaling, K.B. (1989). Marital therapy and spouse involvement in the treatment of depression, agoraphobia, and alcoholism. *Journal of Consulting and Clinical Psychology,* 57, 5-7.

1. English; 2. Clinical/review; 3. Distressed couples; 4. Review of articles on marital therapy and spouse involvement on treatment for anxiety-related psycopathology, showing interrelationship between marital dynamics and outcomes of treatment efficacy; 5. Conclusions indicate marital therapy far superior than individual interventions, and that the disorders are more etiologically attributed to marital stress than to individual client problems. Recommends methodology for follow-up, after using combinations of standard and behavioral methods.

Keso, L., Kivisaari, A. & Salaspuro, M. (1988). Fractures on chest radiographs in detection of alcoholism. *Alcohol and Alcoholism,* 23, 53-56.

1. English & Finnish; 2. Experimental; 3. Seventy-six unmarried or divorced lower class alcoholics with chest fractures, 108 married middle class alcoholics with liver cirrhosis, and randomly chosen hospital patients for control group; 4. Inpatient hospital setting; 5. Fracture prevalence correlations with marital and socioeconomic status; 6., 7. & 8. Group design; 9. No differences appeared between both experimental groups on detectable fractures, although married alcoholics had fewer thoracic fractures than unmarried, divorced or widowed alcoholics. Sensitivity and specificity of the fractures visible on chest radiograph as marker for alcoholism is not sufficient for clinical assessment.

McClelland, M. & Schulberg, H.C. (1987). Recognition of alcoholism and substance abuse in primary care patients. *Archives of Internal Medicine,* 147, 349-352.

1. English; 2. Experimental; 3. Forty-two of 294 adult primary care patients diagnosed alcoholic; 4. Hospital setting; 5. Characteristics of substance abusers and their families; 6., 7. & 8. Structured psychiatric interview identified 17 patients having substance abuse problem at initial clinical evaluation; 9. Clinically significant variables include alcoholics are older, more likely married, users of multiple drugs, and have antisocial personality disorders. Recommendations direct physicians to be trained in recognition and treatment of alcohol-overlapping symptomatology.

Maisto, S.A., O'Farrell, T.J., McKay, J.R., Connors, G.J. & Pelcovits, M. (1988). Alcohol and spouse concordance on attributions about relapse to drinking. *Journal of Substance Abuse Treatment*, 5, 179-181.

1. English; 2. Experiment; 3. Thirty-six couples (alcoholic husbands) followed over a 2-year period; 4. Inpatient setting; 5. Agreement between patients and their spouses on causes of alcoholic relapse; 6. Clinical interviews; 7. Group design; 8. & 9. Results revealed poor agreement between spouses on perception of relapses, with patient seeing their wives as causal factors more frequently than did wives. Recommended is that marital therapy assess and resolve this discrepancy as fundamental to improving marital stability.

Mann, L.M., Sher, K.J. & Chassin, L. (1987). Alcohol expectancies and the risk for alcoholism. *Journal of Consulting and Clinical Psychology*, 55, 411-417.

1. English; 2. Experimental; 3. Study of 979 high school students; 4. School setting; 5. Alcohol expectancies, motivations for drinking, and risk of drinking involvement; 6., 7. & 8. Group design, structured interviews and screening instruments; 9. Measures showed that alcohol expectancy and drinking motives varied as function of risk status. High-risk status correlated with expectancies of enhanced cognitive and motor functioning, tension reduction, deteriorated cognitive and behavioral functioning, personal motives, and power motives. Targets for modification also relate to high-risk status, low-moderation users from alcoholic families or having at least one drinking spouse.

Mathiasen, E.H. & Davenport, Y.B. (1988). Reciprocal depression in recovering alcoholic couples: The efficacy of psychodynamic group treatment. *Group*, 12, 45-55.

1. English; 2. Clinical; 3. Recovering alcoholics; 4. Outpatient clinic; 5. Abstinence and marital stability, and depression; 6. Psychodynamic approach; 7. & 8. Case records; 9. Results reveal that recognition of depression early in psychotherapy increases understanding of marital problems and the alcohol dependence syndrome. Implications offered for a couples group versus pursual of individual alcoholism counseling.

McNabb, J., Der-Karabetian, A. & Rhoads, J. (1989). Alcohol dependence syndrome. *Psychological Reports,* 65, 1327-1330.

1. English; 2. Experimental; 3. 80 adult alcoholic patients; 4. Inpatient hospitalization; 5. Spouse's involvement in treatment of alcoholism; 6. Three groups (Group I involved spouse 3 or fewer times weekly, Group II involved spouse 4 or fewer times weekly, Group III involved spouses treated as inpatient co-alcoholics); 7. Twelve steps and reality-based interventions; 8. Personal interviews, follow-up plans; 9. Greater family involvement correlates with enhanced abstinence and better family relations following discharge and after six months.

Miller, B.A., Downs, W.R. & Gondoli, D.M. (1989). Spousal violence among alcoholic women as compared to a random household sample of women. *Journal of Studies on Alcohol,* 50, 533-540.

1. English; 2. Experimental; 3. 45 alcoholic women (experimental group) and 40 nonalcoholic women (controlled); 4. Outpatient clinic; 5. Conflict behaviors, spouse-to-woman negative verbal behaviors, levels of violence, income, parental violence; 6. Two-hour interview schedules determining predictors of violence; 7 & 8. Conflict Tactics Scale, clinical interview; 9. Multivariate analyses revealed that spouse violence scores were strong indicators of type and sample of violent alcoholics. Implications strongly suggest that outpatient assessments should incorporate devices screening for spousal violence among women and in reaction to marital duress.

Noel, N.E., McCrady, B.S., Stout, R.L. & Fisher-Nelson, H. (1987). Predictors of attrition from an outpatient alcoholism treatment program for couples. *Journal of Studies on Alcohol,* 48, 229-235.

1. English; 2. Experimental; 3. One-hundred and five applicants to outpatient treatment divided into (1) treatment refusals, (2) treatment dropouts, and (3) treated subjects; 4. Outpatient setting; 5. Characteristics associated with treatment recovery; 6. Marriage and family systems interventions; 7. Group design; 8. Clinical interviews; 9. Remaining in treatment most significantly associated with marital factors, assignment of the couple to a marital therapy group versus treatment where spouse not involved, and spouse's initial satisfaction with the marriage. Recommendations for spouse involvement in treatment outlined.

O'Farrell, T.J. (1989). Marital and family therapy in alcoholism treatment. *Journal of Substance Abuse Treatment,* 6, 23-29.

1. English; 2. Theoretical/clinical; 3. Alcoholic couples/families; 4. Literature review on treatment outcome research for couples and family therapy; 5. Three conclusions drawn include (a) intervention with nonalcoholic spouse motivates family or alcoholic spouse seeking treatment, (b) BMT shows strongest therapeutic promise on reduced drinking outcomes and resolution of marital discord, and (c) studies of long-term maintenance suggest that behavioral marital therapy with an alcohol relationship may reduce marital and drinking deterioration better than individual methods during long-term recovery. Recommendations offered on variations of behavioral marital therapy.

O'Farrell, T.J., Cutter, H.S.G. & Floyd, F.J. (1985). Effects of marital adjustment and communication from before to after treatment. *Behavior Therapy,* 26, 147-167.

1. English; 2. Experimental; 3. Male alcoholics and wives; 4. Inpatient hospital; 5. Interpersonal communication, marital stability, and abstinence; 6. Effects of behavioral marital therapy group (BMT) upon routine individualized alcoholism counseling; 7. Group design; 8. Case records; 9. BMT produced better overall marital adjustment than interactional therapy and alcoholics in BMT groups maintained sobriety longer during and after treatment. Limitations of BMT also reviewed for future studies.

Penick, E.C., Powell, B.J., Bingham, S.F., Liskow, B.I., Miller, N.S. & Read, M.R. (1987). Comparative study of familial alcoholism. *Journal of Studies on Alcohol,* 48, 136-146.

1. English; 2. Experimental; 3. Five hundred and sixty-eight male alcoholics; 4. Outpatient setting; 5. Comparisons of patients with positive (65%) or negative (35%) family history of abusive drinking among first degree relatives; 6., 7. & 8.: Structured interviews, group design; 9. Alcoholics with positive family history had early onset of alcoholism, more alcoholic severity, more medical and legal problems, broader range of treatments, increased lifetime prevalence of other psychiatric disorders, and greater diversity of psychiatric disturbance among biological relatives.

Perodeau, G.M. & Kohn, P.M. (1989). Sex differences in the marital functioning of treated alcoholics. *Drug and Alcohol Dependence,* 23, 1-11.

1. English; 2. Experimental; 3. Fifty-five treated alcoholics (31 males, 24 females) and 199 nonalcoholic spouses; 4. Outpatient; 5. Drinking impact on affection and sexual behavior of marriage; 6. Diagnostic assessments; 7. Group design (experimental group tested along dimensions of sex, age, level of education, number of children, alcoholism, and marital satisfaction); 8. Dyadic Adjustment Scale, Areas of Change Questionnaire, Marital Status Inventory; 9. Results showed (a) alcoholics reported poorer marital functioning than non-alcoholics, (b) male alcoholics reported less troubled relationships, (c) spouses of alcoholics reported strained marriages, (d) alcoholic couples were less congruous regarding marital stability, and (e) alcoholic wives had taken more steps toward helping alcoholic husbands, than nonalcoholic husbands had toward helping alcoholic wives.

Perri, M.G. (1988). Improving treatment for alcohol-dependent veterans. *Psychology of Addictive Behaviors,* 2, 82-91.

1. English; 2. Theoretical/clinical; 3. Veterans; 4. Analysis of treatment areas targeted for alcohol-dependent veterans receiving outpatient and inpatient services; 5. Focused components include (a) better definitions of alcoholism, (b) assessment of cognitive influences, (c) involvement of spouse and family in treatment orientation, and (d) development of maintenance programs to enhance long-term effects of treatment.

Ridley, T.D. & Kordinak, S.T. (1988). Reliability and validity of the Quantitative Inventory of Alcohol Disorders (QIAD) and the veracity of self-report by alcoholics. *American Journal of Drug and Alcohol Abuse,* 14, 263-292.

1. English; 2. Experimental; 3. Twenty-five inpatient alcoholics and their spouses, and 21 nonalcoholics and their spouses; 4. Residential treatment; 5. Measuring severity of alcoholism; 6. Diagnostic testing; 7. Group Design; 8. Quantitative Inventory of Alcohol Disorders (QIAD), Michigan Alcoholism Screening Test, Alcohol Severity Rating Scale; 9. QIAD demonstrated construct and concurrent validity showing high correlations with self-reported drinking amounts and types of marital interactions. Validity of test for screening and assessment phases is discussed.

Royce, J.E. (1989). *Alcohol problems and alcoholism: A Comprehensive survey.* NY: Free Press

1. English; 2. Theoretical; 3. Family groups; 4. Critically examines etiology and sociological trends causing individual and marital decay in alcoholic families, covered in 21 chapters, including directions for future rehabilitation; 5. Conclusions suggest physiological or disease model of alcoholism offers identity for struggling families who accept the role of "team" approach in seeking spiritual or medical treatment.

Stebenau, J.R. & Hesselbrock, V.M. (1984). Psychopathology in alcoholics and their families and vulnerability to alcoholism: A review and new findings. In S.M. Mirin (Ed.). *Substance abuse and psychopathology.* Washington, D.C.: American Psychiatric Press (pp. 108-132).

1. English; 2. Theoretical/review; 3. Alcoholics, spouses and family; 4. Review of effects of quantity and frequency of drinking upon family dynamics, focusing on typologies of alcoholism and influences by sex, antisocial personality disorders, and family pedigree for alcoholism; 5. Conclusions suggest 40% of alcoholics concurrently have personality disorders, polydrug abuses, and frequently have family history of alcohol dependence. History of alcoholism on maternal and paternal sides increased probability of developing dependency at younger age.

Sullivan, E.J. (1987). Comparison of chemically dependent and nondependent nurses of familial, personal and professional characteristics. *Journal of Studies on Alcohol,* 48, 563-568.

1. English; 2. Experimental; 3. One hundred and thirty-nine recovering chemically dependent nurses and 384 registered nurses not identified as chemically dependent; 4. Outpatient setting; 5. Traits of family and intergenerational alcoholism; 6., 7. & 8. Group design, mailed questionnaires collecting information on demography, family history, education, employment, medical history, lifestyle, alcohol and drug related behaviors; 9. Significant differences between both groups found in family alcoholism, sexual trauma, sexual preference, parenthood status, marital history, physical health, and depressive illness. No differences found along variables of sibling rank, highest educational degree held, academic achievement, or length of nursing experience.

Thomas, E.J. & Yoshioka, M.R. (1989). Spouse interventive confrontations in unilateral family therapy for alcohol abuse. *Social Casework,* 70, 340-347.

1. English; 2. Clinical; 3. Passive nonalcoholic spouses; 4. Outpatient clinic; 5. Methods of assertiveness and confrontation regarding spousal alcoholism; 6. Monitoring, education, relationship enhancement, neutralization of "old system" and disenabling by spouse; 7. & 8. Group design; 9. Spouses of uncooperative alcoholics can facilitate abuser into treatment or toward drinking moderation and abstinence through abuser-directed interventions focused on specific role changes in the nonalcoholic spouse.

Waterson, E.J. & Murray-Lyon, I.M. (1989). Screening for alcohol related problems in the antenatal clinical: An assessment of different methods. *Alcohol and Alcoholism,* 24, 21-30.

1. English; 2. Experimental; 3. Women drinkers; 4. Antenatal outpatient clinic; 5. Level of alcohol intake relative to pregnancy and family problems; 6. Comparative analysis of different screening devices; 7. Group design; 8. Clinical history, quantity-frequency questions, Brief Michigan Alcohol Screening test, Michigan Alcohol Screening Test; 9. Instruments plus questions regarding binging of alcohol proved reliable to determine consumption rate in populations drinking at a low level.

Chapter 3

Adolescent Addiction

Normal, healthy adolescent behavior can often be surprising or disturbing to parents and other adults. In recent years, however, powerful social factors have combined to produce a range of problem behavior among youth that is a source of even greater concern. The epidemic of youthful drug and alcohol abuse that began in the 1960s and continues into the present is an especially alarming manifestation of this trend.

This chapter carefully surveys major factors underlying this trend and contributing to high health-risk behaviors among today's adolescents. Etiology covers adolescent problem behaviors and predictors of substance abuse. Section two, on effects upon family, reviews literature and behavior patterns linked with family system defects and family violence. In priorities for intervention, the last section, components of prevention and treatment of adolescent addiction receive attention.

ETIOLOGY

Adolescent Problem Behaviors

Not all alcohol and drug use is clearly problem behavior. In fact, if deviant or problem behavior is behavior that a considerable number of people view as reprehensible, then a large experimental and occasional use cannot truly be viewed as deviant. For many youth, experimentation with alcohol and drugs represents a push toward independence and adulthood (Mitchell, 1975). While one may criticize a society that has so few constructive rites of passage to adulthood that adolescents must use smoking, drinking, and getting high to mark the transition, these behaviors in moderation do not appear to be always problematic. Several studies show that while the majority use substances occasionally, only a minority become intensively involved. Yet the more involved minority represents a significant proportion of youth, and the impairment and loss associated with their alcohol and drug use is of considerable consequence.

A number of studies indicate that drug and alcohol use among youth ranges from apparently normal behavior to obviously dysfunctional behavior, accompanied by a wide variety of other behavioral and psychological difficulties. Dysfunctional use tends to be characterized by increasing quantity and the use of increasing varieties of both legal and illegal substances. It is often characterized by onset at an earlier age, and it tends to be associated with other kinds of dysfunctional behavior as well (Hamburg, Kraemer & Hahnke, 1974).

Alcohol and drug use are common among youth who also manifest other forms of dysfunctional behavior. Such youth are deviant in the sense that they participate in activities that are considered contrary to social norms and uniformly defined constructive behavior. Dropping out of school, truancy, running away from home, theft, teenage pregnancy, and mental health problems are examples of such problem behavior. The social costs of these behaviors are high for the individuals involved and for society as a whole. High-risk-taking behaviors regarded as aberrant increasingly predispose adolescents to situations they are not prepared for or which produce consequences leading to greater social isolation. Let us consider this path of aberrancy under *At-risk Health Behaviors* and *Psychosocial Inventory*.

At-risk Health Behaviors

The term *risk-taking* is increasingly used to describe the patterns of behavior initiated during adolescence which are responsible for the majority of negative health outcomes occurring in the second decade of life. Behaviors associated with violent outcomes (e.g., homicide), psychiatric disorders, including suicide and eating disorders, vehicle use, sexual activity, and substance abuse are generally included under the construct of risk-taking. Reviewed here are risk-taking behaviors that are volitional in nature, that is, the outcomes remain uncertain with the possibility of an identifiable negative health outcome. Young people with limited or no experience engage in behaviors with anticipation of benefit without understanding the immediate or long-term consequences of their actions. Behaviors considered include: (a) Sexual behaviors, (b) motor/recreational vehicle use, (c) crime, and (d) substance abuse.

Sexual behaviors. Sexual activity (i.e., coitus) has increased dramatically from 1971 to the early 1980's (Hayes, 1987; Hofferth & Hayes, 1987). In the most recent survey (1983), 77.9% of males and 62.9% of females had experienced intercourse by 19 years of age. These percentages run higher for blacks (92.2% for males and 77% for females) and Hispanics (78.5% for males and 58.6% for females). Recent reports concerning coital activity of adolescents younger than 15 years range from 12% to 55%. Little is known about sexual behaviors other than coitus, including homosexual activity (Irwin & Ryan, 1989; Westney, Jenkins & Butts, 1984).

The number of adolescents at risk for sexually transmitted diseases (STDs) has also grown in number over the past two decades due to an increase in sexual activity among youth. The most common STDs are presumed to be human papilloma virus (HPV) and *Chlamydia trachomatis* infections (Cates, 1987). HPV, the cause of genital warts and of cervical neoplasia, can be found in 3-8% of unselected young women, and colposcopic evidence of HPV has been found in 25% of STD clinic attenders (Becker, Stone & Alexander, 1987). Data from the National Disease and Therapeutic Index suggest a minimum of 650,000 cases of HPV in 15-19 year olds treated in private practitioner's offices between 1979 and 1984. This figure fails to reflect the substantial number of cases treated in public facilities and clinics, and those subclinical cases that have not come to medical attention. While nearly all asymptomatic male partners of women treated for HPV will have evidence of infection themselves, males tend to escape medical detection.

Chlamydia trachomatis, causing nongonococcal urethritis in males and mucopurulent cervicitis in females, is considered to be the most common bacterial STD in the United States. Up to 14% of suburban teenage girls, and 35% of their urban counterparts are infected, many asymptomatically (Soren & Willis, 1989). However, gonorrhea infections decreased in numbers. Overall rates of gonorrhea fell 32% from 1981 to 1988; the rate for teens aged 15-19 fell a modest 8.8%. The rate for the youngest teens, those aged 10 to 14, actually increased over this same period. Equally problematic is the increasing frequency of antibiotic-resistant cases of gonorrhea, which increased six-fold from 1982 to 1987 (USDHHS, 1988).

Relatively few cases of acquired immunodeficiency syndrome (AIDS) have been reported in adolescents. Among youth aged 13 to 19, only 101 cases were reported to the Centers for Disease Control in 1988 and fewer than 400 total cases have been reported (Centers for Disease Control, 1989). These data, however, may underestimate the true magnitude of human immunodeficiency virus (HIV) infection among adolescents. Because of its protracted latency, HIV infection acquired in adolescence is far more likely to manifest itself in the third decade, among persons 20 to 29 years of age, causing prevalence of AIDS to rise dramatically.

Motor/recreational vehicle use. Unintentional injuries are the primary cause of mortality in adolescents. Accidents account for 60% of the deaths in this age group. Motor vehicle injuries account for 80% of these deaths (Bass, Gallagher & Mehta, 1985). The peak time for vehicular accidents among late adolescents occurs on weekends and late at night. Life style factors appear to be primary forces in the injury situation at these times. Acute nonfatal injuries account for the largest number of hospital days for both adolescent males and females and for approximately 16% of outpatient visits. Increasingly, studies have documented that children as early as 10 years of age report engaging or being dared to engage in risky behaviors such as fights and skateboard and bicycle use (Lewis & Lewis, 1984). The National Adolescent Student Health Survey (1987) reports that over 50% of students did not wear a seat-belt the last time they rode in a motor vehicle, 92% never wear a helmet when riding a bike, and 72% never use a light at night when riding a bike. Essentially, data support the lack of basic preventive behaviors during adolescence.

Crime. Homicide and violent crime are central to adolescent risk. Homicide is the third leading cause of death for youth at 14.2 deaths per 100,000 population age 15-24 (USDHHS, 1989). In 1986, the homicide rate doubled that of 1960, which was at 5.9/100,000. Homicide disproportionately affects nonwhite adolescents; the 1986 homicide rate for Black male adolescents was 79.2/100,000, over five times that of white males. Similarly, homicide rates for Black females at 16.2/100,000 was nearly four times that of white peers. Excluding homicides, young persons 12-24 years of age have the highest victimization rates for crime of violence. The 1984 National Crime Survey documented a victimization rate of 60.5 per 1,000 for crimes of violence against youths 12-19 years old (USDJ, 1989). The rate of victimization for those 16-19 years of age was 67.6 per 1,000, higher than for any other age group. Victimization rates for male youths were slightly higher than those for white youth. Fewer than half of the violent crimes were committed by strangers, and more than two thirds were perpetrated by other youth.

Substance abuse. High rates of substance use during adolescence have been documented in national surveys since 1975. Consider trends related to alcohol, drug abuse, and nicotine use.

Alcohol. Experimentation with alcohol is nearly universal among teenagers; by age 18, more than 90% of teenagers drink alcohol. There is no evidence that this proportion is declining. While the period of highest use for alcohol is from 18 to 21 years of age, large proportions of teenagers indicate frequent use of alcohol: 63% of 1988 high school seniors reported alcohol use in the previous 30 days and an alarming 34.7% reported having had five or more drinks in a row within the previous two weeks (Johnston, Bachman & O'Malley, 1989).

Drug use and abuse. National trends of high school seniors show a steady decline in the number who report ever using an illicit drug (see Table 1). In 1980, 65.4% of high school seniors reported ever using illicit substances. Eight years later, 53.9% of 1988 high school seniors reported using some illicit drug, a reduction of nearly 18% (Johnston et al., 1989). In addition, much of the illicit use is experimental and short-lived. Only 38.5% of 1988 high school seniors reported the use of drugs in the preceding year, and only 21.3% of seniors reported use of illicit drugs in the preceding 30 days. For example, of seniors reporting marijuana use, only 18% had used cannabis in the preceding 30 days and only 2.7% of them reported being daily users. Of the 8.9% of seniors reported using hallucinogens, only 2.2% reported using them in the preceding 30 days. Of the 12.1% of seniors ever using cocaine, only 3.4% reported use within the preceding 30 days and 0.2% reported daily use. Stimulants, tranquilizers and sedative drugs follow identical declining trends.

Table 1
Percentage of High School Seniors Reporting Use of Different Drugs, 1988

Substance	Ever use	Preceding 30 days	Daily
Marijuana	47.2	18.0	2.7
Inhalants	16.7	2.6	0.2
Hallucinogens	8.9	2.2	0.0
LSD	7.7	1.8	0.0
Cocaine	12.1	3.4	0.2
Crack	4.8	1.6	0.1
Heroin	1.1	0.2	0.0

Stimulants	19.8	4.6	0.3
Sedatives	7.8	1.4	0.1
Alcohol	92.0	63.9	4.2
Cigarettes	66.4	28.7	18.1

adapted from: Johnston et. al., 1989.

Tobacco use. The deleterious effects of cigarette smoking also are well documented. While few teens suffer from hypertension, chronic lung disease, heart disease and smoking-related cancers, cigarette use in adolescence establishes a behavior that contributes to adult disease. Silvis & Perry (1987) reported that 85% of teenagers who are able to smoke two cigarettes completely will become regular smokers. School surveys reporting overall decreases of drug use may underestimate numbers of adolescent cigarette smokers and particularly adolescents who use smokeless tobacco. Use of smokeless tobacco has risen dramatically in the past two decades. Snuff production in the United States rose 56% from 1970 to 1985 and production of chewing tobacco rose 36%. Because adult use of smokeless tobacco has remained fairly constant, increased consumption has been primarily among juvenile males. Most recent estimates suggest there are three million users of smokeless tobacco less than 21 years old (DHHS, 1986). Five to 8% of adolescent males report daily use of smokeless tobacco, with more than twice this number reporting regular use.

Psychosocial Inventory

Adolescence and risk-taking activities go hand-in-hand owing to a myriad of cognitive, psychological and environmental factors. Effects of drug use and abuse is only one of them. Developmental influences upon growing teens spread from familial into interpersonal relationships and ultimately account for the exploratory and experimental actions resulting in problems. This section regards these actions as continuous, which is consistent with the ecobehavioral framework. Considered is how to identify and define each action etiologically using a *psychosocial inventory.*

Once therapy begins and initial trust is developed between therapist and adolescent, the psychosocial inventory can begin. This should be obtained from both therapist and parents but independently and at separate visits. Assessment covers behavior in three areas: At home, in school, and among peers (dating, substance abuse, and antisocial behavior). Particular emphasis is given to peer behaviors, as this is the arena in which most risk behaviors take place. Table 2 outlines the general points that should be addressed in the inventory.

Table 2
Questions to Ask in the Psychosocial Inventory

Categories and Inventory Questions
Home
Level of communication: degree to which teens confides in parents?
Areas of support/conflict?
Adolescent's feeling toward family members and parental feelings toward adolescent?
Strengths/vulnerabilities of family members?
School
Performance: any recent change?
Adolescent's perception of school: likes, dislikes, and reasons?
Relationship with classmates, teachers?
Educational/vocational plans?
Attention to details; on task?
Peers
Has friends? Has confidant?
Prefers being with friends or alone?
Primary interests and activities in peer groups?
Friends primarily older or younger?
Dating
When started; past and present partners?
Nature of present dating relationships; future plans?
Dating behavior; who else couple goes out with; where do they go?
Sexually active with past or present partner?
Any pregnancies, STDs?
Contraceptive use?
Knowledge about risks of sexual activity?
Perceived level of vulnerability to risks?
Substance Use
Cigarettes, alcohol, marijuana, others drugs (what, when, where, why, how long, how much, how often, with whom, level of of intoxication, use when alone, use in school?)
Knowledge about risks of substance abuse?
Perceived level of personal vulnerability to risks?
Use of alcohol or other drugs while driving?
Alternative transportation if driver intoxicated?
Habituation or addiction?
Accidents due to intoxication?

Physical harm (organ system damage)?
Psychosocial harm (emotional, educational, interpersonal)?
Trouble with law?
Soft drug use as gateway to harder drug use?

Antisocial Behavior

Truancy; pushing drugs; shoplifting; gang membership?
Trouble with the law?
Parent-child conflict?
Seriously aggressive or homicidal tendencies?

---

adapted from: Hofmann, 1990

In school, normal adolescents generally perform satisfactorily with their present level of achievement being consistent with past experience. Deteriorating performance immediately signals potential trouble. Likewise at home. Normal adolescents commonly exhibit some degree of conflict, but it is generally sporadic and limited to such matters as household chores, personal tidiness, dress and hair style, allowance, curfew hours, and the like. Normal adolescents are not likely to confide in their parents about all that goes on in their private lives, particularly what goes on in the peer group. But they commonly do discuss both highly important things and matters that are not parental forbidden behaviors. Signs of dissension beyond the norm are when the youth becomes consistently confrontational, more secretive, spends more time away from home without explanation, frequently condemns and deprecates parents in angry terms, and frequently seems to be hateful and alienated or depressed and withdrawn.

Regarding peers, normal adolescents generally prefer to be with companions their own age. They will affiliate with a particular peer group and have one or two particularly close friends they regularly confide in. The peer group assumes great importance in being the major arbiter of acceptable behavior. What goes in the peer group is a cardinal indicator of what goes on in the adolescent's own life. If the peer group is involved in societally approved behaviors (e.g., earns good grades, attends Saturday or Sunday religious services, etc.), one can reasonably assume the adolescent is engaging in these behaviors as well. The converse applies if the peer group is engaged in negative behaviors, suggesting that imitation may engender antisocial or negative behaviors.

By closely examining current risk levels, two basic questions are answered. First, *is the adolescent engaging in age appropriate behaviors?* Range of deviation depends on the liberal attitude afforded to the definition of adolescence deviancy. In most cases how far extreme behavior is depends on social context. In a metropolitan, urban setting, schools and peer groups tolerate more deviancy as the social norm, whereas in rural, culturally restricted settings there is intolerance to any deviancy. Second, *what are the inappropriate behaviors and why are they occurring?* Clearly identified antisocial actions signal some history of emotional and behavioral deterioration that is harmful to self or to others. Isolating these actions etiologically, however, goes beyond first impressions. Questions must be asked such as *what keeps the behavior going? Who views the behavior as objectionable? And, are there social, physical or interpersonal factors beyond the adolescent's control complicating antisocial behaviors?*

Answering these questions requires the use of a formal *functional analysis*. A functional analysis, like a psychosocial inventory, surveys adolescent behavior relative to peer, home, and school categories, by assessing the dimensionality of behaviors that explain what effect behavior has on other people or surroundings. Analysis narrows down the antisocial patterns through the *topography* and *function* of behaviors. Topography of behavior includes the shape, form or movement of behavior in space and time. An example is hitting behavior. Questions asked about function might include (a) how many times does the adolescent hit (frequency), (b) how long does he hit (duration), and (c) how forceful is hitting (magnitude or intensity)? Function of behavior describes the precipitants and immediate outcomes of behavior. Consider hitting again. Questions asked about function might include (a) who was hit (person), (b) what did that person do (consequence), and (c) what in turn did it do to increase or decrease hitting by the adolescent? Table 3 lists the important questions asked in a functional analysis.

Table 3
Functional Analysis of Adolescent Behaviors

Categories and Inventory Questions
Preliminary Analysis of Behavior
1. What are the adolescent's behavior deficits?
2. What are the adolescent's behavior excesses?
3. What are the adolescent's behavior assets?
Clarification of Problem
1. Who views the problem as objectionable?

2. What are the consequences of the problem for the adolescent and others?
3. What would the consequences be for the adolescent and others if the problem was removed?
4. What are the antecedents (precipitating events) of the problem?
5. Would the adolescent have new problems if the problem was removed?
6. Is the adolescent able to help in the development of a behavior program?
7. What would the adolescent and others gain if the problem was changed?

Analysis of Consequences

1. What kind of reinforcers are most effective for this adolescent?
2. What has been the experience with these consequences?
3. What groups exert the most control over this adolescent?
4. Does the adolescent understand use of reinforcers or punishers?
5. What are the adolescent's unpleasant consequences?
6. Would a program require the adolescent to give up current reinforcers associated with this problem?

Development (maturational) Analysis

1. Does the adolescent have biological limitations that affect this problem?
2. Would these limitations (disabilities) restrict choice of behavior change methods?
3. Is problem behavior more pronounced when the adolescent is hungry, thirsty, or otherwise deprived of something?

Social Change History

1. Describe the adolescent's present social and cultural situation (e,g., rural-urban, economic, ethnic group, education, living quarters, etc.).
2. Can these situations be changed to assist with behavior change?
3. Before the onset of current problem, did the adolescent exhibit similar behavior problems?
4. Can the onset of the current problem be traced to significant models in the adolescent's natural environment (family, friends, etc.)?

Self-control Analysis

1. Are there any situations in which the adolescent can control the problem behavior?
2. What are those situations and how does he control the behavior?
3. Does the adolescent's perception of this problem or self-control correspond with observations by others?
4. Can these people positively influence the adolescent toward behavior change?

Analysis of Interpersonal Relationships

1. Who are the significant others for the adolescent?
2. Do certain people or groups by mistake reinforce problem behavior?
3. What reinforcers can be identified in the adolescent's social relationships?

4. Can these people positively influence the adolescent toward behavior change?

Analysis of Setting and Environment

1. How does the adolescent's problem behavior compare to the norms for this behavior by his peers?
2. Are the norms for this behavior the same in various places (e.g., school, home, in public, etc.)?
3. Are there in the adolescent's world limitations (e.g., school, economic, physical, etc.) that prevent reinforcers for good behavior?
4. Does the adolescent's environment permit the type of changes felt needed?

Predictors of Adolescent Substance Abuse

Predictors of adolescent substance abuse are manifold. The seemingly infinite macro- and microstructures intricately guiding teen behavior are complex, at times undetectable, and largely inseparable from family interactions. Thus far predictors considered have been teenage sexuality, crime, motor/vehicular use, substance abuse and related health-risk behaviors ranked most likely evident at this age group. However, the constellation of adolescent activities including biological development entails more than risk behaviors. As the functional analysis suggests, problem behaviors *covary* with others behaviors or dysfunctional patterns that equally signal trouble. In this section correlates of substance abuse behavior are further explored focusing on group and individual factors.

Behavior Typology

Early predictors of teenage substance abuse frequently are described in a number of studies. Among them is the Woodland study. This study longitudinally tracked elementary school children over 10 years beginning after first grade. In 1963, the first year of the Woodlawn project, 57 first grade teachers in the 12 Woodlawn elementary schools were asked to define those behaviors that they thought would indicate that the child was having task difficulties and performance in the classroom. A four point global scale was made for each classroom task, ranging from adapting within minimal limits to mild, moderate and severe maladapting. Ratings were obtained for each child in the classroom on each task three times in the first grade and again in the third grade. Rated task scores resulted in a representative set of maladaptive behaviors listed by category in Table 4. Under each category are descriptive behaviors inferred by the Woodlawn teachers' report that are commonly observed in problem children.

Table 4
Categories of Maladaptive Behaviors Developed from Woodlawn Project

Categories and Expanded Behavior Descriptors	
Shyness	
Frequently seems anxious or tense	Is self critical
Cries easily or often	Overreacts to small mistakes
Worries a lot	Acts inferior to other children
Is overly dependent	Is always a follower, never a leader
Needs to be reassured frequently	Gives up easily
Feelings are easily hurt	Is pessimistic
Frequently seems sad and depressed	Worries about making mistakes
Feels guilty too easily and too often	Has little self-confidence
Feels inferior	Always gives in to other children
Is easily embarrassed	Is afraid to ask other children to play
Has strong fears	Tries to be too much like other children
Has many fears	Is not interested in learning
Refuses to try new things	Is not curious
Seems uncomfortable in new situations	Never disagrees
Is afraid to show anger	Does not give best effort
Is easily upset	Appears to be uninterested
Seems withdrawn or spends time alone	Is too humble
Needs too much affection	Refuses to talk
Does not respond to affection	Uses baby talk
Is too neat and orderly	Forgets things
Is suspicious	Frequently daydreams
Worries about getting sick	Is too involved in fantasies
Has unusual beliefs	Has overactive imagination
Sees or hears things that others do not	Has trouble reading
Is too involved with certain thoughts or ideas	Has trouble with spelling or writing
Has trouble relaxing	Talks too fast
Seems too serious	Stutters or stammers
Repeats certain behaviors over and over again	Has poor sense of direction
Talks often about death or injury	Misnames things on purpose
Aggressiveness	

Is not friendly to other children
Hurts or teases other children
Does not get along with children same age
Is not liked by other children
Has few friends
Does not compromise with other children
Competes too hard in games
Has no hobbies or interests
Has friends that are mainly of opposite sex
Frequently argues or disagrees
Refuses to listen
Is resentful
Has bad temper
Threatens to run away from home
Is cruel to animals
Is a show-off
Threatens to hurt self
Is demanding
Plays with matches or fire
Has vandalized
Is in trouble with police
Has bad reputation
Cheats at games
Steals things from children or adults
Does not feel guilty for misbehaving
Does not know right from wrong
Is disrespectful to authority

Bullies other children
Does not share with other children
Is teased a lot by other children
Has trouble making friends
Will not play alone
Is a poor loser in games
Has friends who are bad influence
Is socially immature
Is uncooperative
Is disobedient
Is stubborn
Is secretive
Always has to have own way
Intentionally breaks things
Often brags or boasts
Threatens to hurt others
Frequently sulks or pouts
Manipulates others
Swears or uses bad language
Tries risks like grown-ups
Does not respond to punishment
Frequently lies
Takes or uses other children's toys
Blames others for mistakes
Is unaware of other children's feelings
Ignores rules
Has poor sense of loyalty

Concentration Problems (Impulsivity)

Does not pay attention
Has trouble finishing projects
Acts rapidly, spontaneously
Has trouble planning activities
Changes mind often
Is uncoordinated
Bumps into things
Is restless
Is always climbing or running

Is easily distracted
Cannot finish games or puzzles
Has trouble getting organized
Loses interest quickly
Has difficulty following rules
Frequently drops or breaks things
Is overactive
Has trouble sitting still at meals
Has tics and twitches

Underachievement

Does not finish homework

Does not like school

Does not get along with children at school	Does not get along with teachers
Needs too much attention from teachers	Is a discipline problem at school
Blames teacher for problems in school	Is frequently late for school
Skips school	Frequently gets sick in school
Gets poor grades	Quits easily on tough tasks
Is in special education	Hangs out with underachievers

Results of the outcome study generally showed that, despite fairly strong correlations among the first grade teacher ratings, the scales have specific and well-defined patterns of outcomes. Findings fell under four categories: Shyness, Aggressiveness, Concentration Problems or Impulsivity, and Underachievement.

Shyness. Shyness among males in the first grade had different outcomes depending on whether it was combined with aggressiveness. Among males, shyness without aggressiveness inhibited later use of marijuana, hard liquor and cigarettes. Similarly, it inhibited later delinquency patterns. However, shyness in the first grade was associated with higher levels of anxiety in adolescence. Among females, shyness was much less significant for later outcomes. The one correlation was that shyness in females inhibited use of hard liquor in adolescence.

Aggressiveness. For males, aggressiveness in first grade lead to increased levels of use of beer or wine, marijuana, hard liquor, and cigarettes, but also a higher level of antisocial behavior ten years later. Males that are moderately and severely aggressive, but also shy, risk higher levels of substance use and to larger extents are prone to delinquency. For females, outcomes of aggressiveness and shy-aggressiveness were quite different. Aggressiveness in first grade did not lead to overt substance use and delinquency in adolescence. However, these behaviors did lead to paranoid symptoms and clear psychological disturbance.

Concentration problems or impulsivity. Impulsivity scores reflected noncompliance and detachment problems. Noncompliance involved not following instructions, being disrespectful or violating established policies or adult rules. Detachment was the by-product of total immunity from feelings such as shame, guilt or self-resentment regarding inappropriate actions committed toward himself or others. Outcome results showed that impulsive and noncompliant first graders were heavy teenage alcohol users and usually graduated to opiates, barbiturates and other sedative-acting drugs for a calming effect. Cocaine users also had impulsive histories, particularly if the impulsiveness became aggressive.

Underachievement. Underachievement in first grade predicted clear outcomes ten years later, but not in substance abuse. This maladaptation lead to depressive symptoms and progressively worse deterioration of self-confidence, ambition, and interpersonal successes.

These results showed that specific early predictors of drug use also predicted the use of other kinds of substances by teenagers as well as certain others kinds of teenage misbehavior. Maladaptive behavioral responses to first grade tasks apparently had important relationships to outcomes. Theoretically, the results reaffirm the ecobehavioral principle that dysfunctional interactions in early life brought on by systemic limitations and the child's deficits and excesses will remain unchanged as long as there are no significant alterations in events, conditions or the person intervening with life span development.

Adolescent Development

Let us consider more carefully what this life span development entails. Adolescence is a period of great physical and psychological change. Individuals experiment with a variety of behaviors and lifestyle patterns as part of the natural process of separating from parents, developing a sense of autonomy and independence, establishing an identity, and acquiring new skills needed to function effectively in an increasingly adult world.

Profound cognitive-developmental changes occur during the beginning of adolescence which significantly affect adolescents' views of the world, and the manner in which they think. In contrast to the preadolescent's perceptions of concrete things, the budding adolescent is more relative, abstract, and hypothetical. This enables him to conceive of a wide range of possibilities and logical alternatives, to accept deviations from established rules, and to recognize the frequently irrational and inconsistent nature of adult behaviors.

Changes also occur with respect to the relative influence of peers and parents. As individuals approach adolescence, there is a progressive decline in parental influence and a corresponding increase in the influence of peers and other socializing agents. Furthermore, adolescents tend to have a heightened sense of self-consciousness about their appearance, personal qualities, and abilities. These factors increase adolescents' risk of yielding to the various direct and indirect pressures to smoke, drink or use drugs. Use of some substances (e.g., cigarettes, alcohol) is age-graded and may be proscribed for children and adolescents while viewed as acceptable for adults. Thus, using these substances may be an attempt to lay claim to adult status.

While self-consciousness (egocentricity) and increased reliance on the peer group may tend to promote substance use, the cognitive developments occurring prior to and during this period may also influence substance use. For example, a higher cognitive orientation may allow an adolescent to spot inconsistencies or logical flaws in arguments raised by adults concerning the risks of substances, especially if those adults are users themselves. The adolescent forms counter-arguments and rationalizations to ignore the adult warnings. Undermining the adults arguments is also an innocent curiosity fueled by the peer pressures and the strong need adolescents have for independence. As they defect from parental control, curiosity steps boldly into risk-taking and results in rejection of fears previously preventing this curiosity.

Given there are clear transitions in adolescence, let us now consider the experimental research further documenting these effects.

Evidence for early contributions to drug involvement. Prior to about 1970, no systematic empirical work had dealt with questions of early experience with drugs by children, and the ways such experience might serve as precursors to later drug involvement. The first of such studies, reported by Jahoda and Cramond (1972), studied school-aged children in Glasgow (ages 6, 8, and 10) and also collected some data on a small four-year-old sample. Utilizing age appropriate, game-like tasks and interviewing techniques that were enjoyable for the children and that minimized impact of language development on task success, these investigators raised questions about the innocence of young children. They also showed that development of cognitive structures about drugs were already coming into play in the child's language, and that evidence existed to indicate that attitudes about alcohol, as a drug, were already to some degree in place. Since that time several other investigators have elaborated upon what goes on in these earlier years. Summarized below are their results centered around five questions.

When are children able to identify alcoholic beverages? Varying the sensory modality that the child utilizes in identifying a drug like alcohol can help the investigator trace the possible origins of this capacity. Research has focused on when children were able to provide verbal labels based upon visual stimuli (e.g., photographs of beverage containers), and when they are able to make correct discriminations based upon odor information. In the first instance, correct identifications can be attributed to either socially distant, culturally provided opportunities, such as watching television, or to first hand experience in the home. In the latter instance, olfactory detection occurs if one has had direct exposure, within nasal range. This clearly implicates the family as directly supplying the opportunity.

Two studies demonstrated the early visual discriminations. First was a study by Noll (1983), in which 17 children (ages 2 to 6 years) looked at photos of family foods and drinks. All of the children correctly identified photos of milk, and beer, and other alcoholic beverages (wine, gin/vodka, sherry, etc.). A subsequent study (Greenberg, Zucker & Noll, 1985) using 131 children repeated this photo discrimination task and produced similar findings. Older (six years old) children performed better on the tasks than younger children, although even children between 30 and 41 months were reasonably successful.

Verbal labels for alcohol *by smell* represents the research by Jahoda & Cramond (1972). Their initial work showed that a substantial subset of children between ages of 6 and 10 years were able to provide correct verbal labels for alcoholic beverages even when they were only permitted to smell these substances. Using a cross-sectional but developmentally focused design, findings indicated that as one moves from younger to older age groups, children perform better on this task. By age 10, 61% of the children can identify the alcoholic beverage odors, and pilot data on a small sample of 4-years old showed that some children this young could also identify alcoholic beverages by smell.

When do children learn about cultural drinking norms? The sociological and socio-psychological literature on adolescence has historically regarded this time frame as the developmental epoch within which learning to drink and learning one's role as drinker takes place. Peers, as significant socializers, are viewed as the source of knowledge and attitudes about adult behavior, including knowledge about drinking. But learning also derives from principal interactions with the culture itself. One study tapping a child's perception of these interactions used the "Appropriate Beverage Task" (Penrose, 1978). This approach provides data on what beverages children think are appropriate for adults and children to drink on various occasions. Children tested with this approach selected alcohol beverages more often for adult males than adult females. More recently, similar research (Greenberg et. al., 1985) used a sample of preschool children (ages 2 to 6) and found that three-year olds selected alcoholic beverages more often for adults in the pictured scenes.

What is the family's influence on young children's knowledge of, and attitude towards alcoholic beverages? There are few data available that assess the child's knowledge of alcoholic beverages and simultaneously obtain systematic information on parental drinking and parental attitudes toward alcoholic beverages. The first reported work in this area was based on spontaneous verbalizations during testing by Jahoda & Cramond (1972). These verbalizations allowed a small subset of children to be classified as coming either from homes with heavy drinking or homes where no alcohol was consumed. Statements contained explicit mention of the parents' drunkenness or heavy drinking, or that neither parent drank. Jahoda also examined the impact of parental drinking models on children's knowledge of, and attitudes toward alcoholic beverages (Jahoda, Davies & Tagg, 1980). Parental drinking was assessed with a questionnaire asking parents whether they drank regularly, quite frequently, only occasionally, or never. Children were then evaluated on several tasks designed to corroborate the parents' reports. While parent-child reports did correlate to some extent, methodological limitations of the study weaken the validity of the results.

In sum, attempts were made to examine the relationship between children's performance on tasks designed to evaluate the knowledge of and attitudes toward alcoholic beverages and drinking. Data accumulated thus far suggest that parental drinking models have an impact on the developing cognitions of the child toward alcoholic beverages. The weight of findings also suggest that knowledge of alcoholic beverages is in preschool children.

What is known about the development of young children's attitudes toward alcoholic beverages and drinking behavior? How do these attitudes change developmentally? Several of the studies already reviewed have also examined children's attitudes toward drinking behavior, drunkenness, and their expectancies about their own drinking as adults. Similar findings were reported by Spiegler (1983) in her investigation of children's attitudes. Children between ages of six and ten years were shown photographs of men and women involved in various activities, including eating, smoking, talking on the phone, and drinking alcoholic beverages. They were asked to rate each picture based upon how they felt about the person depicted in the photograph. Reports of dislike were greater for men and women who were drinking alcoholic beverages.

What evidence is there for personality and other individual differences contributing to this process? This question has not yet been explored in any great detail. The Greenberg et al. (1985) research showed that individual differences relating to cognitive capacity, as assessed by measures of verbal intelligence, have a low order but significant relationship to the awareness of cultural drinking norms. But there was no relationship between this measure and preschoolers' ability to identify alcohol beverage names. Level of cognitive complexity, already lower at preschool ages, may limit information the child can gather while raised in a drinking household. However, limited cognitions do not mean there are no discriminations taking place or that children simply miss critical stimuli impacted on them.

On the contrary, clinical observations repeatedly reveal that abused, neglected or manipulated preschoolers raised in alcoholic or aggressive households develop acute hypersensitivity to all events transacting around them. Attention to details is at accelerated rates and overincorporated with inferences about why the events must be happening. Higher probabilities exist that such children observe and learn family routines rapidly and formulate rules predicting these routines. Predicted routines prevent that child from being caught off guard or suffering aversive parental consequences. Avoidance of consequences frequently also advances this hypersensitivity to peculiar levels of perceiving subtle, very minor events underneath so-called conscious awareness, where the child feels he or she can see or know things that are premonitions or extra-sensory.

Black Adolescents

Alcohol abuse is considered a major problem among blacks as well as whites in America. Recent reviews of research conducted over the past 35 years on alcohol use among blacks conclude that adverse consequences of alcohol use are at least as great for blacks as for whites in this country (Harper, 1977; Harper & Dawkins, 1976; King, 1982). Analysis of the etiological and epidemiological implications are reviewed under two sections, "Alcohol-related problems among black adults," and "differences in the social contexts of alcohol use."

Alcohol-related problems among black adults. The relative magnitude of alcohol problems among blacks, as in any population, varies in part depending on the type of study and on the measures used. Self-report data collected in a 1979 probability survey of persons 18 years and over, for example, indicated that heavy drinkers and problem drinkers were as common among blacks as among whites who drank. However, a higher number of blacks than whites, especially females, reported alcohol abstention (Clark & Midanik, 1982). Objective measures of the consequences of alcohol use, on the other hand, suggest that some alcohol-related problems may be more severe among blacks than among whites, particularly among young black males. For instance, alcohol-related homicide rates are higher for black males 30 years old and younger. Rates are lower for white counterparts. Even more striking are the figures on deaths from cirrhosis of the liver, generally caused by prolonged heavy drinking. Among black males 25 to 34 years of age, cirrhotic death rates were several times higher than for white males the same age. For all ages, the cirrhotic death rate for black Americans was nearly twice that for white Americans.

A second related problem deals with risk arising from educational and vocational inequities. More black than white youth 18 to 19 years of age are high school dropouts (Bureau of the Census, 1981). Economic disadvantage occurs even earlier than age 18. In 1977, for example, nearly three times as many black youth were unemployed as were white youth--35% compared to 13%. This was attributed in part to the movement of jobs from largely black central cities to predominantly white suburbs as well as to the adverse effects of discrimination and ghetto environment and education. By 1982, the unemployment rate among black youth reached 53% (Wrather, 1982). These findings indicate a need to prepare black youths--both students and their out-of-school peers--for the period of high risk for alcohol problems that begins not long after the high school years.

Differences in the social contexts of alcohol use. Analysis of research on social contexts of alcohol show that drinking among youth was most common in settings where only peers were present--at unsupervised teenage parties and hangouts, at school functions when no adults were visible; and in cars at night (Harford & Speigler, 1982; Lowman, 1981/82). The students who reported they often drank alcoholic beverages in unsupervised settings were among those who reported the highest levels of alcohol use and the most frequent drunkenness.

Findings on alcohol use by black students and white students in various social contexts disclose very different patterns in two subgroups. The most popular setting for alcohol use among black students appeared to be special occasions at home. The most common setting among white students was unsupervised teenage parties. Even though black students reported lower levels of alcohol use in all social settings, the difference did not exceed 9% in contexts supervised by adults--dinner with the family, special occasions at home, and teenage parties with adults present. Differences in alcohol consumption in peer-only contexts, on the other hand, ranged from 15% to 27%. Twice as many whites as black students reported they often drank at unsupervised teenage parties. This index does not tell us how often an individual was exposed to a particular context. It only signifies the frequency of drinking when in that context. The fact that the frequency of drinking in peer-only contexts is highly correlated with reported quantity and frequency of alcohol use suggests that black students attend peer-only parties where alcohol is served less often than do white students.

Despite these findings, research on social and clinical alcohol-related problems among black adults indicates that high risk for such problems can occur in early maturity. Alcohol problems have been found to be associated with work-role instability, school drop-out rates, and faulty prevention strategies insensitive to discrimination issues. This last issue implicates community interventions for lacking integrational components necessary for including black youths at risk in outreach and treatment programs. Reaching these youth apparently is less problematic than is mobilizing the agencies or service providers into the community to establish, develop and maintain formal strategies. The few providers who do effectively locate, isolate and mainstream at-risk users into network services are unfortunately deficient with follow-up or maintenance, largely due to their voluminous caseload.

Gangs

The transition from childhood to adulthood has never been easy either for the adolescent, who must adapt to all the changes taking place at this time, or for the adult, who must tolerate inconsistent and sometimes pseudo-sociopathic behaviors. Adolescence is a time for experimentation, risk taking, and irresponsibility, all mingled with a youthful narcissism. Normal adolescents have a feeling of invincibility, that nothing bad can or will happen to them. Despite being cognitively aware of the consequences of automobile accidents, for instance, many will drive automobiles at excessive speeds. Many more even drink alcohol or use drugs and then drive at excessive speeds. From this unabated bravery evolves a priority for group relationships. Thus, gangs develop during the years between childhood and adulthood, when individuals are looking for an identity, a peer group, and a purpose. Adolescents leave the safety of their families and find security in their peers. Gangs can supply some or all of these needs.

Gangs occur most commonly in cities with large minority populations where the population has not been integrated into the larger U.S. environment. This segregation prevents the minority population from profiting in the social, financial and physical resources available to the larger population. Adolescents may be more sensitive to this inequality or at least more unwilling to accept it. One thing they do have control over is the area that they inhabit. The land may not contain anything of great financial value but its value lies in that it can be possessed, protected, and regulated. Gangs that are territorial consider this area or "turf" as the exclusive property of their gang. This gives the gang a purpose for all members to share.

Although gangs tend to be identified with poor black and Hispanic neighborhoods (Bell, 1987; Campbell, 1987; Fox, 1985; Moore, Vigil & Garcia, 1983) and with dysfunctional families (Bowker & Klein, 1983; Erlanger, 1979; Lowney, 1984), there are examples of gangs in white and middle class societies. In 1985 the news media reported that children of the very rich in Hollywood, California had formed "gangs" and had robbed several banks. The membership and goals of gangs differ from city to city and ethnic group to ethnic group, but most develop out of a frustrated need for a sense of belonging and importance.

In small and mid-sized cities where gang activities used to be minimal, there is now an increasing gang presence (Stover, 1986). Many middle class suburbs are reporting arrests of teens from "affluent gangs" that engage in vandalism, robbery, and drug dealing. Drug dealing in particular brings in money to gangs regardless of socioeconomic status. Gangs have become a major element not only in use of drugs by individual members but also in distribution of drugs within the gangs' territories. Regardless of the original reason for joining a gang, once a member, involvement with drugs may now be inevitable. Adult gang members shield themselves by using juveniles as the street level workforce that brings in new customers, delivers drugs, and collects debts. As involvement with drugs has become big business, violence has increased. The violence extends to the innocent as well as to the gang members.

Adolescent females represent the fastest developing rank of street gangs. They are forming what amounts to ladies' auxiliaries. *Detroit News* recently reported this free-wheeling gang lifestyle frequently includes sex, drugs, and liquor, which contributes to an increase in sexually transmitted disease and teenage pregnancies. Some young girls are forced out in the streets when their association with gangs leads to a showdown with their own families. Other girls become drug runners. Desires for expensive, impulsive material goods lure enrollment and compliance. Girls also join after their boyfriends shower them with lavish gifts, foods, and privileges only fantasized beforehand or entirely unreachable given their parents' low socioeconomic status. However, once with the gang, a girl finds her movement restricted. She cannot associate with friends who might be in other gangs and she may suffer physical punishment if she does. Defection therefore is common. Girls launch their own groups, stealing drug-running business from competitive groups. Teenage girls who drift toward new or male drug gangs are no longer passive, and easily battle for territorial dominance.

Not all members of all gangs are heavily involved with drugs. Multiple studies document dramatically increased involvement of some aspects of drugs among gang members compared with controls who are not members of the gang (Anglin, 1988; Dembo, Allen & Farroll, 1985). The bottom line, however, is that a war on gangs implies a war on drugs. Extending this farther, a war on gangs can be considered to be a war on poverty, minority status, broken homes, physical and sexual abuse, low self-esteem, addiction, and homelessness.

EFFECTS UPON FAMILY

Intergenerational effects of family dysfunction surface in clinical records of adolescent substance abusers. Links to substance abuse include: Family alcoholism, physical or emotional abuse, and sibling aggression. One school of thought blames genetic inheritance as explaining this transmission of disorders. The other school, following a learning theory or ecobehavioral model, rejects inheritance as solely the cause. Genetic or biological (phylogenetic) precipitants clearly influence the learning process but are weaker predictors of dysfunctional problems than are direct experience of consequences.

Current research findings support this position (Belskey, 1984; Carroll, 1977; Elder, Caspi & Downey, 1986; Patterson, DeBaryshe & Ramsey, 1989; Wachs & Gruen, 1982). Ineffective parenting practices account for the first of three steps of behavior degeneration from childhood to adolescence. The second step, the conduct-disordered behaviors, lead to academic failure and peer rejection. These dual failures risk depressed mood problems and involvement in deviant peer groups. The third step is engaging in high risk chronic delinquency behaviors.

This section accepts this three-step model, consistent with the book, that intergenerational effects upon adolescent drug and alcohol abusers primarily result from operant and respondent contingencies within the larger interactional context. Reviewed first are family system defects forming adolescent deviancy, and, second, the severe repercussions of family violence.

Family System Defects

Factors showing a deterioration in the family unit leading to onset of adolescent substance abuse are hard to obtain. Though hypothetically easy to make, empirical collaborative data is frequently unobtainable because parents hide this information or protect the child's integrity by underreporting delinquent acts, suspected drug use incidents, or dismissing their suspicion based on inferred stages of adolescent growth involving criminal, assaultive, or experimental behaviors. Very often parents seem to be trying to keep control over their youngsters, to avoid separation, by giving them money for drugs. They claim this protects the adolescent from having to steal for drug money. But in effect this keeps the youth dependent on his parents--which the parents very much desire, without realizing it.

Research studies clinically able to penetrate this edifice have documented initial findings on family system patterns. Kaufman and Kaufman (1979) compiled the following list of the most frequently reported complaints or observations made among families and clinicians regarding families with adolescent drug abusing members:

1. The addict is the symptom carrier for the family dysfunction.

2. The addict helps to maintain the family homeostasis.

3. The addict member reinforces the parental need to control and continue parenting, yet he finds such parenting inadequate for his needs.

4. The addict provides a displaced battlefield so that implicit and explicit parental strife can continue to be denied.

5. Parental drug and alcohol abuse is common and is directly transmitted to the addict or results in inadequate parenting.

6. The addict forms cross-generational alliances that separate parents from each other.

7. Generational boundaries are diffuse--there is frequent competition between parents. Frequently the crisis created by the drug-dependent member is the only way the family gets together and attempts some problem solving, or is the only opportunity for a "dead" family to experience emotions.

Implications of these seven predictors suggest the abusing adolescent can hold the family together where otherwise it would disintegrate under its own dysfunctional orientation. Examples of this "band-aid" or *adhesion-role* are manifold. Troubled parents suffering repeated losses such as unemployment, child mortality, and financial instability, and whose drug abusing habits are intermittent, may grow so accustomed to crisis-adjustment that the family is discoherent unless there are frequent emergencies. Interspousal support is insufficient or never occurs, in other words, unless the spouses *must solve a problem creating instant need for an alliance.* Even families enjoying financial security, steady employment and that are drug-free may be inadvertent victims of their own or their child's medical illnesses. For example, diabetic children demand unorthodox attention and daily compromises from parents such that *not making those sacrifices* seems unnatural. Upon restoring normalcy, once the ailing child improves his health, re-orienting to an uncomplicated, nonstressful lifestyle may be resisted. The parents instead may *look for ways to prove their child is still sick.*

Personifying the sick or defective child is only one way to maintain family unity and functionality. Reilly (1976) in addition reported nine pathological family interaction patterns and five conflict themes derived from his family therapy work. These include:

1. Negative interactions (family members give negative messages when they do communicate, such as criticisms, put downs, complaints and nagging).

2. Inconsistent limit setting or structuring by parents.

3. A cry for help or attention by the substance abuser (designated patient) advertising drug use and related problems as a way of getting some particular response or structuring or limit-setting by parents.

4. Global or massive parental denial--for example, they manage not to see what is going on, either the evidence of substance abuse or accidents and other evidence that the problem is getting worse.

5. Offspring on drugs provide some vicarious gratification that parents need, either consciously or unconsciously.

6. Use of alcohol and drugs as self-medication or as disinhibitors by substance-abusing member who needs this aid for expressing or acting out certain reactions or feelings.

7. Difficulty in expressing anger between parents and children. There is no appropriate continuum of expression, resulting in either no expression or violence.

8. Pathogenic parents' expectations of substance-abusing child, who is either perceived as a good or bad image of a grandparent or relative of the parent and is not seen as a real person for himself.

9. Family members make statements such as promises about their behavior in the future, that are so unrealistic that they cannot be believed. They don't mean what they say.

Are there recurrent themes generated by these patterns? Reilly (1976) identifies five conflict themes remaining unresolved not only between parent and substance abusing child, but also unresolved from generations of parent-child conflict. Conflicts include the following, along with an expanded description of each:

1. *Attachment and separation.* Bonding relationships underdeveloped or never developed discourage trust and support between parent-child. Parents' refusal of empathic interest in child's activities or personal growth creates distance reacted to by the child's anger, then fear, and then feelings of desertion. Detachment left unresolved destroys the child's sense of compassion, both in giving and receiving, thereby transforming inevitably into a rigid, uncaring, heartless rebel seeking only selfish ends.

2. *Ego diffusion.* Confusion of identity, on knowing right from wrong and conflicting perceptions of adult models deflect youthful observers from appropriate behaviors. Left to their own conceptions of behavior, adolescents never fully develop rules of propriety or understand moral and ethical reasons behind actions. Actions, instead, are inferred as appropriate or inappropriate by degrees of punishment (or absence thereof) that follow behavior, rather than by governing ideals or norms of behavior.

3. *Dependency and autonomy.* This concept largely borrows from Erikson's psychosocial stage of autonomy versus shame and doubt (1963). This is where children learn to be self-sufficient in many activities including toileting, feeding, walking, talking, *or* doubting their own abilities. Accordingly, doubt raised by parental rejection or punishment inhibits the young child who in adolescence resists risking new, even age-appropriate behaviors. By early teens the child may

withdraw from heterosexual contact, may hate talking in front of classmates, or even refuse personal grooming errands such as self-bathing and selection of clothing, or money management. Lack of independence and risk-taking forces dependency on parents. However, too much dependency, while maintained by the child lacking skills to do things on his own, causes resentment and anger, and efforts are made to liberate from parental control. Though rebellious or even legally emancipated youths think they escape parental control, they still have major skill deficits blocking their adaptation to the world. Rather than return home or restore their subordinate role under parents, unskilled adolescents flounder in unguided directions and become prime candidates for drug use.

4. *Nurturance and deprivation.* Parental resources such as affection, money and security supply basic nurturing for healthy adolescent growth. Delay, removal, interruption or prevention of these resources depletes the supply and forces an unusual adaptation by the adolescent, usually responsible for caretaking, aggressive or antisocial behaviors. Deprived love, for instance, especially if this resource was once available or plentiful, sends mixed messages that what the adolescent did was insufficient for receiving love. Efforts suddenly are bolstered to win this love back, restoring the old ways. When this fails, repeated efforts are exhausted not only in adolescence but into adulthood trying to restore the flow of affection. Caretaking spouses, for example, may enter distressful marriages and devote hours upon hours to repairing the marriage.

On the antisocial or aggressive end, parental deprivation of resources, especially when the child initially received them, frustrates the child and forces the survival response of caring for himself. Unfed children, for example, learn rapidly to eat when they can, steal food, or binge large portions. Competitively the child fights off opponents who seek the same food supply (siblings) and regards adults as opponents as well. If securing food or other resources requires anger, threats, bodily harm, or property destruction, the behavior occurs regardless of consequences. Aggression simply becomes the means to survival ends.

5. *Control, leadership, limit setting versus freedom, permissiveness.* Parental protection goes a long way. When parents overly insulate their child from outside influence, be it from friends, school, or just playing outside in the yard, three problems occur. First, already described above, is dependency on the insulating parent. Second, also described above, is a profound retardation or underdevelopment of age-appropriate skills. A third problem, in

addition, is that parents lose touch with the culture or their own social peers who might disapprove of the parents' actions. Working parents, for instance, who share anecdotes about child-raising and the pitfalls of running a busy schedule open up their world to scrutiny by listeners, be they friends or just casual coworkers. Listeners may point out mistakes and ways to correct mistakes and perhaps share their own ordeals, again focusing on "right ways and wrong ways to do it." Exchange of comments in this way establishes a regulating or monitoring mechanism of behavior that the insulated parent lacks. Without regulating mechanisms, insulated parents may believe their deprivations, limit setting, or permissiveness are healthy.

The problem with insularity, however, goes beyond just exclusion of regulatory mechanisms. One of the major forces underlying adolescent deviancy, especially of substance abuse, is parents unknowingly depriving the child of essential opportunities for normal growth and peer adjustment. For that reason a closer look at this insularity phenomenon is warranted.

Parental Insularity and its Effects Upon the Adolescent

Child behavior problems in family settings generally decrease after the introduction of parent training techniques (Boger, Richter, Kuretz & Haas, 1986). Parenting techniques will build behavior control skills, but there are drawbacks. One drawback is lacking skill training that directly guides the parent, himself or herself, to become better adjusted (e.g., Dangel & Polster, 1984). Factors affecting parents vary from family size, to stressors, to community isolation. These factors combined account for the phenomenon investigated by Wahler called the "insularity effect" (1980; Wahler, Leske, & Rogers, 1979).

Insularity refers to parents of poverty level having minimal community contacts who are prone to aversive interactions with children. Wahler (1981) argued that insularity rests not on isolation per se, but rather on the aversive nature of those social contacts that do occur; such contacts contribute indirectly to maintenance of parent-child altercations. Patterson and Reid (1970) argued for a similar phenomenon, calling it a "coercive relationship." By "coercion" was meant the "interaction in which aversive stimuli control the behavior of one person and positive reinforcers maintain the behavior of the other (p 133). Conceptually both Wahler and Patterson & Reid provoked controversy regarding the role of parent, not child, in parent education.

This section briefly examines current trends in insularity research following a systems approach to deviant child behavior.

Sections cover: (a) The role of parental insularity, (b) common parent-training program failures and (c) recommendations for research expansion.

The role of parental insularity. At some point in the child's life, his parents or members of the larger community may decide that aspects of his behavior are deviant or his actions may become distressful to parents. Probably the most common behaviors classified as deviant by parents are those that involve rule breaking or noncompliance with parental instructions. Sometimes these actions involve assertive activities, such as fighting, and sometimes actions are passive, such as ignoring parental instructions. Systems theory speculations on the development of these behaviors fall into two categories: Negative reinforcer trap; and coercion trap. Both theories directly implicate parental mistakes and the origins of insularity.

Negative Reinforcer Trap. This kind of trap is where the child's behavior is aversive to other family members. One caretaker may discover that there are quick and efficient ways of terminating the aversive action. Often the most effortless of these escape methods involves dispensing positive reinforcers to the child. In doing so, unfortunately the child has been reinforced for the very behavior the caretaker wishes to suppress (Wahler, 1975).

Coercion Trap. Patterson and his colleagues (Patterson, 1969, 1982; Patterson, Cobb & Ray, 1970; Patterson & Reid, 1970) explain the coercion trap as children coercing reinforcers from their parents. Actions such as hitting, nagging, and whining appear functionally geared to obtain parental compliance of the child's wish. Patterson's findings based on naturalistic observation support a developmental view of coercion insofar as showing different, sequential stages of coercion. For instance, first coercion attempts are generated; second, parental replies become automatic; third, reciprocal reinforcement results from child obtaining his goal and parent terminating the child's aversive behavior.

Coercion and negative reinforcer traps equally emerge when parent-child interactions are weak; when parental control is weak, and when parents have interpersonal problems beyond child-rearing. Wahler (1980) showed that risk of child neglect and abuse correlated with mothers who felt "cut off" from social contact, or because of low socioeconomic level encountered aversive contacts in social situation. Eighteen mothers participated in a 3-phase parenting program and were interviewed about reasons for their problems. Data also were collected on self-reports and observed parent interactions with social contacts. Nearly 60% of contacts were with social service workers, as opposed to friends. Of these contacts, insular mothers rated 85% of their interactions as highly aversive. Results indicated that aversive interchanges with social contacts (e.g., welfare workers, employers, etc.) appeared to be coercive in much the same manner as those between mother and child.

The social contact (e.g., social worker) responds in ways that direct the mother to start or stop certain behavior. If mothers comply, coercion traps arise because both parties are reinforced. The social worker is reinforced by the mother's compliance, and the mother is reinforced by the social worker not asking her to comply. Further, increased aversive interchanges affects how (insular) mothers treat their children. On days in which contacts were friendly the parents show more tolerance to child noncompliance. On days contacts were aversive the parents consistently resort to immediate punishment over positive ways. Patterson and Fleishman (1979) verified the ubiquity of this correlation based on their review of parent training techniques.

Insular parents who are resistant to social contacts due to contacts being aversive thus become prone to child abuse. Garbarino (1977) first speculated that a mother's social isolation diminishes parental control. Wahler, Leske & Rogers (1979) replicated this finding and also discovered that these limited contacts seldom involved mothers' friends and were usually not initiated by the mothers. In other words, the most severely troubled mothers appeared to avoid interchanges with people outside their families. Withdrawal from the community directly was linked to abused children's social, emotional and cognitive problems.

Absence of social support further magnifies child-rearing stressors (Crockenberg, 1981, 1986). Crockenberg (1988) argued that social support buffered stressors by fostering responsive and nurturant parenting. Supportive members of the nuclear family and outside social providers relieve the mother of maternal pressures and affirm the mother's need to be cared for. Crockenberg & McCluskey (1986a, 1986b) found among sensitive mothers after childbirth that an established support network increased the mother's self-efficacy. This confirms findings reported earlier by Longfellow, Zelkowitz, Saunders & Belle (1979), on 40 low-income women with young children who responded better to children's dependency needs after receiving child care training. Demonstrable improvements in parental affection, attachment (bonding), motivation, and overall maternal competency all positively correlated with availability of social resources.

Insular parents who are abusers characteristically display lower levels of overall interaction with their children. This has been demonstrated with infants, preschoolers, and school-aged children

(Wolfe, 1985). Wahler & Dumas (1986) particularly found parents indiscriminate in their attention to toddlers. Lewis & Schaeffer (1981) concurred, adding from their study that parents are less sensitive auditorily and tactilely to their children. Detached parents, either from society or from caregiving roles, overall demonstrated recurrent symptoms thus predictive of family abuse. Azar, Barnes & Twentyman (1988) identified these characteristics as the following:

1. poor impulse control
2. social skill deficits
3. poor stress coping skills
4. lack of parenting skills
5. inconsistent or random with reactions
6. protective and disguised abusive effects

Inadequacies in caregiving behavior put insular mothers at a great disadvantage because they are unaware of their abuse and probably inaccessible for social workers to draw it to their attention. This leads parents to blame their parenting failures on the child. Belsky, Robins & Gamble (1984) essentially demonstrated this consequence: That abuse children's maladaptive behaviors became the explanation for a mother's low frustration tolerance and inevitable choice of punitive discipline. In short, the variables most often identified as critical to the parent's insular behavior include:

1. Lack of nonviolent child management skills
2. Inadequate knowledge concerning child behavior
3. Anger-control deficits
4. Over-arousal to cues of child misbehavior
5. Limited resources for solving problems
6. Limited social resources that monitor or alter maladaptive functioning

Given this insularity factor and the broad consequences it has on the family, naturally the solution might be a strong parent-training program. We consider why such a solution has many pitfalls.

Common Parent-Training Program Failures. Documented studies on parent-training related to the insular parent typically address child management methods. More recently, several studies have described interventions for teaching abusive parents to use effective, nonviolent child management skills. Training commonly is conducted in groups (Wolf, Sandler & Kaufman, 1981) or with individual families (e.g., Crozier & Katz, 1979; Denicola & Sandler, 1980). While these interventions yield promising results, only a handful of the methods directly address problems beyond child management. Abusive parenting behavior is multi-dimensional, systems-oriented, and skill deficits related to other areas (e.g., interpersonal inhibitions) might influence child-rearing practices.

One exception, by Jeffrey (1976), taught developmental enrichment skills focusing on self-esteem and personal values. In a related study, by Scott, Baer, Christoff & Kelly (1984), skill training broadly covered assertiveness, child management, problem-solving and anger control. In large part, however, omission of this component in parent-training programs leads to training failures, parental noncompliance, and trainers accidentally blame parents for strategy outcomes rather than re-examining the methods themselves. Along these lines, we now briefly examine potential flaws in parenting programs worth correcting if training eventually can benefit the insular mother.

First consider which families are labeled as abusive. Legal definitions of abuse concern perpetrator intentionality or emphasize the level of physical consequences. Those families accessed through this definition may or may not demonstrate insularity effects. Protection by the parents disguises the chronicity, severity and recency of abuse and deflects attention onto more sympathetic problems of the parent such as unemployment or history of mental health.

Second, parenting studies clearly prejudice against gender. Focus primarily is upon mother as insular parent although as caretaking responsibilities broaden, the role of father is equally suspect. Sex of perpetrator may also interact with that of child to produce differential outcomes. Abusive aggressive fathers, for example, may engender more explosive hostility in the offspring whereas aggressive mothers may instill inhibition in offspring (cf . Martin, 1976). Budd & O'Brien (1982) advocated policies for mandatory father involvement at best to support mother's difficult behavior changes and maximize generality of results.

Some methodological issues are of concern as well. Many of the same problems noted in previous reviews of parent-training research (e.g., Johnson & Katz, 1973; Lutzker, McGimsey, McRae & Campbell, 1983) appear in studies involving insular or insular-related parents. First is the serious lack of description of both subjects and procedures. This makes replication and generalization of treatment results difficult, particularly in studies failing to specify their measurement design. Second is that studies neglect to report attrition rates. Parents dropping out of treatment should statistically decrease the overall results of the program, yet efficacy seems at times untouched by this change. Third, specifics about the child population remained unclear. Age group, some history of treatment and nature of parental abuse provided some profile but hardly enough for a general developmental perspective.

As for parental profiles, very little demographic data are presented on them. Details regarding ethnic and cultural group membership, educational background, and whether parents had a history of interpersonal or marital failures all were absent. Details also were scarce for parent trainers. While noting their collegiate level (e.g., freshman, graduate student, etc.), missing was type of training they received prior to being providers.

A final limitation considered is data collection. Recording procedures varied from study to study, and few employed multiple outcome measures. Such types include ongoing objective, direct observations of natural parent-child interactions. Observations range from explicitly timed intervals for spot-checks on behavior to liberal intervals and longer durations of observation. In all cases, recorded are one or many target reactions between parent and child. Most studies, in contrast, employed interview assessments, clinical diagnostics, or relied on referral records from network agencies.

Of the parenting studies examined regarding insularity, few presented enough description to accurately discern effectiveness of training. Statistical significance was frequently the measure of improvement but even these data lacked gravity. Values of p used to calculate significance were high, implying that similar effects might occur by chance or by nonexperimental conditions. Studies employing single-case designs (e.g., reversal design, multiple-baseline design, etc.) showed superior validity and reliability simply because replication of desired effects appeared within the study rather than being a recommendation for future research. Unfortunately the number of single-case design studies was low.

Recommendations for Research Expansion. What can be said about research on insularity? A perusal of the now-extensive literature on parent-training with insular or insular-related parents essentially has focused on two main areas: (1) the effectiveness of parent-training on affecting behavior changes in child, and (2) the content and methods employed in the training itself. Relatively little attention, however, has been focused on the impact of parent training upon the parents themselves. Specifically, what is the effect of parent training programs on the parents' adjustment and functioning and on the family life as a whole? Koegel, Schribman, Britten, Burke & O'Neill (1982) concluded from a review of 30 families that parenting training had superior lasting impact on families compared to that gained from traditional psychotherapy. These results are consistent with those reported by Lovaas, Koegel, Simmons and Long (1973). In both cases, however, positive training outcomes largely derived from self-reports of parents' attitude toward their child's improvement, not from self-reports of benefits to the mother herself.

Does this mean that cessation of a child's misbehavior suffices for parents to feel happy, confident, and readjusted? Does cessation of bad behavior distinguish an effective from ineffective training program? Unfortunately the answer might be yes. Recall that Patterson's coercion hypothesis premised on this very problem: That positively reinforced children who momentarily stopped bad behavior then negatively reinforced their parents for giving that reinforcement. In effect that is what these training results show; that a successful training program was one in which parents regained control over the child by suppressing bad behavior. Outcomes measures do not reflect the number, frequency, or duration of "good" behaviors taught by parents, rather only the number, frequency, and duration of "bad" behaviors suppressed.

Results reported from research reviews thus imply some potential problems for training with insular parents. These include:

1. Parents are more eager to end bad behavior than teach new behavior.

2. Parents do not distinguish between attention for bad and attention for good behavior.

3. Parents lose interest in the program and emphasis is upon their own psychological disturbances.

4. Parents angry in their adult life are unlikely to differentiate between anger toward adults and anger toward their children.

Toward addressing these problems, future parenting research must correct training omissions particularly regarding the mother and father's own dysfunctional behaviors. Specifically, issues to consider include:

1. Methods that help insular parents see that changes in their child's behavior are related to their own efforts.

2. Methods that help increase the parents' confidence in their skill and thus the likelihood that they will use the skills that trainers

teach them. Increased contact time with teaching staff is a beginning but hardly a solution.

3. Methods that, ideally, combine clinic treatment and parent training with enhanced attention to idiographic problems of parents.

4. Methods that address internal family problems such as substance abuse, aggressive disorders, or history of learning and emotional disabilities.

5. Methods that respond to mutliple or family systemic effects such as finances, occupation, housing, and divorce and single parenthood.

6. Methods employing an index by which the parent can measure progress from inception of skills to longterm maintenance of skills. Self-monitoring can include simple recording strategies that naturally fit into daily routines.

7. Methods providing extended support either through identified self-help groups, or by enrolling the parent in state-funded outreach programs to prevent insularity effects from starting or returning.

Applying these strategies largely depends on parenting support groups working in concert with outreach programs. For example, the National Association of Children's Mental Health (NACMH) has many state chapters recruiting parents whose children have a variety of emotional disorders (attentional deficits, hyperactivity, substance abuse). Parents meet monthly to exchange updated information about community agencies and effective clinicians, and to discuss repeated obstacles faced in treatment service delivery. Meetings coordinate with members of adolescent runaway programs and single-parent programs. To the extent NACMH reaches high-risk parents before insularity effects occur, parents can rapidly make behavior changes using the support of peers and backbone of a strong advocacy organization.

Family Violence

Although very young children are frequent targets of physical abuse, abuse is not limited to young children. Preteens and teenagers are experiencing a wide range of violent treatments at the hands of their parents. Victimization also occurs in the reverse. Oppositional teens fed up with unabated abuse retaliate by releasing their aggression on their parents. Violence taken out against parents worsens in proportion to the family disunity and teenager's refusal to stop the terror for fear of again suffering demoralization at the parents' hands. Let us examine more closely this facet of family system defects, first by understanding dynamics of violence toward adolescents, and second, by seeing the negative reciprocal effects it has upon the offspring.

Violence Toward Adolescents

Case reports attesting to child abuse, neglect, and violence examined behaviorally have increased over 30 years (Isaacs, 1982; Wolf, Edwards, Manion & Koverola, 1988). Investigations currently are at advanced levels of isolating, explaining and treating perpetrators engaged in especially severe forms of mistreatment (Barone, Greene & Lutzker, 1986). Together, these developments reflect the rising epidemic of abuse cases warranting not only clinical attention, but that are also becoming unfortunately common in families. Particularly critical are the rising number of reported cases of abuse against teenagers. Toward a better appreciation of the problem, sections cover the extent of this violence epidemiologically, and then the behavioral model of adolescent maltreatment.

Extent of violence toward adolescents. The national survey of officially recognized and reported child maltreatment sponsored by the National Center on Child Abuse and Neglect (Burgdorf, 1980) found that 47% of recognized victims were between the ages of 12 and 17. Data on official reports of child abuse and neglect are collected each year from each individual state by the American Association for Protecting Children, a division of the American Humane Association. These data reveal that adolescents represented about 24% of officially reported victims of maltreatment (American Association of Protecting Children, 1983). While younger children were more likely to be punched, grabbed, slapped, spanked, kicked, bitten, and hit with a fist or an object, teenage children were more likely to be "beat up" and have a knife or gun used against them. Regardless of their size and physical strength, adolescent victims of physical injury rank very high among abuse statistics.

Research findings depicting the relationship between sex and age of adolescents and likelihood of violence and abuse, however, are not always consistent. In a nationwide survey of child abuse, registered reports showed small differences between boys and girls at the younger ages, with boys being slightly more likely to be abused than girls (Gil, 1970). As children grow older, girls are more likely victims of abuse than boys. Gil attributes these results to cultural attitudes regarding child-rearing practices. When children are younger, girls are supposedly more compliant than boys and require less discipline using physical punishment. As children mature sexually, parents become more anxious over daughters' heterosexual relationships. Presumably this anxiety leads to greater restrictions, increased conflict, and more frequent use of physical punishment to ensure parental control. Regarding boys, as they grow older their physical strength increases and parents are less able to exert physical force for fear of retaliation. Also, anxieties about the son's sexual irresponsibility is less intense than for the daughter's. Reverse effects of girls being abused at earlier ages and less abused in later teen years confuse the research literature (e.g., Straus, 1971).

One explanation of parents' use of violence toward teenage children is that they are violent and abusive toward their older children for the same reasons they are violent and abusive toward their younger children. In some instances, abuse of adolescents is an extension of violence that began when the teenager was a young child. A second explanation is provided by Lourie (1977, 1979), who points out that as children grow physically stronger and seek independence, parents may resort to more violent means of control. Another possible factor might be the struggle for independence between adolescents and their parents.

Behavioral model of adolescent maltreatment. Many of these explanations present elegant representations of the multivariate nature of child maltreatment. Traditional models of psychopatholgy focus on parental psychiatric disorders. Socio-cultural models emphasize the role of stress engendered by poverty, unemployment, and educational disadvantage. Social-situational models view child abuse as the result of parental, child, and situational characteristics. But integrative ecological or ecobehavioral models perhaps more operationally than the other approaches draw in variables that are internal and external to maltreatment. Explored are interactions between potentiating factors and compensation factors that increase or decrease the likelihood of maltreatment. Efforts are made to distinguish between enduring and transient factors that differentially affect risk on temporal as well as causative grounds. Factors identified are what the child or parent does that facilitates escalation of conflict or how they have been historically aggressive.

The other advantage of ecobehavioral models is that they can elucidate the process involved in maltreatment. Earlier we considered one of the processes involved: Insularity. Now let us consider some additional process defects fundamental to teenage abuse.

Azar and Siegel (1990) described five broad areas at the root of abusive parental behavior across all periods of childhood. These are listed below and expounded upon behaviorally.

1. *Maladaptive interpretive processes, including unrealistic expectations of children, poor problem solving, and negative interpretations of child behavior.* Parental expectations for adolescent behavior frequently are abstract, very high, and cumulative. Abstract in that the criteria set consists of many overlapping behaviors that are inconsistent directions for the behaviors, and contingencies governing the behavior are inconsistent.

High expectations unrealistically demand mastery of skills that are normally weak or inappropriate for adolescence. Expecting, for instance, a teenager to responsibly coordinate a boy scout or girl scout meeting, assumes a level of intellectual acuity or maturity that most teenagers lack. Failure to coordinate that meeting creates instant conflict instead of parents realizing that the teen is incompetent for this particular challenge.

Cumulative means a perpetual graduation from one unrealistic criterion to a higher criteria without assuring the adolescent's mastery of either criteria. Lack of leadership qualities, for instance, requires starting at a lower step such as following a leader. But impatient parents assuming the child naturally should be a leader might leap over this deficient step and push their teen to run for president of the school student council. Compounding failure upon failure invites opposition.

2. *Poor parenting strategies.* The insular parent was a good example of parenting failures responsible for adolescent delinquency and subsequent substance abuse problems. Treatment initiatives run behaviorally are widely visible in research (e.g., DiGiuseppe, 1988; Rueger & Liberman, 1984; Schellenbach & Guerney, 1987) but they are fraught with shortcomings applied to teenagers. A major obstacle is getting parents into treatment. A second problem is reminding parents

that they are still responsible guardians despite being verbally and physically abused by the teenager or even after they have pursued emancipation for their child.

3. *Poor impulse control.* Anger control is weak or nonexistent for parents who perceive the teenager as invasive upon their lifestyles and destabilizing the family. Intolerance toward a teen's oppositional behavior, however, lies with the parents' problem, not the teenager's. Perfectionistic, highly rigid and synchronized parents dictating their children's lives prevent the most basic form of autonomy. Closed or restricted family systems deny this independence because it threatens to imbalance control in the household and undermine the parent's sacrosanct need for authority.

4. *Poor stress coping.* Demands of busy daily schedules imposed on the average two-family household, let alone upon single parents, are stressful roadblocks to parent-child relationships. Adjusting adult schedules to the energy of an adolescent's schedule requires flexibility in coping with compromises. Parents unwilling to compromise or who negatively react to adjustments discourage open communication with their teens and subsequently parents become upset when that child stops sharing personal needs.

5. *Poor social skills.* There are two reasons that poor social skills are a serious link to teenage delinquency and substance abuse. First is that socially deficient parents overlook early signs of adolescent disintegration or are too afraid of confronting the child lest he or she hate the parent. Second is that social deficits are vicariously contagious around impressionable adolescents. Offspring imitate behavior patterns of their parents. But if imitated behavior is insufficient for societal coping and drug use becomes the remedy for this deficiency, addiction instantly is formed.

Physical abuse during adolescence often goes unreported and is frequently blamed on the adolescent for many deviant behaviors (runaways, truancy, crime, etc.). Patterns of abuse among teenagers are further delineated into seven types. Again, listed below are these types with clarification.

1. *Continuation of abuse occurring in childhood years.* Parental abusers unleashing their corporal punishment upon infants up until preadolescent ages are accustomed to using this discipline. They develop a peculiar immunity against shame or thinking there is

another, more positive approach. Abuse at early ages is highly probable to recur when the child's behavior is verbally more articulate, threatening, and noncompliant.

2. *Maltreatment that occurred in childhood ceased and then began again in adolescence.* Abusing parents who do experience guilt and by seeking therapy or self-discipline cease corporal physical punishment, may re-develop old habits once the child's misbehavior resembles a miniature adult. Maltreatment that disappears and reappears, however, usually is a function of external sources (other spouse, friend, companion, etc.) who interceded the first time and do not do it again or are gone. For instance, divorced parents who rotate raising the teenager during their visitation no longer have the other spouse there to monitor aggressive parenting. Without feedback, aggressive discipline returns in full force.

3. *Escalation of previously used forms of physical punishment.* As indicated in #1 above, episodes of maltreatment during early rearing may continue into periods of rearing teenagers. However, frustrated parents encounter more verbal obstacles from the teens and may escalate their negative discipline, figuring that firmness and harshness are more forceful than empathy and compromise. If yelling alone was sufficient to gain compliance in toddlers, yelling plus threats of physical attack "might be more effective." Of course this reasoning underestimates the integrity of adolescent reactions and ignores the basic principle of punishment: That higher magnitudes of aggression always cause more aggression, *after a period of remission.* Stifled by punishment, angry adolescents may abruptly stop misbehavior in one setting, displacing it in other settings, or resume anger toward the punishing parent at a later time (Deur & Parke, 1970; Engfer & Schneewind, 1982; Parke & Deur, 1972).

4. *Maltreatment that begins in adolescence.* Relatively calm and empathic parents unfortunately are not spared of turning violent. Rising altercations between parent and adolescent may quickly exhaust the repertoire of discipline relied upon during preteen years. Ineffective efforts to plead, reason through logic, and even show authority may leave parents feeling vulnerable, out of control, and defeated. Restoring control, for the sensitive, caring parent, usually involves avoidance of conflict or seeking escape from conflict once it begins. However, avoidance and escape responses frequently come across as aggressive and intimidating in hopes of terminating the argument. A parent who instantly yells when the child refuses to do

homework may not necessarily be angry at that child for academic neglect; the parent yells to immediately *stop, delay or escape from the impending conflict.*

5. *Maltreatment to avoid interspousal conflict.* One unusual form of parental abuse is when physical discipline is used to deflect conflict or anger from another spouse. Timid or passive spouses easily upset by criticism and rejection may attack the teenager with a direct torpedo of aggression so that the child stops misbehaving. The faster misbehavior stops, the faster that spouse prevents the other spouse from insults about incompetent parenting. Addiction families are more prone to maltreatment to avoid interspousal conflict. Enablers keep the household on peaceful ground by arbitrating all disputes with the children and creating the artificial world of happy family.

6. *Maltreatment to adhere to socio-cultural or religious norms.* Many religious cults or even derivations of established religions tinker with the child-discipline realm. Advice is offered on punishing, withholding love, and formation of maturity through guided enforcement of respect for adult authority. In principle all of these socio-cultural and religious guidelines are innocent and seek to eliminate confusion for caring parents. However, actual methods they recommend lack veracity or are prone to aggravate parent-child conflict, if not immediately, then in the very near future. Adherence to these guidelines, frequently, is not even because parents totally agree with the strategies; belief in the philosophy or spiritualism underlying these strategies is the compelling reason to use them. Even after repeated failures, parents refuse dispensing of ineffective methods if it means using scientifically valid methods. Again, the reasons have nothing to do with the methodology. Forfeiture of techniques endorsed by culture or church is like committing hearsay.

7. *Maltreatment that is intergenerationally consistent.* Research evidence is replete with demonstrating that physical abuse occurring in one generation is probable to occur in second and third generations. The reason? Most victims of physical abuse repeat the only discipline they learned growing up in their own parenting strategies. Intergenerational transmission of maltreatment is further thwarted by significant others who marry into the family or other nuclear family members, also abused as a child, who regard the negative discipline as *normal.*

Violence Toward Parents

Adolescents are not only victims of violent attacks in families, they are also offenders. Discussion or reporting of such acts is almost a taboo subject because many parents are ashamed of their own victimization. Parents are afraid that others will blame them for their children's violent behavior. Parents of abusive children are believed to suffer from tremendous anxiety, depression and guilt. Harbin & Madden (1979) examined 15 families identified as having adolescent offenders. All these families were trying desperately to maintain an illusion of family harmony. Parents might occasionally admit to being abused by their children following a particularly aggressive episode, but they denied this assault was continuous. Parents would try endlessly to protect their abusive offspring. This was done in four ways:

1. The families would try to avoid all discussion of the violent episodes.

2. All the family members would attempt to minimize the seriousness of the aggressive behavior.

3. The parents would avoid punishment for the abusive behavior.

4. The families refused to ask for outside help either for themselves or for their child.

Who is violent? Harbin & Maddern (1979) found the majority of children who attack a parent are between the ages of 13 and 24. Researchers agree that sons are slightly more likely to be violent and abusive than daughters. The sons' rates of severe violence against a parent increase with age, whereas for daughters the rates of severe violence decline with age. As far as who gets hit, studies show that mothers are the most likely target of children's aggression (Evans & Warren-Sohlberg, 1988). Why is this the case?

One reason is that attack upon mothers produces less aversive consequences in short-run. Abusing teens figure they are in less danger because the mother is (a) physically inferior to them, (b) aggressively inferior to them, (c) protective of them, and (d) resistant to spreading the bad news to her spouse or extended family. A second mitigating factor is the mother's self-blame. She is tolerant of escalating arguments and even property destruction on the assumption that adolescent aggression is a parenting failure, not abuse. While, scientifically, this may be true, self-blame also precludes asking for help and accepting professional intervention. When abuse explodes into drug using habits in the household, again the veil of denial is raised. The result is that, indirectly, abusing adolescents infer it is appropriate to act this way.

PRIORITIES FOR INTERVENTION

Over the last 20 years research undertaken to investigate treatment effects on adolescent substance abusers has reached similar conclusions. Strategies aimed at achieving sobriety and ensuing changes in societal patterns are difficult unless the adolescents have some, but not all of the prerequisites for a sober lifestyle. Prerequisites usually include awareness of harmful effects of drugs, reasons to overcome peer pressure, and the presence of adult role models at some authority level from whom they can acquire moral guidelines. Establishing these guidelines and assuring minimal prerequisites for informed drug choices requires that there be preventive education at primary levels. *Primary prevention* essentially entails casefinding and training high-risk adolescents before drug use begins. Addicted families naturally comprise the largest class of at-risk offspring. But this group is a minority compared to the macro-level of potentially curious youth dabbling in recreational alcohol and drug use not realizing the dependency possibilities.

Education and prevention at primary levels for adolescents, over adults, is unique in that prevention really means *prevention*. Training programs offered through communities and schools can actually reach students before they ever engage in any chemical use, whereas prevention for adults usually refers to relapse prevention. Because of this early learning, innovative advances in preventive education are especially impressive at the adolescent level. This next section reviews current advances made in primary education, whereas the next section, on treatment, examines secondary and tertiary interventions once drug use or abuse is evident.

Prevention

Primary prevention for adolescents is a sensitive business. Like a science class on creationism versus Darwinism, discussion must delicately take into account the relative ignorance which a student has toward life issues and especially toward experimenting with chemicals. Presenting drug use, misuse and abuse in implosively shocking graphic detail only inspires personal curiosity kept secretive. Shrouded in taboo, persistent interest develops in unveiling the deep mystery of its dark side and experiencing first hand the mind-altering effects. However, taking the opposite extreme poses similar hazards. Presenting drug education in an "above-board" approach, where blatant honesty accompanies explicit testimonies of ex-addicts and actual drug samples are put on visual display, can weaken the seriousness of drug problems and lose its shock value entirely. What, then, is the best approach?

Examined here are options yielding mixed results from repeated application in schools and communities. Options include (a) peer prevention, (b) use of mass media, and (c) health promotion.

Peer Prevention

Peer interaction and influence is a normal, necessary, and healthy part of adolescent development. This natural tendency to rely on peers provides an opportunity to channel that very force toward healthy behavior and the promotion of the survival, maintenance, and growth of the individual. Peer groups have outstanding potential as an effective method for preventing problem behavior because they can readily be tailored to deal with so many of the factors related to stress reduction, building coping skills, and modifying situational constraints. Four generic types of peer programs include: (a) positive peer influence; (b) peer teaching programs; (c) peer counseling and facilitating programs; and (d) peer participation programs.

1. *Positive peer influence.* These programs can help to channel peer pressure in positive directions. They can also help to develop and enhance self-esteem and problem-solving skills. Role-modeled peers assume task of staying drug free and making abstinence a requirement for being popular or member of a group.

2. *Peer teaching programs.* These programs address the need not just for useful information and skills among youth, but also provide youth meaningful roles and real-world responsibilities at a time when youth are increasingly isolated from such roles and responsibilities. Peers voluntarily or by nomination enter into school-sponsored programs, many times in lieu of class electives. Training puts adolescents in semi-adult responsible jobs and in contact with abstinent role models.

3. *Peer counseling and facilitating programs.* These helping programs assist young people in solving problems and coping with some of the challenges with which they are inevitably confronted in modern society. Family problems and problems with friends and school are commonly dealt with by a dyadic group made of peers who offer general experience, their own coping strategies, and empathy while the troubled peer undergoes difficult transitions.

4. *Peer participation programs.* These programs can function to link between the world of peers and the real-world tasks and responsibilities and adult guidance. Much like peer teaching programs, adults volunteer to be a "big brother/big sister" in instructing teens on certain occupational tasks or toward better realizing varieties of enjoyment besides drug use that may be financially unattainable or outside the teen's boundary of experience given their family's limitations.

The growing popularity of peer-group strategies in schools and youth-service programs across the country attests to the appeal of these approaches. One particular approach gaining widespread research support and replicable in many counties is the *peer listening program.* It provides selected students with the information, skill development, and practice to become proficient in the helping relationship. The model which is based on cognitive and affective experiences exposes students to skills necessary to help other students and themselves. Schools essentially reserve a room for peer listeners to take turns being available for "drop-ins." Names of peers are publicized to the student body and school staff. Peer listeners then work with students before or after school, during lunch hours, or during study hall. Peer listeners also are used for new student orientation to make adjustment easier. Peer listeners are used as part of an intervention strategy during a school crisis or for rumor control. When used to facilitate support groups, they can screen or defuse the students' intense feelings on particular emotional topics.

Entering a peer listener program requires a two day training. The first day trainees develop communication and cooperation skills, along with learning basic counseling tactics for removal of emotional barriers from other students. Simple methods of relaxation, of assertiveness, and of problem solving are practiced in role-playing analogues under the watchful supervision of trainers who strongly encourage genuineness and monitor for accuracy. On Day 2 the group exercises teach trainees to understand the dynamics of the following 14 topics:

1. The helping relationship
2. Communication and communicating
3. Developing self-awareness and positive self-esteem
4. Friends and relationships
5. Drugs and society
6. Stress
7. Decision making and problem solving
8. Aspects of getting older
9. Peer pressure, prejudice and put downs
10. Breaking up, divorce, and death and dying
11. Sexual assault
12. Domestic violence and child abuse
13. Suicide
14. Life goals

Use of Mass Media

Peer listening starts right at home, exposing teens to realistic problems that they and their listener experience in similar ways. Television and mass media communicate a similar message but the actors are outside the immediate domestic milieu. However, the impact television actors and the meaning of daytime or nighttime shows can be fundamentally more persuasive than real-life peer advocates. This is because television is the preeminent mass medium among adolescents. The typical American, for instance, spends more time watching television than he will spend at any other single activity, including going to school or interacting with friends (Myerowitz, 1985; Reinhold, 1982; Strasburger, 1990). All this time spent watching television no doubt provides adolescents with many learning opportunities.

Over 30 years ago Cartwright (1949) outlined three stages that a campaign must go through to influence behavior. Television anti-drug campaigns follow similarly. First, to create an appropriate cognitive structure, people must know and understand the message. Second, to create an appropriate motivational structure, people must feel compelled to do something. And third, to create an appropriate action structure, people must know what to do and how it can be done. Television advertisements and shows encapsulating these factors provide the best message structure.

In addition to message structure, other factors that have been emphasized by reviewers (Atkin, 1973, 1978; Wallack, 1981) of the use of mass media for health promotion include:

1. The need for more careful planning of media products, and for more formative evaluation during product development.

2. Program or campaign dissemination issues more pronounced rather than disguised by neon visual effects.

3. The use of multiple channels, including supplementation of media programming with other campaign activities.

4. Audience selectivity and interpersonal communication as mediators of media effects.

5. The need for more frequent and improved summative evaluation.

On analysis, the majority of mass media drug abuse prevention programs have failed to change behavior. One obvious reason for this is that most campaigns literally fail to even reach the audience. Obviously, the campaign cannot affect peoples' behavior if it does not even reach them. Advertisers believe that it requires an average of three exposures for an advertisement to affect purchase behavior (e.g., Hershey, Field, Probst & Theologus, 1982). It probably takes even greater exposure to influence health behavior. Yet most evaluations report the proportion of a surveyed sample who recall seeing *any* ads. Even those studies of purchased counteradvertising drug and alcohol campaigns did not report the proportion of their audience reached by their ads three or more times (e.g., Wallack, 1979). Given the low budgets compared to alcohol and cigarette advertisers, the mediocre effects of these paid counteradvertising campaigns might still be explained by low exposure.

A second major reason for failure of campaigns has been heavy reliance on information and fear messages. As alluded to earlier, teenagers are particularly likely to counterargue against threatening messages. A third problem with anti-drug campaigns is the tendency to be directed to unidentifiable audience segments. Fourth, many past campaigns probably have failed because they were not well disseminated. Airing ads outside of prime time or on non-commercial stations, and then only infrequently, cannot lead to the levels of reach and frequency necessary to ensure adequate exposure.

Obviously there must be successful dissemination of a program before any intended effects can be expected. Primary mediators of successful program dissemination are media "gatekeepers." Television and radio station managers, and newspaper and magazine editors are the most obvious and most proximal examples of gatekeepers. Politicians, trade union representatives, parent-teacher associations, consumer protection groups--all of these are less obvious and more distal, but equally powerful gatekeepers. Media gatekeepers determine what is and is not acceptable for media presentation. As such they are the first that must be convinced of the worth of a media product or campaign if it is ever to be disseminated adequately.

Health Promotion

Antidrug slogans across media airwaves transmit a warning that drug use is harmful and should be avoided at all costs. The *Just Say No* campaign, nationally showcased by former first lady Nancy Reagan, spoke to this cause. Slogans impress the consumer with a vital message but are empty in providing exact behavior substitutes for chemical curiosity. Earlier we mentioned that one alternative was to teach the adolescent consumer productive and viable options against which they can compare the deadly effects of drug allurement. This is what health promotion started at an early age aims to accomplish.

Most definitions of health promotion tend to emphasize variation in illness. Historically, health has been defined as a residual category, that is, as the absence of disease. More recently, definitions such as that of the World Health Organization have a more positive character. This definition emphasizes effective social functioning, adequate role or task performance, realistic personal aspirations, the ability to cope and adapt, and extended longevity (Baranowski, 1981).

Definitions used in health prevention remain even less fully explored. "Health" overlaps considerably with the notion of disease prevention. Thus, health prevention is generally associated with changing particular health practices or health-related behaviors such as smoking, alcohol and drug use, control of stress, diet, and exercise. However, more recently, concepts of health promotion have expanded to include organizational, environmental, and economic interventions designed to support behavior conducive to health. In this way, health promotion is concerned with more than reduction or accretion of specific health-compromising behaviors. It may involve a variety of methods to instigate the adoption of alternative behavior, and it can extend to environmental changes that would serve to support such adoption.

Examples of prevention programs are many. Programs that focus on changes at the larger, impersonal environmental level emphasize awareness, knowledge, motivation, trial behavior, and larger environmental changes. An example of a campaign around smoking, for example, is the community wide *Quit and Win* contest (Pechacek, 1983). The contest encouraged adult smokers to Quit and Win by providing a drawing for a prize (a trip to Disneyworld funded by the local community) to contestants who quit smoking and remained non-smokers throughout the month of January. Adolescents also became involved in this effort through their initiation with *Kwit Smoking This Year.* Adolescents were to tally numbers of interviews with adult participants of the *Quit and Win* contest. The leading adolescent interviewer was recognized and awarded with a 10-speed bicycle.

Educational interventions like *Quit and Win* contest and *Kwit Smoking This Year* are the second modality, and their focus is on changes in the immediate, personal environment of individuals in the community and of targeted subgroups. They include behavioral screening centers and special classes aimed at changing health behavior. The programs for youth tend to be school-based skills training, and behavior change programs.

The next level of health promotion is community-organization programs. This third modality focuses on changes in the social environment through the identification and education of key community leaders, organization of task forces on the overall program, smoking, eating, exercise, and hypertension, and community-initiated projects such as community-wide walks and changes in grocery store food product labeling. On an adolescent level, students in school are elected as health council representatives. They are trained as peer leaders to conduct drug abuse prevention programs and are liaisons to parent-teacher coalitions in the development and implementation stages of new school rules.

Community-based programs tied into the school curricula represent the fourth modality. Initiatives by school systems to upgrade health instruction at primary grade levels have resulted in students receiving more comprehensive background on topics such as disease prevention, nutrition, family health, and consumer health. Among leaders in this movement is the *Michigan Model for Comprehensive School Education.* Let us briefly consider the advancement of this program.

Michigan Model for Comprehensive School Education. This program is a combined effort of seven state agencies--Departments of Education, Public Health, Mental Health, Office of Highway Safety Planning, Commerce, Social Services, and Office of Health and Medical Affairs. It provides 8 to 10 week units each year, Kindergarten through 8th grade, and covers major areas of health education including safety, nutrition, family health, consumer health, community health, growth and development, substance use and abuse, personal health practices, emotional and mental health, and disease control and prevention. The model builds sequentially each year and provides, over the first eight years of schooling, a strong base of positive health-oriented knowledge, attitudes, and skills necessary to maintain health over the child's lifetime.

Table 5 below describes the goals established under each health topic expected for grades K-3 within the comprehensive model. Because health education is considered essential for a balanced school curriculum, skill learning may even supplant regular course requirements and involve grade assignments calculated into a student's overall grade point average. Treated like any other class, students must complete assigned readings, written papers, and verbally participate by expressing opinions that reflect their accurate understanding and application of the tools at home. Frequently parental involvement is requested so the students can receive the needed family support to do the assignments and the social validity to feel the assignments are valuable in the short- and long-run.

Table 5
Michigan Model for Comprehensive School Education Curriculum Goals for Kindergarten through Third Grade: A representative sample

Health Topics and Subheadings

DISEASE PREVENTION AND CONTROL

Characteristics of Disease

1. By the end of third grade, students will distinguish between being "well" and being "ill."
2. By the end of the third grade, students will identify the signs and symptoms of possible illness that should be reported to an adult (e.g., splinters, sore throat, headache, toothache, etc.)
3. By the end of the third grade, students will describe signs and symptoms of common childhood diseases and conditions (e.g., chicken pox, measles, impetigo, head lice, etc.).

Disease Causation

1. By the end of the third grade, students will demonstrate knowledge of causes of illness (e.g., heredity, environment, lifestyle, etc.).
2. By the end of the third grade, students will demonstrate knowledge that germs causing disease are spread in different ways (e..g, people, animals, water, etc.)

Disease Prevention and Control

1. By the end of the third grade, students will exhibit knowledge of ways which prevent diseases from developing (e.g., immunization, good health habits, and knowledge of risk factors.)
2. By the end of third grade, students will demonstrate knowledge of the benefits of early recognition, reporting and prompt treatment of disease.
3. By the end of the third grade, students will demonstrate the relationship between personal health practices and the prevention and control of diseases which affect the health of people.

PERSONAL HEALTH PRACTICES

Dental Health

1. By the end of the third grade, students will demonstrate knowledge of the location and basic function of teeth.
2. By the end of the third grade, students will demonstrate knowledge of how foods affect the health of the teeth and contribute to the formation of plaque.
3. By the end of the third grade, students will apply dental health methods and utensils to the care of their teeth.
4. By the end of the third grade, students will demonstrate knowledge of health services available in a dental office or clinic.
5. By the end of the third grade, students will demonstrate knowledge of the purpose for the use of fluoride in protecting teeth.

Personal Care

1. By the end of the third grade, students will demonstrate knowledge of activities which help promote personal cleanliness and improve appearance.
2. By the end of the third grade, students will demonstrate knowledge of proper clothing selection for various weather conditions.
3. By the end of the third grade, students will demonstrate knowledge of how sleep and rest promotes good health.
4. By the end of the third grade, students will demonstrate knowledge of how regular physical activity promotes good health.

NUTRITION EDUCATION

Foods and Food Groupings

1. By the end of the third grade, students will identify a variety of foods taken from the "Daily Food Guide."
2. By the end of the third grade, students will classify foods according to the "Daily Food Guide."
3. By the end of the third grade, students will recognize the major nutrients.
4. By the end of the third grade, students will recognize that food intake has positive and negative effects on health and growth.

GROWTH AND DEVELOPMENT

Major Body Parts

1. By the end of the third grade, students will identify common body parts by correct name (e.g., arms, legs, stomach, genitals, heart, cells, eyes, and ears, etc.)
2. By the end of the third grade, students will identify simple functions of common body parts (e.g., skin, heart, lungs, uterus, sense organs, etc.).

Origin of Living Things

1. By the end of the third grade, students will demonstrate awareness that all living things come from living things (e.g., all life begins the same way, species reproduce their own kind, etc.).
2. By the end of the third grade, students will demonstrate knowledge that all living things eventually die.
3. By the end of the third grade, students will identify the different ways living beings reproduce themselves (e.g., lower organisms can reproduce by self-diversion, plants come from seeds, some animals reproduce from eggs fertilized outside the mother's body, others reproduce from eggs fertilized inside the mother's body, etc.).

Individual Growth

1. By the end of the third grade, students will identify the major factors which affect physical and social growth (e.g., food, water, climate, habits, family members, self-concept, etc.).
2. By the end of the third grade, students will demonstrate knowledge and acceptance of the different ways a child grows to become unique (e.g., weight, height, and body build, disability, physical appearance, abilities and skills, likes and dislikes, etc.).
3. By the end of the third grade, students will list common differences and similarities of boys and girls (e.g., differences in rate of growth and aging patterns, physical characteristics, similarities in activities, hobbies, interests, feelings, etc.).

FAMILY HEALTH

Types of Families

1. By the end of the third grade, students will demonstrate knowledge of types of families (e.g., one parent, two parents, grandparents, extended and blended families).

Family Roles and Responsibilities

1. By the end of the third grade, students will demonstrate knowledge of the roles within a family.
2. By the end of the third grade, students will identify their contributions and responsibilities as a family member.
3. By the end of the third grade, students will demonstrate knowledge of the support roles of various family members (e.g., parent, grandparent, sibling, a significant other, etc.).

4. By the end of the third grade, students will demonstrate knowledge of how family members contribute to the physical and mental health of each other.

EMOTIONAL AND MENTAL HEALTH

Feelings and Moods

1. By the end of the third grade, students will demonstrate awareness of feelings found in themselves and others.
2. By the end of the third grade, students will accept the fact that it is natural to have a variety of feelings.

Coping

1. By the end of the third grade, students will identify acceptable coping behaviors for a variety of emotions, including the sad feelings that accompany separation and loss.
2. By the end of the third grade, students will identify possible ways that a person can overcome grief caused by death.
3. By the end of the third grade, students will demonstrate the ability to think of alternative solutions to a problem.

Social Health

1. By the end of the third grade, students will identify personal characteristics and behaviors which generally help people develop friendships (e.g., respect for each other, being helpful, sharing, generosity, showing concern, accepting others, open communication).

SUBSTANCE USE AND ABUSE

Substance Use and Abuse

1. By the end of the third grade, students will demonstrate knowledge of the uses of drugs and medicines.
2. By the end of the third grade, students will demonstrate knowledge of factors important to the prevention of poisoning.
3. By the end of the third grade, students will identify the effects of smoking (e.g., immediate and long-term).
4. By the end of the third grade, students will demonstrate knowledge of the consequences of inappropriate use of drugs and medicines.

CONSUMER HEALTH

Health Workers and Agencies

1. By the end of the third grade, students will identify those health workers whose services they might expect to receive.
2. By the end of the third grade, students will demonstrate knowledge of the services provided by community health agencies.

Health Services and Products

1. By the end of the third grade, students will identify factors influencing the purchase of health products.
2. By the end of the third grade, students will demonstrate knowledge of how health products can be used and abused.
3. By the end of the third grade, students will identify sources of reliable information regarding health services and products.

SAFETY AND FIRST AID EDUCATION

Safety and Accident Prevention

1. By the end of the third grade, students will demonstrate knowledge of the methods community workers utilize to help prevent and control accidents and injuries.
2. By the end of the third grade, students will demonstrate knowledge of home safety hazards.
3. By the end of the third grade, students will demonstrate knowledge of school safety practices.
4. By the end of the third grade, students will demonstrate comprehension of fire safety procedures.
5. By the end of the third grade, students will demonstrate knowledge of traffic safety practices.
6. By the end of the third grade, students will demonstrate knowledge of recreation safety practices.

Emergency Readiness

1. By the end of the third grade, students will demonstrate that they can get appropriate help to deal with emergency situations in home, school, and community.
2. By the end of the third grade, students will demonstrate awareness of basic first aid procedures used in emergency situations.

COMMUNITY HEALTH

Community Health Resources

1. By the end of the third grade, students will identify community workers who have responsibility for the public's health.
2. By the end of the third grade, students will identify public health organizations and their services.

Environment and Health

1. By the end of the third grade, students will demonstrate awareness of causes and controls of pollution of air, water, and ground (e.g., sewage, industrial waste, smoke gases, ash, etc.).
2. By the end of the third grade, students will demonstrate knowledge of the relationship between pollution and health.

Adapted from South Central Michigan Substance Abuse Commission (1985). *Adolescent substance abuse services task force report, volume two.* Jackson, MI: South Central Michigan Substance Abuse Commission.

Treatment

This section first considers the state of the art of treatment efficacy for adolescent drug abusers, followed by an analysis of different types of interventions frequently utilized in residential and outpatient programs.

State of the Art

On a national basis, Beschner (1985) reports that very few drug treatment programs are designed specifically to treat adolescents. Only about five percent of treatment facilities in the National Drug and Alcoholism Treatment Utilization Survey (NDATUS) reported adolescents as their main clientele in 1982. In the NDATUS system, which includes 3,018 facilities, about 80% of adolescents are admitted to outpatient, drug-free programs and 11% to residential. Beschner also surveyed adolescent treatment outcome studies. He noted only a few systematic attempts to evaluate which program conditions, settings and methods were most effective with adolescents. The three largest studies reviewed are descriptive rather than controlled and must be viewed with caution. Although some programs report favorable outcomes including reductions in the use of opiates and criminal activities (e.g., Sells & Simpson, 1979), use of marijuana and alcohol were not decreased or even increased.

The Treatment Outcome Prospective Study (TOPS) program was studied by Hubbard, Cavanaugh, Gradock and Rachal (1983). They interviewed 240 adolescents one year after a treatment exposure of at least three months. Large proportions of clients interviewed from outpatient clinics felt their treatment had not helped them to reduce their drug use at all. However, two-thirds of residential program respondents reported that their treatment helped them reduce their drug use. Holland (1983) reported similar findings. She conducted a follow-up study of former residents of a therapeutic community whose mean age was 23 at admission. Her results supported time in treatment as a predictor of improved outcome two years later.

Herrington, Riordan and Jacobson (1981) reported a study of outcome of two different types of adolescent treatments. One group of adolescents was in a mixed unit which included adults and was selected retrospectively. The other group was chosen prospectively for a new unit which treated adolescents. Both were in residential settings. Researchers concluded that the adolescent-only group setting was more effective than the mixed adolescent and adult unit in terms of outcomes such as participation in NA and AA groups, returning to school, likelihood of arrest, and association with non-drug using peers.

Miller and Hess (1986) reviewed numerous controlled studies of residential and nonresidential treatment settings. They pointed out that while inpatient treatment was clearly more expensive, there was no evidence to indicate that it was any more effective than nonresidential types of treatment. They further showed that research studies which they evaluated were methodologically better than the majority of research conducted on alcoholism. Based on their results, identifying the best option for adolescents still remains elusive primarily because adequately designed programs for adolescents are only at the infant level of development, and research capacities to evaluate these new programs are scarce.

Inpatient and Residential Services

Inpatient substance abuse treatment is defined as services offered within a hospital setting under medical supervision. Inpatient care traditionally has included both emergency detoxification services and non-emergency services. In recent years, there has been a movement in the health care field away from the provision of long-term substance abuse services in inpatient settings. While an acute care setting is necessary for detoxification, it is not required clinically, and in fact is the wrong environment for long-term treatment, is not cost effective, and discriminates against individuals who have limited resources to pay for treatment.

One form of inpatient hospitalization is *residential services*. Residential substance abuse treatment is defined as services where the client resides 24 hours per day at the treatment program. Minimum lengths of hospital stays are debatable but research suggests up to 45 days (cf. Feigelman, 1990). Admission to hospital is based on belief that it is imperative to remove the adolescent from the drug-using environment and allow for abstinence under controlled settings before preparing the adolescent for community re-entry. Residential treatment components vary enormously from exclusive focus upon participation at AA or NA meetings to an eclectic foci covering such areas as:

1. Social skills training.

2. Alcohol and drug education, including legal aspects of use and abuse by adolescents.

3. Planned recreation activities focusing on physical fitness training, leisure activities, and other components designed to assist in the development of self-concept.

4. Continuation of the adolescent formal academic education through an agreement with the public education system to accept credits earned by the student while in treatment, or assistance from public education by providing lessons while they are in treatment.

5. Family participation in treatment to include all members of the family system. The family as a whole should be in alcohol and drug education services as well as treatment.

6. Provision of groups as the primary method of therapy including specialized groups for both males and females focusing on issues of substance abuse, incest, rape, physiological concerns, and interpersonal relationships and identity issues.

7. Provision of family therapy as a second level of treatment to focus on substance abuse and relationship issues.

8. Provision of individual therapy on a limited basis to explore issues which are difficult to discuss in a group setting. The utilization of individual therapy should be approached with care, as there is a danger of addressing therapeutic issues which would more appropriately be dealt with in an outpatient setting.

Outpatient Services

Outpatient substance abuse services for adolescents also come in all flavors. Sessions are provided in nonresidential settings and are weekly, biweekly, or follow some intermittent schedule. Two major types of outpatient treatment are the traditional one-hour per week scheduled visit, and the relatively new "intensive" outpatient program requiring client attendance from 3 to 8 hours per day. Intensive outpatient services offer alternatives to residential placement and act as a transition from hospitalization to aftercare programs. Types of services generally provided include individual therapy, group therapy, and family therapy.

Individual Treatment

Trends in individual therapy for adolescent substance abusers reveal a clear shift toward short-term interventions either intensively based on such traditional models as psychodynamic therapy, or using a learning-theory based model. Short-term goals following a behavioral model focus on symptom relief and the construction of new drug-alternative repertoires that have a twofold effect. First, goals aim to strengthen relapse prevention by establishing self-control skills and changes in the drug-prone environment. Second, goals aim to induce the mechanisms allowing newly trained skills to transfer or generalize across different settings, people, and behaviors.

Transfer of skills permits abstinence not only to permeate the family unit and encourage positive sibling and parent-child contact, but also to permeate into other critical settings such as school where it draws reinforcing attention from the same teachers or peers who previously rejected the adolescent. Areas of treatment concentration frequently planned for the adolescent cover *competence of social skills training, anxiety and anger reduction skills, life-skills training* and *control over eating disorders.*

Competence of social skills training. The acquisition of adequate social skills may well play an important role in psychological adjustment and psychosocial development. Basic interpersonal skills are necessary for confident, responsive, and mutually beneficial relationships and are perhaps among the most important skills that an adolescent must learn. Inadequate social skills may cause problems in interpersonal relationships or may interfere with optimal functioning in school, work or recreational situations. More importantly, a lack of social competence may lead to rejection and social isolation.

Acquisition of social skills begins during childhood. By the time individuals become adolescents, they are expected to have established a repertoire of social skills such as those involved in communicating effectively, initiating and maintaining conversations, giving and receiving compliments, asking someone out for a date, denying reasonable requests, and expressing feelings. For the most part, social skills are learned through a combination of imitation and reinforcement. However, development of these skills is dependent upon having the opportunity to observe and practice them.

By far, the most common application of social skills training involves teaching people to be more assertive and expressive of feelings, needs, preferences, and opinions. Assertiveness training focuses on both verbal and nonverbal (paralinguistic) behaviors. Verbal assertive skills involve learning what to say (no-statements, requests, refusals), whereas nonverbal assertive skills include eye contact, loudness of voice, facial expression, distance, and body expression. Assertiveness skills are typically taught using a combination of instruction, modeling, feedback, social reinforcement, and behavioral rehearsal (analogues).

Anxiety and anger reduction skills. Several different techniques have been used to help adolescents cope with anxiety and anger. These techniques fall into two categories: relaxation training and cognitive restructuring. The most widely used relaxation technique is called progressive muscular relaxation and was initially developed by Jacobson (1938). This technique, as it is currently used, involves the systematic tensing and relaxing of specific muscle groups. The main objective of progressive relaxation is to make the patient aware of the presence of even mild tension and to provide a means of eliminating it. The technique is useful in four ways. First, it can be used to generally lower physiological arousal throughout the day. Second, it can be used to respond to specific environmental stressors. Third, it can be used to lower arousal stimulated by drug cues and urges. Fourth, it can be used to eliminate fears or anxiety precipitating needed confrontation with people and situations.

Relaxation offers one effective option. Anxiety reduction strategies that are more cognitive than relaxation deal with reconstructing beliefs. Ellis (e.g., 1962) noted that much anxiety is the result of irrational thinking and has suggested that such problems be solved if changes are made in one's internal dialogues. Internal dialogues consist largely of negative inferences blown out of proportion or impurely derived from lacking the facts of a situation. Without facts, inferred reasons draw from why people have done things in the past, why ever the thinker would do that behavior, and from condemnatory or obligatory beliefs as to why the person should or must do something (e.g., Ruben, in press). Examples of approaches are Rational-Emotive Therapy (RET) or methods supported by the work of Meichenbaum (1972). For example, DiLoreto (1971) taught socially anxious undergraduates to re-evaluate the consequences of their behavior in various social situations and eliminate their irrational thoughts. Results demonstrated thought changes and reaffirmed combined uses of RET and systematic desensitization.

Taken together, relaxation and cognitive restructuring offer an excellent means of reducing anxiety. For anger, similar strategies are applied. Aggression in adolescents continues to be a critically relevant variable in etiology of early drug use, and it can emerge from unresolved anger. Although vast amounts of literature have addressed the topic of aggression, assessment and treatment, the emotional state of anger has frequently been neglected by researchers and clinicians. The scarcity of research concerned with adolescent anger and aggression is somewhat surprising considering the number of theories which implicate anger in the precipitation of aggressive behavior. It has been suggested, for example, that arousal attributed to anger increases the likelihood of aggressive responding and that cognitions and affect associated with anger act as mediators in the relationship between frustration and aggression (Rule & Desdale, 1976).

Anger controlled through cognitive retraining and even construction of self-control skills typically entails a multi-componental approach or "package" of many steps known as *stress inoculation* (Meichenbaum, 1975). Essentially, these strategies describe a combination of self-instruction and modification of cognitions with an emphasis on enhancing skills to deal with predictable stressors. Lichstein, Wagner, Krisak & Steinberg (1987), for instance, devised a self-control program of training modules consisting of (a) relaxation through biofeedback, (b) cognitive restructuring, (c) imagery restructuring, and (d) social skills training. Target training on impulses and urges, likened to addictive urges, required a therapist modeling appropriate anger control steps then imitated by the observing client. Videotaped rehearsals assisted the accuracy and consistency of healthy behaviors, until the subjects developed personal self-instructional (rule-governed) or physical cues alerting them that their self-control efforts were correct.

Feindler (1986; 1987) designed a variation of stress inoculation focusing on emotional and impulsive responding as well as appropriate expressions of anger in an assertive and rational manner. Essentially, high risk adolescents learned to moderate, regulate and prevent anger and aggression, and to implement problem-solving actions in response to provocation. Components of this *art of self-control training* are presented via modeling and role-play strategies. Unlike pioneer programs, precautions are put in place to control competing contingencies that usually undermine an adolescent's progress. Factors addressed include (a) parental involvement or support, (b) residential release requirements, (c) peer norms and culture, (d) severe behavior problems in other areas, (e) involvement in outside activities, (f) other therapeutic goals and objectives, and (g) potential punishments or response costs for uncontrolled anger. Attention also is paid to therapist characteristics germane to working directly with adolescents. Therapists must be (a) people adolescents can identify with, (b) able to show vitality and flexibility with guidelines, and (c) sensitive to interfering parental or sibling problems emerging from a history of family dysfunction.

Life-skills training. Life skills training are general personal and social skills for coping with nondrug use interactions and prosocial influences. As such, training typically utilizes several cognitive-behavioral techniques found to be effective in treating the problems described above. Some of the techniques frequently used include goal setting, cognitive strategies to enhance self-esteem, techniques to resist persuasive (advertising or peer pressure) appeals, techniques for coping with anxiety, and a variety of social skills techniques using modeling, rehearsal, feedback and reinforcement, and extended practice through homework assignments. This prevention approach also describes exact words to use when confronted by drug using peers. Students are taught, for example, how to resist direct interpersonal pressures to smoke, drink or use marijuana. Components of decision making go beyond drug refusal statements to the initiation of new friends, or solicitation of counter-drug discussions with peers.

Control overeating disorders. Shown earlier in the *Etiology* section were behavioral correlates to adolescent alcohol and drug abuse. Crime, sexuality, physical injury represent some, but not all the major behaviors associated with substance abuse or its exacerbation. Eating disorders are another collateral problem. Excessive weight gain (obesity), excessive weight loss (anorexia) or cyclical binging or binge-purge patterns (bulimia) evolve from emotionally ritualistic and physically addictive responses developed over time from social pressure, impulsivity, and absence of alternative healthy repertoires. Although coverage of adolescent eating disorders goes beyond the scope of our present purpose, brief mention should be made of the bulimic cycle because of its strong isomorphism to drug abuse patterns.

Several theoretical models of bulimia nervosa have postulated anxiety due to weight gain as a primary factor in the maintenance and development of the binge-purge cycle. Binge eating assumingly produces anxiety and worry regarding weight gain and purgative behavior, that is, self-induced vomiting or laxative use, is motivated by reduction of such anxiety (Mizes, 1985; Rosen & Leitenberg, 1982). However, anxiety reduction from purging is only one relief mechanism in the response sequence. Also reduced is the aversive or negative physiological arousal evoked by strong urge sensations that resemble drug or alcohol withdrawal symptoms. Relief from withdrawal symptoms may occur either before binging or before purging. Before binging, increased cravings for drugs (e.g., elevated heart rate, increased peripheral vasomotor response and skin temperature, etc.) or sensations resembling that craving may prompt rapid food intake. Consummatory responses instantly lower autonomic or other bodily elevation. After binging, increased heart rate, nausea, or painful stimulation, again resembling drug or alcohol withdrawal, may produce avoidance and escape responses in the form of purging.

In the following case study, the author treated a recovering alcoholic who turned bulimic.

Case study: Systems intervention upon multiple response sequences in the case of bulimarexia. The goal of this study was to treat a young 18 year old high school female (5'6"; 115 lbs) whose history of binge-purging ranged from 2 to 5 years and usually involved snacks and fast foods. Intermittent diets, irregular eating habits, occasional starvation and acute history of cannabis and alcohol abuse strengthened bulimic tendency.

Target behavior. Binge-purge episodes were defined as two multiple-response sequences occurring under three different settings. The first sequence (S1) included (R1) touching face or hair, (R2) overt statements to self or others about body size, and (R3) overt statements to self or others about weight, food, etc. The second sequence (S2) included (R1) touching stomach or middle torso, (R2) overt statements to self or others about body size, and (R3) pressing hands to stomach either to vomit or elicit gastric juices.

Design and recording. The study employed a reversal design. Settings included in the shower, kitchen, and school. Measurement of response sequences involved both self-monitoring and analogues procedures. Also measured was compliance to homework assignments, using food box-tops, purchase seals, and grocery receipts. Grocery receipts not only verified targeted foods purchased, but also revealed "bootleg" or unauthorized foods bought during her only weekly shopping trip. Her work and school schedule and unreliable transportation discouraged visits to the store outside of this weekly grocery trip.

Baseline. Collection of data was regarding functional and history of bulimic episodes including that of antecedent and consequent events, medical contingencies, and setting events. Enactment analogues further enabled data for assessment of response patterns.

Self-monitoring plus overcorrection (SMO). Self-monitoring and overcorrection began under all three settings. Client recorded instances of S1 and S2. Overcorrection involved cleaning or otherwise reversing statements and actions made along each sequence. For example, in S1, touching face or hair, client had to then wash her face, and force her hands by her side for one minute. For negative statements, client had to instantly boast to nearby person or to herself in mirror as to how good she looked or felt. Opposite replies would last up to 1 to 2 minutes.

Baseline. This step was a return to pre-intervention conditions.

SMO + exposure plus response prevention (ERP). Exposure plus response prevention (Leitenberg, Gross, Peterson & Rosen, 1984) involved deliberately overeating until the client felt an urge to vomit. Then she prevented this opportunity to vomit by waiting in a (nonvomit) room for 20 minutes, increasing the duration by 5 minutes until the time reached 30 minutes. ERP was applied to each response in S1 and only to the first response (R1) of S2.

Baseline. Contingencies were withdrawn for the response sequences, although client was not explicitly instructed to binge-purge.

Food regularity. This step established a regular daily eating pattern for breakfast, lunch and dinner, plus food decisions for social eating.

Results. The frequency of multiple response sequences and responses within each sequence decreased mainly as a function of SMO + ERP. The near zero level of vomiting (R3) in S2 sharply contrasted to the marginal changes during SMO alone. However, food regularity apparently continued this normal eating pattern as compared to Baseline levels. Further, the introduction of SMO and re-introduction of SMO (+ ERP) led to reductions of 50% to 60% in the frequencies of S1 and S2, and an almost 80% decrement in pressing hands to stomach (R3 of S2).

These results demonstrated two major changes. First, treatment effects upon the first response (in S1) influenced reductions in two sequential responses (R2 and R3). In fact, each multiple response in S2 decreased more significantly than in S1. Second, treatment effects upon each response in S2 led to decreases in the entire sequence. Findings directly support theories of Kantor (1970) and Kazdin (1985) that behaviors are fundamentally interactive and cannot be reduced to causal units. Clusters of interactive behavior further mutually and reciprocally affect one another, so that as changes occur in one target behavior, these changes have broad or specific consequences for other behaviors. Bulimic patterns, formed from her drug using patterns, finally were eliminated.

Group Therapy

Group therapy offers uniquely peer-supported input on social, interpersonal and biological problems. Insight shared among participants identifies with the teens' world view of himself and the pressures surrounding his drug-prevention struggles. Family hardships, whether from emotional or physical abuse, or ancestrally related to drug using parents or grandparents, are openly expressed in a compassionate forum that is guided by a therapist or nominated client leader. Groups prescribe different solutions, or simply allow an exchange of ideas, but ultimately there are concrete benefits gained from group therapy. Let us briefly consider these benefits and then understand how one type of group therapy, run behaviorally, can maximize these benefits.

Function of groups. Bratter (1989) identifies four curative and crucial functions which provide the necessary conditions to help adolescents escape from pharmacological bondage. These include:

1. The group can serve as rational restraining force for adolescents who elect to engage in potentially dangerous and self-destructive, drug-related behavior. Messages sent by the therapist may deflect their self-injurious ends and force reconsideration of their means.

2. The group collectively learns how to help everyone begin to identify negative attitudes in social contacts, how to avoid placing oneself in a no-win situation, and how to unlearn being dependent on mind-altering psychoactive substances.

3. The group becomes a corrective emotional experience. Adolescent members learn how to care responsibly for each other as persons rather than as objects who can be manipulated to gratify narcissistic needs.

4. The group becomes a caring community. Interpersonal weaknesses are tested and shyness eliminated, frequently leading to extramural relationships and equally leading to disclosure of internal feelings toward specific adolescent members.

Behavioral group therapy. Early studies of behavioral techniques in group therapy focused on the group process. It was felt that, by using operant techniques to increase group participation, conventional group therapy techniques and discussions could be enhanced. Recently, however, behavior modifiers have shifted focus to the content of the group itself and the goals each member aspires to reach. Success of behavioral group interventions with drug abusing adolescents are the exception. Most studies report using traditional peer counseling groups following the twelve steps of Alcoholics Anonymous. However, the most comprehensive behavioral treatment program for hard-core adolescent and young adult drug abusers has been developed by Cheek (1972). Cheek developed a self-control treatment teaching clients anxiety management via relaxation and systematic desensitization, assertiveness skills, problem solving skills, and positive self-imagery. Data obtained from this population indicated that this treatment was more effective than traditional group approaches to the problem. In current practice, behavioral group techniques remain quite similar to those used with adults. The majority of techniques fall under the categories of:

1. *Modeling.* Youths act out scripts which demonstrate appropriate behaviors in problem situations, while other group members observe and summarize the main points of the script.

2. *Behavior Rehearsal.* Sequence of training involves (a) instructions (from therapist or other group members), (b) modeling of appropriate behavior, (c) client rehearsal of new behavior, and (d) feedback from other group members on the client's performance.

3. *Structured Exercises.* A systematic series of logical steps enabling development and feedback of behavior in small units of learning. Tailored, in part, after the self-paced individualized education method, this procedure keeps adolescents attentive to tasks and allows rapid acquisition of new material.

4. *The Buddy System.* A method used to enhance transfer of skills from the group to the natural environment is pairing up each group member with another member or "buddy" who can monitor, teach, and reinforce newly learned behaviors. Employing a buddy system in groups can also facilitate communication and rapid acquisition of difficult social skills.

5. *Peer Counseling.* Similar in function to the buddy system, nominated or designated high school students make themselves available as a "sponsor" or listening ear to new group members struggling with behavior change. Empathic acceptance of the member's frustrations is coupled with advice on following strategy discussed in group therapy and which is specifically appropriate for that member.

Family Therapy

Family therapy assembles the entire family unit or selective members together for a closer inspection of the anatomy of presenting symptoms of adolescent drug users. Purposes of having the family meet on account of one troubled member are similar to family therapy for spousal alcoholism. First, open and honest communication begins regarding the problems, effects upon family members, and consensual objectives for recovery. Second, therapy affords the adolescent a rare opportunity for personal expression without parental retaliation or punishment. Third, spousal resentment must first pass through the therapist who mediates frustrations and can distill aggression into meaningful feelings and productive options. Finally, strategies structured by the therapist are for the entire family to participate in toward making recovery a group effort.

Though principally used for these reasons, family therapies differ greatly depending on therapist orientation, types of related behavior problems, and nature of drug abuse. Among the twelve common approaches are:

1. Psychodynamic family therapy
2. Experiential family therapy
3. Communication family therapy
4. Behavioral family therapy
5. Strategic family therapy
6. Structural family therapy
7. Family systems approach
8. Problem-centered systems family therapy
9. Contextual family therapy
10. Functional family therapy
11. Integrative family therapy
12. Intergenerational (extended family) family therapy

Examined thus far in this book have been variations of systems and contextual family therapies. For now, then, let us turn to an approach nicely integrating behavioral and systems methods, namely, the *functional family therapy approach.*

Functional family therapy . Functional family therapy (FFT) is developed for treating juvenile delinquency. It emphasizes that family therapy does not occur in a vacuum, nor can it by itself modify all the factors that influence delinquent behavior. So, while FFT treats the family as an interdependent unit, it also formally considers extrafamilial factors in both assessment and treatment planning. For example, a learning disabled adolescent's verbal aggression in school may in part result from the adolescent's frustrations with an inappropriate classroom placement. Integrating a focus on school with family therapy covers a representative sample of influences upon the adolescent. However, the individual focus is not lost. The values, needs, and behaviors of each individual family member relate to the global family patterns. Resources each can provide or lack make up the total constellation. Phases of intervention follow a stepwise format from assessment to generalization. But the major goal throughout all phases is reconstructing a positive role for the abusing adolescent to receive approval or at least be given opportunities for approval.

Alternative Care

Besides outpatient, inpatient, and residential options, there are newer options arising on the treatment scene. Lately insurance mandates such as DRGs and cost-containment of health care require an alternative benefit plan that reduces length of hospitalization and reduces numbers of outpatient visits. Even trends in mental health management (HMOs, PPOs) of limiting outpatient benefits to 20 sessions a year fall short of cost-containment goals.

The reasons are twofold. First, therapy strategies are uncontrollable, diverse and usually nonmeasurable other than reports of progress or case termination. Second, even demands for short-term therapy or limited inpatient stay, do not prevent "revolving-door" or constant duplication of services once the benefit has expired. For example, clients limited to 20 outpatient sessions per year may exhaust these near year end, but *it doesn't guarantee therapy is over or that therapy was effective.* Consequently clients receive a renewal of another batch of 20 sessions per annum and continue therapy until the next renewal is possible.

Health care services caught in this bind are looking for an alternative to comprehensive care. This is particularly true for the difficult drug abusing or severely dysfunctional adolescent. One such alternative is currently underway by the author regarding an eleven-year-old female with a chronic oppositional behavior history, raised in a physically abusive environment. Her parents are adult children of alcoholics and she has been in and out of institutions for the last 5 years. This innovative program is called *Domestic Training Intervention (DTI).*

Domestic training intervention (DTI). The purpose of Domestic Training Intervention (DTI) is providing alternative psychiatric care directly in the natural environment in response to four goals: (a) to prevent repeated inpatient hospitalizations required in last 5 years since child left abusive father's care; (b) to prevent recidivism of severe maladaptive behavior that primarily and nearly exclusively occurs within the household setting; (c) to provide critical training resources unavailable through family unit and learnable only through patient's regular adjustment; and (d) to enhance structured behavioral management of maladaptive deficient and excessive behaviors beyond outpatient therapy. Repeated outpatient and inpatient treatment failures dictate an alternative method allowing the most comprehensive yet least restrictive learning opportunities.

DTI proposes in-house one-on-one training provided by behavioral technicians (BTs) who follow prescribed curricula identified through team meetings with the supervising psychologist, called the DTI Coordinator. Skills areas designated by the curricula are taught using behavioral procedures approved on Levels I and II under the Department of Mental Health Ethics Review Board.

Structure of DTI (providers). There are two levels of reimbursed providers. First is the DTI coordinator (author) responsible for (a) development of program goals, (b) development and supervision of behavioral interventions, (c) recruitment and scheduling of BTs for in-house training, and (d) inservice training and preparation of BTs for accurate and consistent in-house applications.

Second level of providers are Behavioral Technicians (BTs). BTs are juniors or seniors (undergraduates) or graduates majoring or minoring in child development, psychology, or special education (emotional impairment, learning disabilities, developmental disabilities), educated in behavioral interventions or earning enough prerequisites to receive instructions on procedures through inservices with the DTI coordinator. Recruitment of BTs expected through local university departments. Responsibilities of DTs include: (a) commitment of 5-hour in-house training at the patient's home; (b) compliance with procedures for program curricula and data recording methods; (c) reporting of unusual incidents to parent and DTI coordinator; (d) notifying DTI coordinator of absence within 24 hours of scheduled time and arranging for replacement (already approved BTs) for that shift, and (d) attending supervision/inservice training on behavioral methods for home application. Number of BTs is expected to be 4 , maximum, allowing for substitution.

Time periods. Estimated time shifts include the following:

Weekdays (Monday through Friday)
During School Year

Shift 1: 2:30 pm to 8:30 pm (6 hrs)

On Weekends, Vacation Days or Summer

Shift 1: 8:30am to 2:30pm (6 hrs)

Shift 2: 2:30pm to 8:30pm (6 hrs)

One-Two hours a week for supervision/Training

Individualized Goals and Interventions. Training goals follow three behavioral categories including (1) interpersonal communication skills, (2) family management skills, (3) homework completion skills. A fourth category targeted for parents/sibling is (4) family responses. Behavioral criteria and their respective interventions are listed under each category. All interventions are repeated daily until target behavior meets criteria as described below. Methods used are variations of elementary discrimination training/reinforcement plus overcorrection and extinction.

Interpersonal Communication Skills

1. Listening skills
    a. Look at person talking
    b. Restate words or phrases
    c. Ask questions
    d. Add statement of feeling

Interventions: Cue training plus imitation and modeling. Technician displays appropriate behavior, requesting imitation, plus prompting kind remarks from speaker as reinforcer. Skills built in chain, with each response shaped separately and then in sequence. Behaviors must occur in sequence (a) on 10 consecutive occasions and then (b) for ten consecutive observational days to meet criteria.

2. Delay of needs
   a. Accept refusals when given
   b. Engage in incompatible behavior (behavior opposite to desired response)
   c. Delay repeating request for 20 mn +

Interventions: Each behavior trained separately. After refusal given, technician prompts statements accepting refusal. Imitation follows. Choice then offered of alternative, competing behaviors, selected by client. Once chosen, activity continued for 20 minutes plus. Reinforcer for incompatible behaviors is opportunity to make request for need. Skills built in chain, with each response taught separately and then in sequence. Behaviors must occur in sequence (a) on 10 consecutive occasions and then (b) for ten consecutive observational days to meet criteria.

3. Anger control
   a. Interruption of anger by muscular relaxation
   b. Reduced speed of motion
   c. No words said for 5 minutes
   d. After 5 minutes, one assertive statement made about feelings
   e. Engage in incompatible behavior for 20 minutes +
   f. Statements aloud that it is not "big deal"

Interventions: Series of behaviors taught separately. Muscular relaxation shown when becoming upset. Technicians interrupt rising anger at onset of tantrum, when profanity begins. Relaxation prompted, along with prompts for slowing movement. Escorted out of contact with person angry at. Prompts for no replies, reinforced by opportunity to engage in desired activity with technician. Incompatible behavior lasting 20 minutes. Prompts and imitation for anger-dismissal statements. Should tantrums occur, interruption of it includes (a) removal of other party from room, (b) isolation of child in room alone, without breakable or self-injurious objects, (c) immediate opportunity for desirable competing behaviors once tantrum subsides. Cessation of behavior followed with opportunity for new behavior + reinforcer. Behaviors must occur in sequence (a) on 10 consecutive occasions and then (b) for ten consecutive observational days to meet criteria.

4. Requests for help
   a. Ask for family member
   b. Describe parts of problem or need in low voice, without blaming or escalation
   c. Clarify parts of need in case person confused
   d. Thank person before and after help given

Interventions: Series of behaviors taught separately. Client prompted to ask family member for assistance. Modeled words are imitated, or correction made of words clients uses. Blaming, anger or escalation requires repetition of request in low voice. Requested person only will listen when client speaks appropriately. Prompt for client to clarify helper's understanding. Prompt for thank you before request met. Fulfillment of request is reinforcer. Behaviors must occur in sequence (a) on 10 consecutive occasions and then (b) for ten consecutive observational days to meet criteria.

5. Sharing skills
   a. Ask family member (or friend) to share task/game
   b. Describe roles each will take
   c. Stick with designated roles for 15 mn +
   d. Positive remarks made to family member/friend
   e. Describe in low tone if problem arises and solution wanted
   f. Thank person for sharing

Interventions: Series of behaviors taught separately. Prompt client to ask family member or friend on task or game lasting short time (15 mn+). Modeled and prompted to describe how each will do it, or accept ideas from family member/friend. Food or activity reward made immediately contingent upon uninterrupted sharing for time, positive remarks prompted toward helper and thank you given for helping. If problem, client must describe it in low tone without escalating. Anger escalation treated two ways. First time, opportunity for correction given. Second time, shared activity terminated, with helper receiving reward only. Behaviors must occur in sequence (a) on 10 consecutive occasions and then (b) for ten consecutive observational days to meet criteria.

6. Correspondence between actions and words
   a. Tell family member of chores will do in next two hours +
   b. Tasks attempted, and approximations of completion

c. After time period, describe to family member tasks done or approximations thereof
d. Steps a-c apply to being told tasks to do and saying them aloud to family member

Interventions: Series of behaviors taught separately. Prompt client to name chores or tasks able to do in short 2-hour interval. Told to family member. Praise by technician for every approximation toward completion of each task. When done or time expired, client reports progress to client member, who offers praise. No criticism given on inaccuracy of the task completed. Amount of tasks or behaviors within tasks completed under time limit can earn opportunity for brief rewarding activity. Behaviors must occur in sequence (a) on 10 consecutive occasions and then (b) for ten consecutive observational days to meet criteria.

Family Responsibility Skills:

1. Follow instructions
   a. Restate basic chore or task
   b. Begin action within 5 minutes of restatement
   c. Ask questions if confused
   d. Stay on-task for 10 mn or until task done
   e. Ask family member to check task/chore when done
   f. Offer to help with other tasks/chores

Interventions: Series of behaviors taught separately. Prompted to rephrase request made in low voice using same words as instructor. If escalation, behavior ignored using extinction + selective attention. Once escalation subsides, prompted again to rephrase request, followed by doing the request. Praise given for remaining on-task for 10 mn or until task done (before 10 mn). Prompted to ask same family member for inspection. If errors found, correction made. Escalation or aggressive blaming also ignored. Once subsides, correction made. Once behavior subsides, client starts all over (step a) and begins overcorrection (does steps a-f, plus must do another task immediately afterwards, delaying reinforcer). Behaviors must occur in sequence (a) on 10 consecutive occasions and then (b) for ten consecutive observational days to meet criteria. Daily chores split up between all siblings can follow this procedure. Different chores will require minor revisions in the format.

2. Volunteer for task assignment
    a. Ask family member if need help on anything
    b. If no, tell them to interrupt if they want something
    c. If yes, agree to do it for 10 mn period of time

Interventions: Series of behaviors taught separately. Prompted to ask family member at different intervals of day if client can help that person with anything. Praise for correct phrasing without sarcasm. If no, prompted to incompatible behavior, away from family member to prevent attention-seeking reactions. If yes, prompted to tell family member help is only for 10 minutes. After completion, client prompted to thank family member. Failure at any step requires repetition of steps plus overcorrection. Escalation warrants extinction + reinforcement schedule as before. Behaviors must occur in sequence (a) on 10 consecutive occasions and then (b) for ten consecutive observational days to meet criteria.

Homework Completion Skills:

1. Describe activities in class
    a. Tell family member material covered in each class (5-10 mn)
    b. Answer question asked by family member, without anger
    c. Agree to display or review material if member is curious
    d. Thank family member for listening

Interventions: Prompted to tell older family member about each class for a minimum of 5 minutes. Answers guided to be specific and not accusatory or digressive. Prompted to show family member materials from class. After discussion, prompted to thank listener, followed by opportunity for reinforcing activity either alone or with that family member. Behaviors must occur in sequence (a) on 10 consecutive occasions and then (b) for ten consecutive observational days to meet criteria.

2. Display notes taken in classes
    a. See #1 above
    b. Class materials shown must include notes taken in at least courses, per day. Notes cover 1-2 pages, decipherable, and explained to family member
    c. Answer questions asked about notes

Interventions: Same intervention as #1 above.

3. Completion of assigned work.
   a. Designate 30 mn to 1 hr per day for homework
   b. On-task for 10-15 mn intervals
   c. Ask questions of family members about homework
   d. Tell family member thank you
   e. At end of time, show completed or approximations of work to family member for correction
   f. Make correction given back
   g. Thank family member giving corrections

Interventions: Series of behaviors taught separately. Prompted to allot homework time each day, same time. Homework begins before snack. On-task (15 mn or smaller intervals for starter) given food rewards/attention after interval expires. New interval begins immediately and method repeated (i.e., subsequent intervals begin/end/reward) until homework done. Prompted to show homework for feedback. Prompted to say thank you, plus on-task for correction. When corrected, given back to family member with another "thank you." Escalation during homework or toward family member requires extinction. Behaviors must occur in sequence (a) on 10 consecutive occasions and then (b) for ten consecutive observational days to meet criteria.

Family Responses:

1. Make clear precise verbal statements
2. Consistency between verbal and physical statements
3. Positive statements for appropriate behaviors
4. Ignore minor disruptions
5. Avoid scolding or yelling or provocations
6. Use quiet, steady voice in normal interactions
7. No acceptance of compensatory apologies

Interventions: Each of these steps encouraged of each family member although using less formal procedures. Reminders made each time angry, aggressive, or provoking remarks made. Technician requests family member to try alternative behavior (listed above), followed by client consenting to their requests. If family members refuse these positive alternatives, permission will be obtained from client's mother to establish procedure for that family member (including for the mother).

Data Recording. Data collection is critical to documentation of behavior change and overall progress. Strategies used for recording are conventional in most behavior modification and intervention programs and consist of *continuous recording, event recording, duration recording, time-sampling, sequence recording,* and variations thereof.

Aftercare: Generalization of Behavior

Aftercare services are those efforts designed for adolescents who are no longer in a formal treatment setting yet require contact with professionals as well as their peers who can provide support in maintaining an alcohol and drug free lifestyle. Many aftercare providers rely on utilization of Alcoholics Anonymous-type support groups for this type of care. Recent research, however, suggests that efforts to better define and evaluate various methods of relapse prevention can result in improvements in treatment outcome.

Litman (1980) reviewed traditional and current approaches to relapse in alcoholism. Noting that 33 to 66% of patients relapse, she expressed concern that the relapse phenomena had not been considered fully. Litman pointed out that psychological models of relapse typically consider the relationship between environmental events and individual coping strategies. However, rarely are changes infused into environmental events as much as they are into the recovering person. As a result, unchanged events threaten the stability of abstinence and can cause recidivism within months after hospital discharge or completion of outpatient therapy. Catalano and Hawkins (1985) identified seven factors strongly jeopardizing abstinence, including:

1. Absence of strong prosocial interpersonal network, including family and friends.

2. Pressure to use drugs from drug-using peers and family.

3. Isolation.

4. Lack of productive work or school roles.

5. Lack of involvement in active leisure or recreational activities.

6. Negative emotional states.

7. Physical discomfort.

High risk of relapse no doubt discourages parents wondering if treatment of any sort is really viable. The answer lies not with how good the program is, but how well the program prepares the adolescent for continuity of progress outside of treatment. Most aftercare programs neglect to incorporate specific tactics allowing for transfer of skills from training environment (hospital, clinic, etc.) to the natural environment. Generalization of skills is by no means a new topic (e.g., Stokes & Baer, 1977). But agencies and many service providers in direct contact with adolescents are just uninformed, misinformed, or omit this crucial component in training. Because there are many unknown variables which can affect adolescents once training ends, specific strategies calculated to anticipate those "unknowns" must be part of therapy.

Stokes and Osnes (1989) nicely describe the critical steps of generalization training necessary for programmed skills to be applied in natural settings. The categories of steps include:

A. *Exploit current functional contingencies:*

1. Contact natural consequences.
2. Recruit natural consequences.
3. Modify maladaptive consequences.
4. Reinforce occurrences of generalization.

B. *Train diversely:*

1. Use sufficient stimulus exemplars.
2. Use sufficient response exemplars.
3. Make antecedents less discriminable.
4. Make consequences less discriminable.

C. *Incorporate functional mediators:*

1. Incorporate common salient physical stimuli.
2. Incorporate common salient social stimuli.
3. Incorporate self-mediated physical stimuli.
4. Incorporate self-mediated verbal and covert stimuli.

Setting up skill transfer steps by simplifying the environment so the adolescent knows exactly what to do and how to do it is a quantum leap toward relapse prevention. This supplies adolescents with immediate behavior choices, easier access to positive consequences (reinforcers), and prompts or reminders of ways to achieve the consequences. Behavior choices occur any time the adolescent faces drug cues and drug urges or experiences physiologic sensations reminiscent of cravings or withdrawal. Timing of these experiences is never entirely predictable since there are so many stimuli--exact and similar--confronting each peer interaction, each new setting, and each difficulty encountered in a day. For this reason, generalization represents a *continuous, not a discrete* relationship between environment and behavior (Ruben & Ruben, 1987; 1989). No one skill is appropriate for one single setting. Programming skill transfer thus requires a sophisticated effort to teach adolescents coping skills *across all settings, including skills in adaptation for settings expected in his lifetime.* In this way, drug prevention and relapse prevention really can give a second chance to a young adult.

REFERENCES

American Association for Protecting Children. (1987). *Highlights of official child neglect and abuse reporting, 1986.* Denver, CO: American Humane Association.

Anglin, M.D. (1988). Ethnic differences in narcotic addictions: Characteristics of Chicano and Anglo methadone maintenance clients. *International Journal of the Addictions,* 23, 4-12.

Atkin, C.K. (1973). Instrumental utilities and information seeking. In P. Clark (Ed.). *New models for mass communication research.* Beverly Hills, CA: Sage Publications.

Atkin, C.K. (1978). Effects of drug commercials on young viewers. *Journal of Communication,* 28, 71-96.

Azar, S.T., Barnes, K.T. & Twentyman, C.T. (1988). Developmental outcomes in physically abused children: Consequences of parental abuse or the effects of a more general breakdown in caregiving behaviors? *The Behavior Therapist,* 11, 27-32.

Azar, S.T. & Siegel, B.R. (1990). Behavioral treatment of child abuse: A developmental perspective. *Behavior Modification,* 14, 279-300.

Association for Advancement of Health Education (1988). *National adolescent student health survey.* Unpublished data.

Baranowski, T. (1981). Toward the definition of concepts of health and disease, wellness and illness. *Health Values,* 5, 246-256.

Barone, V.J., Green, B.F. & Lutzker, J.R. (1986). Home safety with families being treated for child abuse and neglect. *Behavior Modification,* 10, 93-114.

Bell, C. (1987). Preventative strategies for dealing with violence among blacks. *Community Mental Health Journal,* 23, 217-227.

Bass, J.L., Gallagher, S.S. & Mehta, K.A. (1985). Injuries to adolescents and young adults. *Pediatrics in Clinics of North America*, 32, 31.

Becker, T.M., Stone, K.M. & Alexander, E.R. (1987). Genital human papillomavirus infection. *Obstetrics & Gynecology in Clinics of North America*, 14, 389-396.

Beschner, G. (1985). The problem of adolescent drug abuse: An introduction to intervention strategies. In A. Friedman & G. Beschner (Eds.). *Treatment services for adolescent substance abusers*. (DDHS Publication No. ADM 85-1342). Washington, D.C.: U.S. Government Printing Office.

Boger, R., Richter, R., Kuretz, R., & Haas, B. (1986). Perinatal positive parenting: A follow-up evaluation. *Infant Mental Health Journal*, 7, 132-145.

Bowker, L.H., & Klein, M.W. (1983). The etiology of female juvenile delinquency gang activities. *Adolescence*, 15, 509-518.

Belsky, J., Robins, E. & Gamble, W. (1984). The determinants of parental competence: Toward a contextual theory. In M. Lewis (Ed.). *Beyond the dyad*. NY: Plenum.

Bratter, T.E. (1989). Group psychotherapy with alcohol and drug addicted adolescents: Special clinical concerns and challenges. In F.J.C. Azima & L.H. Richmond (Eds.). *Adolescent group psychotherapy*. CT: International Universities Press, Inc., (pp. 163-189).

Budd, K.S. & O'Brien, T.P. (1982). Father involvement in behavioral parent training: An area in need of research. *The Behavior Therapist*, 5, 85-89.

Burgdorf, K. (1980). *Recognition and reporting of child maltreatment*. Rockville, MD: Westat.

Campbell, A. (1987). Self-definition by rejection: The case of the gang girls. *Social Problems*, 34, 451-466.

Cartwright, D. (1949). Some principles of mass communication: Selected findings of research on the sale of United States war bonds. *Human Relations*, 11, 253-267.

Catalano, R. & Hawkins, D. (1985). Project skills: Preliminary results from a theoretically based aftercare experiment. In R. Ashery (Ed.). *Progress in the development of cost-effective treatment for drug abusers.* Washington, D.C.: Government Printing Office.

Cates, W. (1987). Epidemiology and control of sexually transmitted diseases: Strategic evolution. *Infectious Diseases in Clinics of North America,* 1, 1-23.

Cheek, F.E. (1972). *Behavior modification training program.* Princeton, NJ: New Jersey NeuroPsychiatric Institute.

Clark, W. & Midanik, L. (1982). Alcohol use and alcohol problems among U.S. adults: Results of the 1979 national survey. In National Institute on Alcohol Abuse and Alcoholism, *Alcohol consumption and related problems.* Alcohol and Health Monograph No. 1. Washington, D.C.: U.S. Government Printing Office (pp. 3-52).

Crockenberg, S.B. (1981). Infant irritability, mother responsiveness, and social support influences on the security of infant-mother attachment. *Child Development,* 52, 857-865.

Crockenberg, S.B. (1986). Professional support for adolescent mothers: Who gives it, how adolescent mothers evaluate it, and what they would prefer. *Infant Mental Health Journal,* 7, 49-58.

Crockenberg, S.B. (1988). Social support and parenting. In H.E. Fitzgerald, B.M. Lester & M. Yogman (Eds.). *Theory and research in behavioral pediatrics.* NY: Plenum.

Crockenberg, S.B. & McCluskey, K. (1986a). Change in maternal behavior during the baby's first year of life. *Child Development,* 57, 746-753.

Crockenberg, S.B. & McCluskey, K. (1986b). Predicting infant attachment from early and current maternal behavior. Paper presented at the biennial meeting of the Society for Research in Child Development, Toronto.

Crozier, J. & Katz, R.C. (1979). Social learning treatment of child abuse. *Journal of Behavior Therapy and Experimental Psychiatry* 10, 213-220.

Dangel, R.F. & Polster, R.A. (Eds.). (1984). *Parent training*. NY: Guilford Press.

Dembo, R., Allen, N. & Farroll, D. (1985). A causal analysis of early drug involvement in three inner-city neighborhood settings. *International Journal of the Addictions,* 20, 1213-1237.

Denicola, J. & Sandler, J. (1980). Training child abusive parents in child management and self-control skills. *Behavior Therapy,* 11, 263-270.

Deur, J.L. & Parke, R.D. (1970). Effects of inconsistent punishment on aggression in children. *Developmental Psychology,* 2, 403-411.

DiGiuseppe, R. (1988). A cognitive-behavioral approach to the treatment of conduct disorder children and adolescents. In. N. Epstein, S.E. Schlesinge, & W. Dryden (Eds.). *Cognitive-behavior therapy with families.* NY: Brunner/Mazel (pp. 182-214).

DiLoreto, A.O. (1971). *Comparative psychotherapy: An experimental analysis.* Chicago, IL: Aldine-Atherton, Inc.

Ellis, A. (1962). *Reason and emotion in psychotherapy.* NY: Lyle Stuart.

Engfer, A. & Schneewind, K.A. (1982). Causes and consequences of harsh parental punishment. *Child Abuse and Neglect,* 6, 129-139.

Erikson, E.H. (1963). *Childhood and society.* NY: Norton.

Erlanger, H.S. (1989). Estrangement, machismo and gang violence. *Social Science Quarterly,* 60, 235-248.

Evans, E.D. & Warren-Sohlberg, L.A. (1988). A pattern of adolescent abusive behavior towards parents. *Journal of Adolescent Research,* 3, 201-216.

Feigelman, W. (1990). *Treating teenage drug abuse in a day care setting.* NY: Praeger.

Feindler, E.L., & Ecton, R.B. (1986). *Adolescent anger control: Cognitive-behavioral techniques.* Elsford, NY: Pergamon.

Feindler, E.L. (1987). Clinical issues and recommendations in adolescent anger-control training. *Journal of Child and Adolescent Psychotherapy,* 4, 267-274.

Fox, J.R. (1985). Mission impossible?: Social work practice with black urban youth gangs. *Social Work,* 30, 25-31.

Garbarino, J. (1977). The price of privacy in the social dynamics of child abuse. *Child Welfare,* 56, 565-575.

Greenberg, G.S., Zucker, R.A. & Noll, R.B. (1985). *The development of cognitive structures about alcoholic beverages among preschoolers.* Paper presented at the American Psychological Association, Los Angeles, CA.

Gil, D. (1970). *Violence against children: Physical child abuse in the United States.* Cambridge, MA: Harvard University Press.

Hamburg, B.A., Kraemer, H.D. & Hahnke, W. (1974). A hierarchy of drug use in adolescence: Behavioral and attitudinal correlates of substantial drug use. *American Journal of Psychiatry,* 132, 1155-1163.

Harbin, H. & Madden, D. (1979). Battered parents: A new syndrome. *American Journal of Psychiatry,* 136, 1288-1291.

Harford, T.C. & Spiegler, D. (1982). Environmental influences in adolescent drinking. In National Institute on Alcohol Abuse and Alcoholism. *Special population issues.* Alcohol and Health Monograph No. 4. Washington, D.C.: U.S. Government Printing Office (pp. 167-193).

Harper, F.D. (1977). Alcohol use among North American blacks. In Y. Israle, F.B. Glaser, H. Kalant, R.D. Popham, W. Schmidt & R.G. Smart (Eds.). *Research advances in alcohol and drug problems, vol. 4* . NY: Plenum Press (pp. 349-366).

Harper, F.D. & Dawkins, M.P. (1976). Alcohol and blacks: Survey of the periodical literature. *British Journal of Addiction*, 71, 327-334.

Hayes, C.D. (1987). Risking the future: *Adolescent sexuality, pregnancy and childbearing. Vol. 1.* Washington, D.C.: The National Academy Press.

Herrington, R., Riordan, P., & Jacobson, G. (1981). Alcohol and other drug dependence in adolescence: Characteristics of those who seek treatment, and outcome of treatment. *Currents in Alcoholism*, 8. 25-32.

Hersey, J.C., Field, T.A., Probst, J.C. & Theologus, G.C. (1982). *Evaluating public health education: A decision-making approach.* National Institute on Drug Abuse. Washington, D.C.: Kappa Systems.

Hofferth, S.L. & Hayes, C.D. (1987). Risking the future: *Adolescent sexuality, pregnancy and childbearing. Vol. 2.* Washington, D.C.: The National Academy Press.

Hoffmann, A.E. (1990). Clinical assessment and management of health risk behaviors in adolescents. In V.C. Strasburger & D.E. Greydanus (Eds.). *Adolescent medicine (vol. 1. no. 1)* Philadelphia, PA: Hanley & Belfus, Inc. (pp. 33-44).

Holland, S. (1983). Evaluating community-based treatment programmes: A model for strengthening inferences about effectiveness. *International Journal of Therapeutic Communities,* 4. 34-50.

Hubbard, R., Cavanaugh, E., Graddock, S. & Rachal, J. (1983). Characteristics, behaviors and outcomes for youth in TOPS study. Washington, D.C.: National Institute on Drug Abuse.

Irwin, C.E. & Ryan, S.A. (1989). Problem behaviors of adolescence. *Pediatric Review,* 10, 235-246.

Isaacs, C.D. (1982). Treatment of child abuse: A review of the behavioral interventions. *Journal of Applied Behavior Analysis*, 15, 273-294.

Jacobson, E. (1938). *Progressive relaxation.* Chicago, IL: University of Chicago Press.

Jahoda, G. & Cramond, J. (1972). *Children of alcohol.* London: Her Majesty's Stationary Office.

Jahoda, G., Davies, J.B., & Tagg, S. (1980). Parents' alcohol consumption and children's knowledge of drinks and usage patterns. *British Journal of Addiction,* 75, 297-303.

Jeffrey, M. (1976). Practical ways to change parent-child interactions in families of children at risk. In R. E. Helfer & C.H. Kempe (Eds.). *Child abuse and neglect.* Cambridge, MA: Ballinger.

Johnson, C. & Katz, R. (1973). Using parents as change agents for their children: a review. *Journal of Child Psychology and Psychiatry.* 14, 181-200.

Johnston, L., Bachman, J. & O'Malley, P. (1989). *Drug use, drinking and smoking: National survey results from high school, college and young adult populations, 1975-1988.* Washington, D.C.: National Institute of Drug Abuse.

Kantor, J.R. (1970). An analysis of the experimental analysis of behavior (TEAB). *Journal of the Experimental Analysis of Behavior,* 13, 101-108.

Kaufman, E. & Kaufman, P. (1979). From a psychodynamic orientation to a structural family approach to the treatment of drug dependency. In E. Kaufman & P. Kaufman (Eds.). *Family therapy for drug and alcohol abuse.* NY: Gardner Press.

Kazdin, A. E. (1985). Selection of target behaviors: The relationship of the treatment focus to clinical dysfunction. *Behavioral Assessment,* 7, 33-47.

King, L. (1982). Alcoholism: Studies regarding black Americans. In National Institute on Alcohol Abuse and Alcoholism. *Special population issues.* Alcohol Abuse and Health Monograph, No. 4, DHHS Pub. No. 82-1193. Washington, D.C: Government Printing Office (pp. 385-407).

Koegel, R.L., Schreibman, L., Britten, K.R., Burke, J.C. & O'Neill, R.E. (1982). A comparison of parent training to direct child treatment. In R.L. Koegel, A Rincover & A.L. Egel (Eds.). *Educating and understanding autistic children*. CA: College-Hill Press.

Leitenberg, H., Gross, J., Peterson, J. & Rosen, J. (1984). Analysis of an anxiety model and the process of change during exposure plus response prevention treatment of bulimia nervosa. *Behavior Therapy*, 15, 3-20.

Lewis, C.L. & Lewis, M.A. (1984). Peer pressure and risk-taking behaviors in children. *American Journal of Public Health*, 74, 580.

Lewis, M. & Schaeffer, S. (1981). Peer behavior and mother infant interaction in maltreated children. In M. Lewis & L.A. Rosenblum (Eds.). *The uncommon child; The genesis of behavior*. NY: Plenum Press.

Lichstein, K.L., Wagner, M.T., Krisak, J., & Steinberg, F. (1987). Stress management for acting-out, inpatient adolescents. *Journal of Child and Adolescent Psychotherapy*, 4, 19-31.

Litman, G. (1980). Relapse in alcoholism: Traditional and current approaches. In G. Edwards and M. Grand (Eds.). *Alcoholism treatment in transition*. Baltimore, MD: University Park Press.

Longfellow, C., Zelkowitz, P., Saunders, E. & Belle, D. (1979). *The role of support in moderating the effects of stress and depression*. Paper presented at the biennial meeting of the Society for Research in Child Development, San Francisco, CA.

Lourie, I. (1977). The phenomenon of the abused adolescent: A clinical study. *Victimology*, 2, 268-276.

Lourie, I. (1979). Family dynamics and the abuse of adolescents: A case for a developmental phase specific model of child abuse. *Child Abuse and Neglect*, 3, 967-974.

Lovaas, O.I., Koegel, R.L., Simmons, J. Q. & Long, J.S. (1973). Some generalization and follow-up measures on autistic children in behavior therapy. *Journal of Applied Behavior Analysis*, 6, 131-166.

Lowman, C. (1981/82). Facts for planning no. 3: U.S. teenage alcohol use in unsupervised social settings. *Alcohol Health and Research World*, 6, 2.

Lowney, J. (1984). The wall gang: A study of interpersonal process and deviance among twenty-three middle class youths. *Adolescence*, 19, 527-538.

Lutzker, J.R., McGimsey, J.F., McRae, S. & Campell, R.V. (1983). Behavioral parent-training: There's so much more to do. *The Behavior Therapist*, 6, 110-112.

Martin, H.P (1976). *The abused child: A multidisciplinary approach to developmental issues and treatment*. Cambridge, MA: Ballinger.

Meichenbaum, D. (1972). Cognitive modification of test anxious college students. *Journal of Consulting and Clinical Psychology*, 39, 370-380.

Meichenbaum, D. (1975). A self-instructional approach to stress management: a proposal for stress inoculation training. In L. Sarason & C.D. Speilberger (Eds.). *Stress and anxiety*. NY: Wiley (pp. 227-263).

Mitchell, J.J. (1975). *The Adolescent predicament*. Toronto: Holt, Rinehart and Winston of Canada.

Miller, W.R. & Hess, R.K. (1986). Inpatient alcoholism treatment: Who benefits? *American Psychologist*, 41, 794-805.

Mizes, J.S. (1985). Bulimia: A review of its symptomatolgy and treatment. *Advances in Behaviour Research and Therapy*, 7, 91-142.

Moore, J., Vigil, D. & Garcia, R. (1983). Residence and territoriality in Chicano gangs. *Social Problems*, 31, 182-194.

Myerowitz, J. (1985). *No sense of place: The impact of electronic media on social behavior*. NY: Oxford University Press.

Noll, R.B. (1983). *Young male offspring of alcoholic fathers: Early developmental differences from the MSU Vulnerability Study.*

Unpublished doctoral dissertation. Department of Psychology, Michigan State University, East Lansing, MI.

Parke, R.D. & Deur, J.L. (1972). Schedules of punishment and inhibition of aggression in children. *Developmental Psychology,* 7, 266-269.

Patterson, G.R. (1969). Behavioral intervention procedures in the classroom and in the home. In A.E. Bergin & S.L. Garfield (Eds.). *Handbook of psychotherapy and behavior change.* NY: Wiley.

Patterson, G.R. (1982). *Coercive family process.* Oregon: Castalia Press.

Patterson, G.R., Cobb, J.A. & Ray, R.S. (1970). A social engineering technology for retraining aggressive boys. In H. Adams & L. Unikel (Eds.). *Georgia symposium in experimental clinical psychology, Vol. 11.* NY: Pergamon Press.

Patterson, G.R. & Fleischman, M.J. (1979). Maintenance of treatment effects: Some considerations concerning family systems and follow-up data. *Behavior Therapy,* 10, 168-185.

Patterson, G.R. & Reid, J.B. (1970). Reciprocity and coercion: Two facets of social systems. In C. Neuringer and J. Michael (Eds.). *Behavior modification in clinical psychology.* NY: Appleton-Century-Crofts.

Pechacek, T. (1983). *Quit and win: Report of a community smoking campaign.* Minnesota Heart Health Program. Laboratory of Physiological Hygiene, University of Minnesota.

Reilly, D.M. (1976). Family factors in the etiology and treatment of youthful drug abuse. *Family Therapy,* 2, 149-171.

Reinhold, R. (1982). An overwhelming violence-TV tie. *New York Times,* May 6, C-27.

Rosen, J.C. & Leitenberg, J. (1982). Bulimia nervosa: Treatment with exposure and response prevention. *Behavior Therapy,* 13, 117-124.

Ruben, D.H. (in press). *Bratbusters: Say goodbye to tantrums and disobedience.* El Paso, TX: Skidmore-Roth.

Ruben, D.H. & Ruben, M.J. (1987). Assumptions about teaching assertiveness: Training the person or behavior? In D.H. Ruben & D.J. Delprato (Eds.). *New ideas in therapy*. Westport, CT: Greenwood Press (pp. 107-118).

Ruben, D.H. & Ruben, M.J. (1989). Why assertiveness training programs fail. *Small Group Behavior,* 20, 367-380.

Rueger, D.B. & Liberman, R.P. (1984). Behavioral family therapy for delinquent substance abusing adolescents. *Journal of Drug Issues,* 14, 403-418.

Rule, B.G. & Nesdale, A.R. (1976). Emotional arousal and aggressive behavior. *Psychological Bulletin,* 83, 851-863.

Schellenbach, C.J. & Guerney, L.F. (1987). Identification of adolescent abuse and future intervention. *Journal of Adolescence,* 10, 1-12.

Scott, W.O., Baer, G., Christoff, K.A. & Kelly, J.A. (1984). The use of skills training procedures in the treatment of a child-abusive parent. *Journal of Behavior Therapy and Experimental Psychiatry,* 15, 329-336.

Silvis, G.L. & Perry, C.L. (1987). Understanding and deterring tobacco use among adolescents. *Pediatric Clinics of North America,* 34, 363-379.

Soren, K. & Willis, E. (1989). Chlamydia and the adolescent girl. *American Journal of Diseases of Children,* 143, 51-54.

Speigler, D.L. (1983). Children's attitudes toward alcohol. *Journal of Studies on Alcohol,* 44, 545-552.

Stokes, T.F. & Baer, D.M. (1977). An implicit technology of generalization. *Journal of Applied Behavior Analysis,* 10, 349-367.

Stokes, T.F. & Osnes, P.G. (1989). An operant pursuit of generalization. *Behavior Therapy,* 20, 337-355.

Stover, D. (1986). A new breed of youth gang is on the prowl and a bigger threat than ever. *American School Board Journal,* August, 15-20.

Strassburger, V.C. (1990). Television and adolescents: Sex, drugs, rock 'n roll. In V.C. Strasburger & D.E. Greydanus (Eds.). *Adolescent medicine: The at-risk adolescent.* Philadelphia, PA: Hanley & Belfus, Inc. (161-194).

Strauss, M.A. (1971). Some social antecedents of physical punishment: A linkage theory interpretation. *Journal of Marriage and Families,* 33, 658-663.

Surveillance Division of HIV/AIDS (1989), Center for Infectious Diseases, Centers for Disease Control, Atlanta, GA.

United States Bureau of the Census. (1981). *School enrollment--social and economic characteristics of students: October 1977.* Current Population Reports Series. U.S. Department of Commerce.

United States Department of Health and Human Services (1986). *Public health service: The health consequences of using smokeless tobacco: A report of the advisory committee to the Surgeon General. NIH Publication,* 86-2874.

United States Department of Health and Human Services (1988). *Public health service, Centers for Disease Control, sexually transmitted disease statistics, 1987,* Atlanta, GA.

United States Department of Health and Human Services (1989). *Public health service, health United States 1988.* Hyattsville, MD: *DHHS Publication,* 89-1232.

United States Department of Justice (1986). *Bureau of justice statistics, criminal victimization in the United States, 1984.* Washington, D.C.: *Publication NCJ,* 100435.

Wahler, R.G. (1975). Some structural aspects of deviant child behavior. *Journal of Applied Behavior Analysis,* 8, 27-42.

Wahler, R.G. (1980). The insular mother: Her problems in parent-child treatment. *Journal of Applied Behavior Analysis,* 13, 207-219.

Wahler, R.G. (1981). Parent insularity as a determinant of generalization success in family treatment. *The ecosystem of the sick kid: Implications for classroom and intervention*. NY: CUNY Graduate Center.

Wahler, R.G. & Dumas, J.E. (1986). Maintenance factors in coercive mother-child interactions: The compliance and predictability hypotheses. *Journal of Applied Behavior Analysis,* 19, 13-22.

Wahler, R.G., Leske, G. & Rogers, E. (1979). The insular family: A deviance support system for oppositional children. In L.A. Hamerlyhnck (Ed.). *Behavioral systems for the developmentally disabled. I. School and family environments*. NY: Brunner/Mazel.

Wallack, L. (1979). *The California prevention demonstration program evaluation: Description, methods and findings*. Berkeley, CA: Social Research Group, School of Public Health, University of California.

Wallack, L. (1981). Mass media campaigns:The odds against finding behavior change. *Health Education Quarterly,* 8, 209-260.

Westney, Q.E., Jenkins, R.R. & Butts, J.D. (1984). Sexual development and behavior in black adolescents. *Adolescence,* 19, 558.

Wolfe, D.A. (1985). Child abusive parents: An empirical review and analysis. *Psychological Bulletin,* 97, 462-482.

Wolfe, D.A., Edwards, B., Manion, I., & Koverola, C. (1988). Early intervention for parents at risk of child abuse and neglect: A preliminary investigation. *Journal of Consulting and Clinical Psychology,* 56, 40-47.

Wolfe, D.A., Sandler, J. & Kaufman, K. (1981). A competency-based parent training program for child abusers. *Journal of Consulting Clinical Psychology,* 49, 633-640.

Wrather, J. (1982). Social issues are themes for seminars. *Science,* 147, 45-68.

SELECTED ANNOTATED RESOURCES

Ackerman, R.J. (1987). Family response to alcoholism: Effects on children growing up in the shadow. *Focus on Family and Chemical Dependency*, 9, 25-27; 31; 39-44.

1. English; 2. Clinical/review; 3. Nonalcoholic offspring of alcoholic parents; 4. Reactive phases of family response to parental drinking are reviewed in terms of defective relationships, emotional isolationism, and potential suppression of heathy development into adulthood; 5. Children of drinking parents are disproportionately represented in juvenile courts, spouse and child abuse cases, divorce cases, and within populations plagued by psychological and emotional problems.

Bainwol, S. & Gressard, C.F. (1985). Incidence of Jewish alcoholism: A review of the literature. *Journal of Drug Education*, 15, 217-224.

1. English; 2. Review; 3. Adults, adolescents; 4. Critical review of research regarding drinking among Jewish people shows serious methodological flaws while the studies that are methodologically sound report low rates of consumption. General trends examined in terms of types of subjects sampled, randomness, and vulnerability; 5. Authors conclude the reported rate underestimates actual numbers and that incidence of alcoholism may be higher. Problem lies with misdiagnosis or insufficient interviewing, particularly when the interviewed patient neglects to identify himself as Jewish or does not affiliate with the Jewish community.

Brisbane, F.L. (1985). Using contemporary fiction with black children and adolescents in alcoholism treatment. *Alcoholism Treatment Quarterly*, 2, 179-197.

1. English; 2. Clinical; 3. Black children and adolescents; 4. Drug awareness and preventive tactics; 5. Technique described on using bibliotherapy in the form of fiction books as drug education for prevention of high-risk children already abusing or living with alcoholic parents; 5. Outcome effects of bibliotherapy predicted are easier identification with values and less threatening fears of their problems.

Chassin, L., Mann, L.M. & Sher, K.J. (1988). Self-awareness theory, family history of alcoholism, and adolescent alcohol involvement. *Journal of Abnormal Psychology*, 97, 206-217.

1. English; 2. Clinical/review; 3. Early adolescents; 4. Proposal based on Hull's theory of alcohol escaping painful states of awareness, that high risk adolescents drink to prevent confrontations with ongoing problems, particularly for offspring of alcoholics; 5. Comparative analysis of two research studies discount validity of this hypothesis but suggest drinking is predictable given certain demographic variables, low self-awareness, failures of feedback, and alcoholic family history.

Christiansen, B.A. & Goldman, M.S. (1985). Differential development of adolescent alcohol expectancies may predict adult alcoholism. *Addictive Behaviors*, 10, 299-306.

1. English; 2. Experimental; 3. Teenagers (n= 1580) between ages 12 and 14, 15 to 16, and 17 to 19 years old; 4. School; 5. Drinking experiences, sleep inducement, relaxation, sexual enhancement, cognitive activity; 6., 7. & 8. Alcohol-expectancy scales, group design; 9. Results confirm adolescent beliefs that alcohol improves social behavior, increases arousal, and decreases tension. Outcomes concur with prognostic studies showing that cognitive expectancies play a significant role in determining causal attribution and long-term responses to drinking situations.

Dawkins, M.P. (1988). Alcoholism prevention and black youth. *Journal of Drug Issues*, 18, 15-20.

1. English; 2. Theoretical/clinical; 3. Black adolescents; 4. Evaluates internal and external forces to the black community to be considered when developing realistic prevention strategies; 5. Concludes that community-based efforts must emphasize mobilization of major black institutions to be involved in training, as well as address racism and goal prioritization. Racial oppression viewed as considerably retarding the resistance of black youths to drug influence.

Delgado, M. Alcoholism treatment and Hispanic youth. *Journal of Drug Issues*, 18, 59-68.

1. English; 2. Clinical/review; 3. Hispanic youth; 4. Comprehensive overview compares literature on factors clouding Hispanic substance abuse, role of acculturation, and interventions; 5. Results suggest few

studies actually focus on Hispanic adolescents' failures at drug refusal and cultural conflicts confronted. Failure to resolve conflicts between the parents' value systems and those of their peers may result in acting out behavior of which substance abuse is just one type. Recommended is continuum of care designed to meet assessment and treatment needs including culture-specific training for providers.

Drake, R.E. & Vaillant, G.E. (1988). Predicting alcoholism and personality disorder in a 33-year longitudinal study of children of alcoholics. *British Journal of Addiction*, 83, 799-807.

1. English; 2. Experimental; 3. Inner-city nondelinquent sons and alcoholic men; 4. Community; 5. Personality disorder features besides predisposition to drug and alcohol abuse in response to environmental stressors; 6. 7. & 8. 33-year longitudinal study following dependency patterns, using existing records and reports; 9. Observed repeatedly in children of alcoholic (COA) groups were school behavior problems, poor maternal relationships, low IQ, and feelings of inadequacy. Adjustment deficits caused, by midlife, drinking disorder in nearly 28% of group.

Edwards, E.D. & Edwards, M.E. (1988). Alcoholism prevention/treatment and native American youth: A community approach. *Journal of Drug Issues*, 18, 103-114.

1. English; 2. Clinical/review; 3. Native American youth; 4. Reviews current modalities of prevention and treatment approaches in individual and family therapies, suggesting that many programs could be addressed in primary prevention strategies; 5. Emphasized are interventions building self-esteem, supplying accurate alcohol and drug information, and teaching responsible decision-making skills established as steps taken by a task-group approach. Method of pursuing task-group formation and types of issues considered are reviewed.

Galan, F.J. (1988). Alcoholism prevention and Hispanic youth. *Journal of Drug Issues*, 18, 49-58.

1. English; 2. Clinical/review; 3. Hispanic youth living in lower income; 4. Examination made of components of prevention programs generalizable to Hispanic youths, and what type of modifications are necessary; 5. Guides to responsible drinking or drinking diversion should be re-designed to include ethnic identity, biculturality,

language, sex role identification, skin color, family history of alcoholism, sense of self in relation to family, and problem solving, particularly as related to personal leadership and cultural integrations. Suggestions offered on pursuing these changes for program expansion.

Gottesman, I.I. & Prescott, C.A. (1989). Abuses of the MacAndrew MMPI Alcoholism Scale: A critical review. *Clinical Psychology Review*, 9, 223-242.

1. English; 2. Literature review; 3. Adult and adolescent male and female substance abusers; 4. Seventy-four papers published between 1976 and 1978 underwent review to examine their sensitivity, specificity, positive and negative predictive powers for diagnosis and assessment; 5. Results reveal flagrant examples of inaccuracy and insensitivity to core drug-using variables calling into question the validity of the instrument for continued application.

Harford, T.C. & Grant, B.F. (1987). Psychosocial factors in adolescent drinking contexts. *Journal of Studies on Alcohol*, 48, 551-557.

1. English; 2. Experimental; 3. Adolescent students; 4. High schools statewide/nationwide; 5. Drinking contexts; 6., 7. & 8. Cross sectional design using survey questionnaires returned by 4,918 (87%) students; 9. Positive functions of drinking, personal attitudes and values were associated with drinking contexts. Drinking for conformity and status transformation, however, were not relevant to drinking context variables.

Heilbrun, A.B., Cassidy, J.C., Biehl, M., Haas, M. & Heilbrun, M.R. (1986). Psychological vulnerability to alcoholism: Studies in internal scanning deficit. *British Journal of Medical Psychology*, 59, 237-244.

1. English; 2. Experimental; 3. & 4. Male college students and adolescents in juvenile court detention; 5. Sensitivity to internal stimulation and extent to which person utilizes internally generated information; 6., 7. & 8. Internal scanning devices and noncontrol, examined in three studies; 9. First study indicated that more acute alcoholic cases displayed poor scanning than chronic alcoholics. Second and third study investigated predispositional influence of scanning (responsivity to internal stimuli). Results reveal that limited scanning contributes to alcohol vulnerability by depriving the drinker of sensory information vital to control or prevent alcohol toxicity.

Holmes, S.J. & Robins, L.N. (1987). Influence of childhood disciplinary experience on the development of alcoholism and depression. *Journal of Child Psychology and Psychiatry and Allied Disciplines,* 28, 399-415.

1. English; 2. Experimental; 3. Interviewed adults with lifetime diagnoses of major depressive disorder, alcohol abuse or dependence or absence of psychiatric disorder (control group); 4. Large urban city; 5. Types of discipline or punishment interviewees recalled during their childhood of 6-13 years of age; 6., 7. & 8. Case-control study using repeated interviews and scales of parental discipline; 9. Results showed that unfair, harsh and inconsistent parental discipline predicted both alcohol and depressive disorders independently of the influence of parental psychiatric history, the respondent's sex, and childhood behavior problems.

Knop, J., Teasdale, T.W., Schulsinger, F. & Goodwin, D.W. (1985). Prospective study of young men at high risk for alcoholism: School behavior and achievement. *Journal of Studies on Alcohol,* 46, 273-278.

1. English; 2. Experimental; 3. 134 sons of alcoholic fathers selected between ages of 19 to 20; 4. High school; 5. Psychopathology, drinking patterns, and hyperactivity; 6., 7. & 8. Seventy groups randomly assigned and received questionnaires, rated also by students' teachers; 9. Data show high risk group reporting drinking causing more disturbed school careers, repetition of grades, and frequency of different schools. Reports corroborated with teachers' evaluation of these adolescents' showing hyperactivity, impulsivity, poor verbal proficiency, and related premorbid characteristics of risk. Subjects rated impulsive and having low communication skills predicted as future alcoholics unless early prevention steps are taken.

MacDonald, D.I. (1986). How you can help prevent teenage alcoholism. *Contemporary Pediatrics,* November, 50-72.

1. English; 2. Clinical; 3. Children of alcoholic parents, teenage drug abusers, parents; 4. Article espouses that a conducive climate for drug prevention involves attention to fluctuating changes in youth's psychological and physical welfare, inspected by pediatrician; 5. Early recognition of risk factors and warning signs of teenage alcoholism can speed intervention and improve treatment outcome recovery.

Mann, L.M., Sher, K.J. & Chassin, L. (1987). Alcohol expectancies and the risk for alcoholism. *Journal of Consulting and Clinical Psychology,* 55, 411-417.

1. English; 2. Experimental; 3. 979 high school adolescent students; 4. High school; 5. Drinking motives, expectations, thought processes, stress and conflict, and family dysfunction; 6., 7. & 8. Survey interviews, group design; 9. Measures of alcoholic expectancies varied as function of risk status and altered social behavior. Perceptions were high of enhanced cognitive and motor functioning, personal power and tension reduction. Low-risk drinking associated with ambiguous expectations. Recommends clinical detection of alcoholic motives in primary prevention and treatment diagnosis.

Mijuskovic, B. (1988). Loneliness and adolescent alcoholism. *Adolescence,* 23, 503-516.

1. English; 2. Theoretical/clinical; 3. Adolescents; 4. Feelings of separation anxiety, hostility, and loneliness leading to inebriation is described following views of Fromm-Reichmann, Fromm and Erikson; 5. Shown are that lonely people are (a) actively hostile and building aggression, (b) driven to escape behaviors, (c) alienated from social peer groups, and (d) detached from parental interest. Clinical direction is alerting parents to this decompensation and ways they can restore parent-child relationships.

MacAndrew Alcoholism Scale among at-risk adolescent females. *Journal of Clinical Psychology,* 44, 1005-1008.

1. English; 2. Experimental; 3. Marijuana and multiple substance abusing females (n = 160); 4. Schools; 5. Impulsivity and related variables diagnosed on the instrument; 6., 7. & 8. MacAndrew Alcoholism Scale, California Psychological Inventory; 9. Groups tested by both instruments showed alcohol to enhance sense of well-being and coping with interpersonal problems. Group tested on MacAndrew instrument additionally yielded higher sensitivity to interpersonal rejection.

Nace, E.P. (1987). Epidemiology of alcoholism. *Pediatrician,* 14, 2-6.

1. English; 2. Clinical/review; 3. Adolescent and adult males; 4. Epidemiological survey of prevalence, drug dependency, treatment options, and risk factors associated with substance abuse focusing on

effects upon family network and adolescent's adjustment; 5. Risk factors identified such as homosexuality, temperament, and genetic factors may be isolated and drinking patterns diagnosed at early stages toward a health prevention approach.

Pandina, R.J. & Johnson, V. (1990). Serious alcohol and drug problems among adolescents with a family history of alcoholism. *Journal of Studies on Alcoholism*, 51, 278-282.

1. English; 2. Experimental; 3. 1,380 New Jersey youth born between 1961 and 1969, tested, retested (ages 12, 15, 18); 4. Community; 5. Reports of alcohol or drug problems; 6. No treatment; 7. & 8. Clinical samples, longitudinal reports; 9. Data indicated that family history rates were highly predictive of offspring substance abuse but there were no significant differences between drug using males and females. Suggests repeating study under controlled clinical samples rather than relying on retrospective community-based samples.

Plutchik, A. & Plutchik, R. (1989). Psychosocial correlates of alcoholism. *Integrative Psychiatry*, 6, 205-210.

1. English; 2. Experimental; 3. Fifty males and 50 female adolescent and adult outpatients; 4. Comprehensive Alcohol Treatment Center; 5. Correlates including negative family history, anxiety, menstrual problems, lack of socialization; 6., 7. & 8. Michigan Alcoholism Screening Test to total group; 9. Addictive events suggesting chronic psychopathology include genetic predisposition, dependency conflict, adolescent reinforcement, supportive cultural norms, related conditioning experiences, and current stressors.

Priest, K. (1985). Adolescents' response to parents' alcoholism. *Social Casework*, 66, 533-539.

1. English; 2. Clinical; 3. Nonalcoholic offspring of drinking parents; 4. Contends that alcoholic father affects an adolescents' peer and family relationships, school performance, emotions and creates struggles causing fears, anger, grief, low self-esteem, and poor sex identification; 5. Examined variables of sons' responses usually point to onset of antisocial behavior early in teens. Professionals urged to attend to special needs of children and work with nondrinking parent on disrupting the destructive effects.

Rhoades, E.R., Mason, R.D., Eddy, P., Smith, E.M., & Burns, T.R. (1988). Indian health service approach to alcoholism among American Indians and Alaska natives. *Public Health Reports*, 103, 621-627.

1. English; 2. Clinical/review; 3. Adolescents, families at risk in Indian/Alaskan communities; 4. Preventive programs reviewed that emphasize self-improvement, attitude classification, decision-making and information about effects of alcohol and substance abuse. Review undertaken by a Task Force on Indian Alcoholism (created in 1986) toward development of adolescent treatment centers; 5. Strategic plan offered emphasizes prevention of disease and promotion of wellness through combined family-integrated programs and individualized training focused on tribal issues in addition to personal or interpersonal issues.

Room, R. (1989). Alcoholism and Alcoholics Anonymous in U.S. films, 1945-1962: The party ends for the "wet generations." *Journal of Studies on Alcohol*, 50, 368-383.

1. English; 2. Theoretical/review; 3. Thirty-four plus Hollywood films; 4. Comparing films made around 1945 and 1962 in terms of depiction of Alcoholics Anonymous, self-help organizations, and situational factors including treatment interpretation; 5. Will-power and mutual help were each frequently shown as paths to recovery, whereas neither professional treatment nor AA's spiritual side were depicted. Hypothesizes that actors, producers and directors of such pictures came from "wet generation" of middle-class youth who had adopted heavy drinking in their college years. Founders of AA were in cohort generations and thus the alcoholism films may parallel evolutions of new or changed thinking about substance abuse.

Watts, T.D. & Lewis, R.G. (1988). Alcoholism and Native American youth: An overview. *Journal of Drug Issues*, 18, 69-86.

1. English; 2. Clinical/review; 3. Native American youth traced intergenerationally; 4. Examines evolving epidemiologic trends affecting native American youth culture before 1832 up to present time, in comparison to alcohol use patterns among blacks and whites; 5. Espouses that there can be no standard model for understanding Native American drinking consumption patterns. Solutions offered include (a) alcohol education and prevention programs in local tribes, (b) program involving parents and youth, (c) economic development programs on reservations, and (d) leadership from Native American

communities. Modifications recommended for community involvement also detailed.

Wilcox, J.A. (1985). Adolescent alcoholism. *Journal of Psychoactive Drugs*, 17, 77-85.

1. English; 2. Review; 3. Adolescent alcoholics; 4. Archival review of problem drinking among youth regarding etiologies of genetics, and influence of role models in forming aggressive, delinquent, and drug using behaviors; 5. Results find that environmental factors principally account for development of alcoholism over genetic influence, although methodology for genetic study is still controversial and warranting further sophistication.

Workman-Daniels, K.L. & Hellelbrock, V.M. (1987). Childhood problem behavior and neuropsychological functioning in persons at risk for alcoholism. *Journal of Studies on Alcohol*, 48, 187-193.

1. English; 2. Experimental; 3. Young adults; 4. Community; 5. Symptoms of hyperactivity, attentional deficit disorder, and pre-alcoholic patterns; 6., 7. & 8. Three groups (1 control). Nonalcoholic offspring of an alcoholic parent and of nonalcoholic parents administered a battery of neuropsychological tests and checklist of attentional deficit disorder symptoms; 9. Subjects from alcoholic parents performed more poorly on measures of verbal and performance intelligence and reported higher frequency of childhood hyperactivity. Neuropsychological deficits indicated in early development predisposing child to drinking if additionally influenced by alcoholic parent.

Yates, W.R., Meller, W. & Troughton, E.P. (1987). Behavioral complications of alcoholism. *American Family Physician*, 35, 171-175.

1. English; 2. Clinical/review; 3. Adolescent alcoholics; 4. Outlines symptomatology of antisocial behaviors related to high risk actions including aggressive, violent behavior and accidental injury; 5. Reports of increased incidences of trauma in alcoholism should alert family physicians to the role of critical investigator of early drug use and direction for family on treatment options.

Zucker, R.A. & Gomberg, E.S.L. (1986). Etiology of alcoholism reconsidered: The case for a biopsychosocial process. *American Psychologist*, 41, 783-793.

1. English; 2. Clinical/theoretical review; 3. Inner-city youth; 4. Details study of youth followed from 1950 to 1968 regarding childhood influences upon personality and pre-alcoholic tendencies leading to acute and chronic drinking; 5. Parametric analyses reveal continuity between premorbid antisocial behavior and alcoholism, although it plays a less significant etiological role than marital conflict and biopsychosocial variables such as genetic endowment. Conclusions recommend charting this phenomenon more closely across developmental continuum.

Chapter 4

Adult Children of Addiction

When you get what you want, in your struggle for self, and the world makes you king for a day, just go to the mirror and look at yourself and see what that man has to say. For it isn't his parents, or preacher or friend, whose judgment upon you must pass. The fellow whose verdict counts most in your life is the one staring back from the glass. Some people may think you're a straight shootin chum, and call you a wonderful guy. But the man in the glass says you're only a bum, if you can't look him straight in the eye. He's the fellow to please--never mind all the rest. For he's with you clear up to the end. And you have passed the most difficult test, if the man in the glass is your friend. You may fool the whole world down the pathway of life, and get pats on your back as you pass. But your final reward will be heartache and tears, if you cheated the man in the glass (Anonymous).

More than ten percent of the population of the United States is being raised or was raised in an alcoholic house. That accounts for between twenty-five and twenty-eight million children of alcoholics in society. Until recently, however, these statistics remained buried in reports by social service and criminal justice departments. In the past decade these reports surfaced and shed critical light on family trauma resulting from parent or sibling alcoholism or drug abuse. The explosion of interest and awareness of the risks, difficulties, needs and problems of adult children who grew up in addiction families sparked rapid efforts to observe and hypothesize about the phenomenon (Brown, 1988).

Until recently, however, actual research to test out these hypotheses was sparse (El-Guebaly & Offord, 1977; Hindman, 1975; Thomas & Santa, 1982). Now the scientific and human service community shows considerably more interest and commitment to research investigation (Ackerman, 1983)

This chapter furthers this commitment to integrating current information regarding the adult child of alcoholic/addiction (ACOA) syndrome. Viewed ecobehaviorally, ACOA patterns undergo a more comprehensive examination in terms of specific effects of parental abuse reported by the applied and experimental literature on punishment, avoidance and escape behaviors, and family system defects. Quite expectedly, presented is a morbid picture of childhood victimization produced by a series of psychological afflictions that nearly always arise from addiction households (substance abusing) and will absolutely arise from dysfunctional households (aggression with or without substance abuse).

First examined are etiological foundations of ACOA including behavioral typologies and formation of permanent rules about behavior. Second, under *Effects Upon Family,* are the effects of punishment conditioning upon ACOAs relative to the applied and experimental analyses of behavior. Third, treatment issues for ACOAs take into consideration the delicacy of distrust and need for reconstruction or new construction of repertoires for a functionally healthy lifestyle.

ETIOLOGY

One reason for a paucity of research on the ACOA phenomena is disagreement about the actual behavioral parameters determining a dysfunction. Another reason is that when afflicted adults enter adulthood they assume their behaviors are relatively normal unless or until peers or members of society confront their personality defects. Once pointed out, amazing similarities in emotions, behavior and thoughts shared among most ACOAs indicate there must be experiential commonalties during childhood and particularly from effects of deprivation and punishment. Authors documenting these common denominators in personality (e.g., Black, 1981; Cork, 1969; Friel & Friel, 1988; Gravitz & Bowden, 1985; Kritsberg, 1985) eloquently identify early signs and symptoms of adult traumatic reaction.

Uniformity of these patterns clearly presumes the evolving traumatic reactions are predictable and traceable to concrete origins. But lacking are operational or causal reasons explaining not only the behavioral similarities, but also how early family variables developed such severe adult maladjustment. Toward that goal, let us first consider different behavioral typologies of the ACOA phenomenon.

Behavioral Typology

Behavior *typology* refers to specific characteristics repeatedly observed in clinical trials and from reported literature on emerging ACOA reactions. Here we divide these typologies into *functional characteristics, survival characteristics, superstitious characteristics,* and *ecological characteristics.*

Functional characteristics. Functional characteristics of behavior produced from parental punishment and deprivation start in childhood and evolve unchanged to adulthood as long as that child remains exposed to same or similar circumstances. Alcoholic circumstances growing up, for example, may persist while dating or married to alcoholics or engaging in alcohol oneself. In childhood, side effects of punishment include the following predictable patterns, explained behaviorally.

1. *Child learns to react to punishment for attention.* Attention-seeking responses are instantly fueled by negative or aggressive parental discipline. Child learns yelling, anger, interrupting, and tantrums, or noncompliance as his only response to obtain gratification regardless if the consequences are aversive.

2. *Child learns to pair or "associate" the properties of punishment with the person administering the punishment.* Repeated anger, aggression or negativity by parents turns the parent himself into an aversive event. Properties defining the parent such as tone of voice, physical stature, odor, and facial features acquire threatening messages avoided by the child.

3. *Child learns to stay away (avoid) anticipated or actual punishment.* Repeated exposure to aversive situations oversensitizes a child to obvious and subtle stimuli surrounding the parent or punishing situation. Hearing a drunken parent return home late at night might cue the child to hide in his room or remain silent. However, hearing that parent return home at any time, drunken or not, may cue the same response.

4. *Child inhibits appropriate behaviors in anticipation of punishment.* Anticipation of aversive situations interrupts appropriate and inappropriate behaviors. Not only does the frightened child hide underneath his bed during a loud marital argument, but the avoidance prevents him from also (a) saying goodnight to his parents, (b) brushing his teeth or going to the bathroom, and (c) changing clothing. That is, appropriate behaviors that never were punished but are collateral or sequential to punished (avoidance) behaviors now undergo inhibition. Unless corrected, inhibitions develop into routines where that child simply omits steps (a) through (c), even into adulthood, whenever he goes asleep.

5. *Child learns inappropriate behavior in anticipation of punishment.* Suppression of some inappropriate behavior from punishment does not prevent the spontaneous learning of other, more discrete inappropriate behaviors. Inappropriate behaviors "spontaneously" arise for two reasons. First is to replace necessary appropriate behaviors that are inhibited. Second is to replace inappropriate behaviors receiving punishment. A spanked child aggressively told to stay in his bedroom at night and who fears asking to use the bathroom may (a) urinate in his bed (enuresis) out of biological necessity, (b) sneak into the bathroom in late evening or early morning hours forcing himself to awake at odd hours (insomnia), or (c) void the following day on household objects, or outside on the shrubbery. A second example deals with eating food. A child severely hit or verbally assaulted at mealtime (regardless of why punishment happened) may (a) avoid meals altogether, (b) sneak food into his bedroom and leave it under his bed or in secret places, or (c) eat wrong or inedible substances (pica) out of biological necessity.

6. *Child never learns behaviors appropriate for peer group.* Social or interpersonal behaviors suppressed at home prevent learning basic peer skills. Children punished for speaking or freely playing never learn to (a) express feelings, (b) share objects, (c) trust people, (d) make mistakes, (e) ask questions, (f) explore their curiosity and imagination, and (g) dismiss criticism.

7. *Child learns sensitivity to and generalization of avoidance and escape in punishment situations.* Avoidance and escape responses learned at home instantly transfer to other situations where there is no need for avoidance and escape. Abused children refrain from talking, risking changes, and playing with friends at school. Confronted by

these deficits, he may cry, act out, or aggressively attempt to escape the confrontation.

8. *Child learns inappropriate reactions that interfere with not only normal behaviors but also the "opportunities" for normal learning.* Afflicted children suffer two repercussions from constant suppression. One, already described, is development of spontaneous alternative behaviors, many of which are inappropriate but subtle. A second repercussion is when inappropriate behaviors delay, interrupt, or entirely prevent access to learning opportunities for socially appropriate behaviors. For example, aggressively-acting, attention-seeking children tested for special education and who spend the majority of school in a resource or contained classroom, lose precious interactions with peer groups. Mainstreaming into regular classrooms restores some opportunities, but by then prerequisites for proper peer dialogue and play are way below standards.

Adult manifestations of childhood trauma gain unfortunate momentum because of naturally developed cognitions, behavioral and emotional faculties, and complexity of interpersonal social experience that form conceptions of oneself and the world. When early dysfunctions persist into adulthood, the enigma of suffering intensifies and causes unusual excesses and deficits (Ackerman, 1987c; El-Guebaly & Offord, 1977). These are spelled out below, again with behavioral clarification:

1. *Personality is one of two major types: Passive or Aggressive.* Dichotomy of behavior is predictable. ACOAs raised under a random, untrusting and frequently punitive environment adapt by responding in one of two major ways. First, rebellion toward that environment appears in the form of challenging the abusing adults. Expressed anger is outwardly aggressive, violent, or oppositional in terms of severe tantrums, noncompliance, running away, lying, stealing, and hyperactivity. In adolescence, when verbal skills are complex, refusals and defiance intensify as the child completely distrusts his parents and assumes total control over personal goals and gratification. Into adulthood this controlling behavior appears manipulating, domineering, and attractive to inept or deficient partners desperate for caretaking partners. Aggression subsides a bit but the person maintains low tolerance to frustration and is easily upset by disruptions in rigidly-planned schedules or decisions. Hostility shown over disruptions, however, *is not to evoke conflict.* Conflict remains avoided at all costs.

The other extreme is more gentle, docile, passively withdrawn from social decisions, confrontations, and ambitions. In childhood this person withdrew from familial antagonism or turned into a mediator, trying to arbitrate peace among hostile parties. Placating aggressive urges of adult parents denied the child his own personal pleasures, opportunities for peer growth, and instilled fear over being autonomous outside the household. Kept within family boundaries, the frightened child developed hypersensitivity to receiving parental approval through personal sacrifice. Approval becomes identified as the only source of love, affirmation, and proof of the child's worthiness. Seeking approval by pleasing, caretaking or assuming unwanted responsibility further averted conflict.

The irony in both personality patterns is that conflict is absolutely anathema. Conflict threatens the fragile balance of confidence and self-hatred that already is shaken by frequent doubts and distrust among adults. Feared most from adults is criticism for any reason. Aggressively controlling ACOAs anticipate or dismantle conflict by injecting needles of verbal pain against their alleged predators. Rude remarks, hostile provokes, using predators as brunt of jokes, and even "egging on" the predator until he or she explodes, all function to delay or prevent confrontation. Passively controlling ACOAs seek the same goal exactly and thus their behaviors operationally are identical: To defuse rising hostility. However, efforts at defusal involve *satisfying the legitimate or illegitimate needs of predators in anticipation of conflict.* They may surrender unwillingly to peculiar wants and needs imposed upon them by predators, hoping the outcome will instantly restore peace. How long this peace lasts is irrelevant.

2. *Trouble expressing feelings.* Adults stuff their feelings internally and refuse sharing anything personally vulnerable. Expression would risk exposure of faults, of looking incompetent, of being disapproved or causing anger in others. Consequently speech is very selective, labored, edited, and words expressed are replayed in thought over and over to test whether they upset the listener.

3. *Cannot seem to relax.* Adults appear highly active, constantly busy, and unable to slow down their pace for fear of feeling unproductive, wasteful, and lazy. Even sitting is accompanied by fidgeting, working on projects and thoughts are racing. Slow, calming or vegetative actions evoke sudden panic and shame. Panic is from the expectation of punishment coming from an authority or significant other (boyfriend, girlfriend, spouse), even if the person lives alone

Feelings of impending criticism overwhelm the person and mobilizes him into immediate action to relieve the anxiety. Reactions of guilt or shame arise from *wanting to just relax but believing it is awful and immoral.* Anticipatory fears evolved from never having opportunities to relax or play by oneself, if compelled to be responsible for other siblings or constantly helping other people.

4. *Are loyal (codependent) beyond reason.* Adults become dependent personalities who are terrified of abandonment and would do anything to hold onto a relationship not to re-experience the painful separation felt from living with people who never were emotionally there for them. Loyalty also means self-appointed commitment to any cause, group, or friendships no matter how problematic or dysfunctional the situation becomes. The adult must stay aboard that *Titanic* even if every one else abandons ship. This martyrdom affirms beliefs that the adult is incomparably superior in loyalty and well deserves the praise and approval of her recipients.

5. *Are overly responsible.* A corollary to *loyal beyond reason* is taking on far more than the adult can chew. Adults have an overdeveloped sense of responsibility focusing entirely on the welfare of another person rather than on themselves. Shifts from selfishness prevent drawing too much attention to their faults (or assets) and disapproval for being conceited. Helping others, also called *caretaking or enabling,* involves total consumption with organizing, solving, or directing lives of other people to guarantee their unconditional approval and ongoing friendship. Forfeiture of personal needs varies from small sacrifices to complete self-neglect, frequently disintegrating down to living or dying depending on whether it pleases another person. Targets for enablers are generally weak people suffering some emotional or physical disability, or underdeveloped socially. It becomes a natural challenge for enablers to commit to the rehabilitation of that person, not for the victory, but for assurance of their approval.

6. *Fear of losing control.* Loss of control translates to panic over looking vulnerable. *Vulnerability* poses serious threats to inadequacies kept private and below the surface. Lack of leadership, or denied opportunities to direct, coordinate or organize people or things instills a fear of abandonment. That other people do not need this adult or regard his services as unimportant thereby implies the person is incapable, incompetent, and has shortcomings. Inferring this rejection, adults believe they failed certain expectations and may immediately

rebound with double the amount of energy and commitment aspiring to please the person at all costs.

7. *Difficulty with relationships.* There are two types of relationship failures. First is with social interactions. Second involve interpersonal and intimate persuals. Building social peer groups is difficult because the composition of people must be passive, weak or amenable to the adult's peculiar idiosyncracies. For ACOAs who are shy, overprecautious and passive, groups must already identify an assertive leader who commands authority and compliance from members. For ACOAs who are aggressive, perfectionistic, and workaholics, groups must be passively receptive to the rigid guidance and offer a surplus of laudable remarks. In intimacy, forming a cohesive relationship again requires attraction to either extreme in a single person. The *failure* exists from discovering that opposite attractions turn sour very quickly or after a series of conflicts.

8. *Fear of conflict.* Aggressive or passive ACOAs are equally afraid of conflict. Conflict refers to any disagreement, criticism or opinion lodged against the adult for inappropriate behavior. Conflict resembles situations of inescapable and unavoidable parental punishment causing shame, self-criticism, and desperate need for approval. Hatred of conflict becomes so fierce that adults literally say or do anything to avert confrontation even if escaping it will ultimately pay the price of another confrontation.

9. *Are overly self-critical.* Self-insultation develops from replaying what ACOA therapists call "mental tapes." Tapes are essentially obsessive thoughts in the form of religious, moral or powerfully persuasive beliefs on how behavior *should be, ought to be, and must be.* Such "musterbations" (cf., Ellis, 1962) take two forms. One form is constant negative assaults on imperfections or mistakes believed to be preventable or controllable, using the same words, phrases or intonations recalled from the adult's parents when they were verbally assaultive years ago. Replays of parental verbal abuse shift from the object-mistake in question to generalized attacks regarding the adult's integrity ("you're so stupid") or unrealistic perception of life ("who do you think you are anyway, you won't amount to anything"). A second form are internal recitations of anger toward another person for *causing you this grief of making mistakes or looking stupid.* Projected hatred toward another person (usually an innocent bystander or good friend) disguises the adult's own unconfronted faults and protects the adult from feeling vulnerable.

10. *Become addicted to excitement, alcoholics, abusers or compulsive people.* ACOAs either become alcoholic, marry an alcoholic, or both, or find another compulsive personality such as a workaholic or over-eater to fulfill their own compulsive needs. But why is this? Attraction to excitement largely occurs for the passive adult dissatisfied with the monotony of boring daily routines and desperate for escapism but is incapable of achieving this objective without coercion or caretaking for an energetic person. More aggressive ACOAs at first resist excitable, impulsive people and are more inclined to gravitate toward reserved, docile or emotionally disabled persons who repress their abuses until the relationship (in friendship or intimacy) develops fully. ACOAs who are extroverts or introverts do, however, share a reason for addiction to excitement. Whether their parents were drug or alcoholic abusers or nonsubstance abusers, the verbal and physical abuse nonetheless stifled natural childhood impulsivity, playfulness and creativity. They never had a chance to experience these things. Living this fun in adulthood becomes possible around profoundly impulsive adults.

Survival characteristics. Black's theory (1984a) on family survival echoes a number of works on family alcoholism (e.g., Ackerman, 1983, 1986, 1987a, 1987b; Gravitz and Bowden, 1985; Hayes, 1989; Orford & Harwin, 1982; Steinglass, Bennett, Wolin & Reiss, 1987; Towers, 1989; Wegscheider, 1981). Essentially the theory holds that afflicted children must play certain roles around other family members to restore balance to the system. Roles usually take three or four forms, with there always being a (a) leader, (b) follower, (c) placater, and (d) rebel. All family members struggle together in disharmony trying to compensate for loss of parental direction. With no direction, that is, no adult structure or control, children are helpless to develop on their own or by teachings of an elder sibling rules about right and wrong.

Survival means development. For "development" to occur, somebody must steer the course for the trajectory by providing opportunities. This is where the leader or responsible one fits in. He or she dictates family structure, sets the pace and synchronizes action allowing others a blueprint for personal growth. Applying this blueprint is the job of adjusters or followers. However, no matter how docilely they behave, still there is turbulence felt among addicted, irresponsible parents and the "rebel." This child essentially models the parent's detached, uncaring behavior and is unwilling to abide by the leader's orders. Rebellion frustrates the leader and threatens what little family stability exists, until the fire is put out by the placater. He or she has one function: to defuse altercations before they ruin the family and infuriate the parents. Placaters also mediate arguments between rebel and parents aspiring to appease both parties, merely to attain peace. Reaching peace, unfortunately, means the placater must sacrifice personal needs.

Research support. Support for this theory is empirical, but subjective. Experience alone serves a major index proving that "these things really happen." Personal traumatic accounts of family life (Black, 1984b; Brennan, 1986; Burnett, 1986; Wegscheider (D), 1979; Wegscheider, 1979, 1980) trace step by step the foundations of each role player and reasons for retention of the role from early childhood through adolescence and into adulthood. Undisputed "truths" emerge from the lay understanding that parental abuse and family ambiguity breed a Darwinian impulse for survival. But this is not why the research community to date has been impotent on testing these roles. Most writers on survival theory are not scientists by training or at least lack a methodological background or instinct for designing a controlled experimental study. So, very little research exists on the topic.

The results are unfortunate. Survival theory suffers from obscure definitions, subjective bias, and confusion over the developmental trajectory of each role. The "undisputed truths" mentioned a moment ago are hearsay and only seem replicable because those authors recounting their roles are adults when they write the analysis. They begin with a predisposing model or orientation that may contaminate actual details of their childhood experiences. Retrospectively they can only infer characterization of these roles, whereas prospectively, as adults reflecting upon their own current behavior, the analysis is more believable. On purely scientific grounds, then, survival theory desperately needs attention.

Relation to ecobehaviorism. In relation to ecobehaviorsm, survival theory implies a gain-loss ratio. Risks dominate the parent-child interaction so heavily that usually one of two extremes takes place. Either little expenditure of energy is put into the family, or extraordinary expenditures of energy are displayed, but in both cases the net return is small, inconsistent, and never reciprocal. An ecobehavioral approach puts the child's cumulative losses in excellent perspective. It better explains why apathy, depression, and oppositional behavior directly worsen as the goods and services vanish, and expectations for personal (the child's) gain are low to nonexistent.

Superstitious characteristics. ACOAs also display erratic or idiosyncratic behaviors at times discretely connected to ongoing situations. Sensitivity to the suppressive or potentially suppressive environment triggers them to act in stereotyped or routine ways that can be explained behaviorally as *superstitious behavior*. Within the tradition of experimental analysis of behavior, Skinner (1948) first showed patterns of stereotyped responding by food-deprived pigeons given grain on fixed-time schedules of reinforcement. Pigeons developed behaviors not intended for the reinforcer, and accidentally recurred every time that reinforcer was available. Skinner characterized the acquisition of this responding as a "sort of superstition," because responding followed a ritual and by accident received strength from the reinforcer (Ferster & Skinner, 1957).

Superstitious behaviors have been found in humans for the same reasons (Ferster, Culbertson & Boren, 1975; Hollis, 1973; Skinner, 1977). Of particular importance were pathological obsessions, compulsions and phobias (e.g., Herrnstein, 1966; Zeiler, 1972). For adults, superstitious or ritualistic behaviors spontaneously emerged for three reasons. First, if behaviors accidentally paired with target behaviors for reinforcement. For instance, while waiting for a cab, if adults smoke two cigarettes, pace up and back, and sing to themselves and the cab arrives sooner than usual, the exact same sequence or ritual of behaviors occur next time a cab is called. Second, if behaviors immediately follow reinforcement ("adjunctive behaviors"). The person waits for the cab, for example, without peculiar actions. Moments after the cab arrives early and he enters the cab, dialogue immediately starts with the cab driver where previously no dialogue occurred.

A third reason is avoidance and escape behavior. Superstitious rituals strengthen from the delay or removal of aversive events. If it is avoidance, for instance, the person stays inside a building, out of the rain while waiting for the cab. Habits that form are always waiting inside a building, never on the curb. If it is escape, the cab driver speaking in a loud or nasty voice may push the person back into the building or away from the cab. Escape from confrontation becomes a conditioned ritual.

Ultimately the learning of compulsive, ritualistic or avoidance and escape behaviors arises from mistaken or adventitious conditioning occurring during childhood. Substance abusing parents who angrily shock the child into submission and develop generalized fears in them are also accidentally teaching repetitive, stereotyped actions that the person believes will avert the impending punishment. Behaviors never occur for specific reinforcers. Behaviors are not learned for a specific reward or reinforcer simply because (a) there are few or no reinforcers available, (b) if available, they are random, arbitrary and unpredictable, (c) reinforcers always pair with punishers, and (d) reinforcers never are trusted as being reinforcers. That is, after an aggressively violent mother cools down and offers her child ice cream for smiling and being happy, that ice cream hardly functions to motivate smiles and happiness. A very frightened child is doing everything possible to show smiles and happiness to avoid mother's violent repetition. Nothing about the ice cream is rewarding.

Ecological characteristics. Within the ecosystems model certain propositions explain the extent of family adaptability and cohesion depending upon the openness or closeness of boundaries. A boundary, defined simply, is s region between systems and separating one system from another one in either physical, material or symbolic form. Open boundaries (systems) allow for interaction and transaction with other systems. Closed boundaries restrict or prevent interaction with other systems. Boundaries also may be random (arbitrarily closed and open). Given these variations, note the following six propositions on family ecosystems:

1. The adaptability and hence viability of a family system is related positively to the amount of variety in the system.

2. Undue energy demands upon a family result in a lessened ability for adaptive, creative behavior, and can result in stress on the family system.

3. The rigidity of the boundaries around a family system will influence their capacity to adapt to stressful situations.

4. The ambiguity of the boundaries around a family system will influence their adaptability.

5. The family members who control the information coming into the family and who control the family "memory" have greater ability to control the behavior of other family members.

6. Family systems which are moderately cohesive, but which allow for individual autonomy, are more able to adapt to change and stress than either those in which family members are very tightly bound to each other, or those in which there is little cohesion, and everyone goes his or her own way.

Propositions 2, 3, 4, & 5 particularly are germane for alcoholic families. Boundary regulations limit children from autonomously expressing opinion, and from having transactions outside of proximal boundaries. For instance, suspecting parents may questions children on what other adults said to them, on opinions about the parents, and will presume the children are lying. Alcoholic families limit boundaries by limiting "resources." When resources communicated to children are ambiguous, the children never properly develop or satisfy basic needs likely met in nondysfunctional families. Two types of regulated resources are "proximity" (location, distance, frequency) of interaction, and type or "exchange" of interaction. Exchange pertains to parenting styles or discipline used on the children (see Chapter 1 for exchange rules).

In ecological terms, proximity impacts use of negative discipline. Proximity or the "positioning" of parents depends on household structure, access routes (dimensions) through different rooms or hallways, and natural boundaries around certain rooms considered private or special to children such as their bedroom or bathroom. Proximity also includes "frequency" of parent-child contact based on the children learning or not learning to approach their parents during the day.

The second variable is method of exchange or use of discipline. Exchange of resources usually means parents grant money, gifts, or special accolades to children for many reasons. Noneconomic resources such as love and caring also may be transferred. In both cases the exchange is unconditional or noncontingent; the child owes nothing in return for the gift. In alcoholic families the exchange not only is contingent, but noneconomic resources such as love and caring are a rarity. Affection and love, if given, is for a stiff price of compliance to rigid, unrealistic expectations. Such high expectations, however, are rarely reached and instead children receive punishment.

On a systems level, punishment disrupts this exchange system. Denial of support, of affection, and of noneconomic resources distances children from parents, from siblings and from the human behavioral environment outside the family. Punishment also closes boundaries around a child's potential, forcing unavoidable and inescapable fear. While parents believe this maintains family control, in effect the control invalidates the child's self-purpose, stifles his learning opportunities, and largely instills hostility in him toward the parents. Anger reaching a certain peak takes the form of acting out behavior.

Family discordance thus intensifies when proximity and noneconomic exchanges of resources are infrequent. In alcoholic families, systems theory elucidates the steps of this gradual deterioration by viewing each member in relation to each other. As barriers to adaptation rise, psycho-social development within a family crumbles and is replaced by diffuse, non-goal-directed perceptions of the world. A system torn by this chaos loses its core values among the children; the parents, consumed by their own insecurities, lose interest in saving the system. And the inevitable decay sets the stage for children to repeat these defective patterns intergenerationally in their own family life cycles.

Functional Relationships. Several functional relationships may exist between drinking parents and the emotional or acting out behaviors of their offspring. First let us consider some initial hypotheses followed by a discussion on similarities and differences among these hypotheses:

Hypothesis 1. Among alcoholic parents, there is direct relationship between parental discipline and frequency of child acting out behaviors.

Hypothesis 2. Among alcoholic parents, there is an inverse relationship between parental contact and child acting out behaviors.

Hypothesis 3. Among alcoholic parents, there is a direct relationship between parents' drinking and child acting out behaviors.

The first and third hypotheses propose similar interactions. Hypothesis one proposes that as parental punitive discipline intensifies, so will acting out reactions among children. Hypothesis three proposes that increases (or decreases) in parental alcoholic consumption can increase (or decrease) child acting out behaviors. Both hypotheses thus share common properties. Both statements are *irreversible* because acting out behavior alone may or may not cause harsh disciplinary action or increased intake of alcohol.

Both statements do have a *deterministic and causal* value. Punishment contingencies, shown experimentally, can induce attention-seeking or aggressive responses in children. Intoxicated parents are more prone to be punishing. Events are *sequential*. Maladaptive behaviors follow from the parents' persistent discipline and drinking episodes. However, maladaptive behavior is not a linear outcome. The *contingent* relationship can be with infinite variables ranging from a disturbed, alcoholic parent, to dilapidated living conditions. Finally, the relationship is *positive* insofar as increases (decreases) in one variable proportionally affect increases (decreases) in the other variable.

The second hypothesis is a bit different. Increases in parental contact in the form of (a) proximity, and (b) frequency of interaction may decrease child misbehavior. Alcoholic parents are typically aloof from mainstream family needs and usually only respond when levels of misbehavior exceed a tolerance point. This tolerance point being low, negative traps ensue by parent and child wasting what few contacts exist in unpleasant ways. However, when proximity increases, as in physical or verbal affection, attention is provided for appropriate attention-seeking behaviors.

In view of this potential, the statement is different from hypotheses one and three. There is a *reversible* relationship. Reduced acting out tendencies can just as easily produce an increase in proximity and frequency of parental contact. Second, while still *deterministic and sequential,* types of interaction very much are *contingent* upon durations of parents' sobriety, the child's risk-taking potentials, and the number of successful and reinforcing family transactions without punishment.

Support for these hypotheses. Testing these hypotheses using a grounded theory method is perhaps putting the cart before the horse. That is, data is collected after the establishment of some preliminary theories. But at least the support "instances" offered can indicate if the concepts are valid. The empirical indicators derive from clinical intake evaluations that record referral reasons for seeking counseling. One hundred cases of alcoholic families were reviewed. The primary referral reasons for each family along with levels of concepts appear below in Table 1.

Table 1
Referral Reasons of Clinical Cases (n = 100) and
Levels of Ground Theory Concepts

DATA	INITIAL LEVEL	HIGHER LEVEL
1. Our children are perfectionistic.	Kids Work Too Hard	Fear of failure
2. Everybody wants control.	Nobody trusts anyone	Fear of vulnerbility
3. My wife is too passive.	She is afraid	Fear of rejection
4. My husband drinks too much.	He is an alcoholic	Fear of stress
5. We never solve arguments.	Avoiding conflict	Fear of conflict
6. The kids are too dependent on us.	Lack independence	Fear of risks
7. The kids are disruptive at school.	Taking out anger	Fear of friends
8. Our parents ignore us.	Neglectful parents	Fear of love
9. Our parents yell at us.	Harsh discipline used	Fear of control
10. The kids think they're adults.	High responsibility	Fear of play

A major referral reason repeated throughout the interviewing process is that families inherently are afraid to deal with presenting problems. Fear itself is quite prevalent despite parents blaming children or children blaming their parents for the communication breakdown. Family decay attributed to minor members further evinces a need for control. By contrast, parents unafraid of control usually can admit fault in themselves as equally as they might ascribe fault to others. An alcoholic family feeds, however, on control and protection of self-vulnerability even if it means fabricating accusations or ignoring personal problems.

Avoidance and Escape Patterns

Thus far the words "avoidance" and "escape" keep recurring. Traditional learning theorists (e.g., Dollard & Miller, 1950; Mowrer, 1950; Solomon & Wynne, 1954), as well as their applied counterparts (e.g., Eysenck, 1979; Stampfl & Levis, 1967; Wolpe, 1958) have proposed that psychological symptoms can be conceptualized as avoidance behaviors designed to escape from aversive conditioned stimuli. Human laboratory experiments attesting to this phenomenon (Banks, 1965; Malloy & Levis, 1988; Maxwell, Miller & Meyer, 1971) repeatedly show that persistence of avoidance and escape patterns, even in the absence of danger, relates to a history of conditioning and intermittent contact with fearful stimuli. Operationally avoidance and escape refer to response-producing changes that terminate that aversive event. *Termination* takes several forms. Responses may:

1. Delay the impending aversive event.

2. Alter the impending aversive event before it arrives.

3. Eliminate the impending aversive event before it arrives.

4. Interrupt the aversive event while it occurs.

5. Alter the aversive event while it occurs.

6. Eliminate the aversive event while it occurs.

Forms of defusing, dismantling and basically diminishing the impact of aversive events in ACOAs vary along these six lines (cf. Ruben, in press). This is the predictable function of behavior. Less predictable and more infinitely diverse is the response topography, that is, what the behavior actually looks like. Here we attempt to identify major avoidance and escape response patterns clinically reported in several case studies, including over 1,000 patients seen in the author's practice. Examined closely, avoidance and escape patterns account for a large percentage of idiosyncratic or repetitive habits deeply ingrained in ACOAs, given the consequences or effects of these patterns also reviewed below.

Enabling/Caretaking. Already mentioned is the passively-seeking ambition to regulate balance in adult relationships. Adults afraid of conflict and of risking behavior changes causing disapproval will resort to a style of accommodation. Compromising personal needs occurs so frequently and habitually that no longer is the forfeited need or object considered a loss. Sacrifices become a natural, familiar motion in daily interaction much like breathing, eating, and sleeping. Without realizing it, enablers and caretakers entirely operate on negative reinforcement.

Pleasing, satisfying or absorbing grief for people delays, alters and destroys impending aversive events and consequently encourages them to do the same behavior in the future. Confirmation comes in the (a) amount of time elapsed before another conflict (the longer, the better), (b) the mild or diminished intensity of arguments when they occur, (c) the shorter duration of arguments, and (d) the recuperative capacity of the arguer. This last one poses an interesting option. ACOAs unable to avoid or escape aversive conflict may appease the predator hoping he will rapidly restore calmness after the argument.

Because contact with aversive events is awful, false alarms are common mistakes and acted upon in the same way. False alarms are believing there is a potential argument and intercepting it beforehand. Avoidance this far ahead creates the false inference that *had steps not been taken, aversive conflict might appear.* Ensuing conflicts may or may not occur but advanced steps, nonetheless, speed into motion long before risk of conflict. Predators on the receiving end of this intervention neither are perplexed, nor willing to reverse the caretaking tactics. A fearful husband, for example, anticipating his wife's critical words over a recent office purchase, lavished his wife with bouquets, "I love you" cards, and took her out to dinner. All efforts assumingly were designed to avoid his wife's cynical remarks long before she learned of the purchases. This may be called *anticipatory caretaking.* Planning ahead seems safe but it is no guarantee of conflict elimination. In fact, his wife may fully thrive on the voluminous reinforcers and may expect complimentary treatment repeated, regardless of her intentions of conflict.

Anticipatory caretaking usually is a methodical, systematic, and incredibly calibrated effort. ACOAs evaluate potentials for aversive contacts and immediately disinfect them in much the same way as ecologists check the atmosphere or waters for pollutants and proceed with chemical treatment. Every step built into the sequence of avoidance has a history of effectively altering one, many, or all components leading to confrontation. Synchronicity is imperative. A wife expecting her drunken husband to be physically abusive may, ahead of time, rearrange the furniture, call a friend (witness) over, evacuate the children to their bedrooms or out of the house, and prepare a meal of his liking. These tasks all have specific *functional* reasons and must occur in this *precise* order. Calculated risks are intolerable mistakes in the overall organization plan of avoidance.

Aggression. Alluded to earlier were verbal outbursts having a twofold cause. First, anger responded to the ACOAs loss of control and resistance to vulnerability. Second, anticipating conflict, anger cues the predators to stay away (avoidance) or terminate conflict (escape). One way or another, the functions of anger rarely if ever include disclosure of emotional frustrations or disappointment as might occur in most people claiming to be angry. NonACOAs accept vulnerability as the natural outgrowth of making errors, being viewed as incompetent, or voicing opinions. ACOAs, on the other hand, carefully repress anger evoked from vulnerability and only release it as a mechanism to expedite conflict elimination. Threats of physical retaliation, profuse vulgarity, hostile demands, and abrasive criticism on the surface look like an aggressive assault, luring the listener into fierce battle. But just the opposite is occurring. Insulting attacks intend to debilitate and discourage the listener from responding in any way.

One result is *anticipatory aggression*. Less calculated and more reflexive are aggressive assaults made in anticipation of conflict. Like *anticipatory caretaking* inadequate proof exists that there will be a conflict except the ACOAs history of conditioning and incapacity to stressfully wait the time out. Poor control over emotions sets off a series of physiological, cognitive and behavioral responses sequentially followed in this format: (a) autonomic arousal (rapid heart beat, tightness of chest, perspiration, shallow breathing, etc.), (b) negative, paranoid-like statements ("who does he think he is," "nobody will blame me for anything," etc.), and (c) outward aggressive actions (yelling, hitting objects, stomping around, etc.).

Arousal is rapid, progressive, and lacks the self-conscious evaluation and calibration of actions to consequences. In the end, hostile actions produce one of three outcomes upon listeners. First, listeners never approach the aggressor out of shock and perplexity. Second, and during conflict, listeners stop the argument instantly, offended and perplexed by the rude interjections. Or third, annoyed listeners determined to pursue the conflict in spite of obstacles accelerate aggressiveness in both parties until the ACOA resorts to physical property destruction, injury toward another, or threats of self-injury. One way or another, escape from rising confrontation will be achieved in a short time. Rarely, if ever, will the ACOA ride the storm out until the bitter end no matter who is right and who is wrong. Right and wrong are irrelevant.

Anxiety and Panic Disorder. Negative reinforcement occurs in still a third way. When conflict threatens on the horizon, panic and anxiety may set in. Relief of anxiety, by avoiding and escaping conflict, reinforces the ACOA to re-experience the anxiety or panic in future similar situations. Panic, as in *panic attacks,* builds from unregulated excitement of the sympathetic nervous system under fear situations. Rushes of dizziness, loss of breath or rapid breathing, weakness in limbs, tachycardia, ear and eye sensitivity comprise symptomatology that triggers an urgent need for escape. Failure to leave the situation prolongs the physical misery and turns into *catastrophizing* thoughts about fainting, being disabled and the dread of embarrassment. ACOAs expecting conflict, criticism or rejection can react the same way. Rather than face emotional hurt, panic attacks arise moments before or just as conflict starts and shift the predator's actions from possible attack to sympathy and empathy. Panic attacks that are announced receive urgent attention from even a slightly caring spouse; sensitivity to the person's health displaces aggressive actions and restores safety to the ACOAs environment.

Variations of Patterns. Acting on avoidance and escape has more manifestations than simply the three types reviewed thus far. Response types also are never so uniformly "black and white." Overlap among response patterns can be confusing, irritating, and misleading. Misinterpretation of these avoidance and escape patterns also accounts for incorrect diagnoses by physicians, psychologists, social workers and other health care providers faced with strange symptoms that have ambiguous or no certain underlying pathology. Response patterns might include the following:

1. *No communication.* Person simply withdraws and remains mutistic under any impending threat of conflict. Attempts to penetrate this silence is met with poor eye contact, crying, or additional efforts to seek safety in a hidden spot.

2. *Runaway.* Person takes refuge by physically running away to another location. Relocation can be to parents' house, friends' house, bar, or driving long distances in unspecified directions.

3. *Substance abuse.* Person drinks beer, mixed drinks, smokes a joint or other chemical use in anticipation of conflict, rejection or criticism or while it is in progress. *Contingent use of substance abuse* usually means the person only engages in substances under emotional duress or when feeling conflict is unavoidable or inescapable.

4. *Emotional paralysis.* Studies on Learned Helplessness (Seligman & Johnston, 1973) and Tonic Immobility (Ratner, 1958; Ratner & Thompson, 1968) have application here. Panic and fright operate simultaneously upon the confronted person who feels totally helpless under inescapable or unavoidable circumstances. Lacking adaptive alternatives, the person's only repertoire is emotional paralysis, of catatonically remaining in the situation without realistic orientation or thoughts. Numbness overwhelms sensory receptors and inhibits all activating responses to combat or diminish a sense of impending doom.

5. *Selective attention.* This is opposite to emotional paralysis. Discriminative abilities became sharper under threats of conflict, criticism or rejection. Astute perceptions in thought, sensation, and observation alert the person to subtle behavior changes in the predator that appear modifiable and promise avoidance and escape possibilities. Awareness, for instance, that her spouse forgot to call home ahead of his arrival *means* he must have stopped at the bar. Inferring this, she can alter the environment ahead of his return and demobilize confrontation. Heightened sensory discriminations (visual, auditory, olfactory, etc.) further detect and clarify competing stimuli in predators such as sorting alcohol odor from after-shave lotion, and even account for "premonitions" of hearing noises or the spouse saying or doing things even before his arrival.

6. *Passivity.* Quietly assuming a passive posture functions like aggression to expedite unwanted predatory attacks. Persons who electively withhold comments wait for the aggression, criticism, or rejection to finish, then they resurrect pleasant topics or move the discussion rapidly to safe territory. Shifting topics begins by asking about topics interesting or rewarding to the predator and on which he can monologue without relapsing to arguments.

7. *Accusation.* Accusing the predator, ahead of conflict, of inappropriate behavior either starts the conflict or defeats it. Accusations primarily arise for two reasons. First, anxious and annoyed, ACOAs may have improperly inferred information from the

predator or environment. Inferences motivate the person to bullishly blame "alleged" predators for violations that the person finds reprehensible, although little support exists for these accusations. Second, accusations may emotionally injure or intimidate the alleged predator and thereby disable retaliation or further confrontation. Listeners stunned by this attack are equally dumbfounded when they "bite the bait" and politely inquire about proof for the accusation. ACOAs retort with vehemently abrasive jabs that entirely ignore peaceful problem-solving efforts and only serve to fortify resistance. Even reconciliatory efforts from listeners go unnoticed since the ACOA is engulfed in antagonism and proving his point just as he did as an aggressive child growing up.

8. *Feign ignorance.* Passivity, emotional paralysis--all serve to withdraw from perceived conflict. Another avoidance tactic is pretending one simply is ignorant of facts or problems presented in the conflict. Ignorance liberates the anxious person from justifying answers, coming up with solutions, or dealing in any way with surface anger. Usually the alternative reply from ACOAs is offering sympathy, empathy or just listening as the predator ventilates aggravation.

9. *Imposterism.* This is a very serious type of avoidance and escape. Fear of incompetency, of exposing faults and raising eyebrows to criticism and rejection may force a person into a disguise that masks or feels like it masks his true identity. Faking knowledge or nodding in agreement on things about which the person knows very little or nothing creates the impression of strength, pride and intelligence. However, underneath this charade is the anxious ACOA, fearful that other people will *spot their stupidity and discover they are imposters.*

Level of actual integrity, of education or career advancement are irrelevant variables determining how sensitive a person is to imposterism. One woman, an executive director over 200 employees, confident and outspoken lobbyist, and financially secure, struggled against the incipient fear of being discovered by her constituents as incompetent. There was nothing actually incompetent about her, other than her self-imposed, persuasive belief that an approving public wanted her error-free.

10. *Shame.* Avoidance and escape take the form of releasing others from their burdens. Shame does this. A person relieves the predator of anger by blaming himself for causing the conflict and now deserving the punishment. Relief occurs in three ways. First, ACOAs anticipate conflict, criticism or rejection by volunteering their faults in hopes that

they match the predator's concerns. Whether they do or not, predators accept the confession rather than start an argument. Second, ACOAs interrupt predatory attacks with a sympathetic re-interpretation of how they caused the impropriety and inconvenienced the predator. Again, escape from conflict is nearly guaranteed as the predator accepts their testimony. Third, ACOAs blame a third person not present during the conflict or attack who can absorb full responsibility for the damage. By again absolving the predator, ACOAs regain control over the situation and eliminate their own guilt for upsetting the predator.

11. *Depression*. Kazdin's (1990) comprehensive review of childhood depression insightfully describes many convergent symptoms as *comorbidity*. That is, many children meet criteria for more than one disorder, such as overlapping criteria for anxiety, conduct disorders, and oppositional disorders. Entering adulthood, unrelieved childhood fears, anxieties, and disorders act as weak immunity against stressors of conflict, rejection, and criticism. Predisposing emotional disabilities increase the adult's susceptibility to avoidance and escape behaviors. The problem, however, is delineating between avoidance and escape in response to ensuing conflict, and avoidance and escape from endogenous or chronic depression. Most ACOAs who suffered arbitrary and critical punishment in childhood also struggle with depression. It comes on rapidly and after prolonged episodes of uncontrolled anxiety, or entrapment in inescapable, unavoidable situations. Depression in ACOAs also arises for the following reasons:

1. Caretaking and enabling efforts disrupted, violated or replaced by another caretaker or enabler.

2. Caretaking and enabling efforts refused by recipients, misinterpreted as rejection.

3. Caretaking and enabling efforts stifled by absence of any available recipient.

4. Caretaking or aggression fail to avoid or escape conflict, criticism, or rejection.

5. Prolonged or generalized anxiety escalating to panic attacks after physical exhaustion and anxiety subsides.

6. Forced to sit, relax or remain immobile either when alone or around predator.

7. Removal or interruption of food, alcohol or drugs after habitual or excessive use either before, during, or after conflict, criticism or rejection.

8. Removal or interruption of running away or hiding either before, during or after conflict, criticism or rejection.

9. Forced to outwardly express angry, vulnerable or personal feelings around predator even if mediated by therapist.

10. Prolonged guilt or shame from repeatedly upsetting people or inferring disapproval.

11. Prolonged guilt or shame from repeatedly asserting personal ideas, disagreements or refusals and inferring disapproval.

12. Prolonged guilt or shame from repeatedly finding fault in self, treating self as scapegoat for others' problems, and regarding loneliness as abandonment and rejection.

Effects of avoidance and escape. Predictable outcomes of avoidance and escape responses seemingly include removal of fear and restoration of control. But not always. In fact, the irony is that opposite consequences emerge that surprise the daylights out of ACOAs. Upon nonACOAs, such consequences would instantly destroy all caretaking, enabling, even aggressive reactions. ACOAs unfortunately perceive the same consequences, not as lessons to stop dysfunctional behavior, but as an ambitious challenge undertaken to improve their chances of approval and ultimately to fulfill an abstract set of expectations. They keep producing the same behavior, thinking the only reason it works or does not work lies within their control. The consequences that ACOAs frequently encounter include the following:

Exploitation. Generously caretaking the needs of people builds up selfish expectations in people who demand more of the same generosity without reciprocity. Caretakers regard the higher demands, at first, as proof of effectively pleasing the person enough so he or she desires more of them. As demands grow, resentment slowly develops but is kept silent. ACOAs feel ashamed as their resentment and delude themselves into believing their caretaking efforts still are inadequate.

Superstitious behavior. One peculiar consequence of *anticipatory caretaking and anticipatory aggression* is that it reinforces whatever the predator is doing before an alleged conflict. Recall that conflict may or may not be impending and efforts to appease the predator end up accidentally shaping strange or unwanted behaviors. For example, one husband claimed his wife always greeted him with excessive affection that he finally realized might distract him from the mail and discovering her compulsive use of credit cards. He noticed himself more sexually aroused after work and expecting intercourse even after his wife's compulsion stopped and supposedly the need for avoidance gone. However, residual behaviors such as this manufactured from earlier avoidance behavior still continued, which caused more trouble for the wife. She hated his daily sexual demands, but now faced a new obstacle of criticism, rejection and conflict if she denied his wants. Avoidance *had to* continue for another reason that she never bargained for.

Rejection. Extensive caretaking efforts for approval dissatisfy the exploitive, demanding party who expects incessant generosity without reciprocity. Continuous appeasement finds these recipients upset, angry, and rejecting the caretaker no matter how much compensatory effort goes into repairing the broken relationship. ACOAs never quite understand reasons for this rejection, attributing it largely to their own incompetency. Guilt over the rejection perpetuates more caretaking efforts that unknowingly annoy the already disturbed recipient who continues resisting the caretaker's efforts.

Inattention to appropriate behavior. Not all recipients take advantage of caretakers. Recipients, such as spouses, acknowledging the caretaker's generosity may properly reciprocate with rewards but be adamantly refused by the caretaker. Resistance to reciprocity indicates inattention and distrust of appropriate behaviors in other people, no matter how much caretakers insist on receiving reciprocity. Attention drawn to caretakers for their kindness or efforts is embarrassing, suspicious and frequently deflected with criticism or aggression. ACOAs may tease, discount, or directly insult recipients for effort.

Punished attempts at reciprocity by recipients undergo suppression rapidly and set an occasion for the caretaker to again complain that he or she receives nothing in return for doing everything. An example was a controlling wife who lamented that her family never helped out with household chores. On the father's initiative, the family surprised the caretaker by completing the laundry, preparing dinner, and running other odd chores. Rather than appreciate this surprise, she immediately found fault in all family participants for improperly doing the chores. Assessment of faults also suppressed further initiatives by family members to help out with chores or even think of repeating similar surprises in the future.

Why do ACOAs seemingly sabotage good-natured gestures by those whom they accuse of being unsympathetic? The answer is threefold. First, *helping out is perceived as exposing incompetency because the caretaker could not do it alone; perception of fault transforms into believing he or she is being criticized.* Removal of that perception of fault and criticism is by eliminating efforts initiated by others. Second, *helping out is distrustful; treating the caretaker nicely "must have" underlying motives believed to inauthenticate the kind gesture. Nobody ever did things in the past for this person, so why are people doing them now?*

Distrusted efforts receive cautious, even callous reactions that protect ACOA from becoming vulnerable, out of control, and re-experiencing the entrapment reminiscent of childhood. Third, *helping out is never as good as it should be. Expectations for reciprocity far exceed realistic criteria for people returning favors or acting correctly.* ACOAs invest such excessive efforts, even at perfectionistic levels, in helping other people that they expect people to reciprocate in identical manner.

However, indulgent, excessive behaviors are abnormal, highly impractical, and unlikely to be repeated by the average lot of responders unless they, too, are caretakers. Ironically, even identically repeating the same large chunks of behaviors, say, if the person is himself a caretaker, will be rejected because it still does not *meet expectations.* These "expectations" essentially are nonexistent, highly abstract, or unreachable objectives regarding what the caretaker believes is functionally appropriate behavior but has never attained himself. Unrealistic adult expectations derive from never satisfying a parent's needs for approval during a dysfunctional childhood.

Provoking of aggression. Despite pleas for others to treat caretakers with respect and reciprocity, ACOAs will desperately gain attention even if it is aggressive attention. An agreeable spouse is *provoked* by insults, criticisms, teasing, and repetitive threats until he or she replies angrily. The moment anger arises, threatening conflict, ACOAs withdraw and blame the provoked person for mistreatment, negligence, or verbal abuse. Absolutely no other explanation offered by the provoked party is admissible other than the reactive behavior being "grossly selfish and aggressive."

Naturally provoked recipients are terribly perplexed. But there is a critical reason that caretakers provoke aggression. Historically, they expect and know how to "deal with" aggressive attention. Enduring physically or verbally abusive attacks during childhood formed a repertoire for aggressive interactions. Habits were formed that prepared caretakers to anticipate or cope with arbitrarily arising episodes of hostility as part of survival. In adulthood, episodes that do not occur *naturally*, that is, on the recipient's own initiative, are contrived to restore familiar family situations. Once produced, ACOAs regain control, redeem their confidence and feel comfortable in much the same way as couples who gain comfort in repeating certain religious or ethnic practices in the marriage they learned in childhood.

Procrastination. Avoidance and escape nearly always produce a delay, or termination of tasks the person feels are (a) difficult to do, (b) outside their repertoire, or (c) prone to cause conflict, criticism, or rejection. Rarely, if ever, does the person admit deficiency when confronted with impossible odds regarding a task or even a small favor asked of them. Politely they accept the task, rather than refuse to do it and face instant rejection. As time passes the task remains incomplete. Reminders to complete the task or fulfill the favors are responded to with honest apologies, compensatory efforts that relieve the accuser of anger, and essentially these appeasements serve to extend delays even longer.

ACOAs react in one of four ways. First, they show fierce anger, aggression or vehemently deny accusations and their commitment to complete the task or fulfill a promise. Second, they distract the accuser by shifting to incompatible, irrelevant topics likely to upset or please the accuser. One distraction is turning the topic around to blame the accuser for *not reminding them to do the task, and how it is their fault for forgetting*. Other shifts, also called "roadblocks," are to start a new conversation, offer sex or food treats, or simply walk away. Third, they sink into spontaneous depression characterized by crying and self-criticism, promising to stop whatever they are doing that moment to fulfill the promise. Most recipients, however, refuse this spontaneous remediation because it seems preposterous, illogical, impractical, or irrelevant. In other words, for the person to "stop whatever they are doing now" may also interrupt the recipient who is unwilling to stop whatever he or she is doing. Finally, combinations of these reactions are very common. For instance, spontaneous acts of remediation ("fine, I'll do it now") may accompany aggressive, defensive remarks.

Miscommunications. One of the severe repercussions of avoidance and escape is miscommunication. Fear of conflict, criticism and rejection prevents inquiry into suspicious behaviors of other people, resulting in damaging inferences about why and how people do things that are not parallel to real events. Inferences distort and affirm stereotyped beliefs that never get clarified. Recently a man broke out into rage over somebody giving him a gift he did not want. He assaulted the gift by destroying it with a hammer, thinking that the gift was left *on purpose to spite and hurt him.* Never did it occur to him prior to his destructive actions to *check out why the gift was left for him and whether the reason was inconsistent with his inference.* Failure to investigate assumptions diminishes the risk of looking stupid or arousing unwanted conflict whether or not these events would truly occur.

Temporary Relief. Avoidance and escape generates negative reinforcement. In principle this means responses that remove or terminate some aversive or expected aversive event will increase in future probability given similar conditions. The "removal" or "termination" produces temporary relief from either anticipatory fear of aversive events or being exposed directly to those events. Once they are gone, anxiety dissipates and control over actions is restored. However, feeling relieved is a misleading and unproductive consequence if the aversive event was essential for healthy adjustment. Relief, for example, from medical illness allows for healthy adjustment. But not relief from conflict. Escaping conflict is unhealthy and denies opportunities to build proper communication skills, listening skills, and solve problems. Relief at the expense of developing adaptive skills is artificially satisfying but also emotionally injurious since it means avoidance and escape will be the only way to handle future conflict.

Termination of Friendships. "Cutting your nose off to spite your face" is a moral expression. It typically describes a child who aborts or destroys something that is personally gratifying at the time so that it might annoy the parent. This "annoyance" is retaliatory and hopefully will hurt the parent as much as it upset the child. Imagine a child thriving on a juicy hamburger. Told he must eat his vegetables or not get dessert, the stubborn child might stop eating his meal altogether, and proceed to dump the entire plate of vegetables, hamburger and french fries into the garbage can. Consequently his parents yell at him, deny offering more food, or in some way punish these actions. Older children, however, regard the provocation of parental anger as retaliation for interrupting or denying the child his selfish needs. In adulthood, similar behavior patterns occur in response to inferred deprivations of selfish needs. This same person, described a moment ago as smashing a gift with a hammer, is so infuriated that he nearly terminates a relationship with the gift-giver, despite friendship for over 10 years.

Why is this? Why cut his nose off to spite his face? Why, in other words, must the ACOA terminate an otherwise rewarding relationship on account of one upsetting episode? Or, how could he even believe this action truly will hurt the person just as similar actions hurt his parents during childhood? The answers lie in the incapacity to accept rejection, criticism and hatred of conflict. As for retaliation, recipients usually never discern that termination of friendship harbors vindictive motives; they simply perceive the gestalt of events as peculiar and maladaptive. Secondly, the ACOA would rather maintain avoidance and escape patterns than attempt solutions that would defuse false inferences, and ensure continuation of rewarding friendships. Forfeiture of accumulated personal resources at "the drop of the bucket" illustrates severely deficient coping mechanisms for one thing. For another, dispensing with resources so rapidly adds to the person's loneliness and isolationism.

Nature versus Nurture Controversy on Transmission of Alcohol and Drug Problems

Stiff controversy surrounds the legendary debate between nature (inheritance) and nurture (environment) as antecedent forces in substance abuse transmission across generations. Supporters of nature argue that clear genetic trackings evinced in twin-separation studies, among other methods, reveal uncanny similarities in adult personality which strongly credit inheritance as the cause (Plomin & Daniels, 1987). Proponents of the nurture position profess a strong learning history responsible for developmental abnormalities traced to poor parental upbringing and limited opportunities for enrichment (Werner, 1985; Wertheim, 1978).

Opponents of both sides of the argument eagerly dispute methodological flaws in the research and unwillingly agree there is indefinite data for substantial conclusions (Clarke & Clarke, 1984). Ultimately the controversy falls upon two major issues. First is whether parental alcohol and drug abuse automatically is transferrable to offspring. Second is whether early onset antisocial behavior or drug abuse problems evident in childhood necessarily progress to adulthood because of genetic forces, or whether conditioning completes the picture. Continuity of personality holds many mysteries we also will explore.

Transmission of addiction problems from parent to child. Explanatory studies favoring inheritance follow children longitudinally across their lifespan and examine particular biological or genetic changes possibly linked to behavior changes. Gaining widespread attention for this approach was *sociobiology*. Sociobiologists, guided by ideas of Darwin, accept that survival-promoting behavior is passed on from one generation to another. They contend the perpetuation of genes, rather than of the individual organism, is the prime evolutionary tendency. Evolution produces organisms that follow a logical approach, almost calculating genetic gains and losses. One interesting extension is that human altruism is expected to decline. Another is that stronger family members carrying on "survival genes" resist alcoholism easier than weaker family members. Because this theory involves extensions to complex human social behavior, relationships between genes and behavior take on a new perspective.

Genetics as predictors. Borrowing from sociobiologists, impetus for genetic research on predicting antisocial behavior has become more popular. Studies on the etiology of schizophrenia are based on examination of families, twins, and adoptions. Heston (1966) Rosenthal (1970) both found that offspring of a schizophrenic have the same risk for schizophrenia whether or not they are raised by a schizophrenic parent. Studies on etiology of alcoholism echo this same conclusion. Persuasive results largely come from adoption studies where distinctions are supposedly clear between mild and severe alcoholism, and propensity for criminal behavior. Cloninger, Bohman & Sigvardsson (1981), for example, interviewed biological mothers and fathers and step mothers and fathers of adopted monozygotic twin children showing high correlations of alcoholism. Individual differences further attesting to twins' behaviors are altruistic and aggressive tendencies (Rushton, Fulker, Neale, Nias & Eysenck, 1986). Nonshared environments seemingly rule out the artifact of common learning experiences and point to dominance of heredity.

Weakness of learning theories. Another victory for behavioral genetics research lies in discrediting environmental studies. Let us consider the type of methodological pitfalls uncovered in weak or otherwise poorly designed models, as perceived through the critical eyes of genetic analysts. Two studies for consideration are by McCord (1979) and Eron (1982).

McCord's findings were that variables describing early home atmosphere predict later criminality. Methodological and theoretical assumptions inadvertently weaken internal and external validity. Included in these limitations are (a) reification of variables in hypothesis, (b) subject selection and sampling error, and (c) pitfalls of case records .

Reification of variables in hypothesis. McCord's study bases its assumption on variables incorrectly and inoperationally defined. Variables describing home life such as mother's self-confidence, conflict, aggressiveness, affection and so on become "things in themselves." They are given powerful status (reified) rather than defined as one, among many, transactions in daily life. For instance, maternal affection is no more important than earned grades in school, or mother-father compatibility, or sibling affiliation. Secondly, his coding classifications lacked specificity to pass the test of validity. While raters scored high on agreement of coded items, thus achieving high reliability, this rating only suggests that codes either were very general or that one code covered more than one behavior.

Subject selection and sampling error. There were major pitfalls in sample selection. One obvious problem is that subjects came from Massachusetts, an eastern state of enriched resources. A simultaneous study conducted on young children in, for example, the foothills of Kentucky, might yield very different results. A second problem is predisposing characteristics. McCord planned for longitudinal tracking of criminal behavior. But tracking started when subjects already were in delinquent prevention. They had already demonstrated deviant behavior. A more valid assessment might have started when children were living at home and their delinquency risk not established.

Pitfalls of case records. Problems of case study records are well known. Subjective inferences by counselors or social workers on what parents do or do not do rely as much on the natural events as on the observer's misperceptions. Imprecision of data causes further difficulty. Recorded observations, for example, that document a father's alcoholism, describe abbreviated moment by moment actions, excluding key aspects of drinking frequency, consumption rate and history of substance abuse. Besides the fact that data were nearly 40 years old, precious information was lost that has more predictive usefulness.

Eron's findings on television-elicited aggression trace back to research studies conducted during the early 1960s, not only by himself, but also by Bandura (1973). Experimental laboratory evidence for these results additionally can be found in pioneering works by Ulrich & Wolfe (1969a, 1969b). Essentially, Eron reported on follow-up longitudinal interviews corroborating his earlier data from the Rip Van Winkle study and another study on younger children. However, although theoretically his model is valid, his conclusions improperly distinguish between effects of television viewing and "other" immediate aggression-inducing factors. Pitfalls thereby arise in his (a) failure to compare television with other media exposure, (b) lack of discrimination between parental patterns and television controlling patterns, and (c) failure to explain maintenance effects of television on perpetuation of aggressive behavior.

Failure to compare television with other media exposure. One major pitfall overlooked by Eron was that other media sources experienced in a child's (6 to 10 years) life contribute equally if not potentially more to aggression. Radio, movie theaters, advertisement boards, newspapers, and books all present evocative stimuli of a reinforcing or punishing nature.

Lack of discrimination between parental patterns and television controlling patterns. Eron's analysis falls short of sorting between aggression derived from parenting patterns and that derived from television viewing. Extensive parent measures on rejection, nurturance, punishment, self-rated aggression, social mobility, TV violence, and aggressive fantasy were positively correlated with aggression scales for boys and girls. Most notably were Scales 4 and 9 on MMPI and extent of parental punishment. Factoring out frequency of television, chances are reasonably high that level of child aggression would remain just as high from parent-child interaction. Eron neglected to use comparison groups to ferret out effects of different variables.

Failure to explain maintenance effects of television on perpetuation of aggressive behavior. Even if Eron's research supports his own and many precursory theories, long-term aggressive behavior does not seem sufficiently correlated with childhood exposure to television. Take, for instance, the case of Ronald. Interviews at age 19 revealed his being on probation and arrested but unfortunately further study of him was terminated by his death. Longitudinal records are fuzzy on how much violent television cartoons he watched and whether viewing subsided after puberty and into late adolescence. Did he stop watching television and resort to excessive R-rated movies? Perhaps pornographic movies? Cumulative aggression is not supported by television alone.

Learned behavior as predictors. Behavioral genetics rivals the very foundation of conditioning or environmental research. While most environmentalists are open to *integrative interpretations,* that is, where both nature and nurture are equal forces, most argue that environment really is the leading cause. Why is this? One reason is the scientific legitimacy of operant and respondent principles underlying the structure of simple and complex social behavior. Using these principles, often times confusing actions involving emotion, memory, cognition, and behavior can be interpreted relatively easily and the analysis tested under controlled laboratory and natural settings. Heredity, on the other hand, although based in genetic quantitative science, loses its measurability when interpreted as a social phenomena.

Plomin & Daniels (1987) eloquently trace behavioral influences to show how adoptive children from the same family can be so different. Since the children share family environment, not heredity, correlations directly estimate the importance of parental behavioral influences and its precursory effects of psychopathology, particularly of substance abuse. Newlin (1987), as well, traces a sequence of subtle steps of conditioning leading sons of alcoholic parents to explore, drink and develop drinking habits themselves. He articulates how classical conditioning increases offspring's autonomic arousal around "elicitive" cues and thereby increases their tolerance and alcohol consumption levels. Tolerance is a conditioned response to drug cues that also inhibits natural (unconditioned) responses to reject alcohol. Alcohol also is vicariously observed as relieving stress, boredom and for enhancing social recreation.

In both studies there is an explicit conclusion that environmental factors are inherently part of family dynamics and are more influential upon drinking and drug use than any genetic factors. The difficulty, methodologically, is tracing the puzzling route of this conditioning to prove the conclusion true. One way of searching for answers to this problem is by looking at changes in individual personality over time.

Persistence of personality from childhood to adulthood. Constancy of personality has two meanings. First, it refers to relatively unchanging behaviors of individuals or groups over a lifespan. Second, it refers to progression of behavior changes following a predictable trajectory from infancy to old age. Constancy across time, without any fluctuation in behavior, is very unlikely and theories supporting it are antediluvian. They are replaced by developmental theories contending that change, like maturation, is an ongoing process during periods of ontogeny. This change occurs in aggregates. In infancy learning is situational or discriminative, where reflexive or operant responses remain closely connected to antecedents and consequences. As aggregates form complex behavior, behavior is less situation-specific and more generalizable. The question, however, is how much change really takes place? Is the change really a recycled version of early childhood behavior, only aggregated by physical, maturational factors? Or is behavior constant and only situations changed? Clearly there is "something" passing through a social trajectory that the research has not adequately determined.

Addictive and antisocial personalities, in particular, are under greatest scrutiny. Let us consider evidence that, first, supports the position that people are antisocially and addictively constant over time. Second, evidence will suggest that changes in addictive or antisocial personality are natural during lifespan development. Third, taking into account that behavior change *is* predictable, we offer probability statements, also called *interbehavioral potentials* (Ruben, 1983) on the origins of addictive personality.

Antisocial and addictive constancy of personality. First we examine the trait model advanced by Costa & McCrae (1980) that personality is set for life by the time the individual reaches adulthood. Using factor analysis, they screened 2000 male volunteers, mostly veterans, ranging in age from their twenties to nineties. One psychological battery was administered to them between 1965 and 1967 (to 1100 subjects), and again administered between 1975 and 1977. Score results revealed that personalities persisted along three lines including Neuroticism, Extraversion and "Openness to experience," (hence calling it the NEO trait model).

A second source of research confirming this belief were studies on aggressive children. First reviewed is Caspi, Elder & Bem's (1987) findings, followed by findings by Huesmann, Eron, Lefkowitz & Walder (1984). Caspi et al. proposed a variation on personality continuity, that childhood behavior interacts with other events and evokes reciprocal, maintaining responses from others. By this is meant that early learning sustains through a cumulative effect, or "interactional continuity." Interactional continuity accounts for similar behavior styles observed in different situations, but no one single behavior is exactly alike. Clinical data draw from interviews of parents of 102 boys and 112 girls (in 1928) concerning frequency of temper tantrums. Adult assessments taken in 1960 (when subjects were 30 years old), and again between 1960 and 1971 (when subjects were 40 yrs old) showed that ill-tempered boys had unmanageable behavior as adults.

Temper tantrums, barring some change, persisted through the subjects' career causing an erratic worklife. Caspi et al. concluded that stable patterns of tantrums in early and late childhood enter adult interactions regardless of social changes. These findings corresponded to those of Huesmann et al. (1984). Data were collected on 870 8-year olds in 1960 using the peer-nomination index of aggression. This is a tool measuring subjective opinions about which classmates are most offensive. Ten years later 427 of the original subjects, now age 19, were re-interviewed. Records also were obtained from Criminal Justice and Motor Vehicle Services. Correlations were evident between early aggression and criminal and driving offenses (e.g., drunk driving). Overall, conclusions supported early childhood aggressiveness having a stable impact on adult interactions.

Antisocial and addictive changes of personality. First at issue are the many flaws exposed in the research showing personality consistency. Clarke & Clarke (1984) reviewed contemporary studies on genetic/maturational research. They noted problems in measurement and subject selection. First is the reliability of measuring devices, from invalid IQ and personality tests to the ranked positions of scores with repetitive test-taking by subjects (see also Goslin, 1968; Wesman, 1968). On intergenerational research, authors criticized two approaches. First were retrospective studies, and second, the prospective studies. Data collected on 21 and 27 year-olds were compared to records on the subjects as children. Results ran counter to both hypotheses that *personality endures,* and that *change is inevitable.* Clarke & Clarke raised questions especially regarding the traceability of subjects for repeated interviews. Their conclusions were that (a) the definition of constancy affects the interpretation of data, and (b) development of each personality trait is equally constant or variable.

Support for these general claims appeared in Rutter's (1980) review of personality changes relative to (a) language and intelligence, (b) socialization, and (c) stress. Regarding language and intelligence, environmental influence in early and late childhood, even adulthood, improves skills. Authors cited studies on Lebanese orphans, one of whom was removed from a deprived environment. This client showed major gains in language. Also shown were longitudinal data on English-speaking children acquiring Dutch as a second language. Rapid acquisition of the Dutch language in early childhood suggested there is ongoing development rather than a static personality.

Socialization and stress showed similar patterns. Factors affecting personality included (a) bereavement and personal losses, and (b) types of adversity experienced or repeated in childhood and adolescence. Findings replicated results of behavior patterns reported by Quinton & Rutter (1976) and Douglas (1975). Stress in childhood was shown to strengthen or weaken vulnerability to adult stress. Laboratory findings reported nearly four decades earlier (Levine, Chevalier & Korchin, 1956) originally arrived at this conclusion. In the early study, electrically shocked pups showed later resistance to stressors. Consequently, it would be premature to build arguments of personality continuity oblivious to the effects of deprivation or adversity of childhood through adulthood.

Probability statements on the origins of addictive and antisocial personality. Granted that antisocial and addictive behaviors change over time, do they have predictable patterns? Patterns affecting ACOAs are discriminable and follow certain repetitive cycles from infancy to late adulthood. This repetitive cycle can be described using probability statements. Following are several probability statements generated from an ecobehavioral perspective that explain the origins and exacerbation of addictive and antisocial behaviors:

In childhood

1. Basic survival needs (feeding, toileting, etc.) are immediately satisfied without delay.

2. Nonsurvival needs (e.g., affection) are never or rarely satisfied or only after long delays.

3. Nonsurvival needs that are delayed are given negative attention (verbal and/or physical punishment).

4. Crying and aggressive outbursts (tantrums) maintain negative attention.

5. Inattention to details and hyperactivity develop and maintain negative attention.

6. Hyperactivity, impulsivity and persistence for self-gratification continues into nonfamilial settings (school, other families, etc.)

7. Hyperactivity, impulsivity, and persistence dominate peers and receive positive social attention. Negative social attention is substantially lower. Conflict with competitive peers is avoided.

In adolescence

1. Hyperactivity fades, as impulsivity and persistence grow stronger. Control over situations increases. Peer groups are formed around passively dependent, withdrawn people.

2. Sensitivity to people's needs disappear. Moral and ethical responsibility are at moderate to minimal levels. Criticism and rejection are avoided by defensiveness, anger, and aggression.

3. Risk-taking behaviors increase severely. Type of risks range from criminality and drug abuse, to sexual promiscuity, vehicular recklessness, and homicide.

4. Defiance toward adults reaches severe insensitivity, as adolescent feels invincible. Probability remains high of running away, seeking legal emancipation or detachment from family unit.

In adulthood

1. Attraction is toward passively-withdrawn, caretaking others.

2. Mistakes are intolerable, and person becomes highly perfectionistic, rigid, and accusatory.

3. Constantly unpredictable, incapable of finishing tasks, and impulsively angry. Very bad temper.

4. Alcoholic, or drug user of amphetamines, cocaine or other stimulants for maintaining concentration or feeling "normal." Incapable of reducing impulsivity or inducing relaxation without alcohol or drugs like opiate synthetics, cannabis, or barbiturates.

5. High risk behaviors intensify without remorse or sense of moral or social consequence. Adult feels immune to all responsibility.

Acquisition and Retention of Negative Rules

Research advancing theories on continuity or discontinuity of personality clearly takes sides on what causes change. Change is attributed to environmental forces such as social learning, or to genetic inheritance. Thus more momentum rises for the nature-nurture controversy. On the learning side, personalities acquired in childhood may endure the passage of time, but not for the reasons frequently cited.

Social learning theorists focus almost entirely on external contingencies or the events affecting people that negatively and positively shape coping skills. Forces such as family life, school, cultural or religious groups, and socioeconomic status play key roles. But equally contributing to acquisition and continuity or *retention* of behaviors are cognitive road maps, rules or personal beliefs instilled by parents and never corrected. Cognitive rules are self-statements describing *how and why the person should behave in certain ways.* In fact, cognitive rules resist modification more than other behaviors under most situations. This peculiarity entrenches ACOAs deeply into muddy ground without a prayer for escape.

Cognitive rules put to an operational test can be conceptualized as *rule-governed behavior* (Hayes, 1989; Zettle, 1990; Zettle & Hayes, 1982; Zettle & Young, 1987). Rules are set up like cues or discriminative stimuli that parents give to their children in the presence of the cue, such as "Don't touch that, it will burn you," or "Taste this, you'll like it." Most people follow rules specifying direct behaviors, be those behaviors proactive or avoidant. Rules prohibiting action such as "Don't do that!" originally gain support from direct-acting contingencies or experiences where the parent presents instances of right and wrong behavior followed by punishment. A parent sets up a training situation (deliberately or inadvertently) in which good or bad behavior verbally is described. For example, abusive parents might shout, "See, I told you, you shouldn't do that," or "You never do anything right." Stated rules describing the child's actions and its consequences lay the initial foundation.

But it is also important that the person come to state the rule to himself. This is especially important if rule-following action occurs without the external parent being present. Self-generated rules usually begin with the question, "What rule is most appropriate here?" Such a question gives rise to various words and phrases, until the person says something that in turn cues the *right or relevant rule.* For example, on finishing a task, an adult might ask himself the following questions: "How much do I have to do?"; "How long should I spend doing it?"; and "Should I complete it and to what degree of quality?" Such cognitive processes are taken for granted but they are crucial to understanding the damage rules can have upon brutal self-evaluation.

Self-evaluatory rule-governed behavior. One classic symptom of ACOA is incessantly severe self-criticism. Why is this? Reasons for self-criticism equally explain the persistence of other dysfunctional behaviors. Rules instilled by parents produce a blueprint of questions and answers generated during a problem-solving or difficult situation. An adult faced with re-planting a dying shrubbery asks herself, "Why did it die?," "Did I do something wrong?" and "Is replanting the best option?" Answers generated from an abusive parental upbringing might sound like, "It died because I neglected it, therefore it's my fault, it was preventable," and "No, I should punish myself by not replanting it and making myself suffer from being so stupid." In other words, parents who punish children for compliance or noncompliance teach that child inaccurate rules. The accurate rule would be: "Here is how to fix it." The inaccurate rule is: "You can't fix it, you screwed up."

Acquiring negative and inaccurate self-evaluatory rules interferes with effective reasoning, is emotionally injurious, and usually evokes compensatory or avoidant behaviors.

Reasoning is distorted by inflexible rules that force adults to think solutions are one extreme or the other; either it's "Black or White." The more naive a person is about the problem at hand, the harsher the rules. Aversive properties of rules are when self-statements describe *why the person should have known to do better and how their incompetency once again proves how stupid they are, or will never amount to anything.* Such disturbing statements completely obliterate focused attempts to brainstorm realistic compromises.

Emotional injury builds on inaccurate rules or parts of rules dealing with fearful, aversive consequences. Thinking, for instance, that a dead shrubbery will look awful to the neighbors or that the spouse might be angry, carries over rules learned in childhood that mistakes are intolerable and threaten parental rebuke. Internal rules describing imminent rejection, conflict or criticism will evoke fear and avoidance behavior. The adult makes the self-statement, "they'll be angry with me" and instantly hides the dead shrubbery, buys a new one from the nursery and plants it before anybody finds out about the situation. All incriminating evidence is removed.

Avoidance behaviors such as described above also accompany compensatory behaviors. Self-statements anticipating rejection, criticism or conflict may describe an inaccurate rule that "one must make up for stupid mistakes or else pay the piper." Consequently the person engages in excessive pleasing or caretaking responses toward the person or people from whom they expect aversive consequences. Inaccurate rules specifying these aversive consequences and the urgency for caretaking are strongly compulsive and the person will resist any outsider's advice not to follow the rules.

Regardless of effect, rules in general may occur in two ways (Hayes, Brownstein, Zettle, Rosenfarb & Korn, 1986). First, they can be tracked, in which rules are followed because of a past history of a correspondence between the rule and contact with the natural contingencies experienced in childhood. A second type is called *pliance.* Pliance is where rules are followed because of correspondence between *similar rules and relevant behavior.* In other words, generation of rules not only occurs from relevant contingency-shaped experience, but also from experiences having some but not all of the relevant features teaching a rule. Sounds confusing, but consider this example. A child forgets to wake his drunken father for work before the child leaves the house, and is brutally scolded for this error.

Relevant features of the rule here are "you better wake him or else suffer consequences." Two days later, in the evening, the child wants to play outside but cannot decide if he should first wake his drunken father or leave him sleep. He chooses to wake him. While situationally, events are different (evening, not morning), plenty of relevant behaviors exist (father is sleeping, child is leaving the house) and thus its evokes similar rules.

This is exactly what happens to ACOAs who develop inaccurate rules regarding their own and other people's behavior causing emotional suppression, and severe avoidance and escape behaviors.

Rules of ACOA. Suppressive rules that develop from parental abuse expectations and threats of punishment ultimately form inaccurate self-statements about the world. Eight rules and their consequential effects upon ACOAs appear below:

Rule 1: It's not okay to talk about problems.
Effect: Families avoid owning problems and children feel shame. As adults, blame is either entirely absorbed or attributed to others.

Rule 2: Feelings are not expressed openly. Keep them to yourself.
Effect: Child denies feelings and stores it up. As adults, conservation of thoughts and fears deny exposure of vulnerability and foster distrust toward other adults.

Rule 3: Communication is private; say as little as possible.
Effect: Innocent children become victims of self-induced fear. As adults, inferences rapidly develop about reasons, motivations underlying people's actions and why they pose an emotional liability to the person. Secondly, expression is selective, frequently edited and rehearsed for appropriateness, and following an expression the person "replays" the interaction over and over (cognitively), looking for faults.

Rule 4: Nothing is good enough. Even imitating the parent's actions is unreliable for approval.
Effect: Child believes he always fails at tasks and that more exertion of effort will ultimately gain parental (adult) approval. As adults, intolerance to mistakes becomes perfectionistic and person persists toward achieving unattainable goals.

Rule 5: Don't be selfish.
Effect: Self-esteem derives from altruistic caretaking. As adults, feelings of dissatisfaction are constant with a minor reprieve while embarking on a mission to help other people. Self-derived benefits never eliminate dissatisfaction, but may worsen a depression.

Rule 6: Do as I say, not as I do.
Effect: Children receive mixed messages and learn not to trust and not to take risks. As adults, action is methodical, controlled, and person must remain in control or take leadership roles. Failure to do so creates anxiety and social withdrawal.

Rule 7: It's not okay to play.
Effect: Child views self as unlovable, boring and stupid. As adults, activity and productivity remain a constant gauge of self-esteem. Time for oneself is unthinkable, evokes fears of impending aversive consequences, and creates immediate feelings of shame. Adult has difficulty relaxing or acting in a childish, jocular manner.

Rule 8: Don't rock the boat.
Effect: Child withdraws from conflict. As adults, avoidance and escape from conflict becomes a familiar routine.

EFFECTS UPON FAMILY

Etiologically, the most important factor contributing to suppression of many behaviors among ACOAs is punishment. Inhibitions, avoidance and escape behaviors, and irrational or inaccurate rule-governed behaviors defeat healthy adjustment and cause severe emotional disturbance that usually remains unchanged unless therapy is sought. Effects of punishment so greatly limit adaptivity that ACOAs feel imprisoned by inexplicable fears and repeated failures in dealing with people. Escape from the larger picture of life tragedies seems futile, aggravated by dragging along a spouse or children through this psychological mess. How do they feel about it? Do they suffer just as much? This section answers these questions after first describing the ecobehavioral effects of punishment experienced by most ACOAs.

Effects of Punishment

An abundant laboratory and applied literature with both human and nonhuman subjects indicates that delivery of punishment causes decisive short-term changes and recurrent long-term damage upon behavior (Azrin, 1970; Azrin & Holz, 1966; Azrin, Hutchinson & Hake, 1967; Azrin, Hutchinson & Sallery, 1964; Cherek, Spiga, Bennett & Grabowski, 1991; Sidman, 1953; Ulrich, 1967; Weiner, 1969). Punishment used for clinical purposes follows a wide variety of procedures (e.g., visual reprimands, overcorrection, time-out, contingent slap, water mist, electronic shock) aimed at an equally wide variety of inappropriate behaviors (e.g., tantrums, aggression, self-injurious behavior, self-stimulation).

Although clinical effectiveness of punishment clearly has been demonstrated (see Matson & DiLorenzo, 1984; Repp & Deitz, 1970, for a review), side effects frequently arise that defeat any positive benefits of punishment and seriously jeopardize the person's functional skills. By-products of aversive control outlined by Hutchinson (1977) included aggression, post-shock in physical and sensory responses, avoidance and escape, and decrements in response generated effects long after aversive stimulation. Analysis of these by-products offers a critical interpretation of the behavioral dynamics underlying the pathology of most ACOAs.

Parameters of aversive control. Aversive control is essentially any aversive stimuli (electric, noxious, social) which supports responses that eliminate or reduce such stimulation. A contingent relationship between aversive events and responding further denotes a *discriminative* and *consequential* effect such that cues forewarn of ensuing stimulation, whereas outcomes produce an increase or decrease in responding. Discriminative cues may signal onset of aversive stimulation in the form of *time* (when it will occur), *intensity* (how bad it will be), *duration* (how long it will last), *frequency* (how many times it will occur), or *latency* (how much time will elapse before the next onset). Time in between termination of one aversive episode and onset of another aversive episode is called *Inter-trial-interval (ITIs).*

Conditioning of *cues* can be primary or secondary. Primary aversive stimuli (cues) cause naturalistic, biological, or unlearned reactions such as electric shock eliciting pain or a loud noise eliciting a startled reflex. Secondary, also called generalized aversive stimuli, are the product of repeated pairings between primary aversive stimuli and neutral events, where the latter acquires many elicitive properties and can produce exactly the same behavior as the primary stimulus. Most generalized conditioned aversive stimuli are social manifestations in subtle or obvious forms ranging from verbal reprimands (paired with loud yelling) to a glaring stare (paired with painful spanking). Intensity, duration, and other noted properties of the primary stimulus also transfer over to the generalized fearful stimulus, until both stimuli, after many years of intermingling, become nearly indiscriminable. ACOAs simply cannot tell them apart.

Consequences directly alter properties of responses over a period of conditioning. Consequences occur on a *schedule* or order of presentation. Schedules are either *response-contingent* or *time-contingent.* Response-contingent punishment is when aversive stimulation follows an exact (fixed-ratio) or average (variable ratio) number of responses without delay. Time-contingent punishment is when aversive stimulation follows an exact (fixed-interval) or average amount of time (variable-interval) depending on whether at least one response appeared before the time interval ends. Schedules of punishment have a second feature, as well. They rarely occur in isolation.

Most contingencies, be they schedules of punishment or schedules of reinforcement, occur one after the other, or simultaneously. Multiple schedules make it more difficult predicting punishment and are the reason for complex obsessions and fears slowly developing. Where prediction is possible, it is by naming the four basic types of multiple schedules. These include *multiple, mixed, chain,* and *tandem.* Multiple schedules are generically two or more contingencies having their own cues and consequences. Mixed schedules are two or more contingencies having one cue and two consequences. Chain schedules are two or more contingencies having two or more cues but only one consequence. And tandem schedules are two or more contingencies having one cue and one consequence. Table 2 below better schematicizes the relationships and gives examples in an ACOA's life.

Table 2
Multiple Punishment Schedules
(in terms of two contingencies)

TYPE	# OF CUES/CONSEQUENCES	EXAMPLE
Multiple	Two cues, two consequences	Told to help siblings, spanked for doing it wrong. Right after,

		told to clean up, and spanked for being sloppy.
Mixed	One cue, two consequences	Told to make dinner, first spanked for not setting the table, then spanked (right after) for not cooking meal correctly.
Chain	Two cues, one consequence	First told to make dinner, then right after told to clean the house. Spanked for doing neither correctly.
Tandem	One cue, one consequence	Told to make dinner, but the person also cleans his siblings' rooms without instructions. Spanked for doing something without being told first.

Finally, consider response properties. Response properties are similar to discriminative properties and include *intensity* (strength of response), *duration* (length of response), *frequency* (number of responses) and *latency* (time between end of response and onset of aversive stimulus). Properties unique to responding also involve *Inter-response time* (time it takes between two consequence responses, *response concurrence* (simultaneous responses producing identical consequences), and *response sequence* (responses following a distinct pattern that produces the consequence).

Manipulation of these properties abounds in punishment research and has accounted for both fascinating and frightening conclusions regarding the operant or respondent effects of aversive control upon human subjects (Axelrod & Apsche, 1983). Among these findings are certain predictable relationships between stimuli and behavior that are briefly described below, followed by a closer examination of the stages of *post-traumatic stress disorder*.

Findings suggest that:

1. Rapid, intense punishment effectively suppresses behavior (Abramowitz & O'Leary, 1990).

2. Variability of punisher (i.e., changing it) effectively suppresses behavior and maintains suppression (Charlop, Burgio, Iwata & Ivancic, 1988).

3. Superimposing one punisher upon another punisher or upon a reinforcer causes conditioned suppression of the reinforced response (Blackman, 1977; Davis & McIntire, 1969; Hackenberg & Hineline, 1987)

4. Entire situations or the transitions between different situations come to be perceived as entirely aversive (Baum, 1973).

5. Pain produced by aversive stimuli induces aggressive and defensive (escape/avoidance) responding (Blanchard, Blanchard & Takahashi, 1978).

6. The probability of escape behavior under pain is greater when the person has opportunity to physically or emotionally attack (Ulrich & Azrin, 1962; Ulrich, Wolff & Azrin, 1964).

7. Punished behaviors acting concurrently or sequentially to other behaviors may have specific or general effects upon those concurrent or sequential behaviors. This is also true for identical behaviors under two different schedules of punishment. People exposed to multiple schedules of punishment develop distinctly different patterns associated with each schedule despite how similar the behaviors are (Bennett & Cherek, 1990; Reynolds, 1961).

Findings of nearly four decades of applied and experimental investigation clearly are more extensive than the aforementioned list, but these represent the most relevant data for ACOAs. Aggression, avoidance and escape or variations of punished-invoked behavior appear largely to be learned, are maintained by primary and secondary aversive stimulation, and remain unaltered because reinforcers for alternative, healthy behaviors are absent or too elusive for the person accustomed to suppression.

Childhood years of punishing experiences that induce fear responses leave an emotional scar of inhibition found in early adulthood. The response deterioration rapidly permeates into all segments of the person's life, not only destroying opportunities for healthy recovery but also turning the punished person into a person who punishes others. The process from start to finish may be called *post-traumatic stress disorder*.

Post-traumatic stress disorder. Post-traumatic stress disorder (PTSD), behaviorally speaking, is the after-effect of shocking aversive stimulation either entirely unpredictable, unavoidable and inescapable, or predictable but not at the severity and density encountered. Symptoms reportedly suffered span cognitive, emotional, and behavioral reactions including nightmares, flashbacks, disturbance of thought, memory impairment, trouble concentrating, sleep disturbance, fears, obsessions and phobias, and chronic feelings of detachment. Foa, Stekette & Rothbaum (1989) recently reviewed models explaining this phenomena and the delineations made between categories of trauma. For *combat trauma*, exposure to life-threatening experiences becomes conditioned to a wide variety of stimuli present during the trauma. Re-experiencing these stimuli, even longer after the direct experience, triggers the traumatic event via thoughts (Keane, Zimmerlin & Caddell, 1985; Mayor & Ruben, 1991; Wolfe, Keane, Lyons & Gerardi, 1987).

Rape trauma equally evokes fear and anxiety. Sexual assault violates the safety and predictability of familiar surroundings inducing a constant distrust, and life-threatening panic in new situations. Like combat trauma victims, rape victims may be triggered into terror by hearing words, sounds, or experiencing other sensations (odors, tactile force) reminiscent of the traumatic event. Unlike combat PTSD, symptoms endemic to assault victims include hyper-alertness, guilt, symptom intensification around rape-related cues, attempted suicide, and sexual dysfunctions (Fairbank & Brown, 1987).

Other victims suffering transportation accidents, death of loved ones, natural disasters, and fires, to name only a few, react with a similar symptomatology. Child victims, in particular, of abductions, animal attacks, exposure to nuclear accidents, and of violent situations react with sizeable fears and vigilantism. In abuse cases, traumatically exposed children may undergo shock from the unpredictable terror and show rapid signs of behavioral suppression while their cognitive and emotional capacities slowly deteriorate. Even after an interim of calmness and control, repetition of fear-induced (physical abuse) cues will trigger old memories and identical behaviors as displayed under earlier conditions.

Understanding this "condition" of unavoidable, inescapable, unpredictable abuse (shock) is crucial to the link between PTSD and punishment in ACOA. Substantially increasing the number or amount of exposure to parental physical abuse in a given time period (i.e., childhood) will *increase the duration and intensity of stressful reactions in adult victims*. But how this happens is more bizarre. The probability of ACOAs currently perceiving harm as adults depends on four interactions between avoidability, escapability, and predictability that occurred during childhood. Adopted from Foa et al. (1989), they include:

1. The more punishment contingencies contained in the family structure, the more difficult it was to identify and predict them.

2. Anxiety reactions decreased over repeated exposures to abuse (habituation) and then re-activated by new punishers at a later childhood time (facilitation) develop more severe generalized anxiety and somatic problems.

3. Absence of predictability lead to inferences. Inferences produced exaggerated probabilities associated with the feared consequence. When probability estimates came true, no matter how exaggerated, erroneous perceptions continued. Reductions in fear and erroneous perceptions depended on stable, consistent, and predictable interactions.

4. Highly fear-aroused children, having excessive physiological activity, are afraid to calm down unless escape is possible or there are clear signs of abuse termination. When these signs are ambiguous or simply do not occur, arousal continues until physical weakness sets in and the person faints or collapses. In adulthood this might cause a propensity for major medical complications, particularly from abdominal pain, constipation, or diarrhea. Such symptoms occurring without any diagnosable physical cause is called *irritable bowel syndrome* (e.g., Blanchard & Schwarz, 1988).

Anxiety and panic attacks. Many people with anxiety disorders and phobias are afraid of experiencing anxiety. What's worse, they may not know they experience these symptoms at all. Research efforts concerned with development, maintenance and cessation of anxiety (e.g., Reiss, 1987) repeatedly conclude that stress-related illness such as worrying, panic attacks and obsessive compulsions become routine avoidant responses to stressful living. ACOAs suffering immediate or remote effects of PTSD may also regard these symptoms as normal, familiar, and expected. Stress caused by repression of feelings, by social or interpersonal inhibitions, and by avoidance and escape patterns essentially incubate fears in the person without confronting the fears. This "anxiety incubation" (Eysenck, 1968) further arouses more fear and trepidation, not necessarily from known events, but from self-reinforcing anxious statements until the person begins to panic. Another way of saying this is that rule-governed statements specify the person *should feel nervous because they are anxious,* and consequentially there is increased tension.

Panic attacks, however, are more than just self-induced anxiety. Several recent reviews of panic disorder (Dittrich, Houts & Lichstein, 1983; Stampler, 1982) indicate that the "fear of fear" hypothesis or some variant thereof is popular but empirically lacking in scope. The fear of suffering somatic fears-of-fear entirely bases its sequence on rule-governed descriptions to oneself, specifying that the body is out of control and losing strength. Autonomic arousal evoked by these statements guide the body into more exaggerated "fear statements" and the cycle starts over until panic overwhelms the person.

An alternative theory asks if after misperceiving some involuntary respiratory sensation, the person hyperventilates causing cardiovascular abnormalities and intensification of fear (Levy, 1985, 1987). That is, first the sudden, unaccountable somatic consequence of hyperventilation causes fear. Hyperventilation sets off a series of respiratory and circulatory changes including rapid heart beat, dyspnea, dizziness, trembling, difficulty breathing, stomach tension. While somatic changes elevate, the person feels a rush of panic gearing toward avoidance and escape. Attacks worsen if the person believes that further inhalation may produce worse panic or the situation is unavoidable and inescapable. However, attacks subside as respiration returns to normal allowing for conservation of carbon dioxide rather than constant expenditure of it.

Regardless of which comes first, physical (hyperventilation) or cognitions (fear), the core point is that arousal of anxiety cripples functional capacities to readjust and regain control. Two reasons for this debilitating condition lay in *anxiety sensitivity,* and *why nonadaptive symptoms persist in absence of aversive stimulation.*

Anxiety sensitivity. Anxiety sensitivity refers to beliefs that anxiety has undesirable consequences apart from its immediate unpleasantness (Reiss, Peterson, Gursky & McNally, 1986; McNally & Lorenz, 1987). Thus, a person suffering anxiety may believe a rapid heart beat portends a heart attack or other seriously harmful consequences. Even after panic sensations subside, residual anxiety (e.g., minor tachycardia) might cause resurgence not only at that moment, but also later on in the day. Sensory acuity to panic develops after years of continuous or episodic attacks, usually physically devastating, and from which calibrated avoidance and escape tactics derived. Now a single unexplained twitch, ache or pain internally triggers high anxiety monitoring of the entire body, from head to toe (Ahles, Cassens, & Stalling, 1987). Elevated fears persist when unexplained symptoms lead to a full-fledged panic episode that not only is frightening but also confirms the need to keep track of body precipitants in the future.

Why nonadaptive symptoms persist in absence of aversive stimulation. Experimental literature offers relatively compelling proof that avoidance behavior tends to extinguish (disappear) following removal of unconditioned aversive stimulation (Mackintosh, 1974). However, rival theories believe the resistance remains strong or can become stronger upon removal of fearful stimuli because there exist multiple generalized conditioned stimuli motivating anxiety.

For example, why is it that adults whose physically abusive parents are long deceased still avoid and escape conflict with a spouse who neither is verbally nor physically abusive? Past emotional conditioning is paired with so many different stimuli, affecting the entire sensory receptor system (taste, smell, hear, see, touch), that only one of these stimuli need reappear for panic arousal. Symptom maintenance, in other words, gains strength from complex sets of cues ordered sequentially in terms of their accessibility and aversive quality (Levis & Boyd, 1979). Cues that have some but not all of the relevant properties of cues eliciting past fear are more than enough to recall memories of parental abuse. This is why the ACOA high on anxiety and victimized by PTSD cannot see the light at the end of the tunnel. He feels deluged by a torrent of aversive stimuli attacking him from all directions with nowhere to hide.

Living with ACOAs: Effects Upon NonACOAs

Symptoms describing the suffering ACOA recur in clinical case studies reported in the professional literature, even in biographical stories more recently published in *Changes: For and About Children of Alcoholics*. This is a consumer-oriented periodical that regularly features candid opinions, stories of recovery, parenting for recovery, and departments guiding ACOAs into treatment and toward an enhanced understanding of the phenomena. No other periodical really identifies itself so specifically in the ACOA field. However, articles on family life, addiction, parenting, and difficult steps in recovery rarely, if ever, switch perspectives and consider how dysfunctional behaviors impact upon loving partners or family members confused by what they experience and cannot change easily.

This section reviews predictable reactions observed in nonACOAs after they live with ACOAs or are reared by ACOAs. First we cover spousal reactions that explore common coping responses in husbands and wives. Then the review turns to parent-child reactions; inconsistencies in parenting style and inconsistencies in modeled behavior create ambiguity, conflict, and send messages that the child is inadequate, which recycles the dysfunctional behaviors into a second generation.

Spousal reactions. Husband, wives, even significant live-in partners may realize a loved one suffers from a dysfunctional history and that symptoms come and go sporadically. Symptoms range from conspicuous alcohol or drug abuse addiction to unpredictable shifts in moods, to very subtle caretaking and avoidance behaviors. Obvious symptoms, such as panic attacks, addiction, and depression, call attention immediately to the need for treatment.

Sympathetic spouses can respond to this urgency by assisting in the hunt for therapists, psychiatrists, or general practitioners. Assistance moves toward easing the rising tensions and burdens of the affected spouse. However, symptoms well guarded or disguised by avoidance, escape, or entirely private as in obsessions or inaccurate rule-governed behaviors (thoughts) risk remaining unnoticed or being misinterpreted by the spouse as peculiar behaviors, spousal rejection, or deliberate provocations. Camouflaged responses also unfortunately lack a "sound-track" where the dysfunctional spouses explain *why they are doing this behavior.* Without answers known, and responses misleading the spouse, horrible effects occur on the spouse. Among these effects are the following.

Unpredictability of ACOA behavior. One of the worst reaction stems from not predicting how a spouse behaves. Usually a cohabitant couple learns the routines, habits, and daily schedules of each other, even developing a "sixth sense," so to speak, regarding the person's reactivity given certain conditions. Development of this intuitive perception of life events is quite normal in most healthy relationships. However, living with ACOAs disrupts this intuitive sense of prediction in two ways. First, impulsive and inconsistent behaviors eliminate a connection between what the ACOA says and does. Second, emotional instability may cause unprecipitated highs and lows of frustration and residual behaviors following these emotions also are unpredictable. Sometimes the ACOA is apologetic, compensatory, and compassionate. Sometimes he or she is self-critical, withdrawn, and hypersensitive to any caring gestures made by the spouse. Or, a third reaction is hostility, rampaging around house in physical aggression, blaming anything and everything on other people.

Role ambiguity. Unpredictability develops into role ambiguity. Role ambiguity is not knowing which behavior is best for the situation. *Best* may refer to behaviors that defuse, calm, confront, or alter the dysfunctional actions. Several options include caretaking, being aggressive, showing sympathy, or avoiding or escaping. Initially the ambiguity is inconvenient and leaves the spouse upset for a short period of time until prediction of behavior returns.

Prolonged role ambiguity, however, causes serious disintegration of spousal trust, love, and commitment to the marriage or relationship. Spouses first feel (a) annoyed, (b) then angry, (c) then helpless, (d) then seek control and prediction outside the marriage or relationship (friends, infidelity, activities, etc.), and then (e) detach emotionally from the dysfunctional spouse. Detachment results from a paralysis or numbness at *not knowing what to do or how to do it, from protracted ineffectiveness at changing spousal behaviors, and from inescapable and unavoidable contact with the impulsive spouse.* By stages of detachment, emotional investment already is seen not to produce dividends and the spouse is highly prone to extramarital sexual relationships.

Anger. Anger develops for three reasons. First is ignorance about why the behavior is peculiar. Second is intolerance to repetitive episodes of intrusive, aggressive or aversive behaviors. Third is from personalizing the intrusive, aggressive or aversive behaviors as attacks upon the spouse instead of treating the spouse with dignity and compassion. Reactive anger usually is a product of all three at any given time. By the time anger occurs, hurt spouses deeply believe they are scapegoats targeted for emotional homicide by the dysfunctional spouse; and that their innocence must be made known, and protected instantly. Spouses may also retaliate. After hearing why they are so awful, *even though they never did what the ACOA spouse blames them for doing,* assertive spouses may strike back with vigilante tactics of finding numerous faults with the ACOA spouse. Of course, angry ACOAs attacked with criticism, conflict, or rejection become more volatile, and the fighting can grow fierce.

Polarity of affection. Caring and sympathy has its limits. ACOAs, as said earlier, may show polarity of affection in that they either are heavily compassionate, intimate or sexual, or virtually cold and distant. Cues that signal which polarity is likely make prediction easier and the mood swings more tolerable. But when swings in affection are unpredictable, that is, occur for opposite cues, the wrong cues, or no cues, or responses *promise but do not deliver,* spouses ultimately lose physical interest and follow the steps of role ambiguity described above.

Opposite cues are when the ACOA prompts passion at times they never have done so in the past (e.g., in public, around the children, or when the nonACOA spouse first prompts it). Wrong cues are situations or conditions in which the ACOA spouse and nonACOA spouse mutually agree to prohibit intimacy (e.g., in the car, at friends' homes, etc.). No cues are when sexual arousal or sexual rejection occurs without warning, and particularly without *any of the cues that previously stimulated or inhibited intimacy*.

For instance, a male ACOA may want intercourse after not talking to his wife for four hours following a fight. The behavior is odd and does not trace to any historically relevant cue understood by the perplexed wife. Finally, sexual or intimate promises that do not deliver include physical or verbal overtures toward passion, made at times that are grossly inconvenient or unavailable to the nonACOA spouse. One example is calling a spouse while out of town on business with desperate sexual demands that cannot possibly be met by the spouse. Upon return, even by the following morning, the tune changes for the ACOA to disinterest and sexual refusals.

Challenge to change the ACOA. The expression, "a little information can be dangerous," applies to nonACOAs who gain some insight into the spouse's behavior and assume the role of therapist. The challenge to change the dysfunctional spouse goes beyond caretaking and becomes an obsession; every wrong behavior, pattern of avoidance, escape and aggression, and caretaking, is monitored, confined and evaluated, showing the spouse what to do instead. Premised on good intentions, the nonACOA vigorously delves into the spouse's background, comes up with clues to a dysfunctional childhood, and perseveres at teaching positive new skills to replace bad habits. Yet it doesn't work. Not because the clues or etiology are wrong, or even because the positive skills are wrong; these may be right on target. The mistake is confusing *perseverance* of training with *helping*.

ACOA spouses may automatically refuse persistent help by perceiving it as criticism and rejection. Remedial efforts rarely if ever are accepted or perceived as caring and love from the spouse. Instead, ACOAs avoid these kind gestures deluded by beliefs that the spouse really wants control over them, is out to hurt, punish or destroy them, and could not possibly be sympathetic to their troubles.

Avoidance of criticism, conflict and rejection. Assertive and passive spouses can develop habits of the ACOA without knowing it. After dealing ineffectively with unpredictable aggression, spouses may avoid conflict of any sort and either keep the relationship "happy" by pleasing the spouse, or by withdrawal from contact. Distancing is another form of avoidance and escape for spouses not afraid of conflict and disgusted at receiving little in return for their kindness. When emotional charity is exploited, noncaretaking, assertive spouses intentionally withdraw from conflict to maintain their own composure, and to deprive the ACOA spouse of attention for dysfunctional behaviors. Calculated distancing of this sort regulates some balance in the marriage but does not advance it in a healthy direction.

Infidelity. Prolonged detachment that paralyzes or numbs emotions from the nonACOA spouse can destroy a principal commitment of monogamy. Detachment goes beyond polarity of emotions or absence of sexual intimacy. Even if coitus is frequent the couple's mutual emotional support and capacity for sharing, listening and enjoying each other's nonsexual company may be gone. Slow deterioration of physical and emotional cohesion begins to weaken the closed marital boundary and opens interests that both ACOA and nonACOA spouses may have in other individuals. At first nonACOAs threaten infidelity as a push for the ACOA spouse to change behavior rapidly or at least become cognizant of the problem.

Failing at this scheme, nonACOA spouses delicately charter a path of socializing differently, by flirting more with the opposite sex, or accepting invitations for travel, sport activities, or weekend trips without the other spouse or children. Sexuality, in other words, may not play a role in the extramarital activity for some time, in cases perhaps even never. Once activities increase incompatible to spending time at home, the risk-level also increases. NonACOAs seek out, and actively engage in heterosexual and presexual relationships, first by forming close friendships with new partners. Trust develops nearly immediately if the partner is sympathetic and displays caring qualities absent in the ACOA spouse. Confidence gained from the friendship quickly turns to physical satisfaction until an "affair" begins.

Slow movement is common in forming extramarital relationships. The classic stereotype that, say, a male nonACOAs will instantly find relief outside the marriage because his ACOA spouse is frigid, is not only unrealistic, but it defies the principles of codependency. Any spouse adhering to the marital vows for a substantial length of time (10 + years) fulfills some basic need derived from the marriage. Needs either to be cared for, loved, for the financial or material status gained, or purely for want of a partner, remain strong and resist temptation. Chances are slim of breaking the codependency for fear of losing the needed resource and especially without a guarantee that somebody else can replace it. Only until or unless trust develops with another person believed to supply this resource will the nonACOA entertain the notion of infidelity.

Separation and divorce. Intolerance to rising marital discord or prolonged detachment usually urges the nonACOA spouse to physically separate from the ACOA spouse. Assertive spouses regard their lives as stifled, blaming it on the ACOA spouse. Passive spouses regard themselves as abused, ignored, and losing confidence due to a selfish ACOA spouse. All reasons, right or wrong, attribute fault to the unchanging dysfunctional behavior that interrupts attempts to make a normal healthy marriage. By separating, presumably the ACOA spouse will experience panic from fear of abandonment and loneliness, and consequently seek solutions in therapy. Frequently the scenario follows this path exactly.

However, there is another scenario. The abandoned spouse may also retaliate out of feeling vulnerable and desperately needing control; instantly the amicable separation turns to antipathy and involves war-waging attorneys demanding financial restitution for the reprehensible abuses caused by the ACOA spouse. Even if such abuses never existed, the ACOA spouse cannot afford the vulnerability of admitting truth and must feign the role of helpless victim to regain approval from bystanders. Along this hostile path is clear psychological damage upon not only the nonACOA spouse but also any children caught up in the mess. Hearing that their one parent is bad, and the other good, makes no sense to children; it is illogical. Logic breaks down even farther when the ACOA spouse and the attorneys start accusing the kind, compassionate nonACOA spouse of severe crimes of abuse that the children never saw. Even after the dust settles, either in divorce or legal separation, children never fully understand what transpired, the reason for this betrayal or whether either parent is worth trusting.

Parent-child reactions. Abuse, neglect and abandonment are typically legal or court descriptions of parental mistreatment of children. This is looking from the outside in, or from the provider's perspective after observing and judging parent-child interactions. The other perspective is less popular and found in psychological reports of interviewed children suffering the abuse, neglect and abandonment. Inside the family, children view parental actions quite differently and adapt or maladapt to actions as part of normal living. Adaptable children find they cope with parental shortcomings, come to expect little or no affection, attention or assistance, and can responsibly act as society dictates of them. Maladapted children find they compensate for parental shortcomings, trying to replace the mother or father role, becoming over-responsible and deviating from social expectations in one of two ways. Either, first, by high achievement and productivity ranking high above their normative peer group and showing extraordinary talents and ambition. Or, second, by floundering in defeat repeatedly by taking health risks (drug use, alcohol use, promiscuity), and social risks (crime, vehicular accidents), or by exhibiting mental health risks (homicide, suicide, depression, panic and anxiety, etc.). Maladaptation takes several forms that initially were carved from the following predictable reactions to ACOA parents.

Unpredictability of parent. Just as nonACOA spouses lack prediction of ACOA spouses, so it is that children can lose the same prediction. Uncertainty as to when dinner is served, when bad behavior is punished or good behavior rewarded, when clothing is new, old, dirty, fashionable, and when to speak and not to--all describe confusing rules the child develops in response to inconsistent behavior. Unlike adults who already have rules, children are just beginning to form rule-governed behaviors and depend heavily on connections between things parents say, do, and the consequences of action. When things parents say and do are inconsistent, rules also suffer from inconsistency. Rules cannot be consistent or accurate because the rule followed today may or may not produce the same consequences tomorrow. Against this obstacle, children create qualifiers or *meta-rules* that essentially govern when a rule is probable or improbable, given several different parental factors. Sophisticated as it sounds, the process of meta-rules is quite elementary.

Meta-rules consist of a pool of experiences between action and consequences (*contingencies)* that are consulted internally as part of solving a problem as to how to behave. Grooming rules, for instance, have many meta-rules to counter the unplanned shifts in parental behavior confronted daily. The rule "I should wash my face with a washcloth before going to bed" has some reinforcing strength and effectively prompts face-washing behavior around the nonACOA parent. Around the ACOA parent, this rule undergoes slight changes if the following meta-rules are true. If the ACOA parent is father, here are the meta-rules:

AROUND FATHER, *I should wash my face with a washcloth before going to bed,* but:

1. Not if dad is yelling, *then* skip washing my face and head right to bed.

2. Not if dad is very quiet, *then* wash my face twice and ask him how it looks. If he says "okay," *then* go to bed. If he says "no good," *then* get a new washcloth and do it over again. Make sure dad says "okay."

3. Not if dad yells at me while I get ready for bed. Then skip washing my face and ask dad what he wants me to do. If he says get into bed, do it. If he then says, after I'm in bed, "wash your face," do it.

Meta-rules are statements specifying the additional or supplemental action taken to avoid or escape punishment or accelerate reinforcement. Children develop meta-rules out of anticipating and observing the verbal and nonverbal behaviors of their parents regarding routine or daily activities involving themselves, their parents, their siblings, or other significant family members. Rules stabilize once the additional information accurately predicts or controls parental consequences even though the original rule does not. For example, *I should wash my face with a washcloth before going to bed* is unreliable to assure punishment or reinforcement, but any variation of #1, #2, or #3 above increases the probability of either consequence. Around the ACOA parent, meta-rules are thus absolutely necessary for early adjustment.

Denial of autonomy. Children faced with hostile, moody or overly caretaking parents take fewer risks at exploration than children whose parents are predictable. ACOA parents paying too much attention to their children overprotect them from errors, from normal physical falls and injury, and from the trials and tribulations accompanying healthy curiosity. Children avoid independent action because of fearing punishment for leaving the parent. A five-year-old told to sit still at the dinner table around guests was fascinated with the antique napkin ring shaped like a bunny rabbit. He moved to touch it and spilled his water glass, causing momentary confusion. The ACOA parent felt grossly embarrassed and immediately chastised the youngster for his disruption. It left him beside himself and afraid to explore new items again. Denied autonomy prohibits the child's future motivation to risk appropriate exploratory behaviors or even feel comfortable around others who have exploratory behaviors.

Fear of affection. Parents paying little or no attention to their children except for "major"accomplishments, birthdays, or special holidays transmit an inaccurate message that affection is bad, immoral or conditional. There *must be a legitimate reason for it, rather than that it feels good.* Legitimizing affection forces the child to work harder in school or by pleasing the parent hoping to reach that magical criteria for affection.

When repeated efforts fail, no matter how persistent the child, two reactions result. First, either the child fortifies caretaking or pleasing efforts by doing, re-doing and aspiring for perfection on all personal tasks and activities. Or, second, surrendering to defeat, effort deteriorates as the child perceives affection as inaccessible, unavailable, and absent because families are not supposed to share affection. Dismissal of affection creates the opinion that affection is abnormal, inappropriate, immoral, or *not necessary* for expression of love. In later childhood, adolescence, and early adulthood, denied affection manifests as disinterest in presexuality and even feeling in control by resisting temptations for sexuality. The latter, of feeling self-discipline by celibacy, comes from a perverted interpretation of sex and affection as objects of inferiority and weakness that must be resisted to remain a powerfully competent person.

Overdependency. The obverse is equally deleterious. Overaffection and protection of the child from injury, exploring curiosity, and independence may create in the parent's eye a strong parent-child bond. The child always asks the parent before doing things, and is sensitive to parental feelings, consequences and not upsetting balance in the family system. While superficially this sensitivity appears idealistic, that caring children develop perfectly stable personalities, the truth is that some *insensitivity is appropriate for growing children.*

Caring taken to extremes forces children to feel ashamed for causing grief to their parents, other people, and for risking independence against words of authority. When moratoriums are placed on autonomy, the "bond" that appears is actually abnormal and misleading; it is not because children respect and love their parents that they remain emotionally attached. Rather, attachment is strong so the child can *watch how the parent thinks and may react in anticipation of punishment.* Bonding develops as a means of avoidance behavior for the anxious child who stays close to an unpredictable parent and can be ready when criticism occurs. Fear of detachment or "separation anxiety," arises when distance between a punishing parent and anxious child limits access to forewarning signs of anger and the chance of being caught off guard by the parent. Avoiding this vulnerability, anxious children develop overdependency on parents for all decisions, movements, and beliefs they have in life.

Noncompliance. Punished or neglected children are not always seeking approval or engaging in perfectionism. After futile efforts for approval, opposition sets in. A child refuses to follow instructions, is verbally disrespectful, may even damage the parent's property, and very frequently is verbally debative. Arguments escalate when controlling parents work feverishly to restore their control by spanking, yelling or, essentially, repeating the same negative discipline or neglect used for that child during infancy, toddlerhood and preteen years.

Lacking success, exhaustive efforts are repeated, at times threatening the child with disownment and insisting that re-entry into the family for that child will require complete compliance to house rules. Such high demands lack sensitivity, caring and emotional respect for the rebellious child whose very anger started from that same inflexible control being used now. As hostility intensifies, distancing parent and child and without compromises in sight, inaccurate rules form for that child regarding *why all parents are ruthless, distrusting, and controlling*. Feelings of abandonment result and the child in early preteen years may seek artificial comfort through sexual relationships or alcohol and drug abuse to relieve hurt of rejection.

Fear of retaliation. One last reaction arising in children of ACOA parents stems from Freudian concepts of the Oedipal Complex. According to classical interpretation, young boys feeling affection for their mothers are fearful that by showing this love, jealous fathers may castrate the boys and thereby emasculate them. Fear, in other words, is associated with the parent's retaliation. Translated into a behavioral systems model, retaliation by one parent for the child loving or favoring another parent inhibits the child's efforts to love either parent and ultimately leads to the conclusion that showing caring, caretaking or compassion to anybody poses emotional risks. Children caught in this tug-of-war between two controlling jealous parents are constantly doubting their true allies and they avoid starting conflicts between parents at all costs.

If the spousal conflicts are unavoidable, and if by saying "yes" to one parent the other parent erupts aggressively, consequently that child will respond in one of two ways. First, that child may step in the middle of feuds and patch differences by satisfying each parent. Rescuing tactics rapidly keep that child on guard 24 hours a day and feeling responsible for maintaining family peace. Second, that child may escape the spousal conflict by aborting his or her promises to both parents, in this way appearing hostile and recalcitrant. This instantly eliminates parental jealousy, stops the arguments, and draws parents together in the common cause of *dealing with their troubled child*. Outcomes are exactly the same between parents, whether the child resolves arguments by pleasing and rescuing, or by aggressively escaping the situation.

PRIORITIES FOR INTERVENTION

Implications for psychotherapy with ACOAs stem from the critical role that control issues play in their sense of self-esteem, from the existence of PTSD symptoms, and from their co-dependent tendency to equate intimacy with loss of personal boundaries. Therapists who evaluate and treat ACOAs bearing these concerns in mind can significantly increase outcome success. But there are therapeutic fallacies interfering with ACOA treatment. First is believing that ACOAs are simply another class of anxiety conditions treatable by standard interventions. Behaviorally this might consist of only systematic desensitization, anxiety inoculation, and relaxation.

Such methods are valid but seriously insufficient for complete recovery. Second is the belief that ACOAs have a biological disease like alcoholics and require medicine or organically-based interventions. Transmission of ACOA behaviors may have some genetic basis, but environmental learning clearly is the dominant factor. Medicines may eliminate symptoms but will miss core pathology left untreated. Third, that ACOAs are all *one type* or naturally can be pigeon-holed into neat diagnostic categories. Evaluation instead must consider all possible categories no matter how well defined the taxonomy is. Fourth, the belief that ACOAs all are aware they are ACOAs and deeply motivated for behavior change. This is hardly true. In fact, it's rarely true. Clients learn of this ACOA phenomenon by accident or after pursuing counseling for another reason.

Finally, beliefs are strong that effective therapists are themselves ACOAs who can identify with personal experiences internally and understand first-hand the dysfunctional family dynamics. In truth, such close intimacy of knowledge can interfere with needed objectivity, the therapist's ability to assert control, and serving as a healthy role model. While therapists certainly are not infallible, and many have dysfunctional histories, using this information for rapport-building or for interventions damages the validity of treatment and runs head-on into problems of transference and countertransference. Therapists should be selective about personal information disclosed and use this privilege only when it directly facilitates positive learning of healthy behavior. Therapists without an ACOA history have plenty of other skeletons in the closet that, with some discretion, may show just as much understanding of the client's ordeal.

These fallacies aside, treatment strategies still vary widely depending on the therapist's training and orientation. Following an ecobehavioral approach, strategies for short-term treatment must deal with two factors. First is the *construction of new repertoires.* New coping methods the client never learned are taught for the first time or refined for adulthood. Second, strategies must *overcome fear.* Control issues, hate issues, addiction issues, all ultimately derive from fear of rejection, criticism, and conflict. Strategies that directly dismantle avoidance and escape behaviors and concurrently desensitize the client toward risk-taking steps are headed in the right direction. Below we review strategies that meet these criteria and can act as recovery guidelines.

Recovery Guidelines

Structured therapy is one among many approaches guided by principles of science. In structured therapy the therapist plans out the goals and objective subject to client approval, and proceeds in each session to work through exercises, strategies, or emotional obstacles along the path of these goals and objectives.

Diversions from the goals and objectives are normal and usually deal with personal reflections on *why the goals are difficult, events happening that day or recently, or regarding new reactions of other people.* Naturally, attention is paid to client concerns but the discussion should return to the goal or strategy in process, keeping the structure balanced throughout the session. Structure further establishes a milieu for teaching and learning and allows clients to *predict exactly how the session will go, with minor variations.* That predictability, for clients with control issues, provides a strong foundation for trust. Consider the following strategies that enter into structured treatment:

Change beliefs. Altering irrational beliefs or impure inferences begins with identifying the inaccurate rules or meta-rules governing the ACOAs behavior. Beliefs most dangerous are self-critical, condemnatory or compare the person with other people perceived as superior. Efforts made to dispute these beliefs include a series of three steps described in earlier chapters consisting of (a) interrupting the beliefs, (b) asking questions of the person from whom inferences are drawn, and (c) replacement of self-criticism with self-complimentary and realistic statements. Self-complimentary or realistic statements are accurate rules liberating the person from false expectations and need for perfectionism. Statements such as "it's no big deal," or "it's okay for mistakes to happen" seem superficial but combat against "negative tapes" mentally replayed by the ACOA under stress situations.

Basic Assertion + Self-expression. Belief alterations provide the doorway for risking confrontations and self-expression. Basic assertions are questions asked of another person about words or actions possibly misunderstood by observation alone. "Why did you do that?" requires a brief answer that clarifies motives, reasons, and obviates the ACOA's inference that offensive or uncertain action must *be due to something I did.* Self-expression further includes three parts.

These include: *disagreements, opinions.* and *criticism.* Disagreements commit the ACOA to make refusals or give opinions expressed by significant others on many different and relevant topics. Disagreements threaten an ambiance of debate and frequently discourage risky attempts resulting in conflict. But tactics on how to stay on the topic, to resist roadblocks, and remain focused prevent digression onto irrelevant issues and personal defensive remarks. Opinions are unprompted statements regarding a spontaneous idea that contribute to the ongoing discussion, or initiate discussion about some object, person or event. Initiating opinions at first challenges the deeply rooted belief that personal ideas impose upon other people who did not *ask for the opinion and thus will regard it as intrusive.* Opinions that decry an object, event or person are criticisms. Unprompted or prompted statements describing why the ACOA dislikes something are appropriate around significant others.

Beyond belief interferences, other interferences to self-expression are *defusal tactics* aimed to calm, soften, or relieve anticipated criticism, conflict or rejection from listeners. Defusal tactics vary depending on individual history but generally take five forms. These include: (a) apologies, (b) discrediting, disqualifying statements, (c) defensiveness, (d) self-criticism, and (e) compensating.

Apologies. Immediately after asserting an opinion the ACOA may sense dissent from the listener and anticipate impending conflict. Apologies accept blame for assumed discomfort imposed on the listener and relieve the listener of supposedly acting negatively in retaliation for the discomfort. Of course, many assumptions play into this ACOA response that usually are inconsistent with the listener's real events.

Discrediting, disqualifying statements. Inferences again are the misleading motivation for defusal. Perceived discomfort in the listener may trigger the ACOA to dismiss, discredit or disqualify opinions they just made by admitting they may be wrong, or that little validity supports the statement, or by deferring judgment to the listener's alleged expertise. Criticism about a modern painting received poorly by a listener might prompt the client to rescind the statement, offering instead that "well, I don't know much about art anyway, certainly not like you do."

Defensiveness. Personal assaults signal many ACOAs to protect their vulnerability by fighting back with debative justifications or *rationalizations* that seemingly explicate their actions. Retaliatory statements marshall reasons, facts, and other "persuasive" artifacts of proof to satisfy the attacker's curiosity and support the validity of an idea. Defensiveness also rebuilds the ACOA's crumbling confidence against intrusive thoughts of "feeling like an imposter" or "looking stupid."

Self-criticism. Attack against oneself instantly is believed to relieve imminent conflict. ACOAs who expect interpersonal trouble shift to their personal faults, and away from faults of the listener, thereby cleansing the situation of anger, rejection or conflict. Self-criticism further restores control to the listener at the expense of the ACOA feeling inferior.

Compensating. Opinions that leave an immediate negative imprint upon listeners frighten ACOAs into thinking conflict is inevitable and they have severely emotionally hurt the listener. Feeling ashamed of this, efforts instantly go into motion to make up or *compensate* for this inconvenience by generously accommodating the listener in some capacity, either by relieving them of responsibilities or providing them with a service or resource guaranteed to win back their friendship.

All five defusal tactics seriously endanger the psychological profits of self-expression and ultimately of braving assertive remarks in hostile situations. Efforts at teaching opinions, assertiveness and resistance to roadblocks must involve specific steps that block these tactics, despite anxiety levels rising and the ACOA's self-perception of guilt intensifying.

Reversal of guilt. Inferred verbal statements from listeners can be easily translated into *self-shame.* Asked if she went to the grocery store, the ACOA wife might shamefully misinterpret the question to mean *how could you do such a stupid thing as forget to go to the grocery store?* Steps that prevent or interrupt guilty rules are twofold. First step is for client to reverse the question back to the listener, seeking more facts about the matter: "Was I supposed to go to the grocery store?"

Fact-finding serves the dual purpose of collecting critical objective information rather than relying on inferences, and it also puts the onus of responsibility upon the listener's shoulder, who must rephrase or reject the question if the topic expects to continue. Second step is literally to *blame the listener* for mistakes or faults related to the topic in question instead of the ACOA absorbing blame. Telling the person that "You could have let me know we were out of milk" shares burdens of inadequacy and imperfection and keeps the control balanced.

Resisting Rejection. Toughest of all interventions is preparing the ACOA for rejection. Rejection underlies the emotional pathology developed over years of avoidance and escape behaviors to the point where fear of rejection becomes habitual and confrontation of it seems utterly impossible. Steps follow a structured but cautious series of self-restraint actions that begin once ACOAs face anger or criticism from other people. Steps include:

1. Delay responding for 3-5 minutes. Resist engaging in defusal tactics.

2. Assertively state what the person said and your emotional disapproval of it.

3. Walk away and ignore subsequent roadblocks, attacking remarks from listeners.

4. Make self-statements that it is okay for people to be upset with you.

This last rule is crucial but contradicts the very core of caretaking behaviors. Accepting that people get angry, that rejection is normal, and it is even healthy for people to hate the ACOA challenges every rule indoctrinated in the person since childhood. Naturally, then, conversion to this new belief system takes time and is resisted adamantly and doubted to bring about healthy recovery. But applying the belief generates three benefits immediately visible to the risker. First, it relieves the ACOA of defusal tactics that undermine their integrity and leave them angry for being subversive; instead, confidence remains strong and gains momentum by self-restraint. Second, letting others be upset at the ACOA forces those people to *adjust to new behaviors in the ACOA*. Third, walking away teaches the ACOA not to depend on approval for self-esteem. Confidence depends, instead, on individualized risks directly challenging the norms, morals or values of social systems.

Building trust. Development of trust also forces the question, *Why?* Distrust runs deeply into the chronic history of abuse suffered by most ACOAs either from sexual, physical or emotional damage. Slowly abandoning this "comfort zone" of distrust by sharing control or inviting others to control the ACOA faces immediate barriers of fear. First is the fear that trust will repeat abuse. A second fear is that losing control will expose embarrassing imperfections and cause rejection. A third fear comes from literally not knowing how to share control. Adults forced in childhood to care for their siblings and parents and who had accelerated responsibilities imposed on daily chores never let other people, except possibly school teachers, be their benefactors. They have no concept of what it means to be a beneficiary.

Taken in context, fears can impede progress toward building trust unless the fears are identified, briefly explored and replaced by functional alternatives that allow a stepwise strategy for sharing control. Steps generally involve variations of:

1. Telling personal, embarrassing, or humiliating situations to a significant other. Resist using defusal tactics when telling the stories.

2. Asking significant others for favors. Ask them to do jobs you usually do or believe nobody else can do. Accept the product of their efforts regardless of errors or the inconsistency between their efforts and your own efforts.

3. Asking the significant other to interrupt your rigid schedule by that person planning, organizing, or directing social or business events that typically are left up to you.

4. Permitting the person to make decisions or initiate efforts you typically handled yourself, without your interference even if the person recruits your assistance.

Breaking the imposter syndrome. Low self-efficacy maintains as long as ACOAs perceive themselves as constantly averting exposure of faults. Fear of this exposure historically links to assaults of random and arbitrary punishment for unpredictable actions. Anticipating criticism at any time, ACOAs remain on guard for any chance of conflict and they sound the alarm the moment they feel vulnerable. The *imposter syndrome* describes this phobia and protective habitual responding.

Removing the syndrome becomes a delicate process of balancing risk with panic. Steps first prepare the person for desensitization, that is, of making verbal statements or displaying physical actions prone for errors while in a relaxed muscular state. Desensitization requires repeated use of progressive muscular relaxation using in vivo visual imagery followed by the client actually responding in the situations previously imagined. Visual imagery in relaxation, for example, may picture the client telling a stupid joke and forgetting parts of it. Once stress is lower under imagery, analogues are constructed in the clinical office and then in the real world for practice of this very scenario. Comfort gained in the in vivo applications breaks the imposter syndrome.

Imposterism also is treated by having the person just *stay in the unpleasant, aversive or frightening situation.* Less structured, but an equally effective desensitization, is forcing the client to interact verbally or nonverbally around people, events or objects feared as destructive to vulnerability. Around a conference table the ACOA executive stays seated throughout the entire meeting, forces input on topics, and verbally accepts constructive criticisms given to him. While interaction flows among discussants, fears about looking stupid and feeling like an imposter vanish long enough for the person to sustain confidence.

Risk-taking efforts. Following the demise of imposter syndrome are efforts to take spontaneous risks regarded as foolish, childish, and posing further hazards to vulnerability. ACOAs first construct a list of social, sexual, or playful activities they envy in other people or wish they can do themselves. Next is to assess how many of these responses currently appear in the person's repertoire, despite the infrequency, inaccuracy, or overall consequences produced by them (i.e., approval, disapproval). Responses showing some strength are the first to be augmented by changing the rules governing them and, if necessary, involving the significant others they affect.

For example, one lady envied people who could put on a bathing suit regardless of their weight and enjoy the swimming pool. Despite her slender fitness, this client's modesty interfered with pursuing the risk. Already in her repertoire was her ability to swim, plus she was a member of a club having an indoor pool. Steps immediately began where she dressed in the bathing suit around the house for one week until feeling relaxed and unthreathened by social disapproval (desensitization process). Second step involved her wearing the bathing suit to the pool, swimming, and gradually spending longer intervals there, around larger crowds of onlookers.

Anger control. Control over fear involves control over anger. The chapter on adolescents thoroughly reviews a methodology prescribed for anger management that is equally applicable to adults. Essentially the ACOA must first be alert to *cues and urges* motivating autonomic arousal, and the trajectory patterns building up to a *threshold* and *peak.* Changes in self-statements, in muscular tension, in visible cues, and toward altering time pressures represent steps in arresting anger.

Disabling enabling. Like eliminating distrust, eliminating the habit of caretaking provokes severe emotional resistance. Many ACOAs expect and automatically accept this dutiful obligation without reservation and depend on *doing for others* as a bloodline to self-preservation. However, repercussions of enabling are devastating enough to reconsider the lifelong habit. Toward this end, *disabling enabling* is a three step approach requiring the client to (a) resist rescuing, (b) resist pleasing, and (c) demand reciprocity.

Resist rescuing. ACOAs have a remarkable talent of being acutely aware of people in distress who must be saved. Rescue efforts launched to relieve the emotional grief, burdens and responsibilities of the victim supposedly earn respect, gratitude and approval from the rescuer. When told to refuse temptations to rescue, thereby allowing victims to suffer, it means the ACOA must also resist vicariously suffering the emotional grief and the guilt associated with ignoring people. Alternatively, ACOAs learn the belief that *people must suffer inconvenience to make changes themselves.* Steps teach the client to literally become distracted or refuse to help others when imposed upon.

Resist pleasing. Just as rescuing relieves grief observed in others, so *pleasing* relieves conflict, criticism or impending rejection. ACOAs make concessions to avoid or escape arguments or interpersonal turmoil while gaining secondary benefits from the approval of seeing others happy. Giving gifts, surprises, parties, or accommodations guaranteed to maintain peace and happiness in a family or friendship all are pleasing gestures. When told to resist temptations to please, even the thought of refusing induces panic reactions because it involves enduring anger and acrimony that historically has been intolerable. Refusals instantly would upset the balance causing distress, complaints, and abandonment of the ACOA by persons dependent on their caretaking. That is why refusals never occur until the client already demonstrates relative mastery of assertiveness, overcoming roadblocks, and expression of opinions. Secondly, withholding pleasing gestures occurs at the same time the client begins satisfying selfish needs. Personal gratification shifts the pendulum away from being the benefactor to becoming a beneficiary of others' efforts.

Demand reciprocity. Disabling enabling further requires the demand for an exchange system. Reciprocity between the client and significant others assures that for every personal sacrifice or concession made there is a dividend earned. Resources returned by other people can vary and need not parallel the quality, quantity or frequency of resources supplied by the caretaker, as long as timing of the reciprocal resource is *proximal.* It must be given shortly after the caretaker gives a resource. While this sounds logical, ACOAs struggle with asking for rewards from people fearing that it looks rude, conceited and selfish. Rewards also are fake; rewards or resources that ACOAs ask for are released reluctantly and stimulate anger in people. This is based on beliefs that requested or *contrived* rewards are inauthentic whereas rewards or resources given on the person's own accord are genuine. However, unprompted rewards for the caretaker's efforts are infrequent and usually nonexistent. Consequently, clients fight internal messages that their actions are wrong and immoral as they modestly ask for *something in return for their efforts.*

Construction of emotions. Anger, fear, anxiety and depression comprise the emotional constellation of most ACOAs. Emotions beyond these types are unusual and command a knowledge base that is severely deficient or absent. Feelings such as love, passion, and intimacy may resemble the *compassion* ACOAs show in their caretaking gestures but it is different. Love, passion and intimacy develop from a trusting and vulnerable relationship built between two independent people whose needs are mutually satisfied and whose ambitions are largely compatible. By contrast, co-dependent, unilateral love shown by the ACOA without much gained in return is *not love,* but rather a pleaser. In teasing out the difference, clients are shocked at mistaking love for pleasing and then are deeply frightened they *have no idea what love is.*

Construction of emotions thus begins as a threefold process. First is the step, described above, of trusting another person and relinquishing control. Second is learning basic touching, from simple hand-holding or extended hand gestures to simple kissing (with a spouse or intimate). Affection in private is broadened to public displays of touching, embracing and even kissing. Physical forms of exchange accompany verbal compliments and self-affirmations of looking and feeling feminine or masculine and looking attractive to a partner.

Disinhibited touching moves to the next step of sexual intimacy. Arousal first is attempted by self-stimulation and by letting a partner caress erogenous areas around upper and lower torso. Foreplay that is excitatory continues for longer intervals instead of being a boring prelude to coitus. After foreplay is satisfactory, strategies are described for building up plateaus (for women) and stability of erection (for men) prior to and during intromission. Sustaining arousal during intercourse involves mutual selfish and benevolent efforts, shifted with balance and without one partner feeling disgraced by the other partner. Lastly, timing and satisfaction of single and multiple climaxes involves both knowledge of the biological process (refractory period, types of excitatory stimuli, etc.), and restraint from criticisms following completion of intercourse.

Third, affection is developed and practiced around children and around persons perceived since childhood as uncaring and cold. Physical embracing, kissing, and verbal compliments toward children usually are easy and ACOAs welcome this exercise for two reasons. First is that it releases tenderness with *special people who they desperately want to love.* Second, showing affection to children breaks the intergenerational lineage of repressed or limited displays of emotion, in that the ACOA's offspring can perceive and understand touching as wonderful (not abusive, fearful or wrong), and plan to freely exhibit it for years into their own adulthood.

Overcoming avoidance and escape. Repeatedly emphasized in this chapter is that underlying most of ACOA behavior is avoidance and escape. Actions averting criticism, conflict and rejection constantly occupy the person's mind and keep them alert to interpersonal social situations. Because this pattern is habitual, much like caretaking, cessation of the behavior must start with *awareness.* Clients learn self-monitoring methods to physically or "mentally" record instances of avoidance and escape and the consequences (types of relief) generated from these patterns. Interruption of the pattern is a twofold process.

First, clients deliberately enter into apprehensive or high anxiety-prone situations and remain stationary until the situation runs its course and naturally ends. For instance, visiting friends who the ACOA believes hate him entails staying at the house, if invited, for a couple of hours or until there is a natural lull to leave. Confronting the *awful feeling that this person hates me* desensitizes the client's fears and allows for functional social behavior. Second, clients next do what intuitively they regard is impossible. They create conflict situations through criticism or disagreements, again feeling afraid, and midway through the argument start to problem-solve a compromise; seeking compromise of issues is diametrical to the habit of either *forcing (controlling) a decision or surrendering to another's decision.*

Accepting compliments. Highly modest, shameful, and intimidated ACOAs resist drawing attention to themselves partly due to imposterism and partly due to risks of conflict, criticism, and rejection. For one reason or another, drawing compliments is especially difficult. Efforts to combat this phobia follow a structured approach consisting of three different types of compliments: *Conversions, directing the conversation,* and *solicitations.*

Conversions are when the client listens to what somebody else is talking about. Then he takes their last statement or phrase and transforms it into a compliment or strength about himself. The statement describes an ability, accomplishment or success related to the last phrase. Melanie says, "That snow outside is so ugly I just can't stand it." The client chimes in with, "I don't know, I kind of like the snow. I love skiing and getting outside with the kids." Another example: Bruce observes, "Can't get any secretarial help around here and typing your own work is tedious." The client replies, "Not for everybody, I type pretty fast, thank God, and can do it myself when the clerical staff are busy."

Next is *directing the conversation.* Directing topics is control on the one hand, and tooting the client's horn on the other. Moments into the dialogue or at a natural breaking point, have the client shift talking to something of personal interest to himself. Expand upon the personal interest for a couple of sentences or until the listener changes topic. For instance, while conversing about budgetary cuts, the client waits for a pause and adds, " you know, it's a good thing we're not being laid off, I think my job is pretty secure." Two or three more sentences embellishing the client's point is enough. Nothing more thereafter. By shifting gears the client draws attention to issues or values important to himself without sounding pompous.

The third method is more direct. Subtlety is wonderful for beginners. But by now the client tries soliciting a compliment about some physical feature or activity she recently completed. "What do you think of this new dress?" Or, "Don't you think I got them to listen to me at that meeting?" Pointed questions regarding the client's appearance or actions waste little time getting to the issue. Egos inflate rapidly from friendly praise and approval that others typically give. Even if feedback is negative or none at all, just hearing himself verbalize the words puts into thought the client's pride in certain attributes.

Practice of compliments without slipping into old habits is tricky and can lead to common traps such as when the client (a) disqualifies the compliment, (b) is self-critical after the compliment, (c) returns a compliment right away, and (d) laughs at himself. Examples of each appear below:

Disqualify your compliments:	"I'm good at that—well not really."
Be self-critical after the compliment:	"I'm good at that, and that's all I'm good at."
Return a compliment right away:	"I'm good at that—but so are you."
Laugh at yourself:	"I'm good at that—isn't that a scream?"

New criteria for selecting new relationships. Above all else, intimacy is a dark secret unless the ACOA already is married or has a significant other. Otherwise, forming new relationships or preventing repetition of bad relationships poses major obstacles because of inexperience and fear of failure. *Inexperience* literally means lacking the prerequisite knowledge concerning how to date, what to look for in a partner, how to engage in small talk, and remaining focused. Focus digresses to obsessive worries of what the "date" thinks of the ACOA and whether they will fail this person's test. *Fear of failure* suggests some history of dating, forming relationships, and intimacy, except the track record is negative. One dysfunctional relationship after the other repeats the cycle until the ACOA gets discouraged that all potential partners are infectious. Attempts at breaking the vicious cycle are ineffective, especially during early dating or honeymoon periods, when first impressions signal a green light for the ACOA to pursue the relationship, only to discover problems later on.

Repeated failures create distrust, feelings of futility, and disrespect for the opposite sex (if heterosexual). The person develops cynical and stereotyped attitudes about inherent defects of the gender; for example, "all men can't be trusted," or "all women are ditsy." Machoism, feminism, and other liberal extremes egocentrically boasting the superiority of its gender may temporarily boost confidence and disguise fears, but ultimately disintegrate the person's capacity for a genuinely caring relationship.

Disguises fade away when the ACOA realizes the world is a lonely place and needs for a companion reach desperation. At this or an earlier point, clients should construct new criteria for selecting partners (heterosexual or homosexual) that challenge their intuitive criteria and force the risk of considering new behaviors. Table 3 lists criteria for healthy relationships based on three typologies described as *Person A, Person B,* and *Person C.* Each typology contains pervasive personality traits along the continuum of addictive, codependent behaviors, from *Person A* (no addiction, well-adjusted) to *Persons B & C* (severely maladjusted, highly prone to addiction).

In addition to applying these criteria, clients must undergo another change of rules. The rule of "when a partner feels right" collides with reality because instinctive feelings are untrustworthy and usually lead to repetitive dysfunctional relationships. Replacing instinctual feelings is a new rule that goes something like:

If you meet somebody and instantly feel "you've known him all your life or you can't believe how comfortable you are around him," that's a warning sign. It means you're doing things that are too familiar, because you did them before in a bad relationship. Instead, if you feel nervous, intimidated or even inferior around somebody, thinking he's so much better than you--you probably are on to a good relationship. He's not any better than you are. But his actions are making you do

new things you are not familiar with and should learn for a healthy relationship.

Table 3
Criteria for Healthy Relationships

PERSON A	PERSON B	PERSON C
Assertive	*Aggressive*	*Passive*
Expresses opinions	Criticizes only you	Is a "good listener"
Criticizes self and you	Boasts	Likes all that you do
Can be vulnerable	Not a listener	Discloses nothing
Admits mistakes	Makes demands	Edits remarks
Compliments self	Angry	Always sorry
Compliments you	Very serious	Afraid to say things
Listens and talks		
Flexible	*Rigid*	*Overflexible*
Easy going	Can't break schedules	Gives in to pressure
Handles mean/nice people	Perfectionistic	Always agrees
Good with all age groups	Compulsive	Afraid of rejection
Offers to compromise	"My way or highway"	Afraid of criticism
Looks for reciprocity	Blames you	Eager to please
Adjusts to new situations	Never admits fault	
Asks for your help		
Consistent	*Impulsive*	*Inconsistent*
What he says he does	Lots of energy	Afraid to do things
Always follows through	Never follows through	Appears lazy
Admits he forgot	Blames you for forgetting	Procrastinates

Clarifying criteria for relationships neither guarantees perfect spouse selection nor lifelong compatibility even if the partner meets all the criteria for *Person A*. What these typologies do offer are safe guidelines for re-entry into the scary dating world that many ACOAs have all but obliterated. As the risks begin, and the optimism for new relationships is stronger, ACOAs will finally discover there really is a light at the end of the tunnel.

REFERENCES

Abramowitz, A. & O'Leary, S.G. (1990). Effectiveness of delayed punishment in an applied setting. *Behavior Therapy,* 21, 231-239.

Ackerman, R.J. (1983). *Children of alcoholics: A guidebook for educators, therapists and parents.* Holmes Beach, FL: Learning Publications, Inc.

Ackerman, R.J. (Ed.). (1986). *Growing up in the shadow.* Holmes Beach, FL: Health Communications.

Ackerman, R.J. (1987a). *Children of alcoholics.* NY: Simon & Schuster, Inc.

Ackerman, R.J. (1987b). *Let go and grow: recovery for adult children.* Holmes Beach, FL: Health Communications.

Ackerman, R.J. (1987c). *Children of alcoholics: Bibliography and resource guide.* Pompano Beach, FL: Health Communications.

Ahles, T.A., Cassens, H.L. & Stalling, R.B. (1987). *Journal of Behavior Therapy and Experimental Psychiatry,* 18, 215-222.

Azrin, N.H. (1970). Punishment of elicited aggression. *Journal of the Experimental Analysis of Behavior,* 14, 7-10.

Azrin, N.H. & Holz, W.C. (1966). Punishment. In W. K. Honig (Ed.). *Operant behavior: Areas of research and application.* NY: Appleton-Century Crofts (pp. 380-447).

Azrin, N.H., Hutchinson, R.R. & Hake, D.F. (1967). Attack, avoidance and escape reactions to aversive shock. *Journal of the Experimental Analysis of Behavior,* 10, 131-148.

Azrin, N.H., Hutchinson, R.R. & Sallery, R.D. (1964). Pain aggression toward inanimate objects. *Journal of the Experimental Analysis of Behavior,* 7, 223-229.

Axelrod, S. & Apsche, J. (1983). *The effects of punishment on human behavior*. Orlando, FL: Academic Press.

Bandura, A. (1973). *Aggression: A social learning analysis*. Englewood Cliffs, NJ: Prentice-Hall.

Banks, R.K. (1965). Effect of pairing a stimulus with presentations of the UCS on extinction of an avoidance response in humans. *Journal of Experimental Psychology*, 70, 294-299.

Baum, W.M. (1973). The correlation-based law of effect. *Journal of the Experimental Analysis of Behavior*, 20, 137-153.

Bennett, R.H. & Cherek, D.R. (1990). Punished and nonpunished responding in a multiple schedule in humans: A brief report. *Psychological Record*, 40, 187-196.

Black, C. (1981). *It will never happen to me*. Denver, CO: MAC Printing.

Black, C. (1984). Children of alcoholics. *NCA Catalyst*, 1, 15-21.

Blackman, D. (1977). Conditioned suppression and the effects of classical conditioning on operant behavior. In W.K. Honig & J.E.R. Staddon (Eds.). *Handbook of operant behavior*. Englewood Cliffs, NJ: Prentice-Hall (pp. 340-363).

Blanchard, E.B. & Schwarz, S.P. (1988). Two-year follow-up of behavioral treatment of irritable bowel syndrome. *Behavior Therapy*, 19, 67-73.

Blanchard, R.J., Blanchard, D.C. & Takahashi, L.K. (1978). Pain and aggression in the rat. *Behavioral Biology*, 23, 291-305.

Block, J. (1971). *Lives through time*. Berkeley, CA: Bancroft Books.

Brennen, G.P. (1986). *I know they love me anyway*. WI: DePaul Rehabilitation Hospital.

Brown, S. (1988). *Treating adult children of alcoholics*. NJ: John Wiley & Sons.

Burnett, C. (1986). *One more time*. NY: Random House.

Caspi, A., Elder, G. & Bem, D. (1987). Moving against the world: Life-course patterns of explosive children. *Developmental Psychology*, 23, 308-313.

Charlop, M.H., Burgio, L.D., Iwata, B.A. & Ivancic, M.T. (1988). Stimulus variation as a means of enhancing punishment effects. *Journal of the Experimental Analysis of Behavior,* 21, 89-95.

Clark, A.D.B. & Clarke, A.M. (1984). Constancy and change in the growth of human characteristics. *Journal of Child Psychology and Psychiatry*, 25, 191-210.

Clonginger, C.R., Bohman, M. & Sigvardsson, S. (1981). Inheritance of alcohol abuse. *Archives of General Psychiatry*, 38, 861-868.

Cork, R.M. (1969). *The forgotten children.* Toronto: Paperjacks.

Costa, P.T. & McCrae, R.R. (1980). Still stable after all these years: Personality as a key to some issues in adulthood and old age. In P. Baltes (Ed.). *Life-span development and behavior.* Orlando, FL: Academic Press (65-102).

Davis, H. & McIntire, R.W. (1969). Conditioned suppression under positive, negative, and no contingency between conditioned and unconditioned stimuli. *Journal of the Experimental Analysis of Behavior,* 12, 633-640.

Dittrich, J., Houts, A. & Lichstein, K. (1983). Panic disorder: Assessment and treatment. *Clinical Psychology Review*, 3, 215-225.

Dollard, J. & Miller, N.W. (1950). *Personality and psychotherapy.* NY: McGraw-Hill.

Douglas, J.W.B. (1975). Early hospital admissions and later disturbances of behaviour and learning. *Developmental Medicine and Child Neurology*, 17, 456-480.

El-Guebaly, N. & Offord, D. (1977). The offspring of alcoholics: A critical review. *American Journal of Psychiatry*, 134, 357-365.

Ellis, A. (1962). *Reason and emotion in psychotherapy.* Secaucus, NJ: Citadel Press.

Eron, L.D. (1982). Parent-child interaction, television, violence, and aggression of children. *American Psychologist, 37*, 197-211.

Eysenck, H.J. (1979). The conditioning model of neurosis. *The Behavioral and Brain Sciences,* 2, 155-166.

Eysenck, H.J. (1968). A theory of incubation of anxiety/fear response. *Behaviour Research and Therapy,* 6, 319-321.

Fairbank, J.A. & Brown, T.A. (1987). Current behavioral approaches to the treatment of postraumatic stress disorder. *The Behavior Therapist,* 3, 57-64.

Ferster, C.B. & Skinner, B.F. (1957). *Schedules of reinforcement.* Englewood Cliffs, NJ: Prentice-Hall.

Ferster, C.B., Culberston, S. & Boren, M.C.P. (1975). *Behavior principles.* Englewood Cliffs, NJ: Prentice-Hall.

Foa, E.B., Steketee, G. & Rothbaum, B.O. (1989). Behavioral/cognitive conceptualizations of post-traumatic stress disorder. *Behavior Therapy,* 20, 155-176.

Friel, J. & Friel, L. (1988). *Adult children: Secrets of dysfunctional families.* Holmes Beach, FL: Health Communications.

Goslin, D. (1968). Standardized ability tests and testing. *Science,* 159, 851-855.

Gravitz, H.L. & Bowden, J.D. (1985). *Guide to recovery: A book for adult children of alcoholics.* Holmes Beach, FL: Learning Publications Inc.

Hackenberg, T.D. & Hineline, P.N. (1987). Remote effects of aversive contingencies: Disruption of appetitive behavior by adjacent avoidance sessions. *Journal of the Experimental Analysis of Behavior,* 48, 161-173.

Hayes, E.N. (1989). *Adult children of alcoholics remember.* NY: Harmony Books.

Hayes, S.C. (Ed.). (1989). *Rule-governed behavior: Cognition, contingencies, and instructional control.* NY: Plenum.

Hayes, S.C., Brownstein, A.J., Zettle, R.D., Rosenfarb, I., & Korn, Z. (1986). Rule-governed behavior and sensitivity to changing consequences of responding. *Journal of the Experimental Analysis of Behavior,* 45, 237-256.

Herrnstein, R.J. (1966). Superstition: A corollary of the principles of operant conditioning. In W.K. Honig (Ed.). *Operant behavior: Areas of research and application.* NY: Appleton-Century-Crofts (33-51).

Heston, L.L. (1966). Psychiatric disorders in foster home reared children of schizophrenic mothers. *British Journal of Psychiatry,* 112, 819-825.

Hindman, M. (1975). Children of alcoholic parents. *Alcohol, Health and Research World,* 6, 2-6.

Hollis, J.H. (1973). "Superstition": The effects of independent and contingent events on free operant responses in retarded children. *American Journal of Mental Deficiency,* 77, 585-596.

Huesmann, L.R., Eron, L. & Lefkowitz, M. (1984). Stability of aggression over time and generations. *Developmental Psychology,* 20, 1120-1134.

Hutchinson, R.R. (1977). By-products of aversive control. In W. K. Honig & J.E.R. Staddon (Eds.). *Handbook of operant behavior.* Englewood Cliffs, NJ: Prentice-Hall (pp. 415-431).

Kazdin, A.E. (1990). Childhood depression. *Journal of Child Psychology and Psychiatry and Allied Disciplines.* 31, 121-160.

Keane, T.M., Zimmerling, R.T. & Caddell, J.M. (1985). A behavioral formulation of post-traumatic stress disorder in Vietnam Veterans. *The Behavior Therapist,* 8, 9-12.

Kritsberg, W. (1985). *Adult children of alcoholic syndrome.* NY: Bantam.

Levine, S., Chevalier, J.A. & Korchin, S.J. (1956). The effects of early shock and handling on later avoidance learning. *Journal of Personality,* 24, 475-493.

Levis, D.J. & Boyd, T.L. (1979). Symptom maintenance: An infrahuman analysis and extension of the conservation of anxiety principle. *Journal of Abnormal Psychology,* 88, 107-120.

Levy, R. (1985). Blood, breath, and fears: A hyperventilation theory of panic attacks and agoraphobia. *Clinical Psychology Review,* 5, 271-285.

Levy, R. (1987). Panic disorder and agoraphobia: Fear of fear or fear of the symptoms produced by hyperventilation? *Journal of Behavior Therapy and Experimental Psychiatry,* 18, 305-316.

Mackintosh, N.J. (1974). *The psychology of animal learning.* NY: Academic Press.

McNally, R.J. & Lorenz, M. (1987). Anxiety sensitivity in agoraphobics. *Journal of Behavior Therapy and Experimental Psychiatry,* 18, 3-11.

McCord, J. (1979). Some child-rearing antecedents of criminal behavior in adult men. *Journal of Personality and Social Psychology,* 37, 1477-1486.

Mallow, P. & Levis, D.J. (1988). A laboratory demonstration of persistent human avoidance. *Behavior Therapy,* 19, 229-241.

Matson, J.L. & DiLorenzo, T.M. (1984). *Punishment and its alternatives.* NY: Springer.

Maxwell, W.A., Miller, F.D. & Meyer, P.A. (1971). The relationship between punishment and unavoidability in eliminating avoidance behavior in humans. *Psychonomic Science,* 23, 435-436.

Mayor, J. & Ruben, D.H. (1991). *After war: Overcoming post-traumatic stress syndrome.* Okemos, MI: Best Impressions International, Inc.

Morgan, P. (1982). Alcohol and family violence: Review of the interaction. In *Alcohol consumption and related problems.* Alcohol and Health Monograph 1. Rockville, MD: National Institute on Alcohol Abuse and Alcoholism (pp. 223-259).

Mowrer, O.H. (1950). *Learning theory and personality dynamics.* NY: Roland Press.

Newberger, E.H. & Bourne, R. (Eds.). (1985). *Unhappy families: Clinical research perspectives on family violence.* Littleton, MA: PSG Publishing Co., Inc.

Newlin, D.B. (1987). Alcohol expectancy and conditioning in sons of alcoholics. *Advances in Alcohol and Substance Abuse,* 6, 33-57.

Plomin, R. & Daniels, D. (1987). Why are children in the same family so different from one another? *Behavioral and Brain Sciences,* 10, 1-60.

Potter-Efron, R.T. & Potter-Efron, P.S. (1985). Family violence as a treatment issue with chemically dependent adolescents. *Alcoholism Treatment Quarterly,* 2, 1-15.

Quinton, D. & Rutter, M. (1976). Early hospital admissions and later disturbances of behaviour: An attempted replication of Douglas' findings. *Developmental Medicine and Child Neurology,* 18, 447-459.

Ratner, S.C. (1958). Hypnotic reactions of rabbits. *Psychological Reports,* 4, 209-210.

Ratner, S.C. & Thompson, R.W. (1960). Immobility reactions (fear) of domestic fowl as a function of age and prior experience. *Animal Behaviour,* 8, 186-191.

Reiss, S. (1987). Theoretical perspectives on the fear of anxiety. *Clinical Psychology Review,* 7, 585-596.

Reiss, S., Peterson, R.A., Gursky, D.M. & McNally, R.J. (1986). Anxiety sensitivity, anxiety frequency, and the prediction of fearfulness. *Behaviour Research and Therapy,* 24, 1-8.

Repp, A.C. & Deitz, D.E. (1978). On the selective use of punishment--suggested guidelines for administrators. *Mental Retardation,* 16, 250-254.

Reynolds, G.S. (1961). Behavioral contrast. *Journal of the Experimental Analysis of Behavior,* 4, 57-71.

Rosenthal, D. (1970). *Genetic theory and abnormal behavior.* NY: McGraw Hill.

Ruben, D.H. (1983). Interbehavioral implications for behavior therapy: Clinical perspective. In N.W. Smith, P.T. Mountjoy & D.H. Ruben (Eds.). *Reassessment in psychology: The interbehavioral alternative.* Washington, D.C.: University Press of America.

Ruben, D.H. (in press). *Avoidance syndrome: Doing things out of fear.* St. Louis, MO: Warren Green Publishers.

Rushton, J.P., Fulker, D.W., Neale, M.C., Nias, D.K.B. & Eysenck, H.J. (1986). Altruism and aggression: The heritability of individual differences. *Journal of Personality and Social Psychology,* 50, 1192-1198.

Rutter, M. (1980). The long-term effects of early experience. *Developmental Medicine and Child Neurology,* 22, 800-815.

Seligman, M.E.P. & Johnston, J.C.. (1973). A cognitive theory of avoidance learning. In F.J. McGuigan and D.B. Lumsden (Eds.). *Contemporary approaches to learning and conditioning.* Washington DC: Winston & Sons.

Skinner, B.F. (1948). Superstition in the pigeon. *Journal of Experimental Psychology,* 38, 168-172.

Skinner, B.F. (1977). The force of coincidence. In B.C. Etzel, J.M. LeBlanc, & D.M. Baer (Eds.). *New developments in behavioral psychology: Theory, methods and applications.* Hillsdale, NJ: Lawrence Erlbaum (pp. 3-6).

Solomon, R.W. & Wynne, L.C. (1954). Traumatic avoidance learning: The principle of anxiety conservation and partial irreversibility. *Psychological Review,* 61, 353-385.

Stampfl, T.G. & Levis, D.J. (1967). The essentials of implosive therapy: A learning-theory-based psychodynamic behavioral therapy. *Journal of Abnormal Psychology,* 72, 496-503.

Stampler, F.M. (1982). Panic disorder: Description, conceptualization, and implications for treatment. *Psychological Review,* 2, 469-486.

Steinglass, D., Bennett, L.A., Wolin, S.J. & Reiss, D. (Eds.). (1989). *The alcoholic family.* NY: Basic Books, Inc.

Thomas, E.J. & Santa, C. (1982). Unilateral family therapy for alcohol abuse: A working conception. *The American Journal of Family Therapy,* 10, 49-58.

Towers, R.L. (1989). *Children of alcoholics/addicts.* Washington, D.C.: National Education Association.

Tzeng, O.C.S. & Jacobsen, J.J. (Eds.). (1988). *Sourcebook for child abuse and neglect.* Springfield, IL: Charles C. Thomas.

Ulrich, R. (1967). Interactions between reflexive fighting and cooperative escape. *Journal of the Experimental Analysis of Behavior,* 10, 311-317.

Ulrich, R. & Azrin, (1962). Reflexive fighting in response to aversive stimulation. *Journal of the Experimental Analysis of Behavior,* 5, 511-520.

Ulrich, R. & Wolfe, M. (1969a). Research and theory on aggression and violence. *Science Teacher,* 36, 24-28.

Ulrich, R. & Wolfe, M. (1969b). Punishment and shock-induced aggression. *Journal of the Experimental Analysis of Behavior,* 12, 1009-1015.

Ulrich, R., Wolff, P.C. & Azrin, N.A. (1964). Shock as an elicitor of intra- and inter-species fighting behaviour. *Animal Behaviour,* 12, 14-15

Wegsheider, D. (1979). *If only my family understood me.* MN: CompCare Publications.

Wegscheider, D. (1979). *The family trap.* MN: Nurturing Networks.

Wegscheider, D. (1980). *A second chance.* CA: Science and Behavior Books.

Wegscheider, S. (1981). *Another chance: hope and health for the alcoholic family.* CA: Science and Behavior Books.

Weiner, H. (1969). Conditioning history and the control of human avoidance and escape responding. *Journal of the Experimental Analysis of Behavior,* 12, 1039-1043.

Werner, E.E. (1985). Stress and protective factors in children's lives. In A.R. Nicol (Ed.). *Longitudinal studies in child psychology and psychiatry.* NY: John Wiley & Sons.

Wertheim, E.S. (1978). Developmental genesis of human vulnerability: Conceptual re-evaluation. In E.J. Anthony, C. Koupernik & C. Chilan (Eds.). *The child in his family: Vulnerable children.* NY: John Wiley & Sons (pp. 17-36).

Wesman, A.G. (1968). Intelligence testing. *American Psychologist,* 23, 267-274.

Wilson, E.D. (1975). *Sociobiology: The new synthesis.* Cambridge, MA: Harvard University Press.

Wolfe, J., Keane, T.M., Lyons, J.A. & Gerardi, R.J. (1987). Current trends in the assessment of combat-related posttraumatic stress disorder. *The Behavior Therapist,* 10, 27-32.

Wolpe, J. (1958). *Psychotherapy by reciprocal inhibition.* Stanford, CA: Stanford University Press.

Zeiler, M.D. (1972). Superstitious behavior in children: An experimental analysis. In H.W. Reese (Ed.). *Advances in child development and behavior.* NY: Academic Press (pp. 1-29).

Zettle, R.D. (1990). Rule-governed behavior: A radical behavioral answer to the cognitive challenge. *Psychological Record,* 40, 41-49.

Zettle, R.D. & Hayes, S.C. (1982). Rule-governed behavior: A potential theoretical framework for cognitive-behavioral therapy. In P.C. Kendall (Ed.). *Advances in cognitive-behavioral research and therapy.* (Vol. 1). NY: Academic Press (pp. 73-118).

Zettle, R.D. & Young, M.J. (1987). Rule-following and human operant responding: Conceptual and methodological considerations. *The Analysis of Verbal Behavior*, 5, 33-39.

SELECTED ANNOTATIONS

Assur, E.R., Jackson, G.W. & Muncy, T. (1987). Probation counselors and the adult children of alcoholics. *Federal Probation*, 51, 41-46.

1. English; 2. Clinical/review; 3. ACOAs on probation; 4. Explores special concerns faced by probation officers who recognize ACOA symptoms in probationers including denial of crimes or problems, susceptibility to substance abuse, high rate of repeated offenses, insecurity, blame, anger, and dissolution among sibling or parent relationships; 5. Detection of clients at increased risk can reduce crime recidivism and lead to counseling or diversion services tailored for emotionally unadjusted offenders.

Baker, J.D. & Williamson, D.A. (1989). Psychological profiles of adult children of alcoholics in search of therapy. *Counselling Psychology Quarterly*, 2, 451-457.

1. English; 2. Experimental; 3. Sixty-nine adult children of alcoholics; 4. Community; 5. Demography, psychopathology, at-risk health behaviors, dysfunctional family relationships; 6. & 7. Group Design comparing ACOA with children from homes with other dysfunctions; 8. Beck Depression Inventory, Irrational Beliefs Test; 9. Both groups showed diversity of clinical problems, with depression and personality disorders being most prevalent.

Beidler, R.J. (1989). Adult children of alcoholics: Is it really a separate field for study? *Drugs and Society*, 3, 133-141.

1. English; 2. Theoretical; 3. ACOAs, general; 4. Examines cores issues underlying maladjustment of ACOAs in terms of individual development, interaction of alcoholism and sociopathy, and relationship of mental disorders to dysfunctional familial roots; 5. Concludes the field deserves special recognition as unique complications outside of traditional mental health study are presented as treatment issues and ultimately warrant retailored methods of intervention.

Benson, C.S. & Heller, K. (1987). Factors in the current adjustment of young adult daughters of alcoholic and problem drinking fathers. *Journal of Abnormal Psychology*, 96, 305-312.

1. English; 2. Experimental; 3. University women with alcoholic and problem drinking fathers (n = 114), women with normal fathers (n = 81), women with psychiatrically disturbed fathers (n = 30), and women with both parents who were alcoholic or problem drinkers (n = 15); 4. College; 5. Conflict, consumption rates, stress adjustment, interpersonal characteristics; 6. 7. & 8. Group design, response to surveys; 9. Daughters of alcoholic and problem drinking fathers reported more neurotic, acting out and psychiatric problems than did daughters of normal fathers and dysfunctional families. Daughters' rate of alcohol intake, however, did not distinguish groups.

Chandler, C.J. (1987). ACAs: The paradox and the dilemma. *EAP Digest*, 8, 46-50.

1. English; 2. Review/clinical; 3. Working ACOAs; 4. Article alerts service providers, managers, and EAP personnel of the unique demands of ACOA employees and alternative methods of coping with their lowered energy, reduced productivity, and interpersonal problems akin to family issues; 5. Standard disciplinary methodology is ineffective, has irreversible effects, and backfires against performance, whereas new strategies are introduced to overcome their higher risk of burnout and job failure.

Churchill, J.C., Broida, J.P. & Nicholson, N.L. (1990). Locus of control and self-esteem of adult children of alcoholics. *Journal of Studies on Alcohol*, 5, 373-376.

1. English; 2. Experimental. 3. 497 college students; 4. University; 5. Locus of control, self-esteem, adult offspring, fears; 6. & 7. Group design of children from alcoholic and nonalcoholic families; 8. Rotter's Internal-External Locus of Control Scale, Self-Esteem Scale from Jackson Personality Inventory, Children of Alcoholics Screening Test; 9. Conclusions showed no significant correlations between locus of control and offspring of alcoholics, suggesting caution when stereotyping loss of control or fears of abandonment in early adult-age children.

Crandell, J.S. (1989). Brief treatment for adult children of alcoholics: Accessing resources for self-care. *Psychotherapy*, 26, 510-513.

1. English; 2. Clinical case study; 3. 57-year-old female adult child of alcoholic; 4. Illustrates how ACOAs possess the requisites for effective self-care but have been blocked from using them; 5. Treatment interventions derived from neurolinguistic programming reviewed that can mobilize personal resources and revive latent skills before they deteriorate beyond repair.

Crawford, R.L. & Phyfer, A.Q. (1988). Adult children of alcoholics: A counseling model. *Journal of College Student Development*, 29, 105-111.

1. English; 2. Clinical/review; 3. College students; 4. Conceptual framework described of different roles family members play in survival of alcoholic families, including family hero, scapegoat, lost child and mascot. Based on adapted model, interventions are shown to dismantle and deregulate these dynamics while transforming the family to a healthier interaction; 5. Problems faced by students suffering effects of childhood "roles" must be considered when using this and other developmental approaches.

Davenport, Y.B. & Mathiasen, E.H. (1988). Couples psychotherapy group: Treatment of the married alcoholic. *Group*, 12, 67-75.

1. English; 2. Experimental; 3. Nine married couples with ten alcoholic members; 4. Outpatient clinic; 5. Family duress, marital issues; 6. Open-ended outpatient psychotherapy; 7. & 8. Group design; 9. Group therapy found effective for both alcoholic spouse and nonalcoholic spouse dealing with familial processes, and removal of defense mechanism. Implications offered for adult children of alcoholics receiving individual therapy over conjoint or group meetings.

Delaney, E.S., Phillips, P., & Chandler, C.K. (1989). Leading an Adlerian group for adult children of alcoholics. *Individual Psychology: Journal of Adlerian Theory, Research and Practice*, 45, 490-499.

1. English; 2. Clinical/intervention; 3. Adult children of alcoholics; 4. Describes treatment method for understanding, confronting, and changing mistaken beliefs, negative behaviors and counterproductive life goals in Adlerian-based group therapy focused on life patterns and early childhood memories; 5. Group procedure follows similar strategies to most therapy models but more introspection spent on feelings of inferiority, background, and confrontability.

Fischer, B. (1988). Process of healing shame. *Alcoholism Treatment Quarterly*, 4, 25-38.

1. English; 2. Theoretical; 3. ACOAs, general; 4. Examines conceptual scheme for healing internalized shame as a manifestation of unresolved anger, and denial of love; 5. Individual therapy described that follows stages of self-reconstruction in a group or family.

Glaus, K.O. (1988). Alcoholism, chemical dependency and the lesbian client. *Women and Therapy*, 8, 131-144.

1. English; 2. Clinical/review; 3. Lesbian ACOAs; 4. Carefully examines alcoholic risk factors pointing to a larger than expected proportion of ACOAs in the lesbian community and relying on lesbian/gay bar for social opportunities of acceptance; 5. Treatment issues explored include emotional denial, defense mechanisms (rationalization, negative affect), internalized homophobia, repressed sexuality, and compulsive need to find partner for family security.

Haack, M.R. (1990). Collaborative investigation of adult children of alcoholics with anxiety. *Archives of Psychiatric Nursing*, 4, 62-66.

1. English; 2. Clinical/review; 3. Children of alcoholic families; 4. Article describes integrative analysis between demography and psychiatric medicine toward understanding types of anxiety and predisposition to substance abuse; 5. Integrative model implicates genetic, social and intergenerational factors in influencing drug use or behavior maladjustment.

Hesselbrock, V.M., O'Brien, J., Weinstein, M., & Carter-Menendez, N. (1987). Reasons for drinking and alcohol use in young adults at high risk and at low risk for alcoholism. *British Journal of Addiction*, 82, 1335-1339.

1. English; 2. Experimental; 3. Teenage to adult offspring of alcoholics (n = 130) and non-alcoholic parents (n = 75); 4. Community; 5. Attitudes, consumption rates, health risk behaviors; 6. 7.& 8. Group design, social interview surveys; 9. Reasons for drinking were not significantly different between both groups, whereas higher consumption rates for offspring of alcoholic parents was largely due to social enhancement and relief of unpleasant affect.

Hibbard, S. (1989). Personality and object relational psychology in young adult children of alcoholics. *Psychotherapy*, 26, 504-509.

1. English; 2. Experimental; 3. 15 ACOAs and 15 non-ACOAs; 4. Clinic; 5. Characterological disorders such as defensive adaptation, impulsivity; 6., 7. & 8. Group design, Millon Clinical Multiaxial Inventory, Rorschach; 9. Results confirmed previous findings that personality disorders relate to deficits in object identification and low self-esteem (poor egocentricity).

Hirshfeld, R.M.A., Kosier, T., Keller, M.B., Lavori, P.W. & Endicott, J. (1989). Influence on alcoholism on the course of depression. *Journal of Affective Disorders*, 16, 151-158.

1. English; 2. Experimental; 3. 268 inpatients and outpatients diagnosed with moderate to severe depression, with and without concurrent alcoholism; 4. Hospital; 5. Depression, relapse potential, sobriety vs. rate of drinking, interpersonal relationships; 6., 7. & 8. Group design, longitudinally followed for 5 years; 9. Groups differed significantly on psychosocial status, with alcoholic depressives reporting lower levels of psychosocial functioning through the 2-year follow-up, particularly in interpersonal relationships and marriages. Implications offered on problems of marital adjustment affecting recovering and current drinkers intergenerationally related to drinking parents.

Jacobson, S.B. (1987). Twelve-step program and group therapy for adult children of alcoholics. *Journal of Psychoactive Drugs*, 19, 253-255.

1. English; 2. Clinical/review; 3. ACOAs, general population; 4. Summarizes the 12-step ACOA program adapted from traditions of AA spiritual recovery program that offers an alternative to structured therapy by focusing on loss of security, trust, love, and teachings in humor, respect and reparenting; 5. Advantages of 12-step program for group support to newcomers and elimination of drug dependency add further meaning to the experience.

Knoblauch, D.L. & Bowers, N.D. (1989). A therapeutic conceptualization of adult children of alcoholics. *Journal of College Student Psychotherapy*, 4, 37-52.

1. English; 2. Experimental; 3. 289 males and 366 female ACOAs; 4. University; 5. Health risk behaviors, locus of control, drinking patterns; 6., 7. & 8. Group design, Michigan Alcoholism Screening Test, Ego

Grasping Orientation; 9. Results suggest routine problem drinking among high risk students showing elevated needs for control, and common ACOA personality deviations. Implications for campus therapy discussed.

Landers, D. & Hollingdale, L. (1988). Working with children of alcoholics on a college campus: A rationale and strategies for success. *Journal of College Student Psychotherapy*, 2, 205-222.

1. English; 2. Theoretical; 3. ACOA students; 4. Needs for campus intervention offered to students of dysfunctional families are discussed relative to effective strategies; 5. Group therapy and support groups in dormitories and classes. Concludes that strategies reach greater strata of affected population than for noncampus populations.

Mathiasen, E.H. & Davenport, Y.B. (1988). Reciprocal depression in recovering alcoholic couples: The efficacy of psychodynamic group treatment. *Group*, 12, 45-55.

1. English; 2. Clinical/review; 3. Recovering alcoholics; 4. Alcoholics' group run psychodynamically is reviewed in terms of the clients' vulnerability to depression, fear and denial, and clinical implications and efficacy of couples group model; 5. Treatment of alcoholic or nonalcoholic spouse must consider depression in both partners as part of dependency syndrome. Short-term traditional therapy more directly acknowledges emotional limitations and allows clients a grasp on priorities for personality changes.

Meacham, A., & Ackerman, R. (1987) Surviving in the alcoholic family. *Changes*, 2, 24-55.

1. English; 2. Review/clinical; 3. ACOAs; 4. Author Robert Ackerman, founding board member of the National Association of Children of Alcoholics, is interviewed about family roles attributed to alcoholic homes and implications they have for adjustment to healthy adult lives; 5. Vulnerabilities suffered in childhood must undergo modification either through supportive, nurturing families of their own or through treatment.

Mitchell, C.E. (1989). A plea for compassion toward the adult child of a functional family. *TACD-Journal*, 17, 121-124.

1. English; 2. Theoretical; 3. ACOAs, all ages; 4. Argues that avant garde therapies pursued by ACOAs indirectly and insensitively address underlying inhibitions requiring more intensive psychotherapy; 5. Fears of decreased attention by therapist and differential attitudes from treatment providers of adult children of alcoholic versus other types of dysfunctional families.

Mylant-Scavnicky, M. (1990). The process of coping among young adult children of alcoholics. *Issues in Mental Health Nursing*, 11, 125-139.

1. English; 2. Experimental; 3. Thirty adult children (ages 18-28); 4. Outpatient clinic; 5. Role-perception, coping behaviors, confrontability; 6. & 7. Group design with semistructured interviews; 8. Jalowiec Coping Scale, different Confrontive Measures; 9. Results show coping deficits preponderant in younger (18-year-olds) subjects and only improving after therapy or through caretaking relationships.

Parker, D.A. & Harford, T.C. (1987). Alcohol-related problems of children of heavy-drinking parents. *Journal of Studies on Alcohol*, 48, 265-268.

1. English; 2. Experimental; 3. Household data of daughters and sons of heavy drinking parents in metropolitan city; 4. Urban city; 5. Risk factors, occupational status, parental influences, and drug and alcohol dependency problems; 6., 7. & 8. Retrospective demographic and survey data from 1978; 9. ACOAs with blue-collar occupations had higher percentages of drug and alcohol dependence and social dysfunction (e.g., criminality or family violence) than for white-collar occupations. Female offspring showed highest risk for alcohol-related problems.

Plescia-Pikus, M., Long-Suter, E. & Wilson, J.P. (1988). Achievement, well-being, intelligence, and stress reaction in adult children of alcoholics. *Psychological Reports*, 62, 603-609.

1. English; 2. Experimental; 3. 44 ACOAs and 92 controls; 4. University; 5. Aptitude, personal satisfaction, achievement status; 6. 7. & 8. Group Design, California Psychological Inventory, Sixteen Personality Factor Questionnaire (16PF), Impact of Even Scale; 9. Subjects showed overall lower personal satisfaction and achievement than controls, and high achievement scoring ACOAs did not have corresponding high stress scores on the Impact scale.

Potter-Efron, P. (1987). Creative approaches to shame and guilt: Helping the adult child of an alcoholic. *Alcoholism Treatment Quarterly*, 4, 39-56.

1. English; 2. Theoretical/clinical; 3. ACOAs, general; 4. Reviews definitions and treatment methodology for unraveling the dynamics of internalized shame and guilt distorted by ACOAs who currently struggle with intimate relationships; 5. Treatment techniques include elimination of irrational beliefs (broadening perspectives), increasing self-acceptance, and experimentation between therapist and client to locate new solutions for anxious feelings.

Richards, T.M. (1989). Recovery for adult children of alcoholics: Education, support, psychotherapy. *Alcoholism Treatment Quarterly*, 6, 87-110.

1. English; 2. Theoretical/review; 3. ACOAs; 4. Author contends that codependents suffer levels of emotional severity (mild, moderate or severe) depending on emotional support or absence of support in parental rearing; 5. Interventions described for building self-esteem and concepts of personal responsibility and sexual/aggressive drives, rely on attendance at groups (peer support) in addition to intensive, structured psychotherapy.

Roush, K.L. & DeBlassie, R.R. (1989). Structured group counseling for college students of alcoholic parents. *Journal of College Student Development*, 30, 276-277.

1. English; 2. Experimental; 3. 12 undergraduate and 12 graduate ACOAs; 4. University; 5. Adaptivity, behavior change, attitudinal changes; 6. 11 two-hour weekly group sessions thematically focused; 7. & 8. Group design, with one month follow-up; 9. Reports positive treatment outcomes with significant improvements in coping strategy and screening of healthy interpersonal relationships.

Schumrum, T. & Hartman, B.W. (1988). Adult children of alcoholics and chronic career indecision. *Career Development Quarterly*, 37, 118-126.

1. English; 2. Theoretical; 3. Unemployed ACOAs; 4. Repeated unemployed and resultant career indecision among ACOAs are explored in relation to traits and patterns, attribution of causality, and types of occupational information received by them; 5. ACOAs require

more than career facts or perfunctory occupational services because undermining their ambitions, despite high aptitudes, are unrealistic expectations, and external blaming that interferes with healthy decision making. Approaches to enhance occupational training are discussed.

Thomas, E.J. & Yoshioka, M.R. (1989). Spouse interventive confrontations in unilateral family therapy for alcohol abuse. *Social Casework*, 70, 340-347.

1. English; 2. Clinical/review; 3. Alcoholic spouses and marriage; 4. Describes steps in the programmed confrontation method of dealing with unmotivated drinking spouse, when decision for treatment is made by rest of family members. Attempts to change role of spouse are carried out independently from and in advance of efforts to alter drinking behavior of the abuser. Interventions include monitoring, alcohol education, relationship enhancement, neutralization of old influence systems, and disenabling by the spouse; 5. Spouse of uncooperative abuser can be assisted in positive rehabilitative way by getting himself or herself in treatment, without the spouse, and accepting risk-taking steps involved.

Wilson, J.R. & Nagoshi, C.T. (1988). Adult children of alcoholics: Cognitive and psychomotor characteristics. *British Journal of Behavioral Genetics*, 83, 809-820.

1. English; 2. Experimental; 3. 350 twins, non-twin siblings and unrelated persons raised in same home relative to alcohol using parent; 4. Clinic; 5. Cognitive and motor responses; 6., 7. & 8. Group design, medical evaluations (metabolic, behavioral and mood measures) before and after alcohol consumption; 9. Biological markers for alcohol-prone addiction are high among tolerance levels and low cognitive abilities. At risk factors requiring further investigation are discussed.

Chapter 5

Elderly Addicts

Old alcoholics never reform, they just fade away. This is just one of many damaging myths about elderly addicts. Hidden and forgotten, they are often ignored by the outside world as their drinking increases and they take too many pills. Ailments of old age conceal this addiction and conceal a serious family problem. But elderly addicts are grandmothers and grandfathers. They play visible roles in lives of their children, grandchildren, great grandchildren, and entire extended family system. Ignoring the addiction not only deceives caring family members but it also destroys respect accorded to the older individual.

Theories abound that alcohol use is dangerous at any age, particularly older age, and when there are drug problems the interactive effects remain undiagnosed. Hospital studies show rising numbers of aged abusers whose symptoms are overlooked. In 1967, over two decades ago, 6% of people over 65 admitted to state and county mental hospitals suffered alcoholism. Of those diagnosed alcoholic, some 80% of them drank heavily longer than 10 years but never were noticed. Today the number staggers at about 12% of elderly seen in state and county mental hospitals.

Of the non-institutionalized elderly, nearly 80% suffering chronic diseases either drink or take prescription medications. Drugs and medical sundries represent as high as 5.1 billion dollars (per total population) and $192 (per capita) during a single year. In other words, elderly consumers who spend way beyond their affordable budgets for medication refills are very susceptible targets for drug abuse, misuse, overuse and underuse.

This chapter overviews critical points of etiology and treatment of elderly alcoholism and medication (drug) abuse documented in the last twenty years (e.g., Barnes, Abel & Ernst, 1980; Maddox, Robins & Rosenberg, 1984; Petersen, Whittington & Payne, 1979; Ruben, 1984, 1986a, 1990). Areas covered provide an introduction to biobehavioral issues facing family members, with guidelines on early detection and treatment options.

ETIOLOGY

Patterns of Alcohol Abuse

Acute and chronic alcohol use evolves over time and is an integrative part of the person's entire lifestyle. Problems during childhood, adolescence, early and late adulthood increase the person's risk of alcoholism but are not absolute causes of it. Current problems in the elderly person's life also directly bear upon addiction and are considered in this section. Conditions increasing risk include: (a) additive qualities; (b) increased use of medications; (c) drinking as a moral issue; (d) lack of knowledge about alcohol; (e) confused or overlooked symptoms; (f) maintaining drinking patterns; (g) overprotective care providers; and (h) myths about alcoholism.

Additive Qualities

Because alcohol is an additive drug, frequent use increases alcohol tolerance. This means that the body requires more alcohol to achieve the same effect and that the visible, behavioral effects are less obvious. Increased tolerance is an initial step toward a longterm addiction. As the addiction controls the person, the tolerance level drops and the visible effects increase. Older drinkers, in particular, show serious additive effects. They likely have been drinking for 30, 40 or more years and age-related problems consequently are more severe than their nondrinking counterparts.

Increased Use of Medications

Older adults are more prone to chronic illness and take prescriptions and Over The Counter (OTC) remedies for their illnesses. For those who drink, increased use of medication contributes to the danger of alcohol-drug interactions.

Drinking Viewed as a Moral Issue

For many older people the teachings of religion and the influence or prohibition era have implanted the concept that drinking to excess is immoral. For some this is a deterrent. However, older chronic drinkers may feel guilty about this and try to deny or hide the drinking from others. Alcohol treated as a moral issue only compounds the guilt the drinker already feels and usually results in continued abuse.

Lack of Knowledge about Alcohol

Physicians, service providers, family members and older adults all may not know enough about the effects of alcohol. They are unfamiliar with the symptoms of an alcohol problem. As a result many alcohol symptoms go unnoticed. Without sufficient knowledge, the people close to drinkers accidentally may enable or encourage the abuse.

Confused or Overlooked Symptoms

Loss of appetite, depression, confusion, bruises, and memory loss are symptoms of an alcohol problem, but they may also be symptoms of severe depression, organic brain syndrome, or prescription drug abuse. Many people overlook alcohol as a possible source of these symptoms. Others simply attribute the symptoms to old age or senility. Multiple chronic or acute conditions may overshadow or camouflage an alcohol problem. When the amount and frequency of alcohol is examined, older people usually drink less but more frequently than a younger person and may not exhibit obnoxious, intoxicated behaviors.

Maintaining Drinking Patterns

The older person who maintains a moderate or heavy drinking pattern from the middle years into old age may deceive those around him. Most people begin to reduce their consumption because of the increased effects of alcohol. In a sense, maintaining an earlier pattern in the later years is similar to increasing alcohol consumption. The effect is the same and the danger of developing a drinking problem is increased.

Overprotective Care Providers

Some people in caring roles, such as family and counselors, overprotect their clients. They assume full responsibility when a client is capable of being fully or partially responsible for his actions. When families overcare for the alcoholic they prevent crises from occurring and they protect users from the consequences of drinking. Care providers mistakenly may buy the alcohol as well as prepare meals, clean up the messes, straighten out financial and legal matters, and make excuses. Overcaring is basically "enabling" continuation of the addiction. Enablers usually are unaware their actions reinforce drinking or they consider this action normal based on how their parents did the same thing.

Myths about Alcoholism

Negative attitudes perpetuated about alcoholics through the years gave rise to false beliefs regarding what alcohol can do to a person. Eleven of the most prevalent myths reviewed by Sherouse (1983, pp. 41-43) include the following:

Myth 1: *There is some other method of sobering up someone who is intoxicated besides just time.* Of course, even the mild stimulation of giving coffee or a cold shower to somebody still does not eliminate the hangover.

Myth 2: *If a person sticks to beer they'll never became an alcoholic.* However, beer contains as much ethyl alcohol as an ounce of liquor and will act on the body in the same way.

Myth 3: *Switching drinks will make you drunk faster or conversely help you stay sober longer than if you stick with just one alcohol beverage.* The fact is the amount of alcohol in a drink determines level of intoxication, not the mixture that contains alcohol.

Myth 4: *Drinking helps overcome depression.* While sedative effects may relieve anxiety for a short time, the person then is left feeling irritated, upset, paranoid and inferior. Depression can become worse from alcohol.

Myth 5: *Every older drinker is a chronic alcoholic.* This clearly is not true. With the aging population increasing, normal stress from adjustment can cause later life alcoholism. Secondly, symptoms of organic illness (polymorbidity) may resemble or duplicate alcoholic symptoms supporting the myth that the person is a chronic drinker.

Myth 6: *Few women become alcoholics.* The ratio was once ten men for every two women who were alcoholics. The ratio is now three men to every one woman.

Myth 7: *Certain races or religions are more prone to produce alcoholics.* The fact is alcoholism is not indigenous to socioeconomic, racial, religious, ethnic or cultural groups but instead widespread among all people.

Myth 8: *People who really can hold their liquor should be envied.* Ironically this ignores the basic toxicology of alcoholism. Increasing amounts of drinks proportionally elevates the tolerance level until a physical dependency develops.

Myth 9: *Drunkenness and alcoholism are the same thing.* Teenagers, in particular, experiment with alcohol tolerance and may get drunk after several beers or mixed drinks. Adults are no different in this respect. Incidences of inebriety, however, only show lack of control and not a physical or psychological dependency. Repeated episodes of drunkenness, with higher doses of alcohol consumed, are a better indicator of addiction.

Myth 10: *Once an alcoholic recovers, the person can drink again socially.* Heavy drinkers who abstain threaten their physical safety by tempting fate. When Sobell & Sobell published their controversial research on "controlled drinking" (1973, 1976, 1978; Mills, Sobel & Schaefer, 1971), chronic drinkers including recovered alcoholics misinterpreted the findings to mean social drinking was again possible. The sobering truth is that controlled drinking is still an experimental infant extremely limited to certain types of drinkers and far from being a revolutionary form of therapy.

Myth 11: *Most alcoholics are skid row bums.* Only 3 to 5 percent of all known alcoholics in the USA are actually of the "skid row" or extremely chronic variety. The remainder sample a cross-section of socioeconomic levels and are married, employed, and capable of functioning in day-to-day life.

Patterns of Prescriptive Drug Abuse

Previous to this new age of drug use, substance abuse among the elderly primarily meant alcoholism. Manufactured Over-The-Counter (OTC) drugs were fewer and tailored more for young and early age adults. But as life-sustaining preparations advanced, so did the potential problems resulting from improper use of medications. This section covers common problems and patterns under the broad topic of drug misuse and drug mismanagement. Medication errors generally fall into six categories: Overuse, underuse, erratic use, contraindicated use, abuse, and improper prescribing practices. First is a brief definition of each problem followed by a review of its causes.

1. *Overuse:* Overuse is mistakenly taking several doses of the same medication or taking medication when it is not needed.

2. *Underuse:* Underuse includes both the failure to fill prescriptions and forgetting to take the medications. Signs are the individual's stretching out the medication to last longer or discontinuing use of it earlier than directed.

3. *Erratic use:* Erratic use refers to the failure to follow instructions. This includes missing doses, taking double doses, taking doses at the wrong time, and confusion over which drug to take at which interval.

4. *Contraindicated use:* This occurs due to incorrect storage of medications, using outdated drugs, or not monitoring side effects. A second cause is sharing or borrowing drugs, frequently termed the "Grey Market." Contraindicated drugs in addition can produce harmful side effects in interaction with the person's other drugs.

5. *Abuse:* Abuse is drug misuse with intent to hurt self or toward addictive purposes.

6. *Improper prescribing practices:* Improper prescribing is primarily a communication problem between physician and client (e.g., Ruben, 1987), but also the mistake of overprescribing or underprescribing drugs inconsistent with biological needs.

Overuse and Erratic Use

Overuse and erratic use are less prevalent than other problems but important enough to review. Prescriptions stating "prn" (take as needed) can lead the person to misuse the drug. When the choice of medications is left to the user's own judgment, medications might be taken when not really needed. This is particularly serious when there already is dependency on substances.

Underuse

Underuse of medication is largely responsible for most medication errors. Some common reasons for underuse by the elderly include the following:

1. *Forgetting*: Not knowing for sure what medications have been taken.

2. *Economics*: Not filling the prescription or reducing the dosage due to cost savings.

3. *Physiological Disorders*: The person cannot swallow the pill or feels ill.

4. *Physiological Recovery:* The person feels better and decides to stop or reduce medication.

5. *Misplaced Medication:* The elderly individual cannot find the appropriate medication if needed.

6. *Mixing up Medications:* Not knowing for sure which medication is correct to take and on what schedule.

7. *Drug-Drug Interactions:* The person experiences an adverse drug effect due to ingestion of two or more drugs.

8. *Side, Allergic, Toxic, Idiosyncratic Effects:* These effects can lead to severe underuse problems.

Contraindicated Use

Another type of misuse is contraindicated use. Contraindicated use refers to several characteristics of the medications or its medical delivery systems jeopardizing proper use. Following are frequent problems cited:

1. *Exchange of Drugs:* Seniors exchange medications with someone who has a similar symptom or has extra (leftover) pills of a prescription also used by the borrower. Unfortunately dosage levels vary for each person despite its being the same medication. Use of somebody else's medication risks harmful effects such as a symptom aggravation or sickness.

2. *Outdated Drugs:* An elderly person may retain unused pills for a later time only to discover the pills lose their effectiveness after an expiration date.

3. *Automatic Refills:* This is when elderly persons continually have prescriptions refilled over the telephone or, essentially, without consulting the physician or receiving a full medical examination.

4. *Duplication:* This where people simultaneously receive two or more prescriptions for the same drug from different physicians or pharmacies, called "polypharmacy."

Improper Prescribing Practices

Improper prescribing practices occur at an astounding rate. Reasons for this problem range from using many pharmacies to inadequate physician-client communication. Among these circumstances include:

1. The client does not provide the physician with enough information about the health problem, other drugs being taken or the side effects experienced.

2. The physician does not adjust the dosage to a level appropriate for the older client.

3. The physician prescribes a drug without sufficiently informing the client about possible side effects or without instructions for taking the drug accurately.

4. The physician repeatedly prescribes an addictive drug without informing the client or addressing the addiction.

A variety of interrelated factors underlie problems of medication mismanagement beyond the six categories just covered. Twelve factors in particular raise concern for direct care providers because their harmful effects are difficult to prevent. Included among these are:

1. Sources of Misinformation
2. Self-care Practices
3. High Cost of Medications
4. Brand and Generic Names
5. Mixed Endorsement of Drugs
6. Lack of Medication Monitoring
7. Geriatric Dosage
8. Drug Pyramiding
9. Prescription Advice
10. Television Advertising
11. Style of Institutional Care
12. Myths about Medications

Sources of misinformation. Most older people are not fully aware of the age-related changes that affect drug use. For health and drug information, they rely on their spouses, family members and friends, physicians, and other service providers.

Self-care practices. Chronic diseases like arthritis and heart conditions now total more than 80% of all illnesses. Modern medicine has no quick cures for these chronic conditions and health care costs have skyrocketed. One result is that client or family is responsible for coordinating their own health care at a time when the level of medical technology is more sophisticated and complicated than ever before. Self-care of health care services is so cumbersome that typically the elderly resort to personal remedies. Self-diagnosis, self-prescribing OTC drugs, and sharing medicines become easier interventions.

High cost of medications. The high cost of medications is one of the greatest deterrents for compliance with prescribed regimens. Many people do not fill a prescription once they know of its cost. Others have to wait until their social security check comes in at the beginning of the month. Then they decide what bill will not be paid or what they cannot afford that month. Others purchase the medication and reduce the amount they should take so the prescription lasts longer.

Brand and generic drugs. The dual system of brand and generic names is a problem. If Haldol and Dilantin sound strange, try their respective generic names, Haloperidol and Phenytoin. With over 7,000 commonly prescribed medications, multiplied by two, there is an overwhelming list of strange names. Confusion abounds by the names of drugs being unpronounceable and too complicated to even try. There is little incentive to master the art of drug information.

Mixed endorsement of drugs. Generic drugs get mixed reviews. Pharmacists and physicians vary in their opinions. Some generic drugs may not be suitable surrogates in special cases or simply may not be available. This uncertainty has been passed on to the older consumer. Other reasons physicians may not endorse generic drugs is that they know the salesman of drug companies, because they may be uncertain of the quality of a certain drug pharmacy selected, or because they wish to support the research efforts of certain drugs.

Lack of medication monitoring. The lack of medication monitoring is another common problem. Residents of nursing homes, hospitals, and mental health facilities, and recipients of home health services are the most likely victims. Medication monitoring should occur whenever the health care or distribution of medication is conducted or supervised by someone other than the medication user. Problems occur when there is no medication monitoring or when the lines of authority are unclear due to shortage of staff and lack of training in geriatric medicine.

Geriatric dosage. Most medications are tested on healthy males in their twenties. The recommended adult dosage is derived from these tests. Older people can change substantially from their young adult years and often should not be prescribed the "normal" adult dose. This is why prescribing medications for older people is a trial process. It may take a while to find the proper dosage level.

Drug pyramiding. Drug pyramiding occurs when a drug is prescribed for a presenting problem and other drugs also are prescribed to treat the side-effects caused by the first drug. The list of prescribed drugs keeps multiplying. In some cases, the drugs prescribed for side effects can block the action of the drug prescribed for the initial problem.

Prescription advice. Prescription advice and directions are frequently given at the doctor's office after diagnosis of a problem or after discharge from the hospital. These are not the best times for clients to comprehend the advice given. Immediately after a diagnosis, the client is likely absorbing details about illness and symptoms. Sadness and anger compound the anxiety most clients feel. Emotions are also strong after clients leave the hospital. Older people are affected more than other age groups by relocation trauma, even if it means returning home. The client may not be ready for technical discourse on when to take medications, how often, with which foods and what side effects may occur.

Television advertising. The problem with television ads as an information source is that they are made to sell a product. They do not give absolutely accurate advice on alternative therapies and they downplay the cautionary information. Ads also normalize self-diagnosis and OTC drugs. Manufacturers and distributors spend approximately $1.2 billion annually to advertise and promote the use of OTC medications, with many targeted to the older consumer.

Style of institutional care. In most general hospitals, nursing homes and psychiatric hospitals, the client's care is important but must fit into the framework of the institution. Because older people in hospitals frequently become disoriented, more effort goes into management of them. Faced with staff shortages, long work shifts, and client overload, short-cuts in management unfortunately sacrifice quality care for the elderly client. This may involve overuse of sedatives, for example, for more rapid regiment compliance.

Myths about medication. Research demonstrates that drug effects are partly or wholly determined by what a person believes the drug will do for him (cf., Einstein, 1989; Ewing & Rouse, 1978). Will it help the person sleep better? Make them feel better? Some beliefs start as true statements about drug effects but in conversation are diluted with false information. Older people who say, for instance, "drugs are different from medicine," truly are convinced of this distinction even though the belief is more fiction than fact. Fictions or "myths" distort actual drug information and potentially misguide people on self-diagnosis and OTC medications. Below are listed some of the common myths and facts about generic and brand name drugs:

Myth 1: *There is a distinction between drugs and medicine.* The myth holds that drugs are used by some people and usually obtained on the street. Medicines are obtained from the doctor and used for curative purposes.

Fact: Chemicals involved in both cases affect the body regardless of source, and the effects can be both pleasant and unpleasant.

Myth 2: *The doctor wouldn't give me anything that would harm me.* The myth is that doctors generally do not prescribe medications which will harm a client.

Fact: In the doctor's opinion, the benefits of a drug may outweigh the potential negative side effects. The doctor cannot control overuse nor can he anticipate allergic or idiosyncratic effects. Thus the client may continue to use medications that the doctor would stop or at least alter the dosage of if he knew problems arose.

Myth 3: *I don't like this medication's effects, or it isn't helping me.* This belief says clients often cease a medication regimen because they do not like the adverse drug reactions or medications do not relieve symptoms as expected.

Fact: This attitude can be countered by thorough explanation of drug side effects and the length of time required to produce noticeable results.

Myth 4: *I'm ill and need help, so give me something.* This is the belief that deciding to see the doctor is a healthy and beneficial step to instant recovery.

Fact: Seeing the physician is a major psychological event for some elderly people because they "admit an illness" and expect that help will be given. Typically clients overtly and covertly pressure the doctor for medication of one sort or another.

Myth 5: *If it looks good, smells good, and tastes good, it can't be good for you.* Many consumers seriously believe that medicines must look bad or taste bad as a measure of effectiveness.

Fact: They recall the awful taste of medicines as a child or parent and are not cognizant of taste improvements made in consumer products over the last 20 years. Corrected expectations involves an explanation from the nurse, physician, pharmacist or health worker.

Myth 6: *Over-the-counter drugs are not medicine.* There is a common belief that OTC drugs are not medications and therefore need not be discussed with the physician.

Fact: OTC drugs are in fact complex preparations containing a variety of compounds which may be contraindicated, including alcohol, aspirin, belladonna alkaloyds and atropine derivatives.

Myth 7: *If this doctor is any good, he will be able to tell what's wrong with the client.* Clients often assume the doctor can make definitive diagnosis with little or no help from them.

Fact: Doctors run into many obstacles in diagnosis. When older persons forget to describe symptoms and do not identify OTC or other drugs they are taking, it complicates the diagnosis.

Myth 8: *If one pill is good, two are better.* It is common for people to increase the frequency or dosage of medication prescribed in an effort to alleviate their suffering as rapidly as possible.

Fact: Increasing the medication at one's own discretion alters the medication regimen and is harmful to the body.

Myth 9: *I'm not ill, I'm just getting older.* Older persons may misattribute a disease state to growing older. Clients may delay seeking help until the illness requires multiple drugs or increased dosages.

Fact: Perceptions of illness and the need for medication are subject to distortion. Invented are beliefs that growing old is automatic license to obtain pills.

Myth 10: *Generic drugs just won't work as well as brand-name drugs.*

Fact: Under the 1984 Drug Price Competition and Patent Restoration Act, generic drugs must be "bioequivalent" to their brand-name counterparts to gain FDA approval. This means that generics must contain the same active ingredients and must be identical in strength, dosage and route of administration.

As care providers, the first step is realizing myths are widespread and greatly influence decisions on drug usage. Beliefs too often multiply when accurate drug information is absent, ambiguous or conflicts with expectations of symptom relief. By presenting the facts, at least clients can stand a better chance of recognizing these beliefs and can be prepared to ask questions of physicians and pharmacists.

Social Causes of Alcohol and Drug Abuse

Ageistic thinking undermines many of the reasons for aged alcoholic and drug abuse. Stereotypical profiles of skid-row bums and "drunken old men" deflect attention away from truths about the etiology, many of which are hard to confront. This section moves beyond drug and alcoholic patterns by reviewing prevalent social causes related to (a) bereavement, (b) marriage, (c) family relations, (d) retirement, (e) tax expenditures, and (f) relocation.

Bereavement

Clinical thanatology has achieved a new status for the elderly community (Sobel, 1981). Thanatologists view their objective as dismantling twentieth century medicine which discourages the naturalness of dying. Clinical care of bereaved friends and relatives thus is typically left to the physician and biomedical services. While survivors of friends and relatives may seek medical guidance, their biophysical changes caused by anger and confusion are best approached by counselors. Many widowed aged, for example, who pass through bereavement with rheumatoid arthritis and asthmas also develop chronic drinking.

Marriage

Many retired couples find that for the first time in their marriages they must live twenty-four hours a day with each other on a permanent basis. Marital stability up to this point maintains because spouses are separated at least eight to ten hours a day in their respective jobs. After retirement, wives may find their husbands interfere with routine chores or that both spouses squabble over trivial differences. Fighting between spouses invokes an eventual aversive home life from which husband and wife may seek avoidance and escape. Elderly couples who turn to drinking resist the seemingly logical solutions of divorce or marital therapy because the costs are expensive and there is the risk of family embarrassment.

Family Relations

Families are no longer the centralized and closely-allied groups present during the turn of the century. About four of every five noninstitutionalized persons over 65 may have living children, but roughly 18% of those children still live in the same household. As a result, the proportion of old people living ten minutes to seven hours away from their children has been constant while the frequency of contacts and visits by siblings and other relatives has seriously dwindled. Widowed persons and old persons who have never married, for instance, are especially at risk (Shanas, 1982).

Retirement

The decline in income and social status after retirement leads to major social adjustments. After retirement, opportunities to generate an affordable income or to remain busy are complicated by legal and social discrimination, of which the worst is age. Even the Age Discrimination Employment Act of 1967, altering mandatory retirement laws, provides insufficient labor opportunities for the aged.

The authorization of the Older Americans Act offers some opportunities, but hardly compensates for the rising cost of inflation during the past three years. For example, reimbursement for volunteer and foster grandparent programs is too low to meet special physical and psychosocial needs. The result is depletion of funds corresponding to poor adaptivity to environmental tensions. Unemployed elderly drinkers who neither enter nor complete such opportunity programs further exacerbate their risk for chronic disease (Atkinson, 1981; Lutterotti, 1969).

Tax Expenditures

Fixed incomes, low educational levels, and declining physical health place the elderly in competition for existing services. The reduction in federal spending also contributes to limited availability of services, especially to those services designed for welfare recipients. Bush's Congressional budget cuts are shrinking funds out of welfare programs and limiting tax provisions. Some major tax expenditures are the exemptions, exclusions and credits. Such exclusions include (a) social security benefits for retired workers, (b) railroad retirement benefits, (c) veteran's pensions, (d) tax credits, and (e) capital gains on home sales.

Such exclusions presumably alter the income distribution between the aged in a manner favorable to low-income aged. But, in fact, these benefits from taxation are heavily weighted toward assisting a minority of high-income elderly rather than individuals who are in need. Because of this inequity, the monies currently allotted under exemption provisions do not parallel direct costs for the elderly. Expenditures for one segment of the elderly population prevents expenditures for another segment, which creates spending habits and higher taxes for elderly poor.

Relocation

Relocation involves moving from one neighborhood to another, from one city to another, or to another state. When relocation is voluntary, the person generally plans the move well in advance and looks forward to the change. Mandatory relocation, however, can have a damaging effect on the mental and physical well-being of the older person.

Whether relocation sustains the survival of the elderly or causes a "transfer trauma" depends on the acceptance or rejection of the *relocation-mortality hypothesis* (e.g., Coffman, 1983; Horowitz & Schulz, 1977; Schulz & Brenner, 1977). This hypothesis suggests that relocation increases the amenability to physical disease since individuals are exposed to adverse housing effects. Coffman (1983) dismisses this hypothesis as an excuse to keep elderly clients in inferior and deteriorating facilities. Ironically, both sides of the controversy militate against successful de-institutionalization. However, emotionality does depend on the individual's health and the quality of the transitional living process (Ruben, 1983a). Elder cottages, for example, offer direction for reaching the underserved and benefit the infirm alcoholic unable to pay for physical therapy and other medical services.

EFFECTS UPON FAMILY

Concerned family members alert to the aging person's habits can exercise many choices. Confronting the person clearly is the best choice and involves several layers of planning steps. One planning step is adopting healthy attitudes regarding older people and increasing sensitivity to their lifestyles, needs and physical limitations. A second planning step is a checklist of questions about medication history and potential problems. Third, guardians, family and service providers of elderly should be familiar with common physician mistakes.

First Step: Healthy Positive Attitudes

There are certain general views allowing for productive, healthy interaction with the elderly. Primarily they are nonageistic, that is, nonstereotypical, and deal with exact actions of the person rather than inferences about those actions. Below are guidelines to develop this healthy outlook:

1. Treat the person as an "individual."

2. Recognize how biological, psychological and socioeconomic factors affect the person. See if the person's physician, pharmacist or other service workers are aware of these changes.

3. Talk to the person about the normal aging process.

4. Help the person understand their natural losses.

5. Be sensitive to their eating habits, particularly if they follow special diets.

6. Be sensitive to complaints and unusual symptoms.

7. Learn to recognize that functioning and responses may depend upon factors such as fatigue, mood or loss.

8. Be patient with people who are slow to respond.

9. Be flexible and accepting of the person.

10. In some instances, just being around and lending a sympathetic ear can be of great assistance.

Since a large proportion of elderly have hearing impairments, the following are suggestions to bear in mind while talking to a hearing impaired older person:

11. Make sure that you have the person's attention before beginning to speak.

12. Be sure the person is able to see your face.

13. Speak at a moderate tone level—not too high or low.

14. Do not cover your mouth with your hands or any other object.

15. Do not chew gum or food when speaking.

16. Do not shuffle papers or other objects while speaking. Background noises may disrupt the listener.

17. When possible, use gestures or other visual stimuli to aid in communication.

18. If necessary, repeat the message, using the same words.

19. If the person does not appear to understand, rephrase the question or statement.

20. Encourage questions from the person.

21. Make an attempt to learn something about hearing aids. Learn how to make simple adjustments such as changing the cord or battery.

Second Step: Questions about Medication History and Potential Problems

Below is a list of suggestions for working with the elderly in the area of medication use. This is not meant to be a complete list. Rather, it contains some basic suggestions that should be incorporated in the family or service providers' activities:

1. Know the names of drugs commonly prescribed for the elderly and know what conditions they are intended to treat.

2. Educate the person to know the names and dosages of their drugs.

3. Know that medications can cause side effects, interaction effects and adverse drug reactions.

4. Know that people *and* the environment can contribute to the way in which drugs are used and misused.

5. Assist the person in following a diet, if one has been recommended with their drug regimen.

6. Know the type and names of commonly used OTC preparations and that they *are* drugs.

7. Educate the person to tell their doctors and pharmacists about the OTC preparations they are using.

8. Caution the person against self-diagnosis and self-medication with OTC's, especially when prescribed drugs are taken as well.

9. Assist the person in finding alternatives to self-medication with OTC's, through balanced diets, rest, exercise, social activity, relaxation, and avoidance of stress.

10. Watch carefully for signs and symptoms of possible medication problems.

11. Educate the person to request a re-evaluation of the medications to determine whether certain medicines should be continued indefinitely or changed.

Third Step: Common Physician Mistakes

Physicians trained in geriatrics (or geropsychiatry) offer expertise in differentiating symptoms of biological aging from drug and alcohol effects. However, many physicians, including psychiatrists, lack this expertise and may unintentionally commit errors that direct care providers should be aware of (Salzman, 1990). Frequent physician mistakes include (a) inattention to the client's medical condition, (b) failure to perform supporting laboratory tests, (c) prescribing too low or high a dose, (d) inadequate drug trial, (e) overreacting to changes in the client's condition, (f) inept use of many drugs versus skillful use of few, (g) failure to monitor drug use, (h) failure to re-evaluate clients periodically, and (i) failure to counsel clients about drug effects.

Inattention to the client's medical condition. Basic medical practice requires that physicians prescribing medicine take into account the elderly's developmental status, medical conditions and any specific physical problems. Particular attention should be paid to prior medication history to obtain clues to previously effective or ineffective treatments. When the client's condition is in doubt, the physician should not hesitate to consult previous doctors or appropriate medical specialists.

Failure to perform supporting laboratory tests. During the initial medical evaluation it is usually important to perform routine blood tests and electrocardiograms to ensure the client is not at risk. This is especially necessary if the client is to receive drug therapy. Ordered tests should be followed-up by the physician or his office staff.

Prescribing too low or high a dose. Perhaps the most common error made in prescription of drugs is incorrect doses. Uncertain physicians may express ambivalence by prescribing inadequate doses. Inexperienced physicians may prescribe an elderly client a regular adult dose or in anticipation of drug side effects, may counter the side effects with other medications. Low adult doses on the slow metabolism of aging bodies will be too weak for relief and instead distress the client. High adult doses may cause unwanted side effects or overdose.

Inadequate drug trial. In addition to proper dosage levels, it is necessary to continue medication for a sufficient length of time to determine if the drug is effective. Treatment plans should include a dosage build-up schedule and specific time periods after which therapeutic effects will be assessed. Should the drug prove ineffective, a second drug, preferably from a different class, then should be tried.

Overreacting to changes in the client's condition. Another common error is when physicians immediately raise or lower dosage with every complaint from the client. Overreaction usually takes place at two stages in the client's course of treatment. First is during the initial phase of treatment, when physicians are building up therapeutic levels. Premature leveling or reduction of drug dosage may yield only modest gains. Second is midway through treatment when physicians decrease or terminate medication in clients who require some stabilizing agent to prevent relapse of a recurrent disorder (physical or psychological).

Inept use of many drugs versus skillful use of few. Most seasoned physicians develop some favorite drugs or drug combinations whose activity and proper dosage indications have become familiar. Consequently they are reluctant to consider or prescribe drugs with whose actions they are unfamiliar. While a conservative practice, it overlooks new drugs on the market with probable benefits or benefits surpassing the action of routine drugs. Physicians who do agree to try new medications should indicate their inexperience with it, the available alternatives, and risks and benefits likely incurred from the dosage.

Failure to monitor drug use. A serious assumption is that because medication is prescribed, clients are taking it. Or for that matter, taking it correctly. When there are signs of deterioration in clinical state, physicians should consider noncompliance of regimen as a leading variable. Once it has been determined that this is the problem, solutions may include: (a) encouraging the family, hospital, or clinic staff to help in overseeing medications administered; (b) using liquid medications, instead of tablets or capsules that are not swallowed; and (c) using long-acting preparations which require fewer administrations than other drugs.

Failure to re-evaluate clients periodically. Once a client's condition is stabilized, physicians may discontinue drug treatment or place the client on maintenance medication. Providers usually are put into place then to monitor continual progress and report any decay of condition. But it is a good practice for physicians to schedule follow-up interviews at regular intervals.

Failure to counsel clients about drug effects. Confident physicians generally regard relief of client symptoms a reliable index to regulate dosage. But what about how the elderly person feels, or side effects they experience? Physicians need to spend more time telling the client about the treatment course and soliciting feedback from them during phases of improvement. An unfortunate but common practice is assigning this duty to ancillary staff such as nurses and physician assistants. While these professionals may have the competency, trust first and foremost is with the physician and it is his obligation to reassure elderly clients of his or her active interest in their welfare.

PRIORITIES FOR INTERVENTION

Competency goes beyond the physician's territory. The family and service providers face equal challenges to competency when trying to identify a *potential* alcoholic or addicted elderly person. Early detection naturally is preferable but harder to accomplish on a grassroots level, and it involves carefully crafted methods of prevention. Reviewed here are two approaches to isolating the problem: Primary prevention *and* secondary prevention (treatment).

Primary Prevention

This section briefly overviews primary prevention, including general recommendations currently undertaken to counter the epidemic proportion of elderly addiction. Sections covered include: (a) What is primary prevention?; and (b) recommendations for professional-client prevention.

What is Primary Prevention?

Primary prevention is when the potential for problems exist without problems being evident. Efforts focus upon programs and strategies put in place before older adults develop alcohol or medication problems. The National Institute of Drug Abuse (NIDA) and National Institute of Alcohol Abuse and Alcoholism (NIAAA) have identified six modalities of primary drug abuse prevention (NIDA, 1981). These include: Information, education, alternatives, intervention, environmental change programs, and social policy change programs.

Information programs. These are designed to provide accurate and timely information about drugs and their effects on the human system. Programs are based on the human potential for self-improvement through responsible decision-making.

Education programs. These are designed to develop critical life skills such as decision-making, problem-solving and communication. These programs premise on the theory that people are motivated to satisfy certain needs (e.g., love, security, self-identity) and that those who are deficient in critical skills may satisfy their needs through drug abuse.

Alternative programs. These provide positive growth experiences in which people can develop the self-discipline, confidence and personal awareness they need to become socially mature individuals. Programs involve participation in activities which foster awareness of self and others and which offer exposure to a wide range of rewarding nondrug activities.

Intervention programs. These provide assistance and support to people during critical periods of their lives. Programs involve person-to-person dyads, sharing of experiences, and empathic listening aiding adjustment to personal and family problems. Techniques used are diverse but usually include counseling, hotline assistance, topical workshops and peer-supported activities.

Environmental change programs. These seek to identify and change social and physical environmental factors that directly influence behaviors and patterns of drug use and abuse. Examples include petition drives to beautify a park, or evicting drug users from it.

Social policy change programs. These attempt to modify social policies, including laws, regulations and enforcement procedures governing drug availability and distribution. Lobbying efforts further modify advertising policies and reduce possible negative consequences through consumer product safety regulation.

Secondary Prevention (Treatment)

Secondary prevention is identifying and reducing existing substance abuse problems at the earliest stage possible. Early symptom detection in elderly addicts is unfortunately difficult given their social isolationism and disguise of major symptoms. Casefinding efforts may locate high-risk individuals, but the next step of treatment decision faces several confusing routes from which to choose.

Treatment programs vary from individual and group counseling to self-help and bibliotherapy groups. Currently, models of counseling show renewed interest in education and aftercare programs. Two prolific movements inspired by this trend combine pharmacology with behavioral interventions. The first deals with what is known as *behavioral pharmacology*, and the second with *behavioral psychotherapy*.

Behavioral Pharmacology

Recent studies in behavioral effects of drugs offer new hope for clinical interpretation of how environmental and pharmacologic variables interact (Breuning, Davis & Poling, 1982; Breuning, Poling & Matson, 1984; Poling, 1986; Poling, Picker & Hall-Johnson, 1983). In the human research, certain principles of drug action make it clear that drugs that are self-administered (and abused) (1) serve as positive reinforcers, and (2) reinforce drug-seeking "operant" responses. These operants are also influenced by the same set of variables that "control" nondrug responses.

There are meaningful correlations between advances in behavioral pharmacology and elderly alcohol and drug addiction. For example, considerable pharmacokinetic properties that determine drug disposition may or may not be age-related. Reduced plasma or decline in renal excretion, usually attributed to aging, may be instead a function of ethanol selectively influencing the person's sensitivity to one kind of stimulus (auditory, visual, olfactory, etc.) and nonselectively influencing sensitivity to other stimuli. Changes in stimulus selection ("discrimination") account for the loss or disruption of stimulus control (tendency to respond to certain stimuli, and not others) and eventual nonresponsiveness to common stimuli. Another operating influence may be levels of deprivation (hunger, time-limitations, thirst, etc.) (cf. Michael, 1982, 1983). For example, elderly with anorexia nervosa (hunger deprivation) may consume higher concentrations of ethanol which would affect their sensory orientation (Ruben, 1984).

Behavioral pharmacology holds important implications for behavioral and biomedical interventions for elders. For example, the physiological benefits of detoxification and disulfiram (antabuse) are limited against producing recidivism. This is because, in strictly medical treatments, there are several untreated events in the natural environment reconditioning substance abuse after the patient's discharge from the hospital. This is why treatment emphasis must always be "multicausal" and "transactional." Multicausal by considering several simultaneous reasons for addiction, and transactional by the fact that addiction develops *over a period of time.*

Behavioral Psychotherapy

Behavioral psychotherapies for elderly addicts usually contain two distinct parts: Assessment and integration. Relatively improved systems are available to assess drinking behavior and may involve mechanical recording devices or the coordination of professionals and paraprofessionals to monitor target responses (cf. Hersen & Barlow, 1976; Ruben, 1990). One such recording system in a nursing home also employed computers to rate validity and reliability of observational data (Schnelle & Traughber, 1983). This involves use of "simulations" or *analogues* (Ruben, 1983b , 1989). These, in effect, attempt to structure events in the clinic so they resemble nonclinic events and thus produce "naturalistic" drinking and medication-taking behaviors. Role-play, enactment, and audio-visual recording provide the usual means of measuring behavior that transfers from the person's natural environment into the clinic or hospital setting.

In treatment design, behavioral methods have assisted the movement of educational programs into alcohol prevention. Outreach projects allow counselors to visit elderly in nursing homes, community senior centers, and in the elderly's own home. On-site behavioral counseling employs contingency management, homework assignments, and direct skill application (Burgio & Burgio, 1986; Cartensen & Edelstein, 1987; Patterson, Dupree, Eberly, Jackson & O'Sullivan, 1982; Pinkston & Linsk, 1984; Ruben, in press; Skinner, 1983).

Frequently behavioral skills training involves direct modeling and imitation exercises. Instructors demonstrate, for instance, pill preparation, and drug-taking steps using a step-by-step or task analysis approach. Each step in the task is brief, easy to implement, and immediately follows with skill repetition and feedback. Once steps are learned in order, one after the other, they are combined into a full sequence comprising the task.

For example, tasks that can be split up into tiny parts for keeping track of different daily medicines might involve the following list:

1. Use an egg carton and electric alarm clock.

2. Label the outside of the egg cup with numbers signifying the time of day to take the drug ("1" = "1:00 pm").

3. Each morning put the day's pills in the proper egg cups. Number of pills for each drug at that hour are put in the cup. If more than one drug is taken at the hour, have separate cups for each drug and labeled with the same time (e.g., all at 1:00).

4. Now, set alarm clock to go off at first pill time (e.g., 1:00)

5. Turn alarm off, open egg carton, and take pills from any cup labeled that time (1:00).

6. Re-fasten egg carton and re-set alarm clock for next time interval.

Constructing a task analysis is an easy process by following basic steps. Consider these six steps:

1. Select a behavior or "response class" and watch carefully how the elderly person does it.

2. Break down the behavior or skill into tiny parts that are all observable, measurable, and easy to say the client has completed.

3. Prompt the client at each step, using imitation and modeling exercises where necessary.

4. Once the client does a step, reinforce him with praise.

5. Move slowly and systematically to the next step. Each step combines each of the previous steps learned.

6. When the client fails or has trouble with a new step, return to the previous step and redo it until he is ready to move on.

One final feature of behavioral treatment refers to "integration." By "integration" is meant a linking between all relevant factors of the elderly addict's *field* that contribute to alcohol and drug problems. Pioneered by the work of J.R. Kantor (1959; Ruben, 1983c, 1986b), this integrative-field concept is like behavioral medicine in that it pulls together biophysiological agents into a holistic model. It is different from behavioral medicine in the same respect; this holism is really a multidisciplinary approach that considers medical, behavioral, as well as *historical, cultural* and *physical science* variables.

All in all, growing concern for the elderly drug and alcohol abuser affects a labyrinth of services, treatment philosophies and scientific research. But the general picture of older abusers has been rather negative. One reason is that traditional views of elderly addiction support a unicausal, rather than multicausal analysis of the problem. Of course, nobody disputes that elderly persons undergo transitions and face multiple health risks. The difficulty, however, lies in professional awareness of *how* these multiple variables interact and of the behavioral outcomes of these interactions.

REFERENCES

Atkinson, J. H. (1981). Alcoholism and geriatric problems. *Advances in Alcoholism,* 2, 5-8.

Barnes, G.M., Abel, E.L. & Ernst, C.A.S. (Eds.) (1980). *Alcohol and the elderly: A comprehensive bibliography.* Westport, CT: Greenwood Press.

Breuning, S.E., Davis, V.J. & Poling, A.D. (1982). Pharmacotherapy with the mentally retarded: Implications for clinical psychologists. *Clinical Psychology Review,* 2, 79-114.

Breuning, S.E., Poling, A.D. & Matson, J.E. (Eds.). (1984). *Applied psychopharmacology: Assessment of medication effects.* NY: Grune & Stratton.

Burgio, L.D. & Burgo, K.L. (1986). Behavioral gerontology: Application of behavioral methods to problems of older adults. *Journal of Applied Behavior Analysis,* 19, 321-328.

Carstensen, L.L. & Edelstein, B.A. (1987). *Handbook of clinical gerontology.* NY: Pergamon.

Coffman, T.L. (1983). Toward an understanding of geriatric relocation. *Gerontologist,* 23, 453-459.

Einstein, S. (Ed.). (1979). *Drug and alcohol use: Issues and factors.* NY: Plenum.

Ewing, J.A. & Rouse, B.A. (Eds.). (1978). *Drinking: Alcohol in American society-issues and current research.* Chicago, IL: Nelson Hall.

Hersen, M. & Barlow, D.H. (1976). *Single-case experimental designs: Strategies for studying behavior change.* NY: Pergamon Press.

Horowitz, M.J. & Schulz, R. (1983). The relocation controversy: Criticism and commentary on five recent studies. *Gerontologist,* 23, 229-235.

Kantor, J.R. (1959). *Interbehavioral psychology*. Granville, OH: Principia Press.

Lutterotti, A. (1969). L'aspect social de l'alcoolisme dans la vieillesse. *Revue Alcoolisme,* 15, 49-57.

Maddox, G., Robins, L. N. & Rosenberg, N. (Eds.). (1984). *Nature and extent of alcohol problems among the elderly*. NY: Springer Publishing.

Michael, J. (1982). Distinguishing between discriminative and motivational functions of stimuli. *Journal of the Experimental Analysis of Behavior,* 37, 149-155.

Michael, J. (1983). Evocative and repertoire altering effects of an environmental event. *Verbal Behavior News,* 2, 21-23.

Mills, K.C., Sobell, M.B. & Schaefer, H.H. (1971). Training social drinking as an alternative to abstinence for alcoholics. *Behavior Therapy,* 2, 18-27.

National Institute on Drug Abuse (NIDA) (1981). *Prevention planning workbook: Volume 1*. Rockville, MD: National Institute on Drug Abuse.

Patterson, R.L., Dupree, L.W., Eberly, D.A., Jackson, G.M., O'Sullivan, M.J., Penner, L.A. & Dee-Kelly, C. (1982). *Overcoming deficits of aging: A Behavioral treatment*. NY: Plenum.

Petersen, D.M., Whittington, F.J. & Payne, B.P. (Eds.). (1979). *Drugs and the elderly: Social and pharmacological issues*. Springfield, IL: Charles C. Thomas.

Pinkston, E.M. & Linsk, N.L. (1984). *Care of the elderly: A family approach*. NY: Pergamon.

Poling, A.D. (1986). *A primer of human behavioral pharmacology*. NY: Plenum.

Poling, A.D. , Picker, M., & Hall-Johnson, E. (1983). Human behavioral pharmacology. *Psychological Record,* 33, 473-493.

Ruben, D.H. (1983a). Assessment and setting events and interbehavioral history for dispelling myths about aging residential elderly. *Interbehaviorist,* 12, 9-11.

Ruben, D.H. (1983b). Analogue assessments in the behavioral treatment of drug addictions. *Catalyst,* 2, 69-77.

Ruben, D.H. (1983c). Interbehavioral implications for behavior: Clinical perspectives. In N.W. Smith, P.T. Mountjoy & D.H. Ruben (Eds.) *Reassessment in Psychology: The interbehavioral alternative.* Washington, D.C.: University Press of America (pp. 445-469).

Ruben, D.H. (1984). *Drug abuse and the elderly: An annotated bibliography.* Metuchen, NJ: Scarecrow Press.

Ruben, D.H. (1986a). The elderly alcoholic: Some current dimensions. *Advances in Alcohol & Substance Abuse* 5, 59-70.

Ruben, D.H. (1986b). What is the "interbehavioral" approach to treatment? *Journal of Contemporary Psychotherapy,* 16, 62-71.

Ruben, D.H. (1987). Improving communication between the elderly and pharmacies: A self-initiative training program. *Journal of Alcohol and Drug Education,* 32, 7-12.

Ruben, D.H. (1989). Behavioral predictors of alcoholics: A systems alternative. *Alcoholism Treatment Quarterly,* 5, 137-162.

Ruben, D.H. (1990). *The aging and drug effects: A planning manual for medication and alcohol abuse treatment of the elderly.* Jefferson, NC: McFarland & Company.

Ruben, D.H. (in press). Reducing interruptions in functional activity through control of self-medication and habit-reversal. *Corrective and Social Psychiatry and Journal of Behavior Technology, Methods and Therapy,* 34.

Salzman, C. (1990). Principles of psychopharmacology. In D. Bienenfeld (Ed). *Clinical geropsychiatry.* Baltimore, MD: Williams & Wilkins (234-249).

Schulz, R. & Brenner, G. (1977). Relocation of the aged: A review and theoretical analysis. *Journal of Gerontology,* 32, 323-333

Schnelle, J.F. & Traughber, B. (1983). A behavioral assessment system applicable to geriatric nursing facility residents. *Behavioral Assessment,* 5, 231-243.

Shanas, E. (1982). The family relations of old people. *National Forum,* 62, 9-11.

Sherouse, D.L. (1983). *Professional's handbook on geriatric alcoholism.* Springfield, IL: Charles C. Thomas.

Skinner, B.F. (1983). Intellectual self-management in old age. *American Psychologist,* 38, 239-244.

Sobel, H.J. (Ed.). (1981). *Behavior therapy in terminal care: A humanistic approach.* Boston, MA: Ballinger.

Sobell, M.B. & Sobell, L.C. (1973). Individualized behavior therapy for alcoholics. *Behavior Therapy,* 4, 49-72.

Sobell, M.B. & Sobell, L.C. (1976). Second year treatment outcome of alcoholics treated by individualized behavior therapy. *Behaviour Research and Therapy,* 14, 195-215.

Sobell, M.B. & Sobell, L.C. (1978). *Behavioral treatment of alcohol problems: Individualized therapy and controlled drinking.* NY: Plenum Press.

SELECTED ANNOTATED RESOURCES

ATKINSON, R.M. (1984). Substance use and abuse in late life. In R. Atkinson (Ed.). *Alcohol and drug abuse in old age* (pp. 1-21). Washington, D.C.: American Psychiatric Press.

1. English; 2. Clinical/review; 3. Elderly drug users; 4. Overviews typologies of alcohol and drug use and misuse relevant to the rising aging population. Complicating problems include misdiagnosis, early mortality, underreporting, genetic factors, biological sensitivity, psychosocial stressors, and natural aging ailments; 5. Concludes that early intervention, while ideal, overlooks potential abuse patterns with medication and drug-drug interactions.

BROWN, N. (1986). Mainstreaming reduces elderly isolation. *Alcoholism & Addiction*, 7, 41-42.

1. English; 2. Experimental/review; 3. Elderly alcoholics; 4. Reports on New Haven, CT study on attracting and treating elderly alcoholics on Medicare, involving outreach and intervention steps; 5. Results showed that removal of isolationism through the health care system fostered more rapid improvement than through traditional drug therapy or therapy alone.

CARTENSEN, L.K., RYCHTARIK, R.G. & PRUE, D.M. (1985). Behavioral treatment of the geriatric alcohol abuser: Long term follow-up study. *Addictive Behaviors*, 10, 307-311.

1. English; 2. Experimental; 3. Male elderly ages 65-70 years-old; 4. Treatment outpatient program; 5. Post-treatment maintenance and benefits; 6. Behavioral treatment modalities; 7. Interview surveys conducted in person; 8. Self-reports of improvement and medical stability; 9. Of the 16 subjects located, 8 were abstinent and an additional two decreased drinking, suggesting that abusive drinking is changeable in later life.

CROSS, P.S. (1982). Epidemiology of psychopathology in old age: Some implications for clinical services. *Psychiatric Clinics of North America*, 5, 11-26.

1. English; 2. Theoretical/review; 3. Mentally ill elderly; 4. Examines that (a) prevalence of alcoholism among elderly ranges from 2 to 10 percent, (b) that drop of alcohol use relates to generational effects, lack of purchasing power, physiological intolerance from hepatic dysfunction and attrition from institutional admission, and (c) early onset cases of alcoholism never survive to old age; 5. Despite lower reported rates, findings still show alcoholism greatest among psychiatric and medically ambulatory and in acute care settings.

DOUGLAS, R.L. (1984). Aging and alcohol problems: Opportunities for socioepidemiological research. In *Recent developments in alcoholism: volume 2* (pp. 251-266). NY: Plenum Press.

1. English; 2. Clinical/theoretical; 3. Elderly; 4. State of the art review of social dynamics bearing on epidemiological research as the population of the United States ages. Demographic reports examined regarding prevalence of alcoholism and efficacy of outreach programs; 5. Recommendations for research recommended include role of elderly in society, changes caused by retirement, historical factors, and diseases of elderly.

DUNHAM, R.O. (1986). Noticing alcoholism in the elderly and women: A nationwide examination of referral behavior. *Journal of Drug Issues*, 16, 397-406.

1. English; 2. Experimental; 3. 305,000 elderly and nonelderly treatment patients through period of October 1977 to March 1979; 4. Treatment programs nationwide; 5. Different referral sources used and effects of gender upon them; 6. & 7. National statistical data base drawn from (a) patient profile data and (b) program activities data; 8. Statistical analysis comparing groups of elderly and types of symptoms; 9. Elderly had more personal and medical referrals, while non-elderly had legal referrals.

FINLAYSON, R.E. (1984). Prescription drug abuse in older persons. In R. Atkinson (Ed.). *Alcohol and drug abuse in old age* (pp. 61-70). Washington, D.C.: American Psychiatric Press.

1. English; 2. Clinical/review; 3. Elderly medication abusers; 4. Prescription drug misuse is major cause of drug induced illnesses, obscured behind actual medical conditions and complaints that resemble normal aging. Reviews symptoms of pain and insomnia

leading to greatest abuse; 5. Author provides guidelines for physicians on prescriptive practices and indications for prevention strategies.

FREEMAN, E.M. (1985). *Social work practice with clients who have alcohol problems.* Springfield, IL: Charles C. Thomas.

1. English; 2. Clinical/review; 3. Adolescents, adults, elderly alcoholics; 4. Monograph clarifies physiology, biochemistry, etiology, and counseling interventions of alcoholic clients referred through prevention, community and EAP services and who typically come from dysfunctional families. A section on research highlights current trends primarily affecting minority clients; 5. Orientation of book calls for systemic approach toward drinking problems with intense family involvement.

GALLANT, D.M. (1983). Alcohol abuse in the aging population. *Alcoholism: Clinical and Experimental Research*, 7, 244.

1. English; 2. Experimental/review; 3. Elderly, hospitalized and nonhospitalized; 4. Data from latitudinal study of elderly population showed increased use of alcohol due to premature retirement, poor health with limitation of routine activities, and loneliness with increased risk of depression; 5. Findings indicated that alcoholic elderly or those at risk of developing abuse are hospitalized or institutionalized.

GERBINO, P.P. (1982). Complications of alcohol use combined with drug therapy in the elderly. *Journal of the American Geriatrics Society*, 31, 888-893.

1. English; 2. Clinical/review; 3. Elderly; 4. Discusses chronic ingestion of alcohol interfering with drug regimens and causing (a) hazardous drug interactions, (b) poor compliance, (c) contraindicated effects; 5. Advice offered that medication recipients abstain from alcohol or that drug schedules be modified with drinking levels in mind.

GILBERT, R. (1986). Drugs and aging. *Journal*, 15, 5.

1. English; 2. Theoretical; 3. Adult and elderly drug misusers; 4. Reviews preponderance of OTC medicine and prescriptive medicine abuse among older persons increasing polymorbidity (increased fat, liver enzymes, smaller kidneys, central nervous system sensitivity,

toxic effects); 5. Encourages practitioners through different steps to spot polydrug abuse and confront family of the elderly.

GOTTHEIL, E., DRULEY, K.A., SKOLODA, T.E. & WAXMAN, H.M. (1985). *Combined problems of alcoholism, drug addiction and aging.* Springfield, IL: Charles C. Thomas.

1. English; 2. Clinical/review; 3. Elderly polydrug abusers; 4. Monograph reports on biomedical, behavioral and sociological reasons behind aging addiction, focusing on misdiagnosis, epidemiological trends, and diverse issues endemic to elderly; 5. Guidelines identify tactics for providers and family on addressing elderly substance abuse, speculating on future psychosocial problems if the epidemic of abuse spreads.

GRAHAM, K. (1986). Identifying and measuring alcohol abuse among the elderly: Serious problems with existing instrumentation. *Journal of Studies on Alcohol, 47,* 322-326.

1. English; 2. Theoretical/review; 3. Elderly alcoholics; 4. Comprehensive review of pitfalls in self-report questionnaires asking about social or legal problems, self-recognition, drinking levels, health problems and dependency. Low reliability due to misleading categories and nonexclusive diagnosis of acute versus chronic drinkers. Impairment in elderly consists of societal factors missed in instruments; 5. Future studies employing measures of alcohol consumption are advised to run validity samples prior to experimentation and delineate more precisely alcohol-related problems from age-related problems.

HASDAY, J.D. & KARCH, F.E. (1981). Benzodiazepine prescribing in a family medicine center. *Journal of the American Medical Association,* 246, 1321-1325.

1. English; 2. Experiment; 3. 1886 prescriptions to adults ages 25 to 44-years-old; 4. Medical center; 5. Prescription of diazepam, chlordizepoxide, oxazepam, and clorazepate; 6. Prescriptions for frequent diagnoses of anxiety, hysterical neurosis, vertebral column disorder, and acute alcohol withdrawal; 7. Quasi-control study; 8. Case reports; 9. Prescriptions written more frequently during the summer, more frequently for women, and recipients usually had multiple medications.

HOFFMAN, A.L. & HEINEMANN, M.E. (1986). Alcohol problems in elderly persons. In N.J. Estes & M.E. Heinemann (Eds.). *Alcoholism: Development, consequences and interventions* (pp. 257-272). St. Louis, MO: Mosby.

1. English; 2. Theoretical; 3. Elderly; 4. Prevalence and patterns of alcohol problems discussed relative to physiologic, psychosocial, and pathophysiologic consequences; 5. Recommends method to delineate diagnosis problems for early prevention.

HORTON, A.M. (1986). *Alcohol and the elderly.* Maryland Medical Journal, 35, 916-918.

1. English; 2. Clinical/review; 3. Elderly alcoholics; 4. Demographic analyses indicate two typologies of elderly drinkers, those with lifelong patterns and late life onset of abuse in response to age-related stressors; 5. Findings suggest that groups made up of elderly alcoholics are more amenable to treatment than mixed groups of young and old drinkers.

HUSAIN, S. (1982). Drug problems among the elderly. *SPADA SAGE,* 3, 2-5.

1. English; 2. Theoretical; 3. Elderly; 4. Alcohol represents the highest abused drug compared to problems of medication mismanagement. Examined are clinical and administrative aspects of alcohol and drug misuse contributing to problems; 5. Correction of drug or alcohol misuse begins at prevention level of alerting at-risk elders of warnings and side-effects of medicine, and proper self-administration strategies.

KING, G., ALTPETER, M. & SPADA, M. (1986). Alcoholism and the elderly: A training model. *Alcoholism Treatment Quarterly,* 3, 81-94.

1. English; 2. Experimental/review; 3. Elderly alcoholics; 4. Summarizes national study estimates that only 15 percent of elderly alcoholics receive treatment because of such obstacles as (a) trainer unavailability, (b) misdiagnosis, (c) inaccessibility of elderly, and (d) drug interactions; 5. New training model introduces strategies for counselor preparation and outreach services that increase alcoholism identification.

KOLA, L. A. & KOSBERG, J. I. (1981). Model to assess community services for the elderly alcoholic. *Public Health Reports,* 96, 458-463.

1. English; 2. Theoretical/clinical; 3. Elderly alcoholics; 4. Assessment model presented based on three levels including client level, agency level and community level. On client levels five kinds of services are explored. On agency levels, areas examined are competency, policy formation, continuity of care, and accessibility of resources. On community level focus is upon consumer awareness and unity to disseminate warnings about alcohol abuse; 5. Recommendations for implementation and anticipated pitfalls are explored.

LADEWIG, D. & GRAW, P. (1986). New manifestations and theoretical aspects of addiction from the viewpoint of the clinician. In (no editor) *Suchtproblematik: Theorie der sucht* (pp. 58-70). NY: Springer-Verlag.

1. German; 2. Clinical/review; 3. Elderly drug abusers; 4. Outlines problems of etiology, diagnosis and clinical manifestations of addiction, requiring a re-evaluation of policies and particularly of the causal social acceptance of so-called soft drugs (types of prescription drugs). Argues that no comprehensive model of intervention exists for clinical practice; 5. Proposes that one direction is expansion upon the addictive personality model looking at cognitive and behavioral variables.

LAMY, P.P. (1984). Alcohol misuse and abuse among the elderly. *Drug Intelligence and Clinical Pharmacy*, 18, 649-651.

1. English; 2. Theoretical; 3. Elderly; 4. Contends that 2.5 million elderly are alcohol abusers leading to somatic, psychological, social and other serious consequences. Alcohol misuse interferes with management of chronic diseases and drug interactions. Draws relationship between heavy drinkers with European ancestry and external causes, with focus on woman drinkers; 5. Concludes that alcohol abuse increases in severity when mixed with improperly self-administered prescription drugs.

LEX, B.W. (1985). Alcohol problems in special populations. In J.H. Mendelson & N.K. Mello (Eds.). *The diagnosis and treatment of alcoholism* (pp. 89-187). NY: McGraw-Hill.

1. English; 2. Clinical/review; 3. Elderly, youth, racial and ethnic groups, native Americans; 4. Chapter assails the prevalence of factors affecting elderly, Blacks, Hispanics and Native American drinkers and their culturalization; 5. Heterogeneity among groups accounts for improperly constructed treatment services, unprepared service

providers, and severe misdiagnoses owing to physicians unaware of indigenous psychopathologies.

LOVINFOSSE, M. (1984). TAPS: Hidden costs of elderly alcoholics. *Alcoholism: The National Magazine*, 5, 28.

1. English; 2. Theoretical; 3. Elderly; 4. Increasing numbers of elderly alcoholics becoming polydrug abusers through prescription drugs and requiring community services. Intervention called Tenant Assistance Program (TAPS) assists individuals with alcohol and drug problems thereby reducing costs such as residential fire, flood, and other hazards; 5. Advantages of TAPS for network state programs outlined.

LUKE, E., NORTON, W. & DENBIGH, K. (1982). Prevalence of psychologic impairment in an advanced age population. *Journal of the American Geriatric Society*, 30, 114-122.

1. English; 2. Experimental; 3. 200 elderly persons, 80 years and older; 4. Vancouver and Victoria, Canada; 5. Emotional and behavioral problems affecting lifestyle; 6. Interview method; 7. Data on depression, functional disabilities, suicidal ideation, social interaction, demography, and psychological distress; 7. One to five percent of subjects interviewed drank constantly; one percent expressed alcohol accounting for psychological problems.

NATHAN, P. E. (1983). Failures in prevention: Why we can't prevent the devastating effects of alcoholism and drug abuse. *American Psychologist*, 38, 459-467.

1. English; 2. Theoretical; 3. Elderly, adults, adolescents; 4. Proposed that among all policies established by U.S. government for intervention, prevention is last priority. This reduces impact upon high risk alcoholics and overlooks special needs of elderly, women, and other minorities; 5. Concludes that until legislation ranks drug prevention a worthy cause, incident rate probably will double and measure of change will remain minimal.

OSGOOD, N. J. (1982). Suicide in the elderly: Are we heeding the warning? *Postgraduate Medicine*, 72, 123-130.

1. English; 2. Theoretical/clinical; 3. Elderly alcoholics; 4. Contends that loneliness and depression are overlooked warning signs of suicidality that remain hidden behind myths of old age. Responsibility

upon physician is to detect symptoms as a form of prevention working together with family members; 5. Author laments that if society recognized its elderly citizens more attention likely would be paid to early diagnosis and treatment strategies.

PENIN, F. (1984). Alcoholism in the elderly. In *Alcoologie*, (pp. 202-206). Riom, Cedex, France: Riom Laboratoires.

1. French; 2. Theoretical/review; 3. Elderly alcoholics; 4. Reviews causes of long-term and recent onset of alcoholics age 65 and over, compared to younger alcoholics in terms of culturalization, heredity, psychosocial and medical factors. Identifies that alcohol accelerates organic and psychiatric deterioration; 5. Results show these predisposing factors are not indigenous to countries but rather internationally prevalent and equally as influential as psychotropic medicines mixing with alcohol. Implications for geropsychiatric research offered.

ROSENBLOOM, A.J. (1986). Optimizing drug treatment of alcohol withdrawal. *American Journal of Medicine*, 81, 901-904.

1. English; 2. Clinical/review; 3. Elderly alcoholics; 4. Surveys medical complications of withdrawal including renal and hepatic disease that are poorly monitored; 5. Formulates a more efficient treatment regimen minimizing risks while stabilizing medical condition both during and immediately following a withdrawal syndrome.

RUBEN, D.H. (1986). Elderly alcoholics: Some current dimensions. *Advances in Alcoholism and Substance Abuse*, 5, 59-70.

1. English; 2. Clinical/review; 3. Elderly alcoholics; 4. Problems affecting elderly drinkers examined in terms of etiology and treatment. Etiology covers bereavement, marital problems, retirement, decline in income, taxation provisions, and adverse effects on health caused by relocation. Also examined is paucity of technical understanding among practitioners about the aged and potential alcoholic symptomatology. Treatment covers behavioral psychotherapy with emphasis upon systems or integrative-field theory application; 5. Networking a prevention approach depends on practitioners being educated along with methods for early detection.

SCHOOLAR, J. C. (1984). Introduction/alcoholism: Perspectives for the 1980s. In J.T. Hartford & T. Samorajski (Eds.). *Alcoholism in the elderly: Social and biomedical issues* (pp. 1-4). NY: Raven Press.

1. English; 2. Theoretical/clinical; 3. Elderly alcoholics; 4. Examines approaches to reducing cardiovascular disease and alcohol abuse by outlining advanced research in the area, as preface to book; 5. Author concludes that conscious-raising attitudes currently underlie effective prevention programs but it is inadequate at reaching elderly consumers.

SHANAHAN, P.M. (1984). Alcoholism and aging: A challenge. In M. Goby (Ed.). *Alcoholism: Treatment and recovery* (pp. 83-99). St. Louis, MO: Mosby.

1. English; 2. Theoretical; 3. Elderly; 4. Literature review on aging and alcoholism showing the paucity of substance abuse research in gerontology and geriatric medicine. Ageistic attitudes further prevent priority shift to alcohol focus. Attributes of elderly addict examined include physical handicaps, negative attitudes, and myths of senility; 5. Proposed are directives for members of the health community on disseminating accurate information.

SMITH, J.W. (1985). Alcohol and the aging population. *Senior Life*, January, 5-6.

1. English; 2. Clinical/theoretical; 3. Elderly; 4. Reviews alcohol use and alcoholism interacted with medications and drugs. Overviews population trends affected by disease; 5. Proposes that difficulties in diagnosis during early and late onset delay or prevent proper intervention and relief of later problems.

STEPHENS, R.C., HANEY, C.A. & UNDERWOOD, S. (1982). *Drug taking among the elderly*. Rockville, MD: National Institute on Drug Abuse.

1. English; 2. Experimental/review; 3. Noninstitutionalized adults over age 55; 4. Monograph reports results of Houston study on drug use and misuse, closely examining rate of psychotropics prescribed; 5. Sixty percent of medication using sample reported frequent inebriety and fewer than two percent of sample reported using any illicit drugs in their lifetimes.

SUMBERG, D. (1985). Social work with elderly alcoholics: Some practical considerations. *Journal of Gerontological Social Work*, 8, 169-180.

1. English; 2. Clinical/review; 3. Elderly alcoholics; 4. Examines parameters of social work issues facing therapy with older drinkers including (a) denial, (b) hopelessness, (c) diagnosis and outreach, and (d) sensitivity to holistic problems; 5. Support usually entails integration of family members into treatment plan and operational objectives for both early recovery and aftercare steps.

WATTIS, J.P. (1983). Alcohol and old people. *British Journal of Psychiatry*, 143, 306-307.

1. English; 2. Experimental/review; 3. Drinking elderly in several countries; 4. Findings from international research indicates the increasing visibility of older alcoholics unchanged by aging, and particularly affecting women; 5. Survey methods used to assess data face bias because of difficulties in alcoholic diagnosis and confusion with symptoms of illness and disability.

WELLS-PARKER, E., MILES, S. & SPENCER, B. (1983). Stress experiences and drinking histories of elderly drunken-driving offenders. *Journal of Studies on Alcohol*, 44, 429-437.

1. English; 2. Experimental; 3. Two samples: 92 repeated DWI male offenders, 60 years and older, in experimental and 68 nonoffender males as control groups; 4. Clinic; 5. Assess treatment modalities in reducing incidence of driving rearrests; 6. Retrospective data on treatment interventions recorded from case files; 7. Group design; 8. Data on the timing, perceived magnitude, and duration of DWI events, including situational variables affecting arrest; 9. Results indicate that relationships exist between first-time elderly DWI offenders and stressful life events, particularly losses of significant others. Second correlation is between problem drinking and lower levels of social support.

WEST, L.J., MAXWELL, D.S, NOBLE, E.P. & SOLOMON, D.H. (1984). Alcoholism. *Annals of Internal Medicine*, 100, 405-416.

1. English; 2. Clinical/theoretical; 3. Infants, pregnant mothers, elderly; 4. Reviews epidemiology of the 10 million people afflicted with alcoholism, causing such high rate problems as murders, suicides,

motor vehicle accidents, fires, and polymorbidity. Covers fetal alcohol syndrome complications. For elderly, analyzes problems of misdiagnosis, tissue sensitivity, and pharmacokinetic variables; 5. Concludes that aging and alcohol are additive and raise health risks that typically are overlooked by health professionals.

WILLIAMS, M. (1984). Alcohol and the elderly: An overview. *Alcohol Health and Research World*, 8, 3-9.

1. English; 2. Clinical/review; 3. Elderly; 4. Discusses majority of elderly suffering loss of productive lives, alienation, and anxiety, causally linked to alcohol problems. Cites statistics showing increase in alcoholism due to lifestyle changes and higher consumption rate of medicines. Types of elderly at risk reviewed; 5. Blames epidemic spread of problem on policy failures and lack of network support that can monitor both professionals serving elderly, as well as elderly themselves.

WINSTEAD, D.K. (1982). Psychotropic drug use in the elderly. *Journal of the Louisiana State Medical Society*, 134, 88-93.

1. English; 2. Clinical/review; 3. Elderly medication abusers; 4. Describes problems of medication use following diagnosis of organic mental disorders (dementia, delirium), depression, and alcoholism; 5. Steps for differential diagnosis increasing accurate treatment with psychotropics are outlined along with taxonomy of common symptoms of alcoholism.

ZIMBERG, S. (1985). Alcoholism in the elderly: Diagnosis and management. *Rivista Italiana di Alcologia*, 4, 4-8.

1. English; 2. Clinical/review; 3. Elderly alcoholics; 4. Presents epidemiologic issues of elderly alcoholism in United States, stressing symptom confusion with early and late-onset alcoholism and treatment efficacy of antidepressants, family case work, and group therapy; 5. Treatment shown most effective when delivered through senior citizen programs, nursing homes, home care programs, and physician-patient conversation.

ZIMBERG, S. (1985). Psychosocial treatment of elderly alcoholics. In S. Zimberg, J. Wallace & S. Blume (Eds.). *Practical approaches to alcoholism psychotherapy* (pp. 347-363). NY: Plenum Press.

1. English; 2. Clinical/review; 3. Elderly alcoholics; 4. Reviews evidence of effective and ineffective treatment interventions for elderly, classified into early-onset and late-onset drinkers. Focus is upon supportive and problem-solving group therapy, antidepressant medications, group socialization and recreational activities; 5. Case histories document the range of techniques currently adopted by community health agencies and institutions.

Subject Index